DAYTIME SHOOTING STAR

Story & Art by
Mika Yamamori

CONTENTS

STORY THUS FAR

Suzume Yosano is a first-year in high school. Born in the country, she grew up living a free and easy life. When she learns her father is being transferred abroad, she moves to Tokyo to live with her uncle Yukichi. On her first day in the city, she gets lost and passes out, but a man carries her on his back to her uncle's home. A freckle on the back of his neck reminds Suzume of when she was lost as a child and a shooting star in broad daylight showed her the way home.

At her new school, she runs into the man again: he is her homeroom teacher, Mr. Shishio. Suzume has trouble making friends, but with some advice from him, she befriends Mamura and Yuyuka. Nothing is straightforward between Suzume and her teacher, but the distance between them gradually lessens.

When Suzume comes home with a failing test result, her uncle hires Mr. Shishio to tutor her. While studying with Mr. Shishio in her room, she finds herself drawn to him...

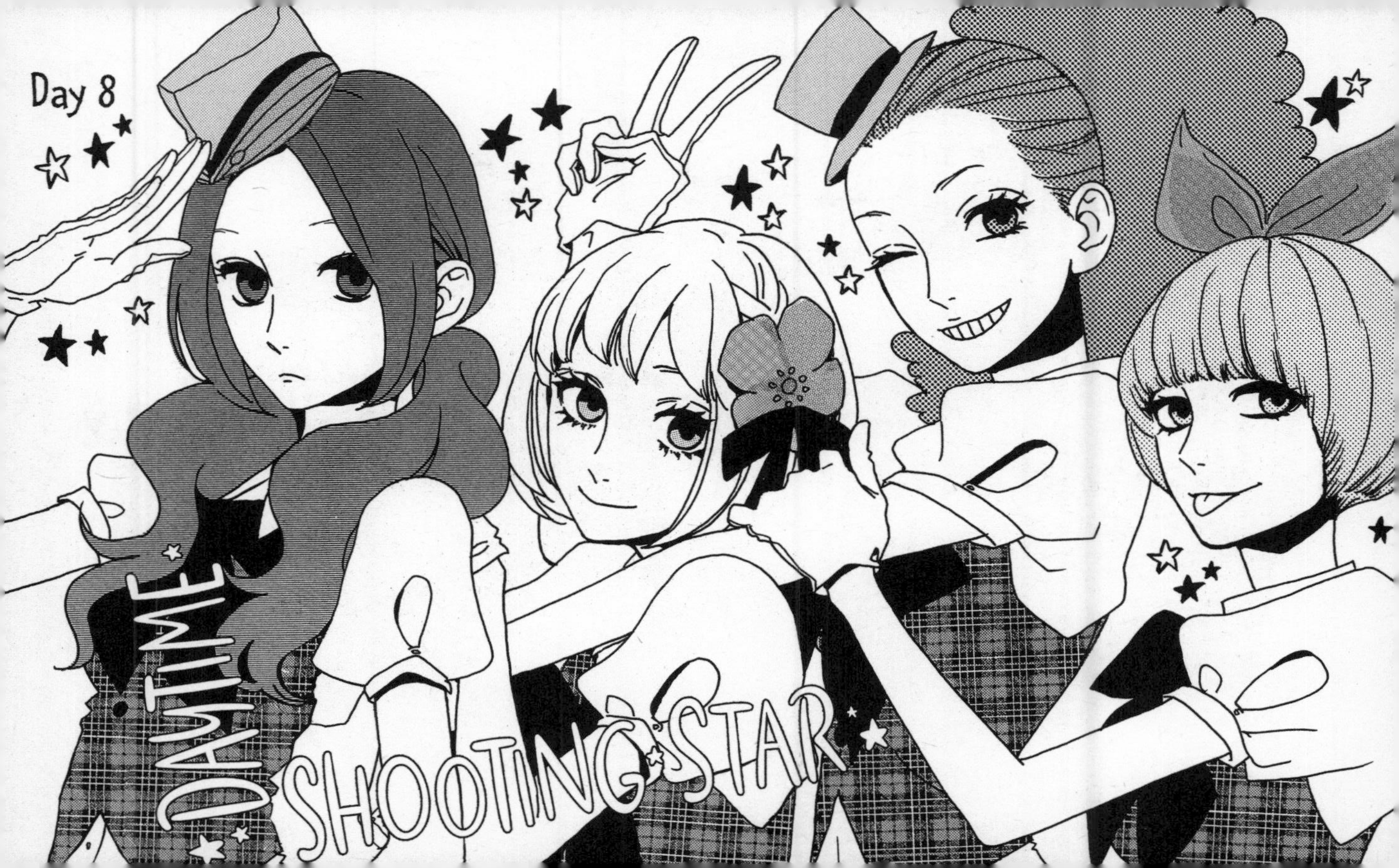
Day 8
DAYTIME SHOOTING STAR

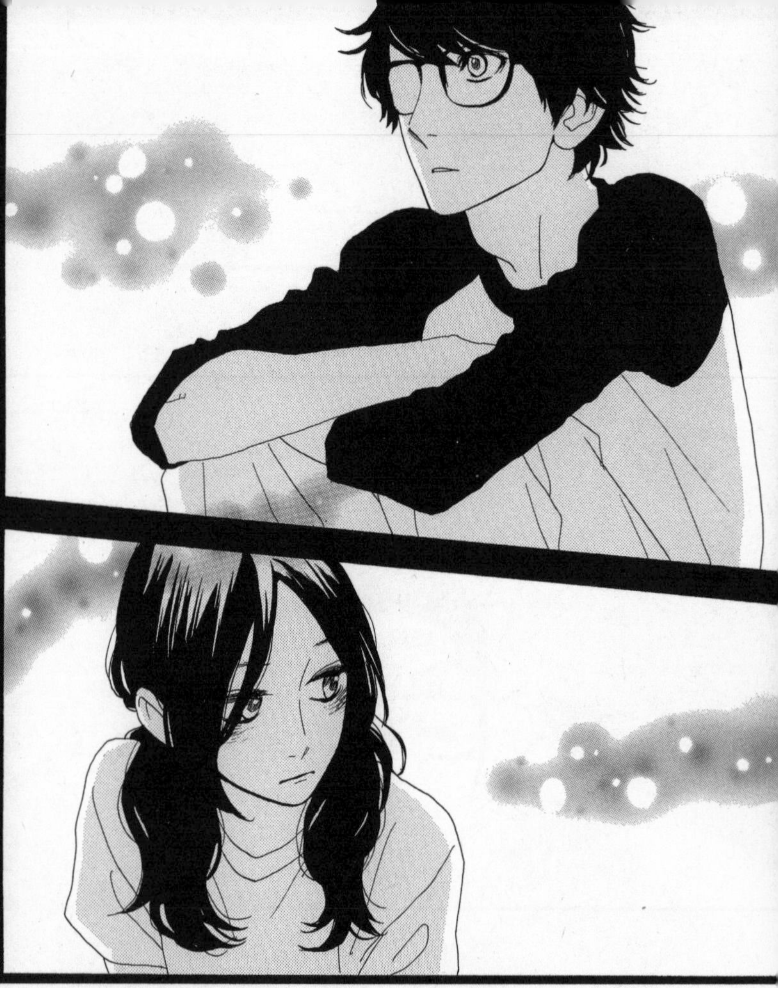

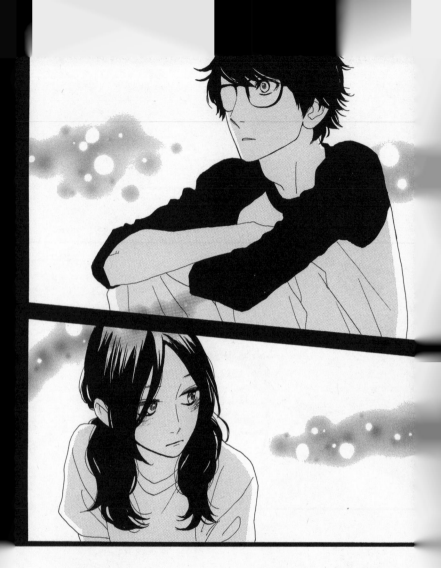

Yuyuka's Monologue

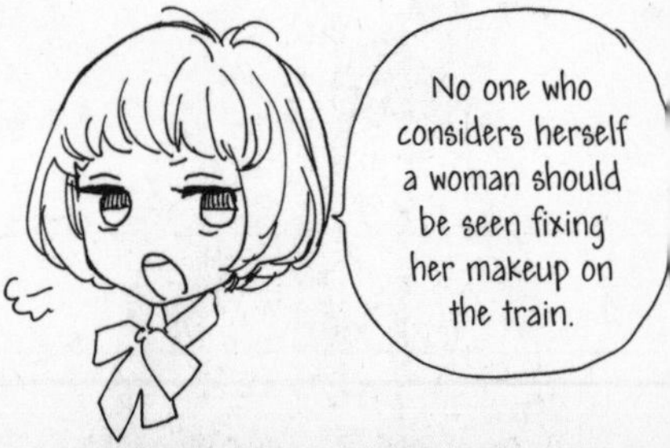
No one who considers herself a woman should be seen fixing her makeup on the train.

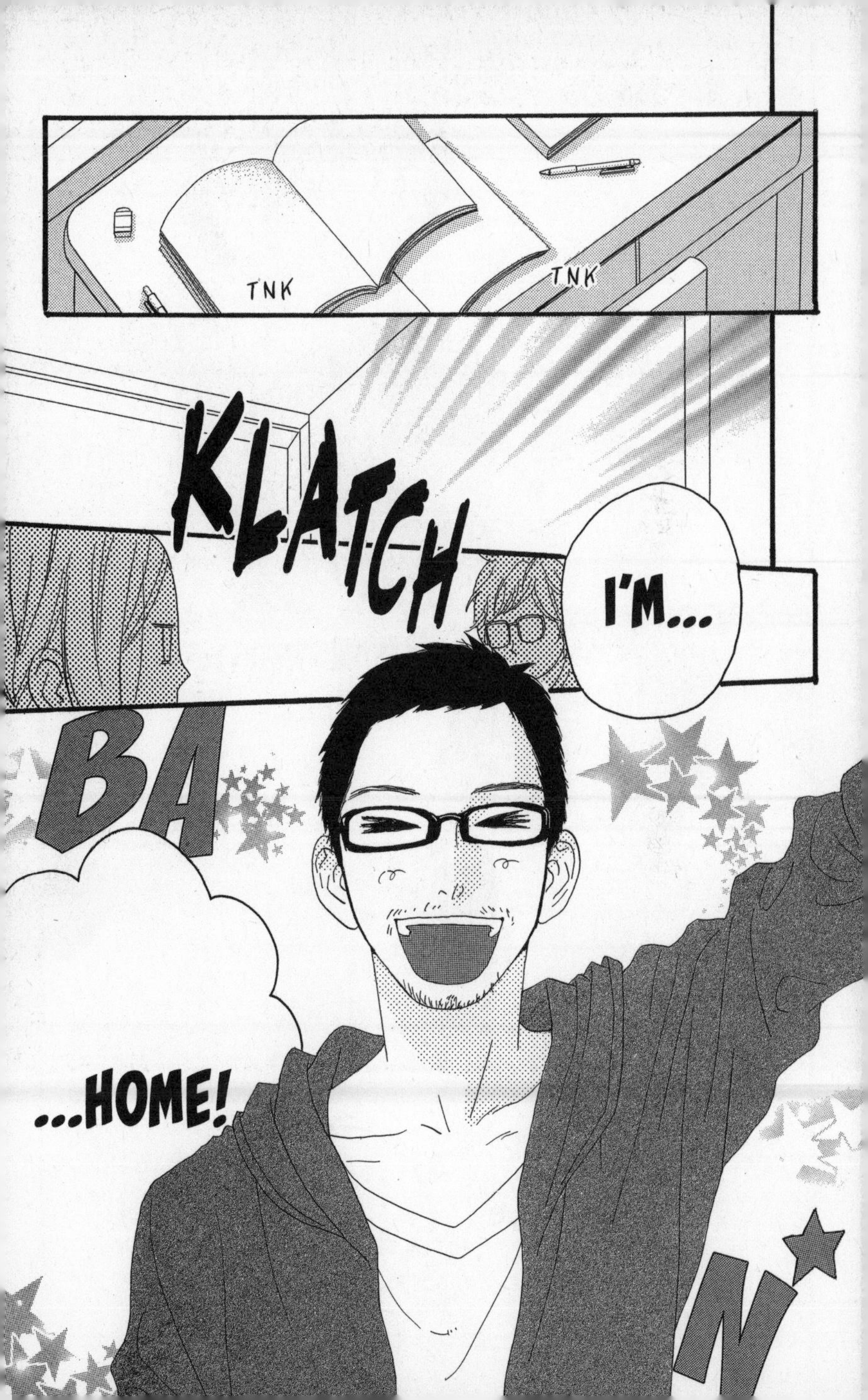
TNK
TNK
KLATCH
I'M...
BA
...HOME!
N

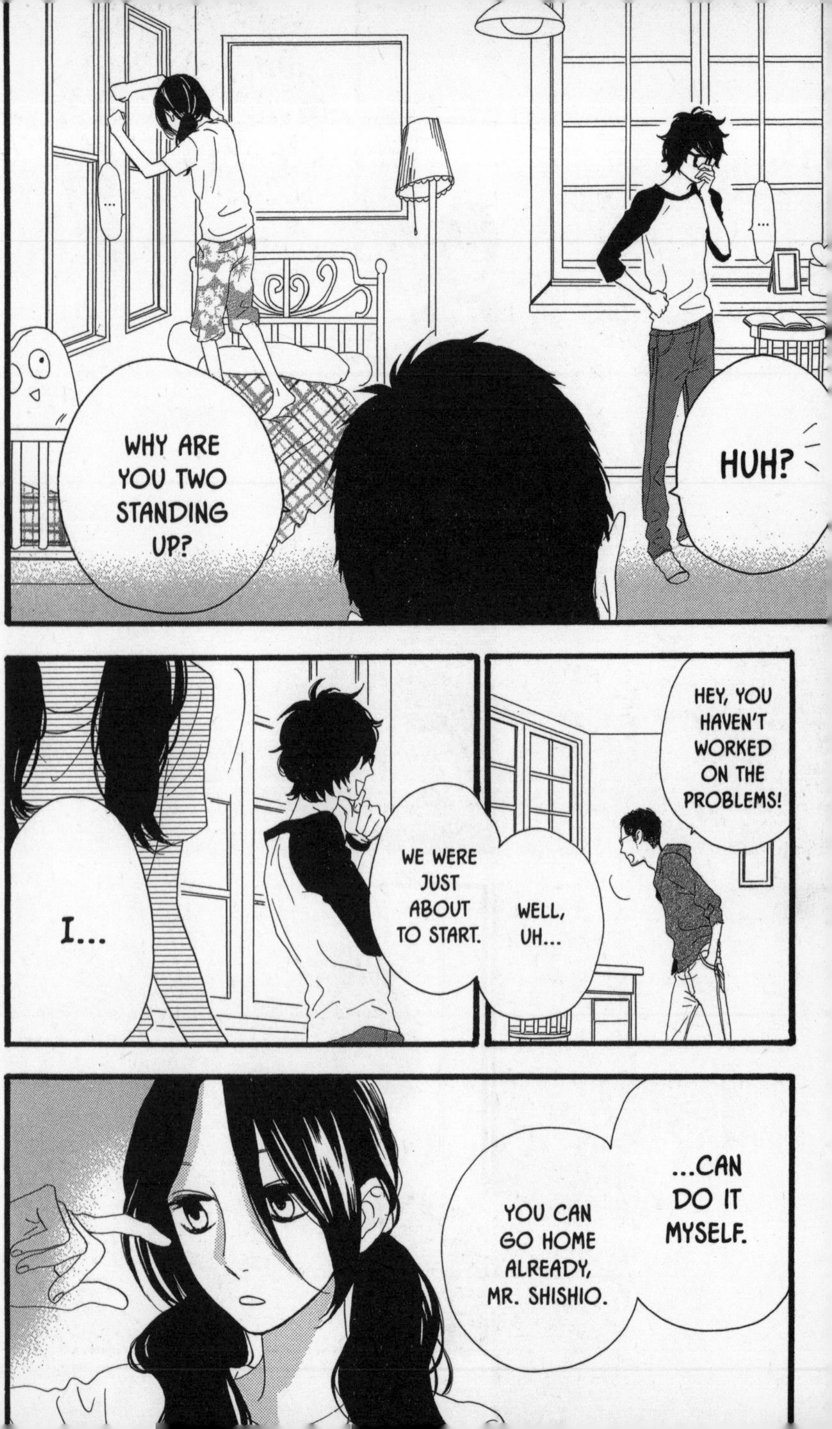
...
...
WHY ARE YOU TWO STANDING UP?
HUH?
HEY, YOU HAVEN'T WORKED ON THE PROBLEMS!
WELL, UH...
WE WERE JUST ABOUT TO START.
I...
...CAN DO IT MYSELF.
YOU CAN GO HOME ALREADY, MR. SHISHIO.

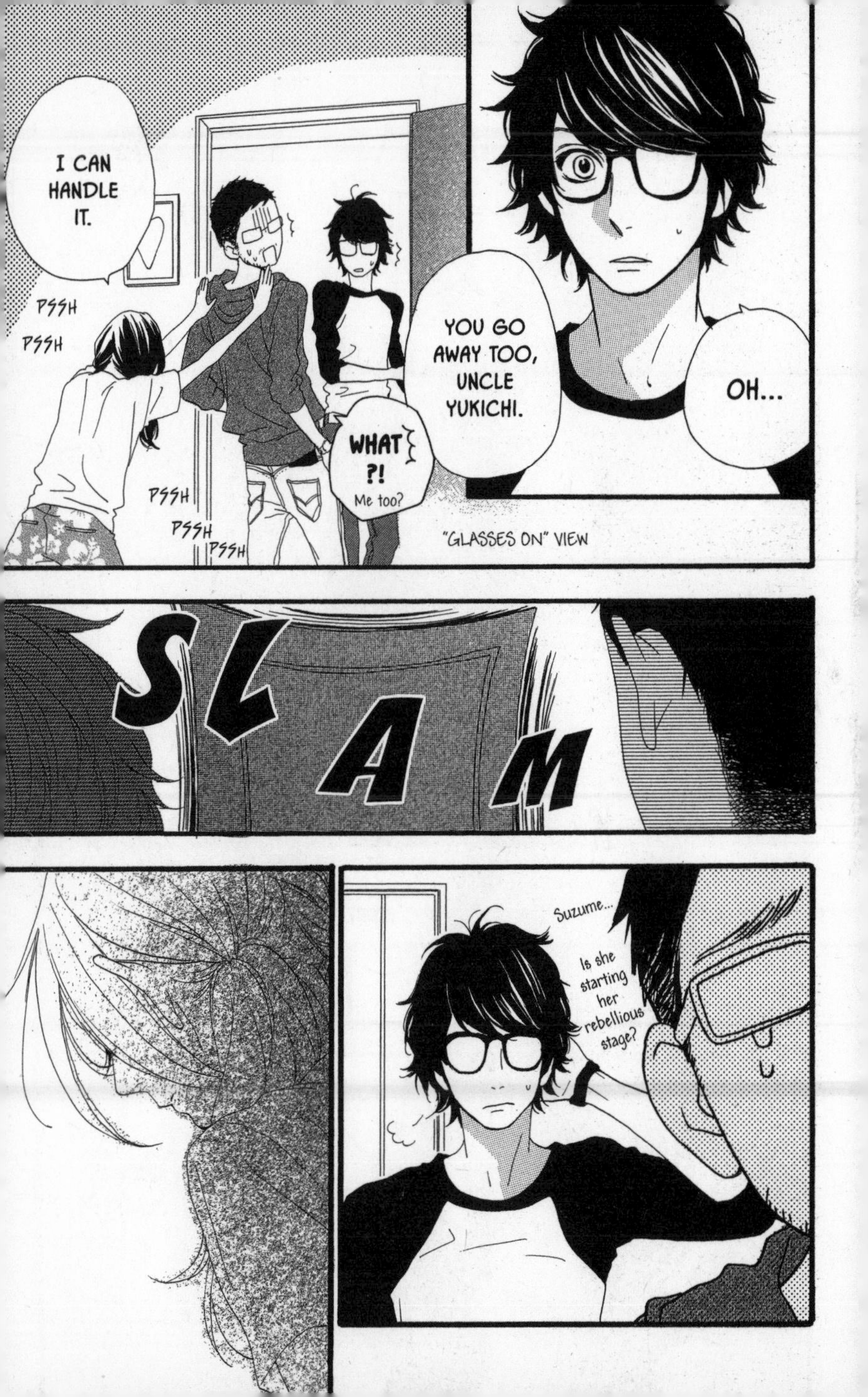
OH...
YOU GO AWAY TOO, UNCLE YUKICHI.
"GLASSES ON" VIEW
WHAT ?! Me too?
I CAN HANDLE IT.
PSSH PSSH
PSSH PSSH PSSH
SLAM
Suzume...
Is she starting her rebellious stage?

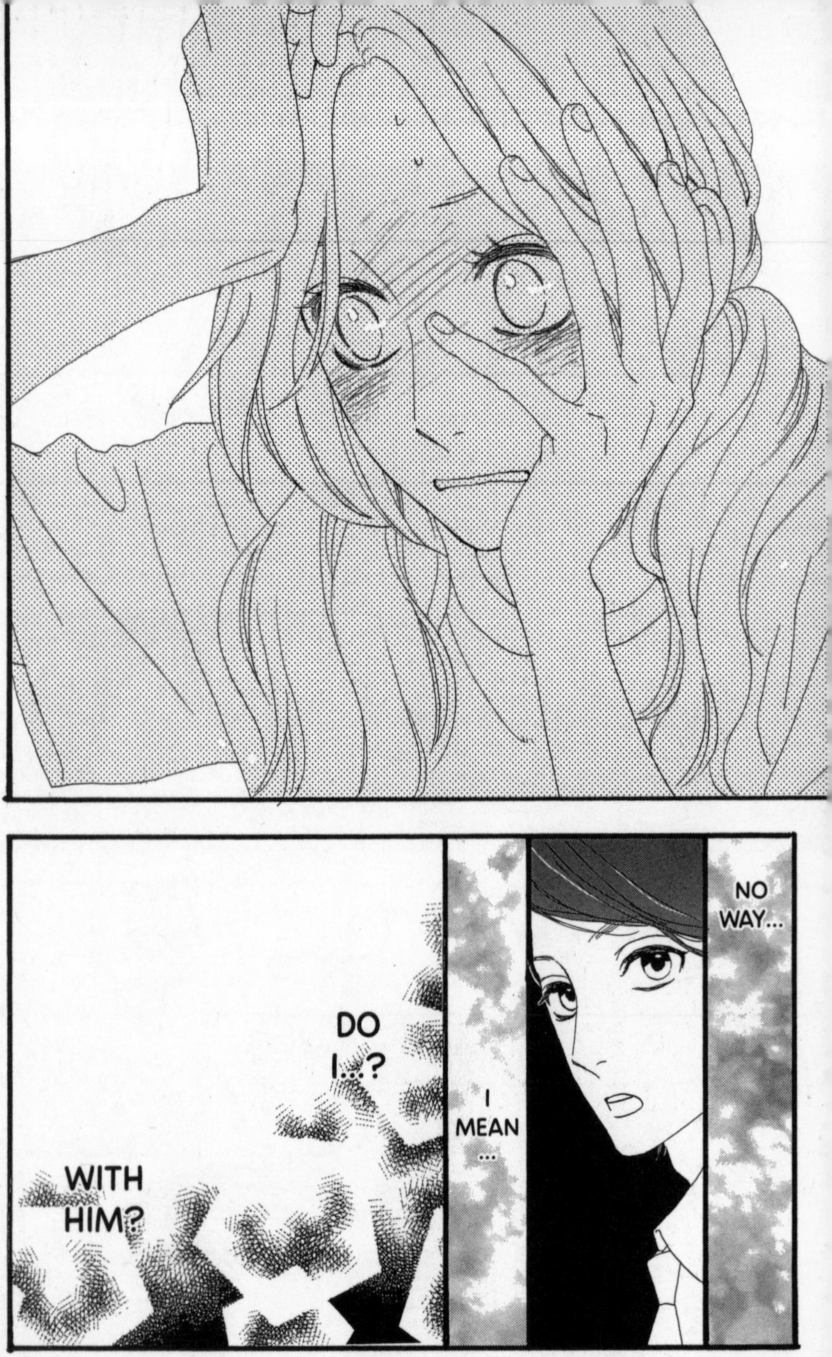
NO WAY...
I MEAN ...
DO I...?
WITH HIM?

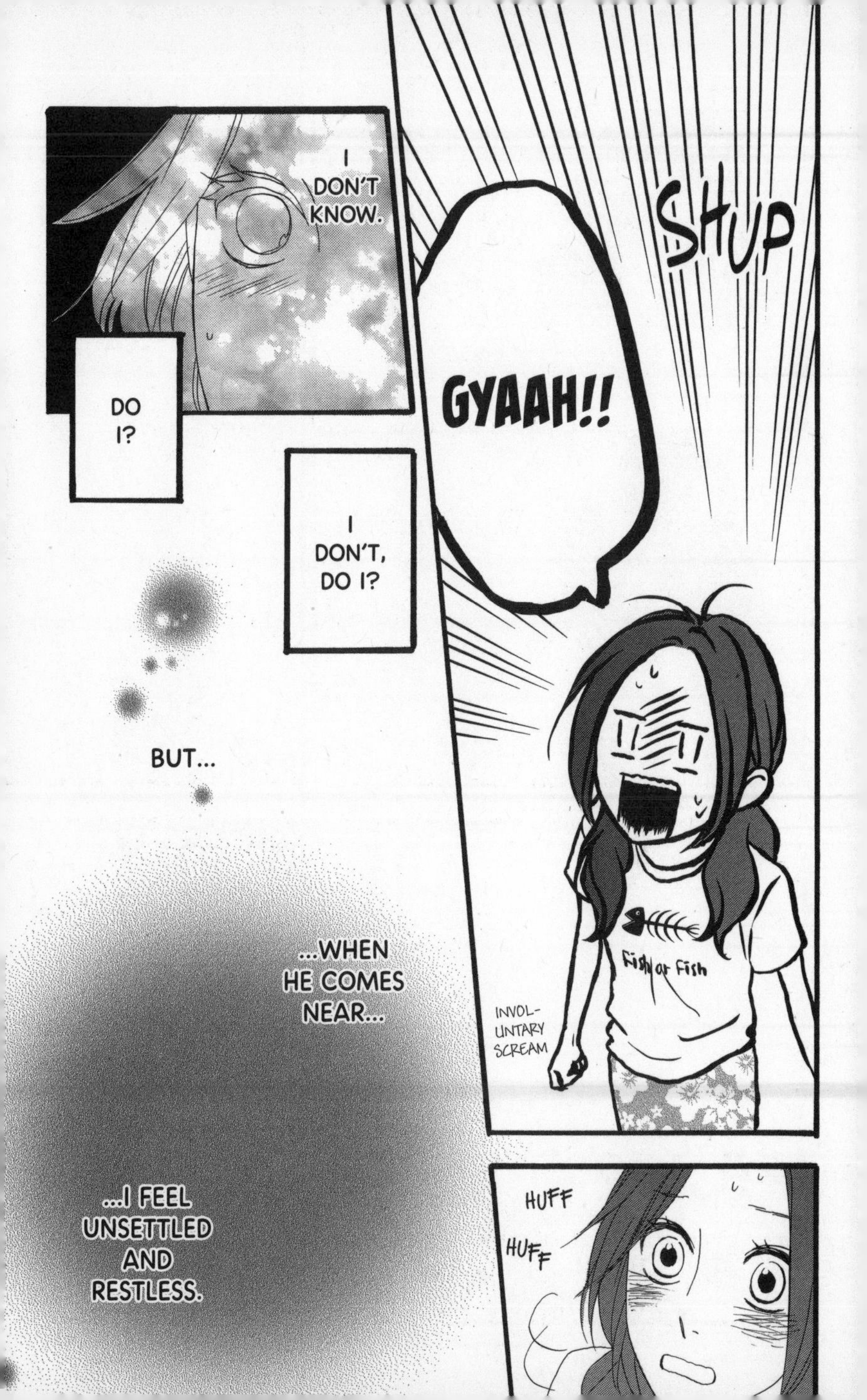
SHUP
GYAAH!!
INVOL-
UNTARY
SCREAM
Fish or Fish
HUFF
HUFF
I DON'T KNOW.
DO I?
I DON'T, DO I?
BUT...
...WHEN HE COMES NEAR...
...I FEEL UNSETTLED AND RESTLESS.

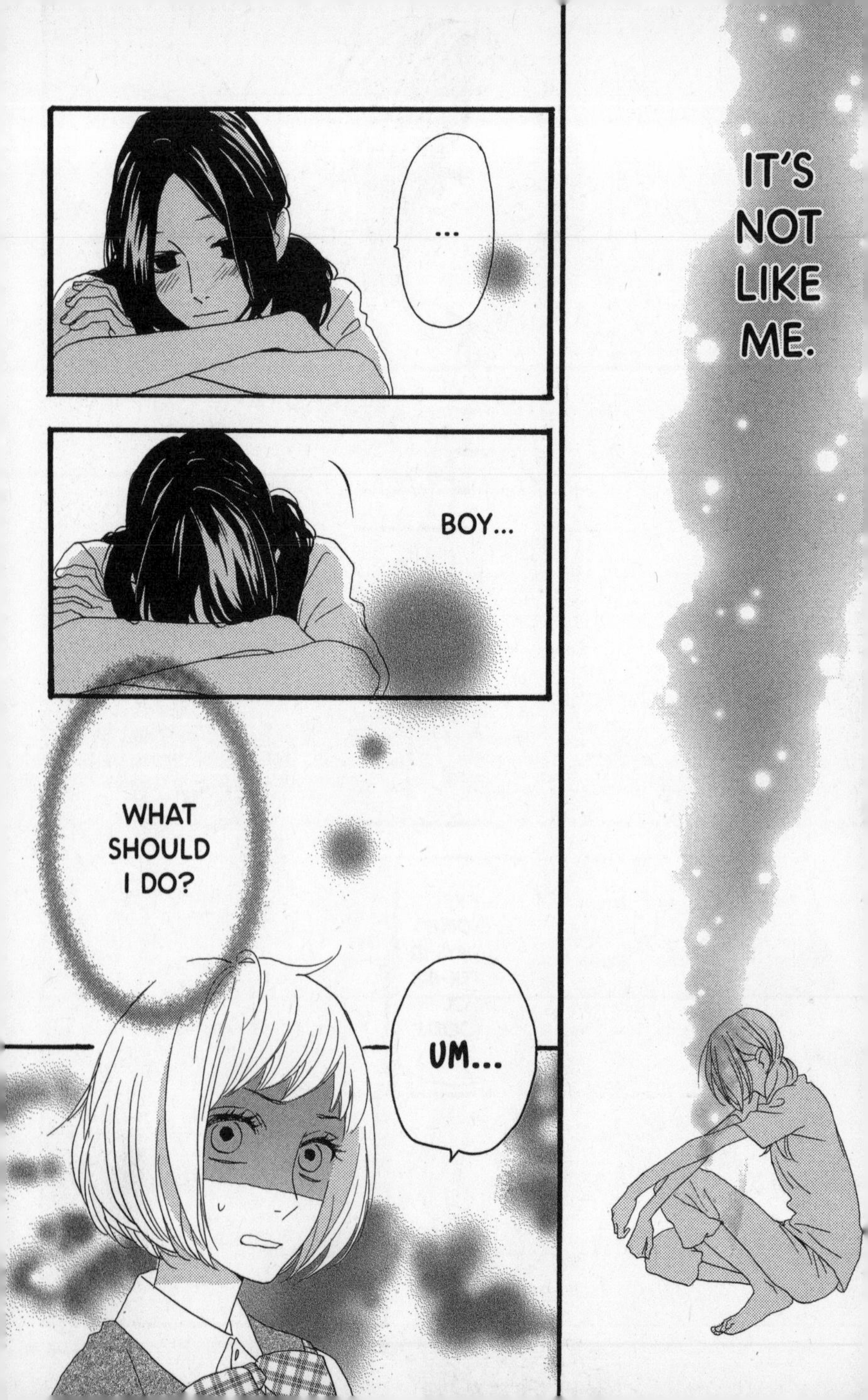
IT'S NOT LIKE ME.
...
BOY...
WHAT SHOULD I DO?
UM...

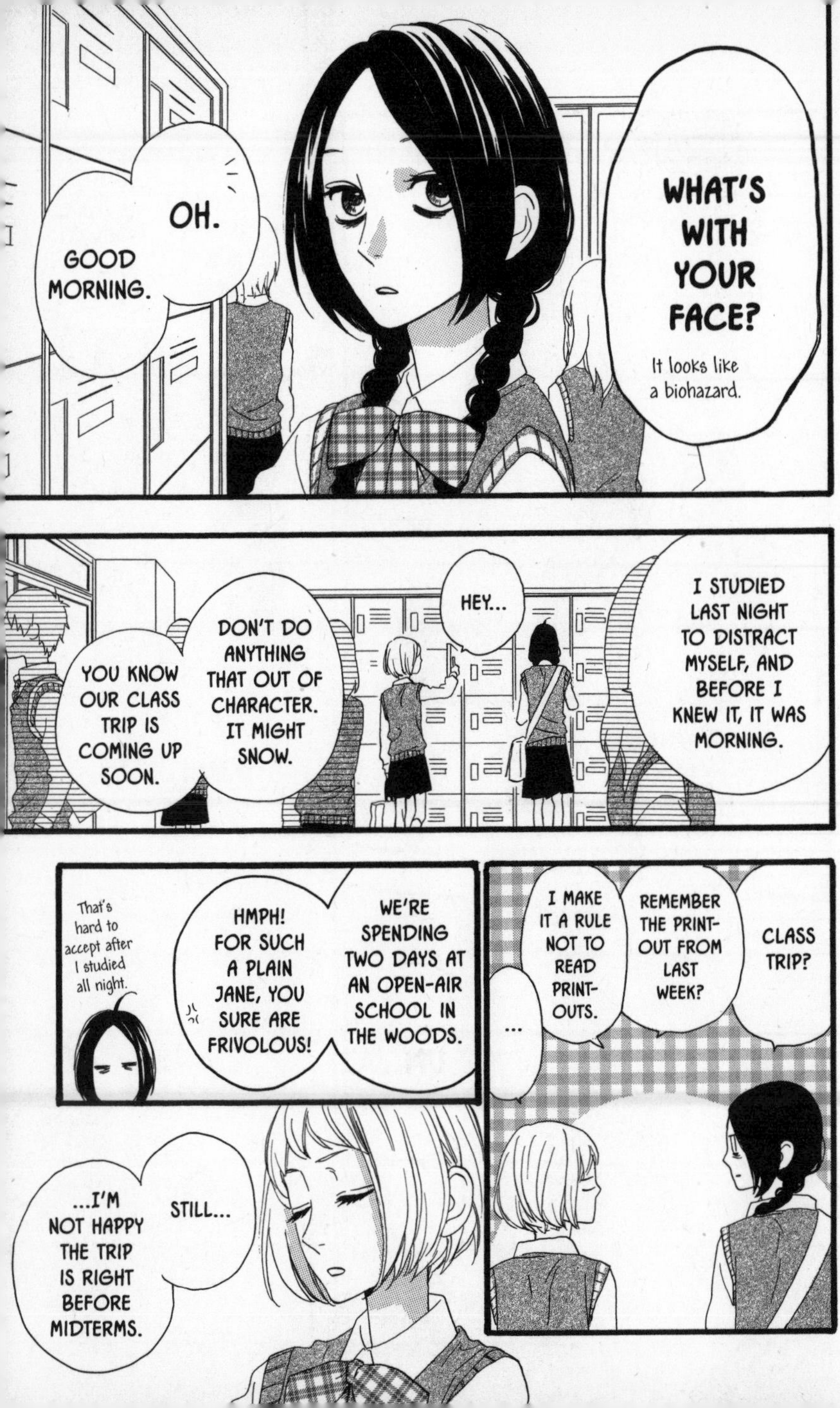
WHAT'S WITH YOUR FACE?
It looks like a biohazard.
OH.
GOOD MORNING.
I STUDIED LAST NIGHT TO DISTRACT MYSELF, AND BEFORE I KNEW IT, IT WAS MORNING.
HEY...
DON'T DO ANYTHING THAT OUT OF CHARACTER. IT MIGHT SNOW.
YOU KNOW OUR CLASS TRIP IS COMING UP SOON.
CLASS TRIP?
REMEMBER THE PRINT-OUT FROM LAST WEEK?
I MAKE IT A RULE NOT TO READ PRINT-OUTS.
...
WE'RE SPENDING TWO DAYS AT AN OPEN-AIR SCHOOL IN THE WOODS.
HMPH! FOR SUCH A PLAIN JANE, YOU SURE ARE FRIVOLOUS!
That's hard to accept after I studied all night.
STILL...
...I'M NOT HAPPY THE TRIP IS RIGHT BEFORE MIDTERMS.

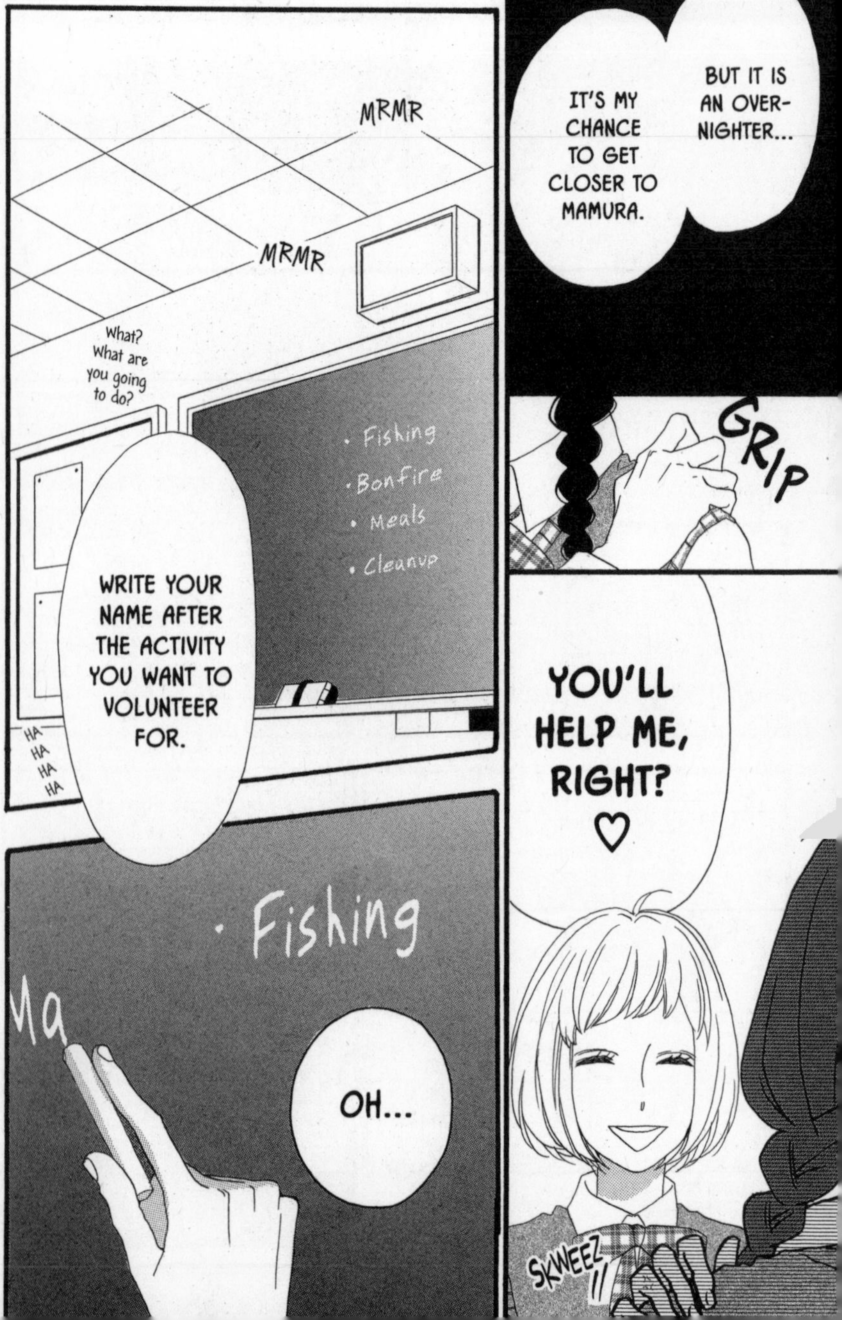
BUT IT IS AN OVER-NIGHTER...
IT'S MY CHANCE TO GET CLOSER TO MAMURA.
GRIP
YOU'LL HELP ME, RIGHT? ♡
SKWEEZ
MRMR
MRMR
What? What are you going to do?
• Fishing
• Bonfire
• Meals
• Cleanup
WRITE YOUR NAME AFTER THE ACTIVITY YOU WANT TO VOLUNTEER FOR.
HA HA HA HA
• Fishing
Ma
OH...

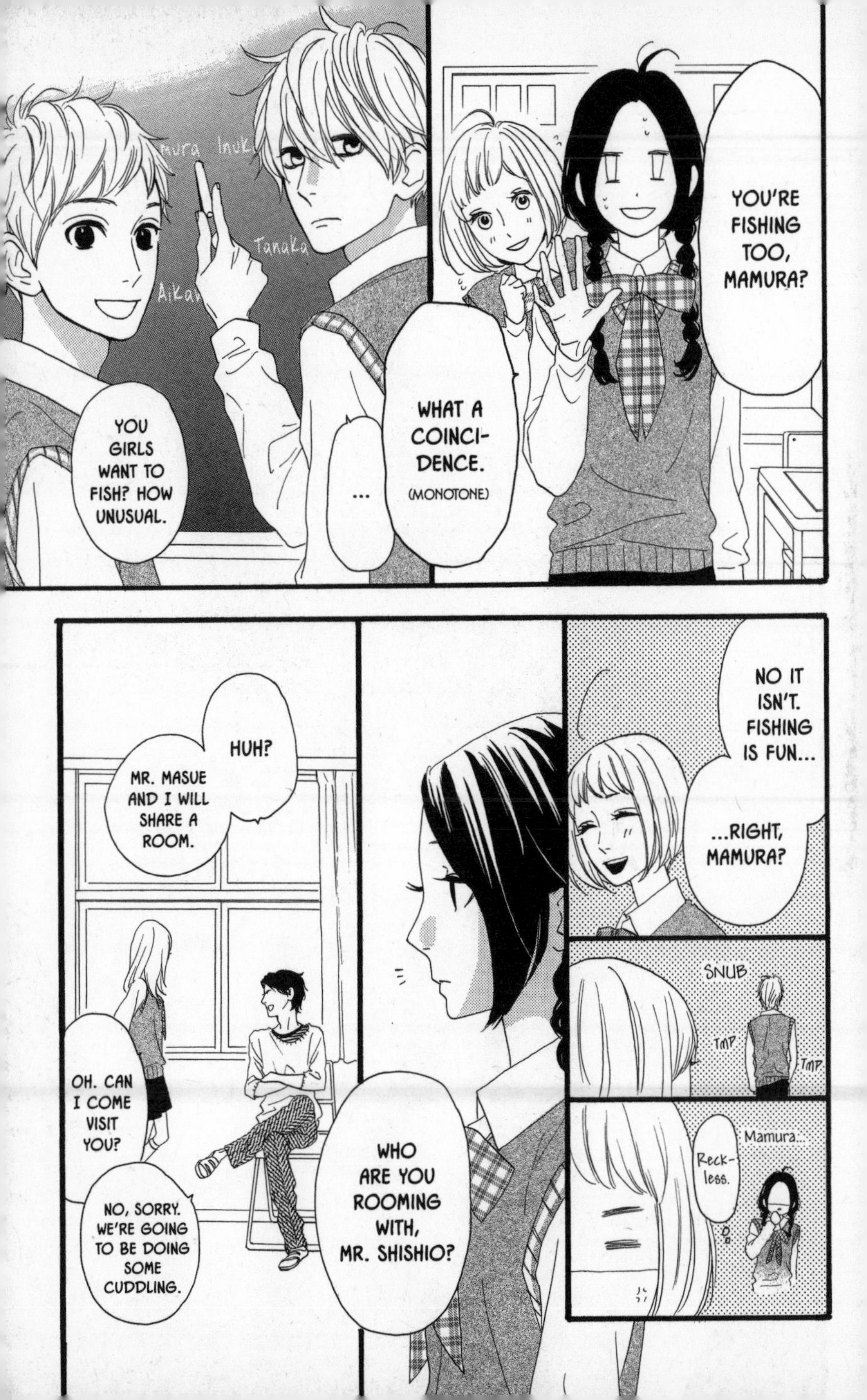
YOU'RE FISHING TOO, MAMURA?
WHAT A COINCI-DENCE.
(MONOTONE)
...
Tanaka
YOU GIRLS WANT TO FISH? HOW UNUSUAL.
NO IT ISN'T. FISHING IS FUN...
...RIGHT, MAMURA?
SNUB
TMP
TMP
Mamura...
Reck-less.
WHO ARE YOU ROOMING WITH, MR. SHISHIO?
HUH?
MR. MASUE AND I WILL SHARE A ROOM.
OH. CAN I COME VISIT YOU?
NO, SORRY. WE'RE GOING TO BE DOING SOME CUDDLING.

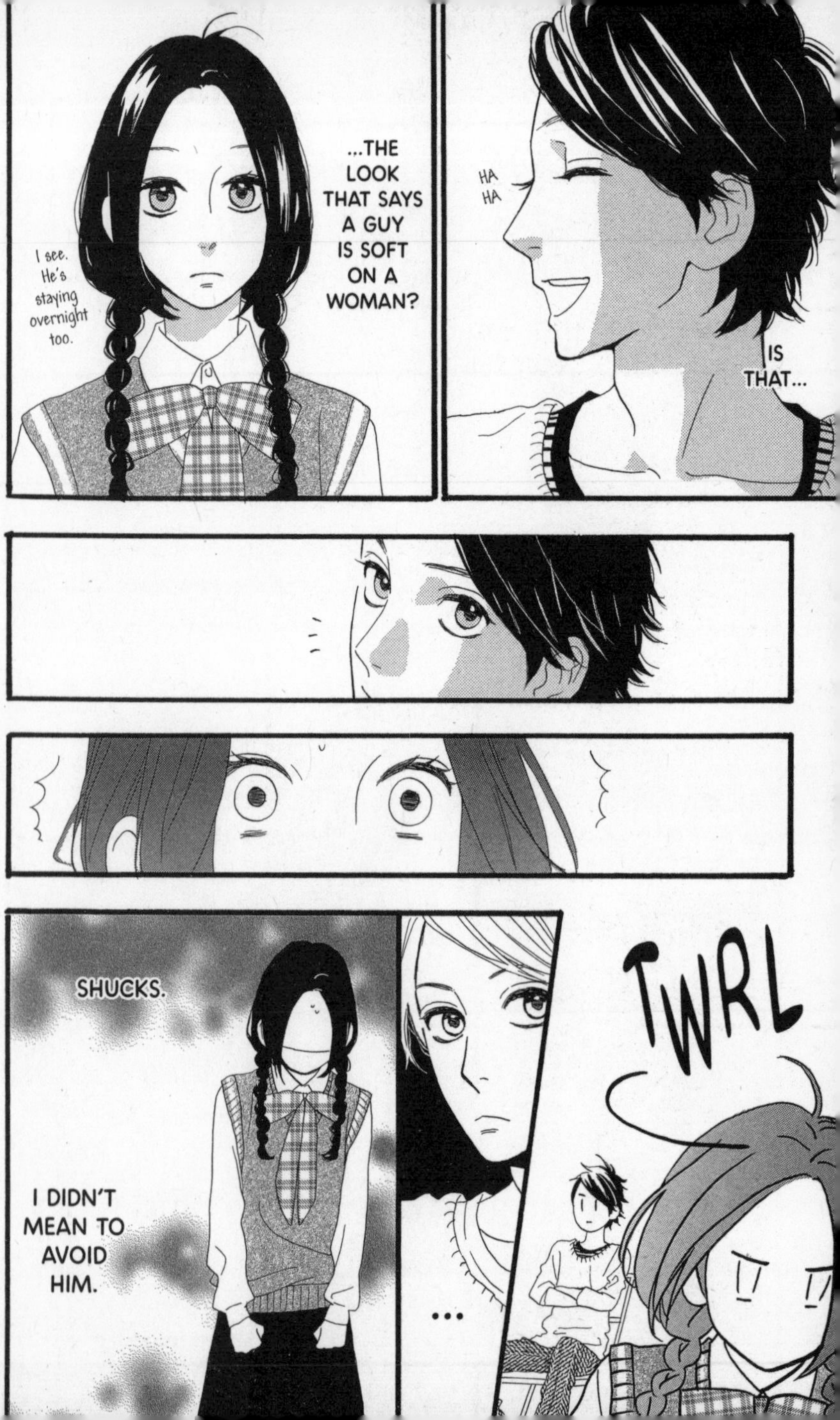
HA
HA
IS THAT...
...THE LOOK THAT SAYS A GUY IS SOFT ON A WOMAN?
I see. He's staying overnight too.
TWRL
...
SHUCKS.
I DIDN'T MEAN TO AVOID HIM.

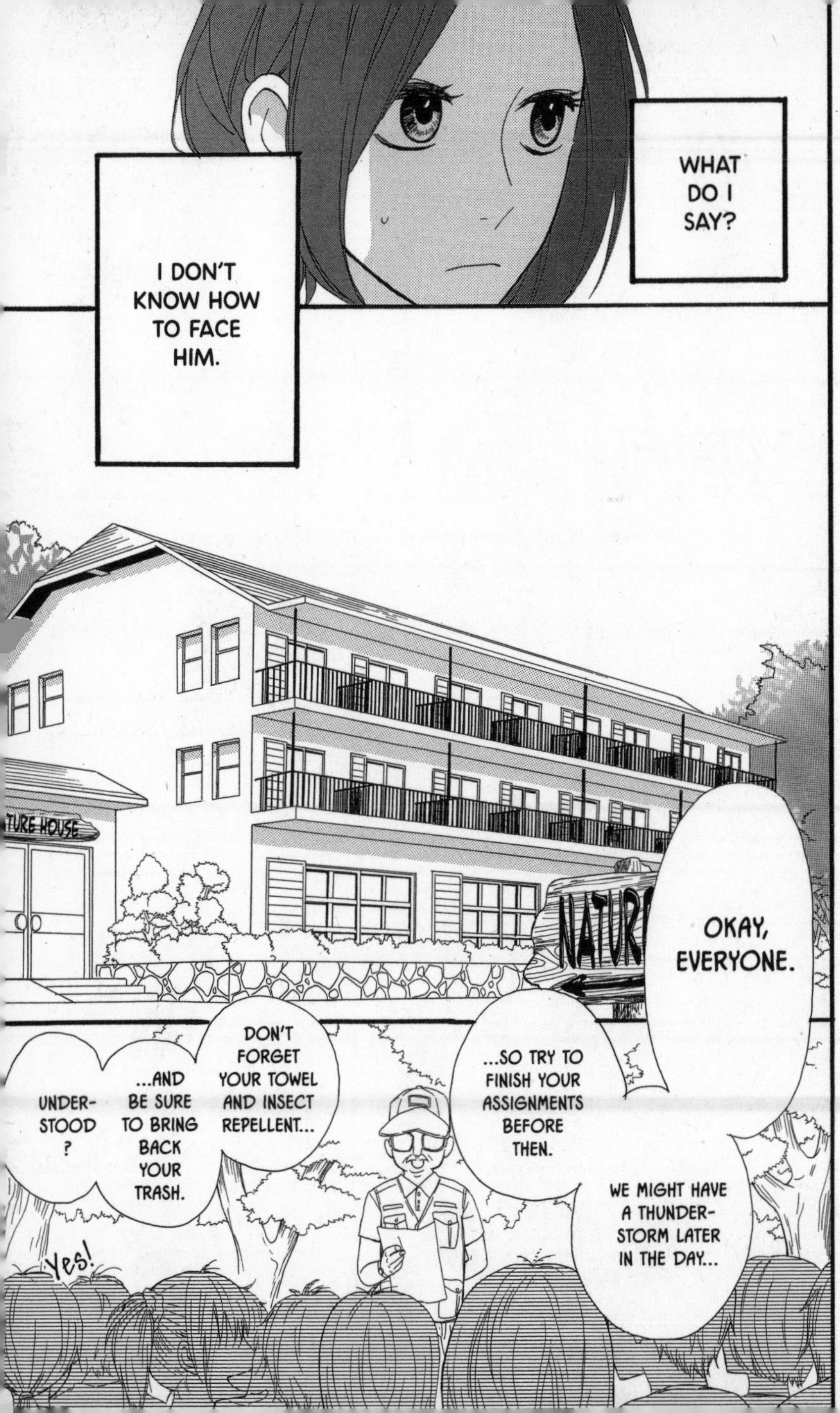
WHAT DO I SAY?
I DON'T KNOW HOW TO FACE HIM.
OKAY, EVERYONE.
WE MIGHT HAVE A THUNDER-STORM LATER IN THE DAY...
...SO TRY TO FINISH YOUR ASSIGNMENTS BEFORE THEN.
DON'T FORGET YOUR TOWEL AND INSECT REPELLENT...
...AND BE SURE TO BRING BACK YOUR TRASH.
UNDER-STOOD?
Yes!

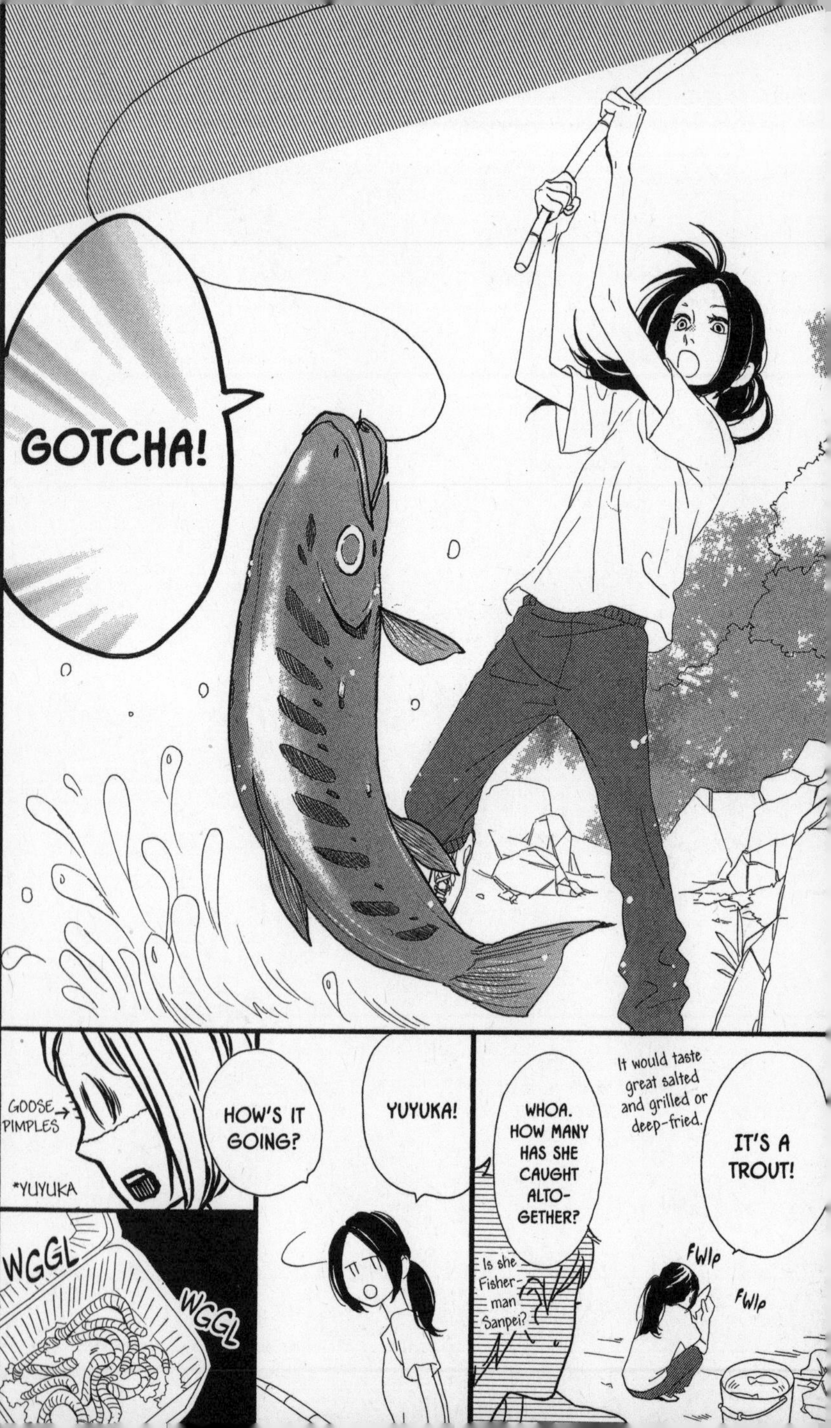
GOTCHA!
IT'S A TROUT!
It would taste great salted and grilled or deep-fried.
WHOA. HOW MANY HAS SHE CAUGHT ALTO-GETHER?
FWlp
FWlp
Is she Fisher-man Sanpei?
YUYUKA!
HOW'S IT GOING?
GOOSE PIMPLES
*YUYUKA
WGGL
WGGL

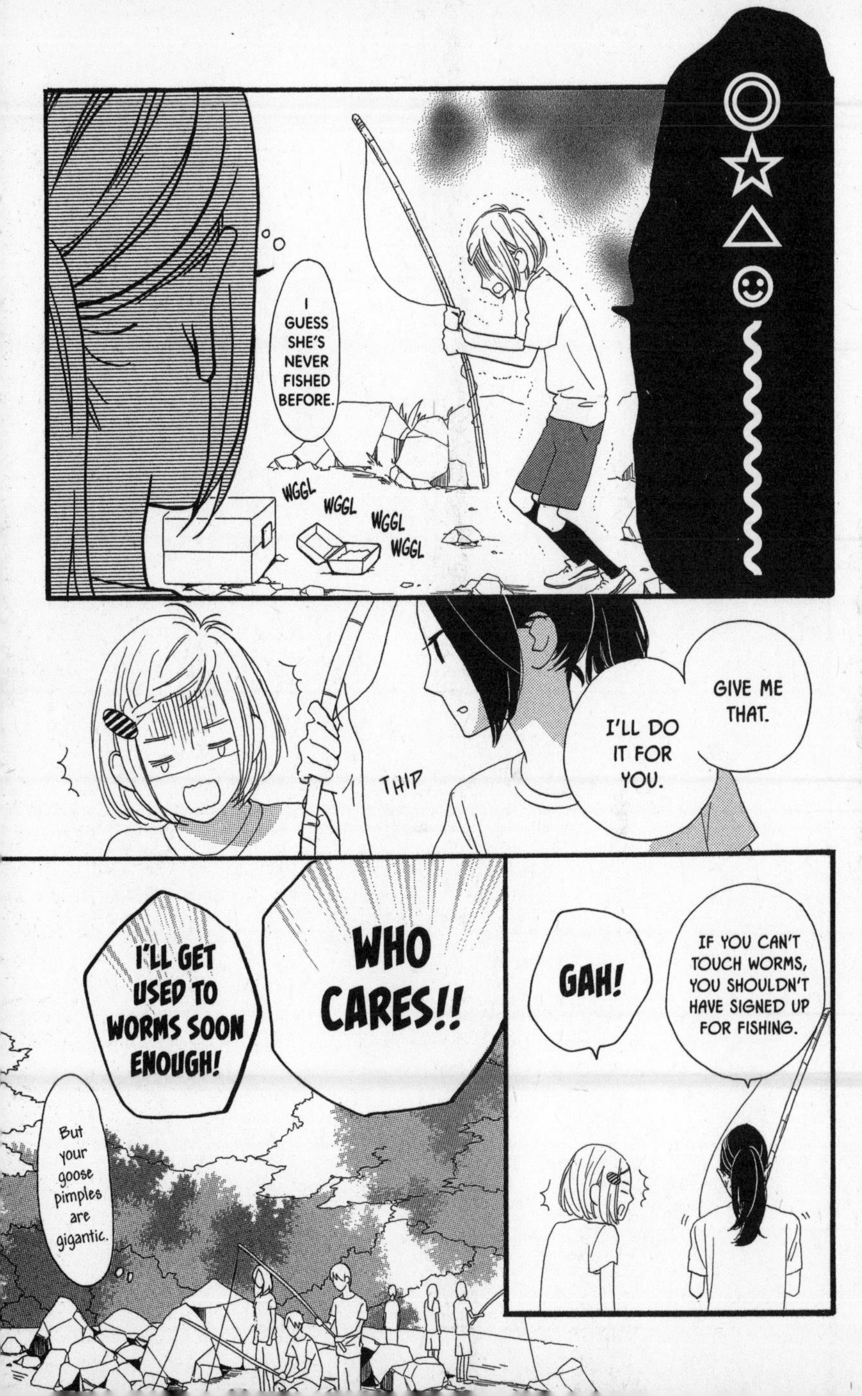

I GUESS SHE'S NEVER FISHED BEFORE.
WGGL
WGGL
WGGL
WGGL
GIVE ME THAT.
I'LL DO IT FOR YOU.
THIP
IF YOU CAN'T TOUCH WORMS, YOU SHOULDN'T HAVE SIGNED UP FOR FISHING.
GAH!
WHO CARES!!
I'LL GET USED TO WORMS SOON ENOUGH!
But your goose pimples are gigantic.

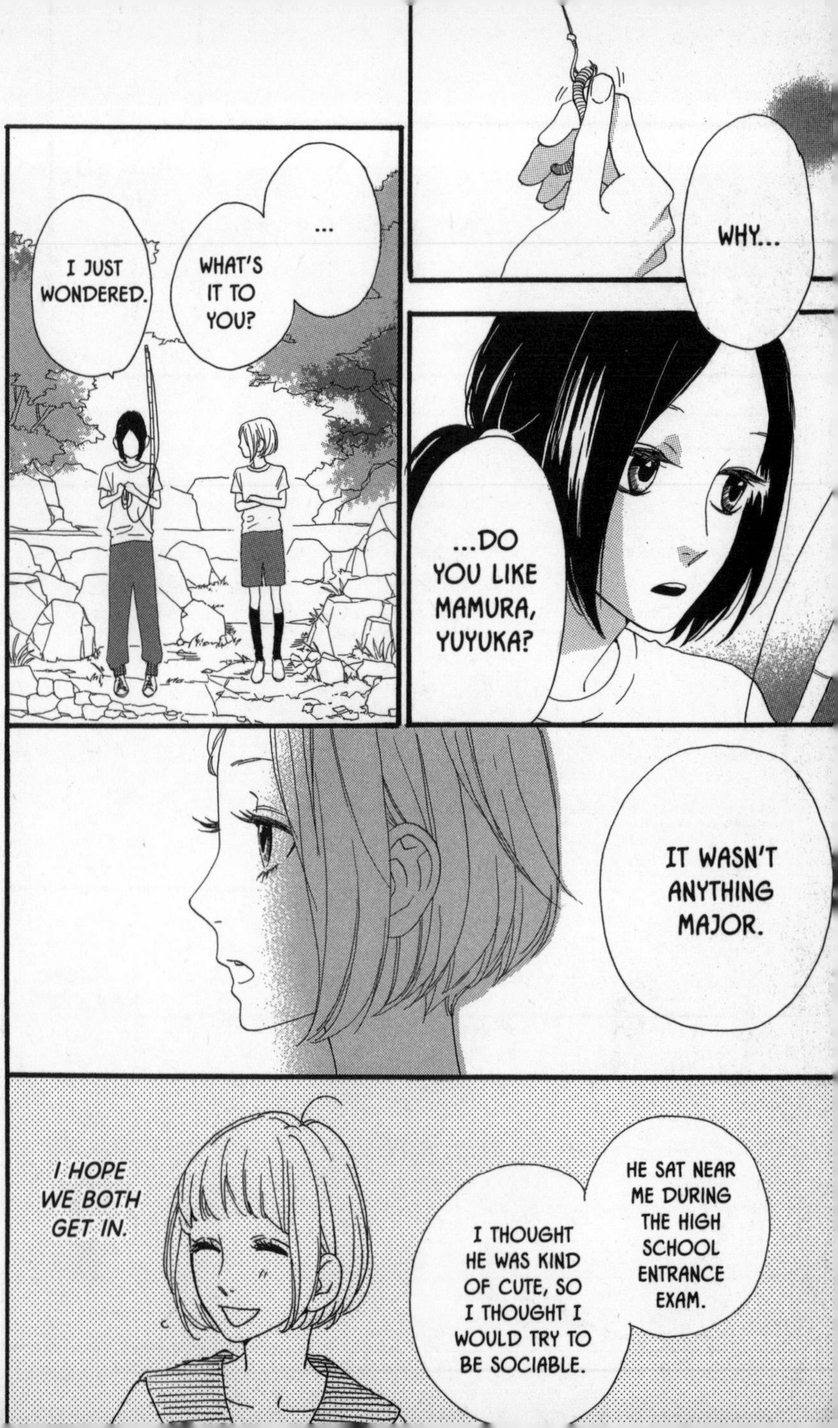
WHY...
...DO YOU LIKE MAMURA, YUYUKA?
...
WHAT'S IT TO YOU?
I JUST WONDERED.
IT WASN'T ANYTHING MAJOR.
HE SAT NEAR ME DURING THE HIGH SCHOOL ENTRANCE EXAM.
I THOUGHT HE WAS KIND OF CUTE, SO I THOUGHT I WOULD TRY TO BE SOCIABLE.
I HOPE WE BOTH GET IN.

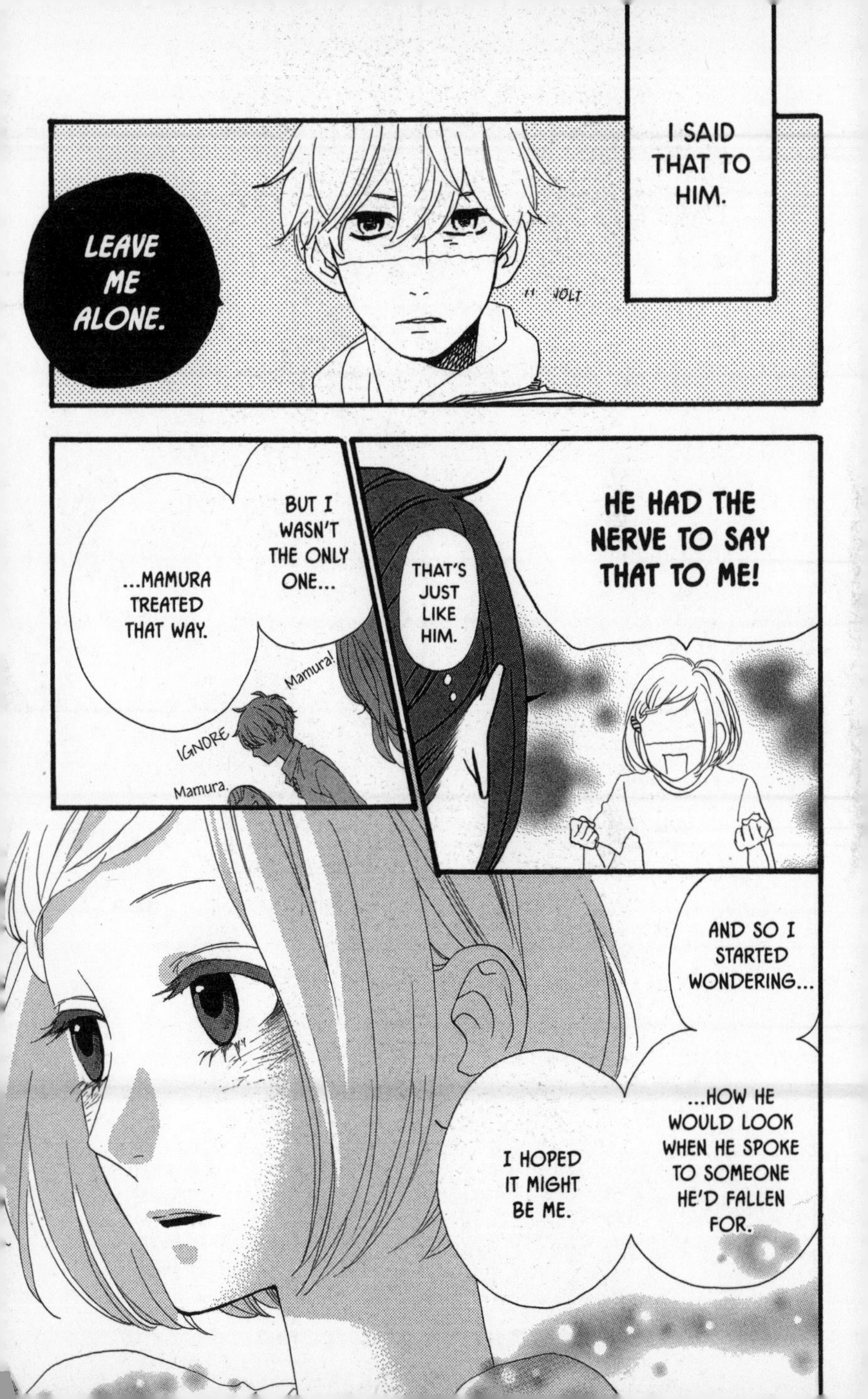
I SAID THAT TO HIM.
LEAVE ME ALONE.
JOLT
HE HAD THE NERVE TO SAY THAT TO ME!
THAT'S JUST LIKE HIM.
BUT I WASN'T THE ONLY ONE...
...MAMURA TREATED THAT WAY.
Mamura!
IGNORE
Mamura.
AND SO I STARTED WONDERING...
...HOW HE WOULD LOOK WHEN HE SPOKE TO SOMEONE HE'D FALLEN FOR.
I HOPED IT MIGHT BE ME.

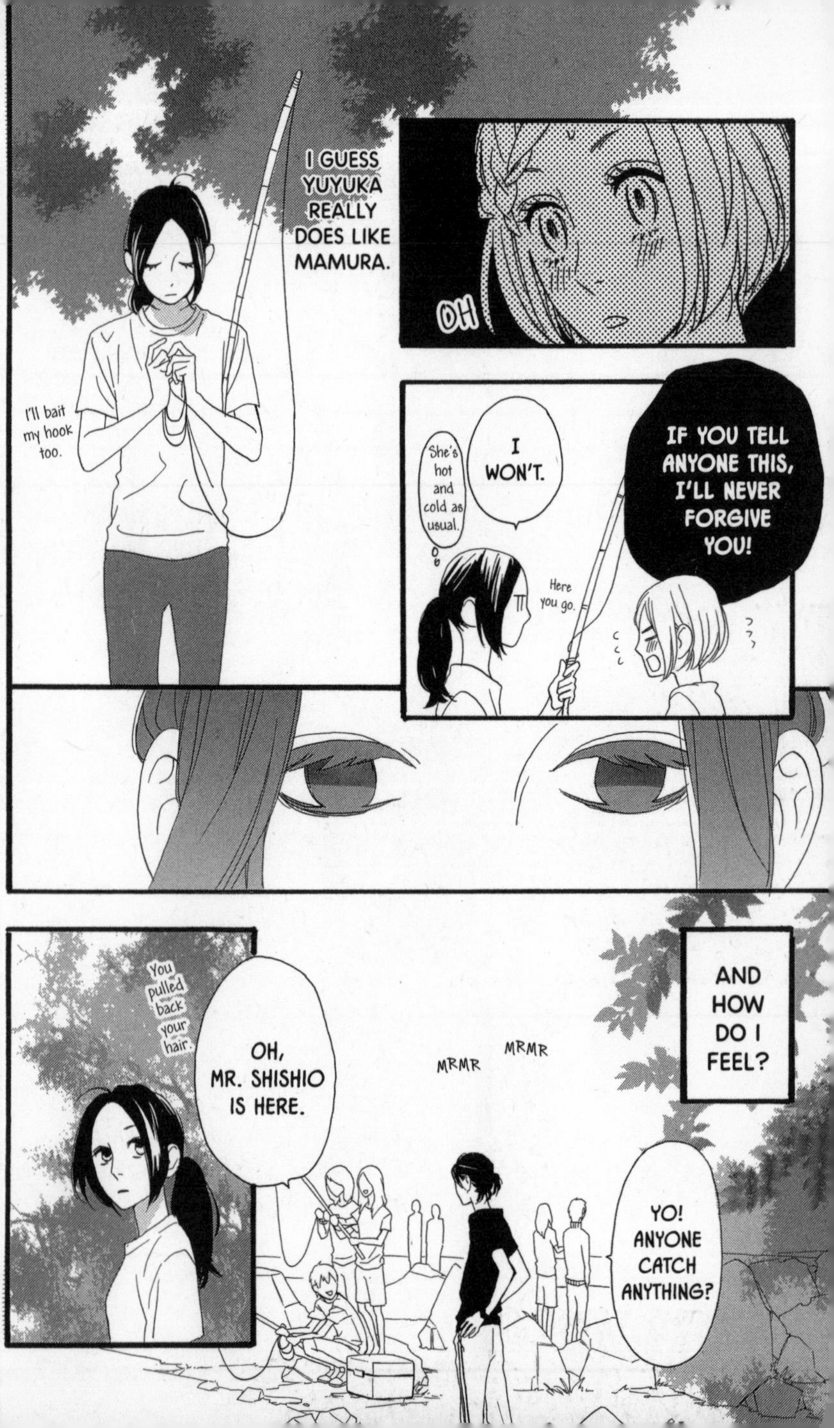
OH
IF YOU TELL ANYONE THIS, I'LL NEVER FORGIVE YOU!
Here you go.
I WON'T.
She's hot and cold as usual.
I GUESS YUYUKA REALLY DOES LIKE MAMURA.
I'll bait my hook too.
AND HOW DO I FEEL?
YO! ANYONE CATCH ANYTHING?
MRMR
MRMR
OH, MR. SHISHIO IS HERE.
You pulled back your hair.

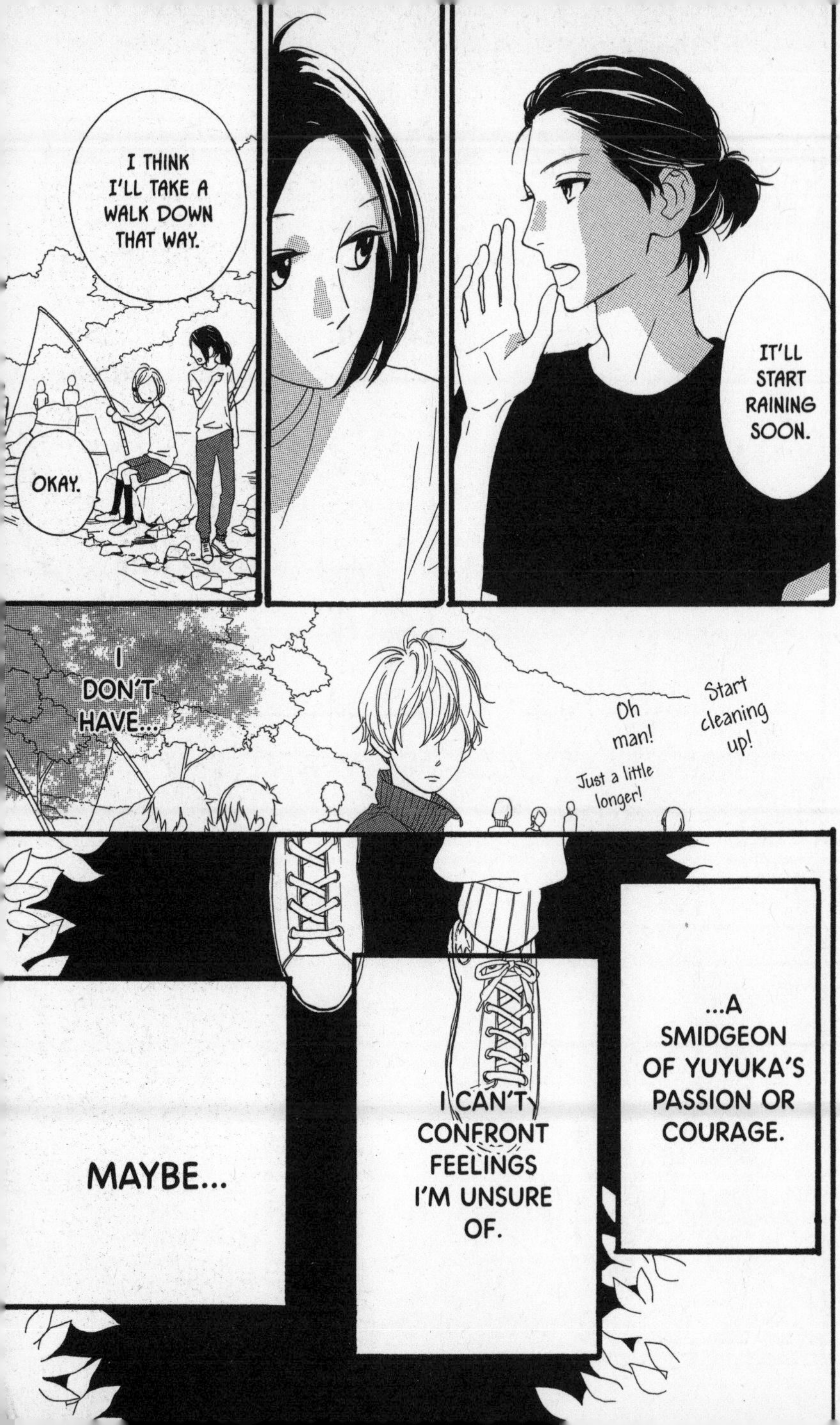
IT'LL START RAINING SOON.
I THINK I'LL TAKE A WALK DOWN THAT WAY.
OKAY.
Start cleaning up!
Oh man!
Just a little longer!
I DON'T HAVE...
...A SMIDGEON OF YUYUKA'S PASSION OR COURAGE.
I CAN'T CONFRONT FEELINGS I'M UNSURE OF.
MAYBE...

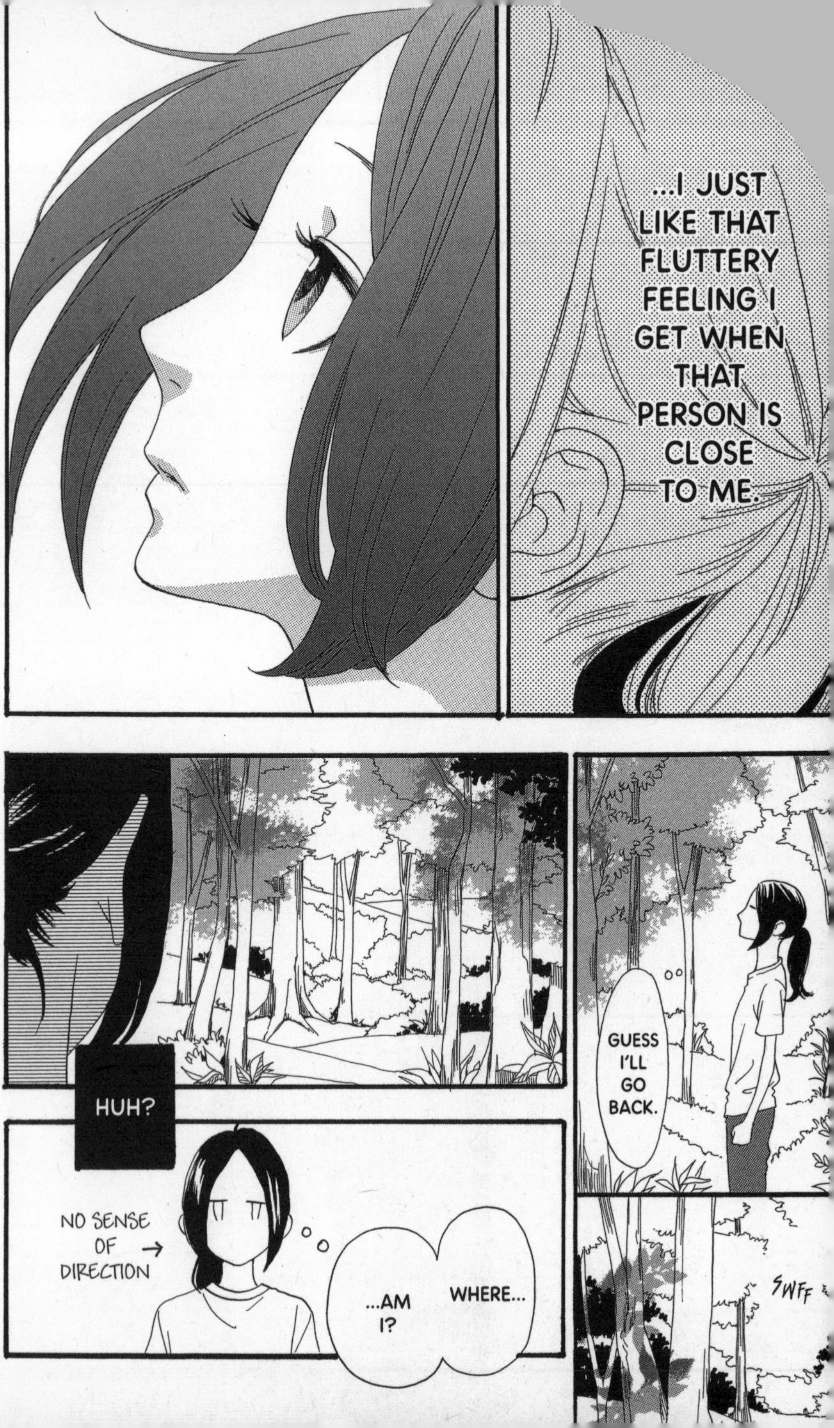
...I JUST LIKE THAT FLUTTERY FEELING I GET WHEN THAT PERSON IS CLOSE TO ME.
GUESS I'LL GO BACK.
HUH?
SWFF
WHERE...
...AM I?
NO SENSE OF DIRECTION

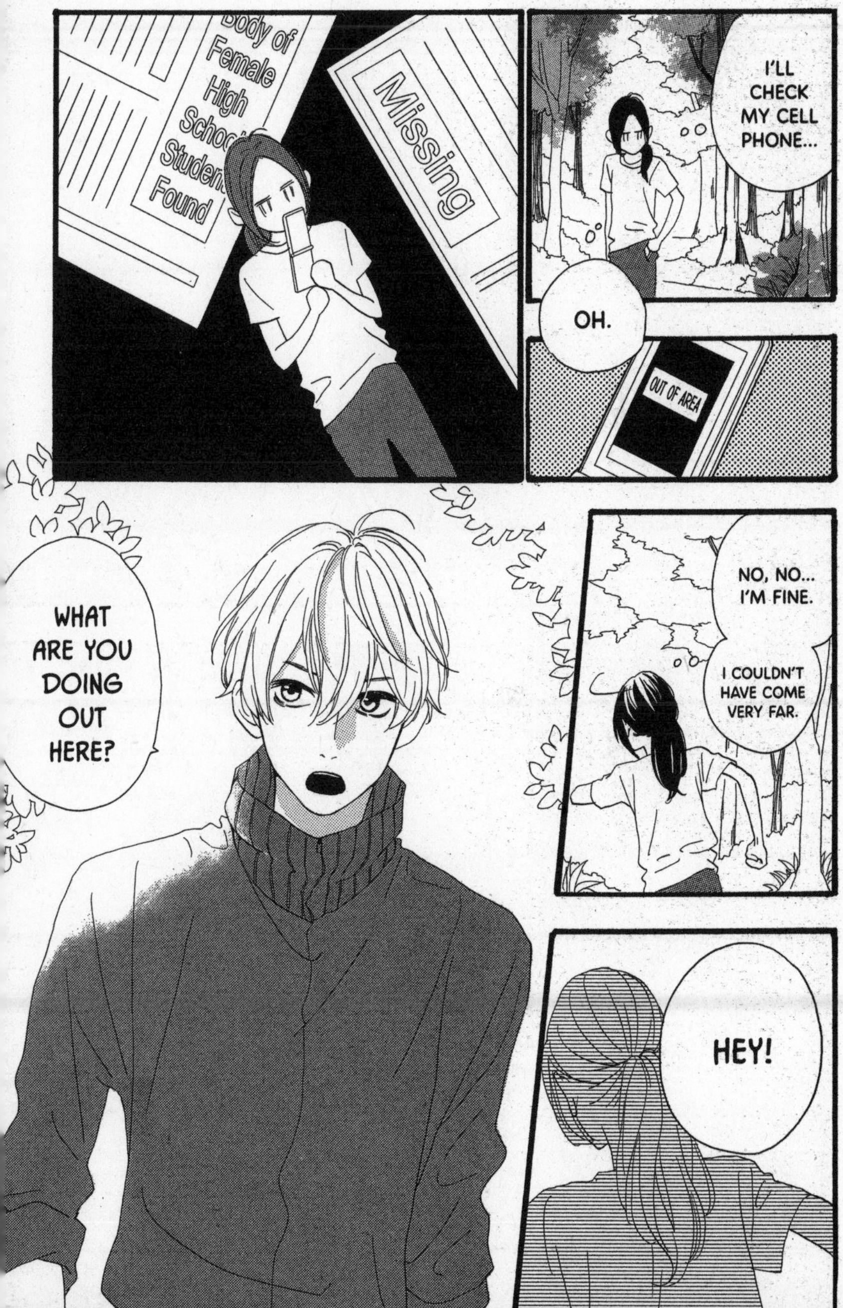

I'LL CHECK MY CELL PHONE...
OH.
OUT OF AREA
Body of Female High
Found
Missing
NO, NO... I'M FINE.
I COULDN'T HAVE COME VERY FAR.
HEY!
WHAT ARE YOU DOING OUT HERE?

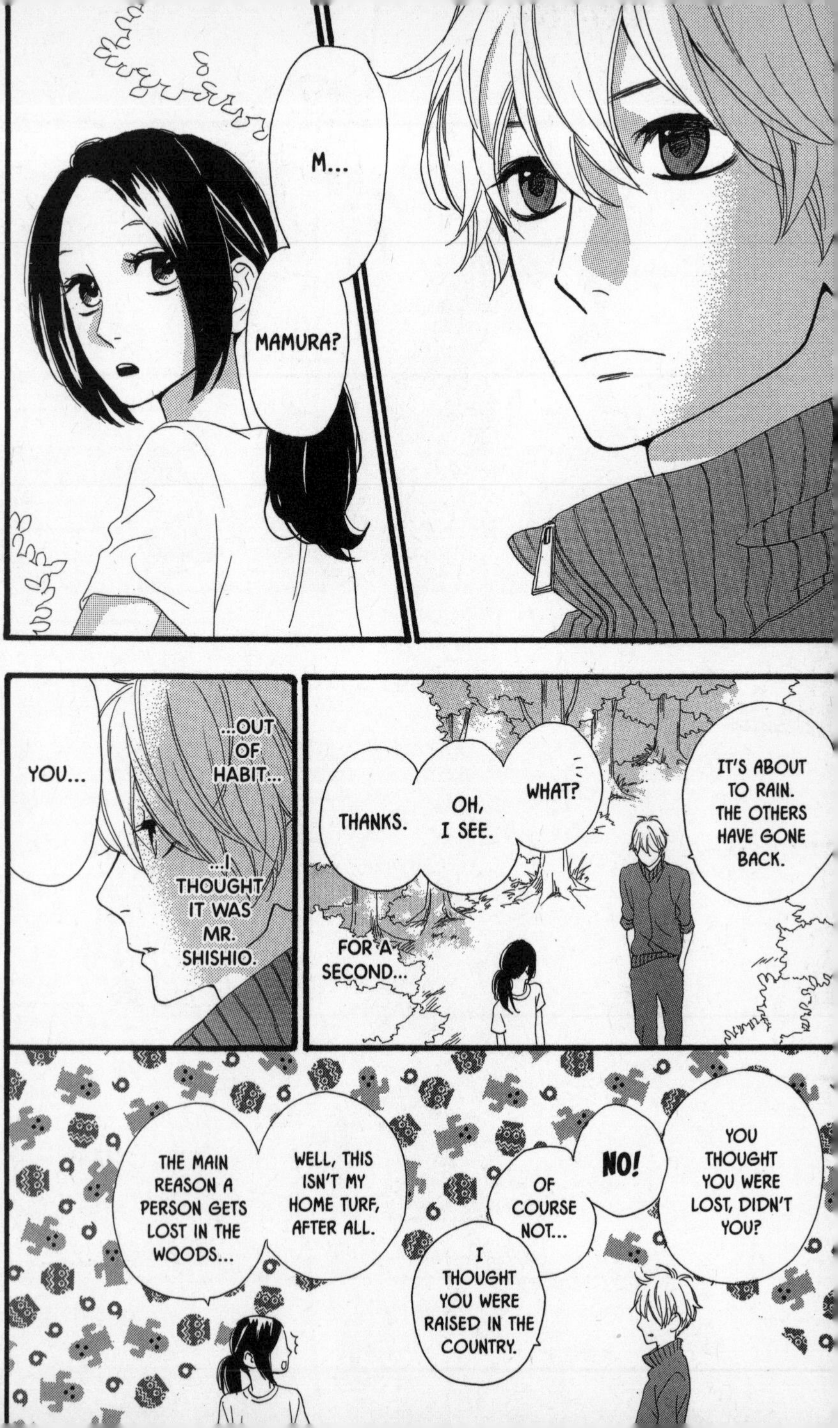
M...
MAMURA?
IT'S ABOUT TO RAIN. THE OTHERS HAVE GONE BACK.
WHAT?
OH, I SEE.
THANKS.
FOR A SECOND...
...OUT OF HABIT...
...I THOUGHT IT WAS MR. SHISHIO.
YOU...
YOU THOUGHT YOU WERE LOST, DIDN'T YOU?
NO!
OF COURSE NOT...
I THOUGHT YOU WERE RAISED IN THE COUNTRY.
WELL, THIS ISN'T MY HOME TURF, AFTER ALL.
THE MAIN REASON A PERSON GETS LOST IN THE WOODS...

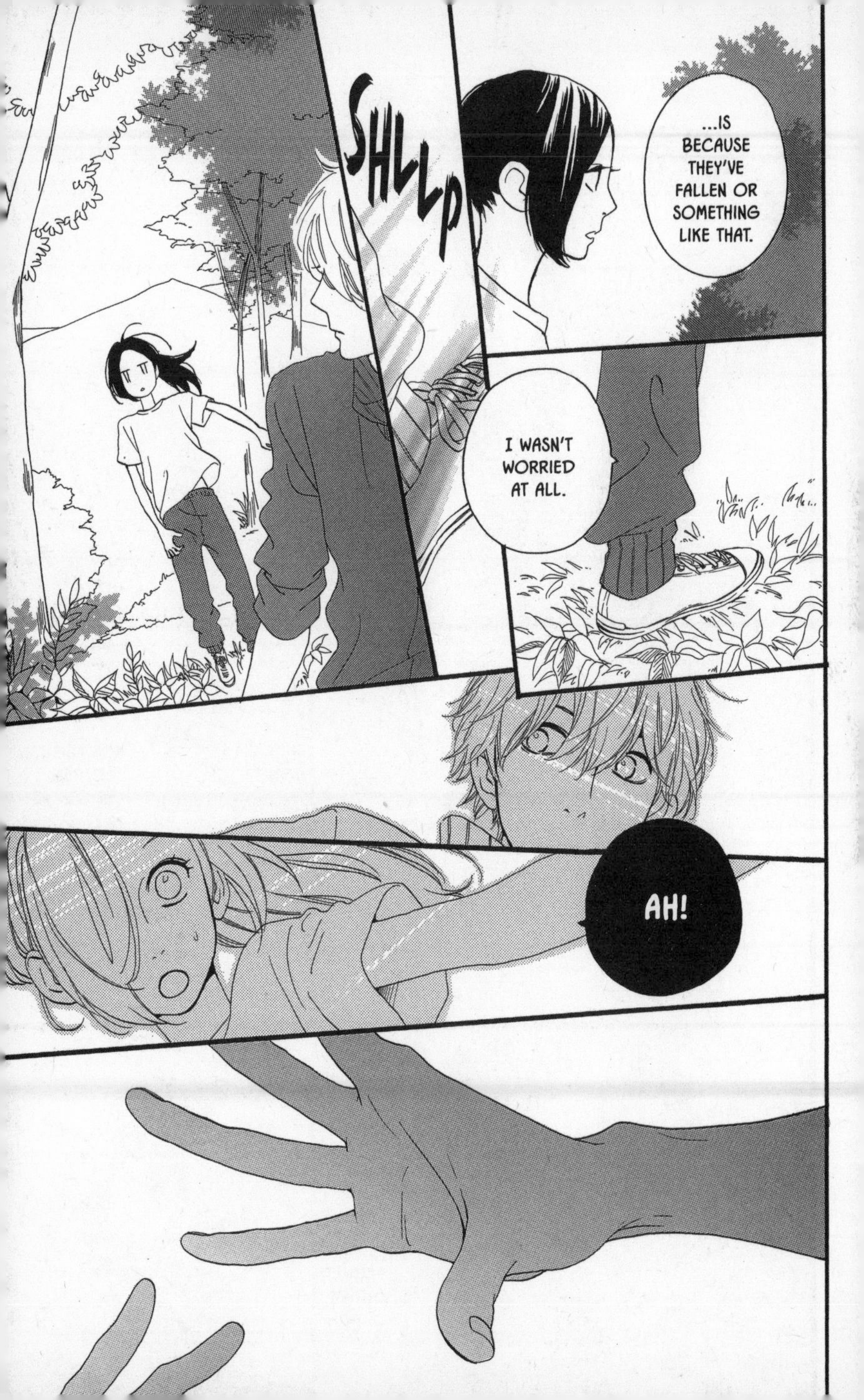
...IS BECAUSE THEY'VE FALLEN OR SOMETHING LIKE THAT.
SHLLP
I WASN'T WORRIED AT ALL.
AH!

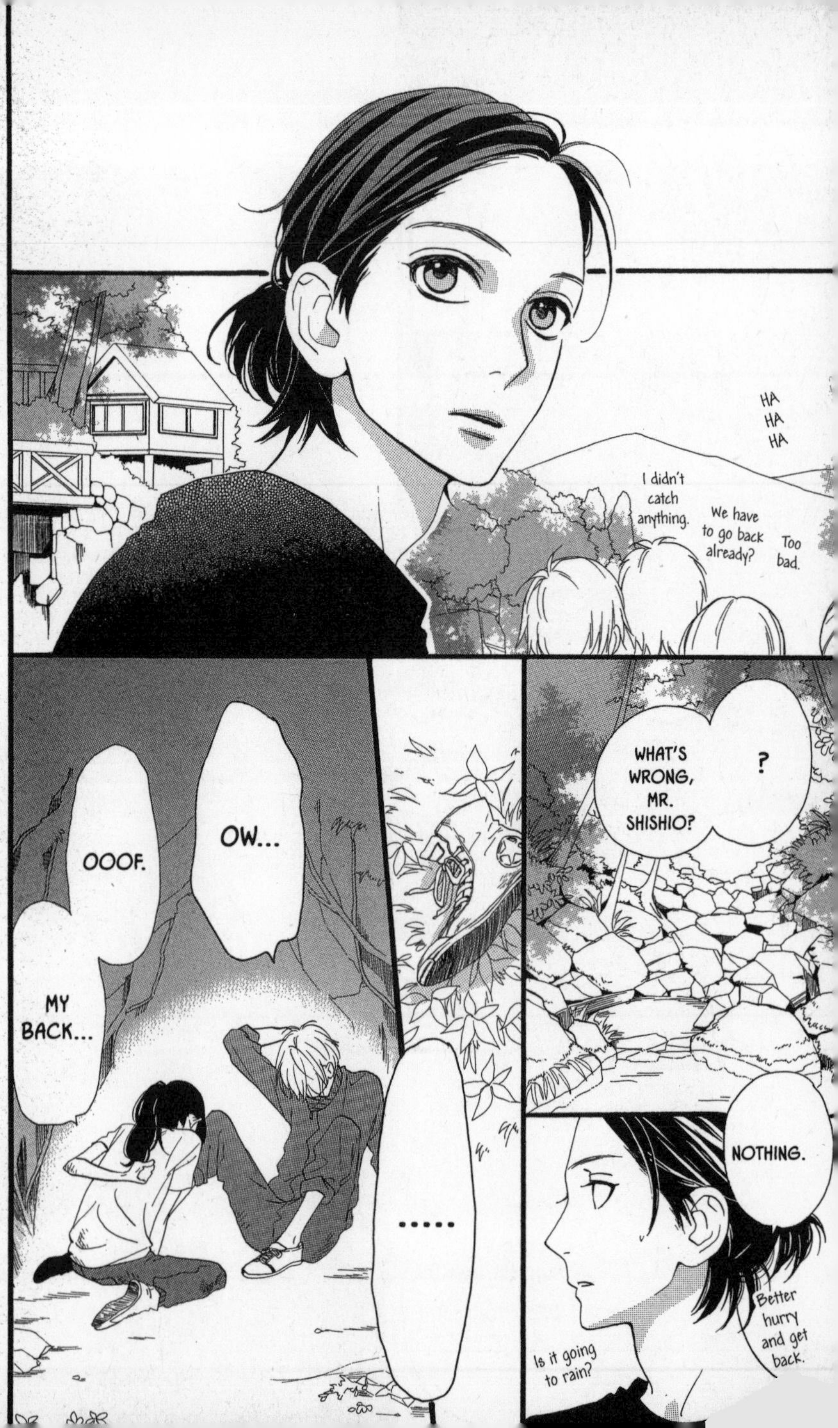
HA
HA
HA
Too bad.
We have to go back already?
I didn't catch anything.
WHAT'S WRONG, MR. SHISHIO?
?
NOTHING.
Better hurry and get back.
Is it going to rain?
.....
OW...
OOOF.
MY BACK...

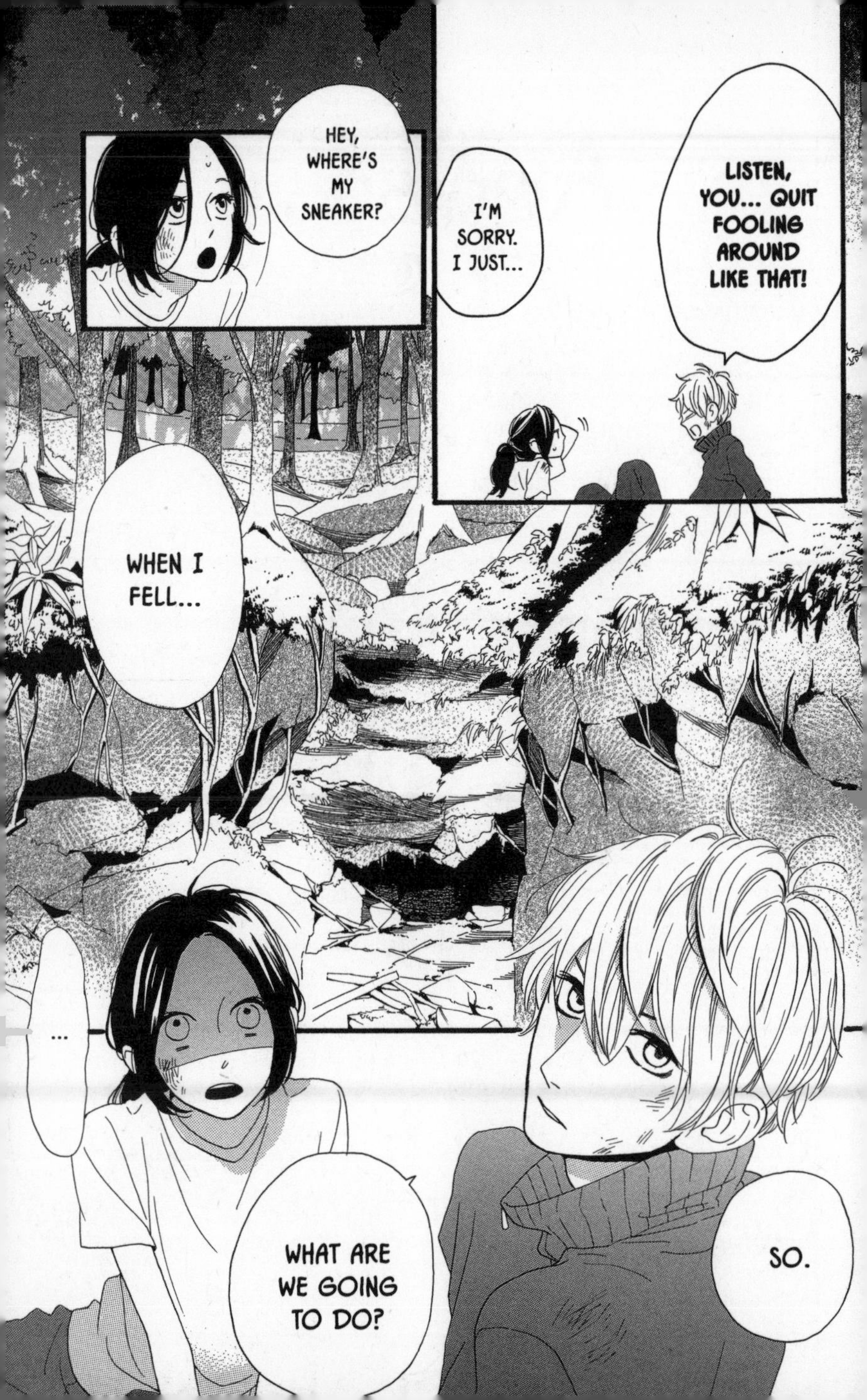
LISTEN, YOU... QUIT FOOLING AROUND LIKE THAT!
I'M SORRY. I JUST...
HEY, WHERE'S MY SNEAKER?
WHEN I FELL...
...
SO.
WHAT ARE WE GOING TO DO?

And so...

Volume 2 is safely (?) done. ✿✿ Hurray—!!
Thank you very much! I truly owe it all to you! I have slowly grown accustomed to publishing twice a month. (Still, my deadlines are a bit iffy. ↗)
Anyway, if you get some enjoyment out of this series, I will be happy!

★SPECIAL Thanks★

- Editorial department • Editor K • Sakochan • Ms. Noboria
- Printer's staff • Graphic designers • Friends & family
- All my readers!!!

With all my love!
From Paulo Silver (just kidding)

Those in the know will understand.
From *New Horizon* (English textbook).
Forgive me.

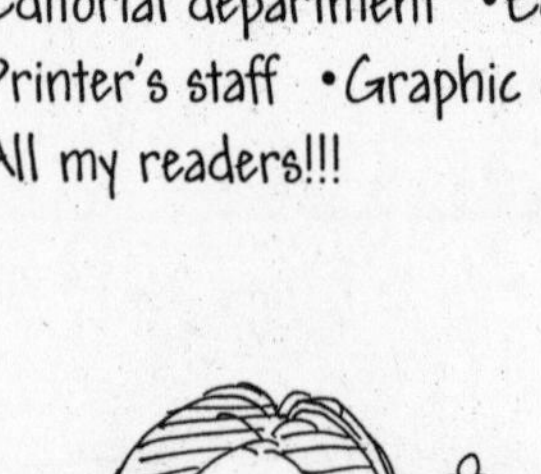

My hair has grown so quickly.

Mika☆

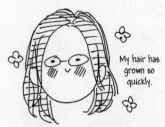

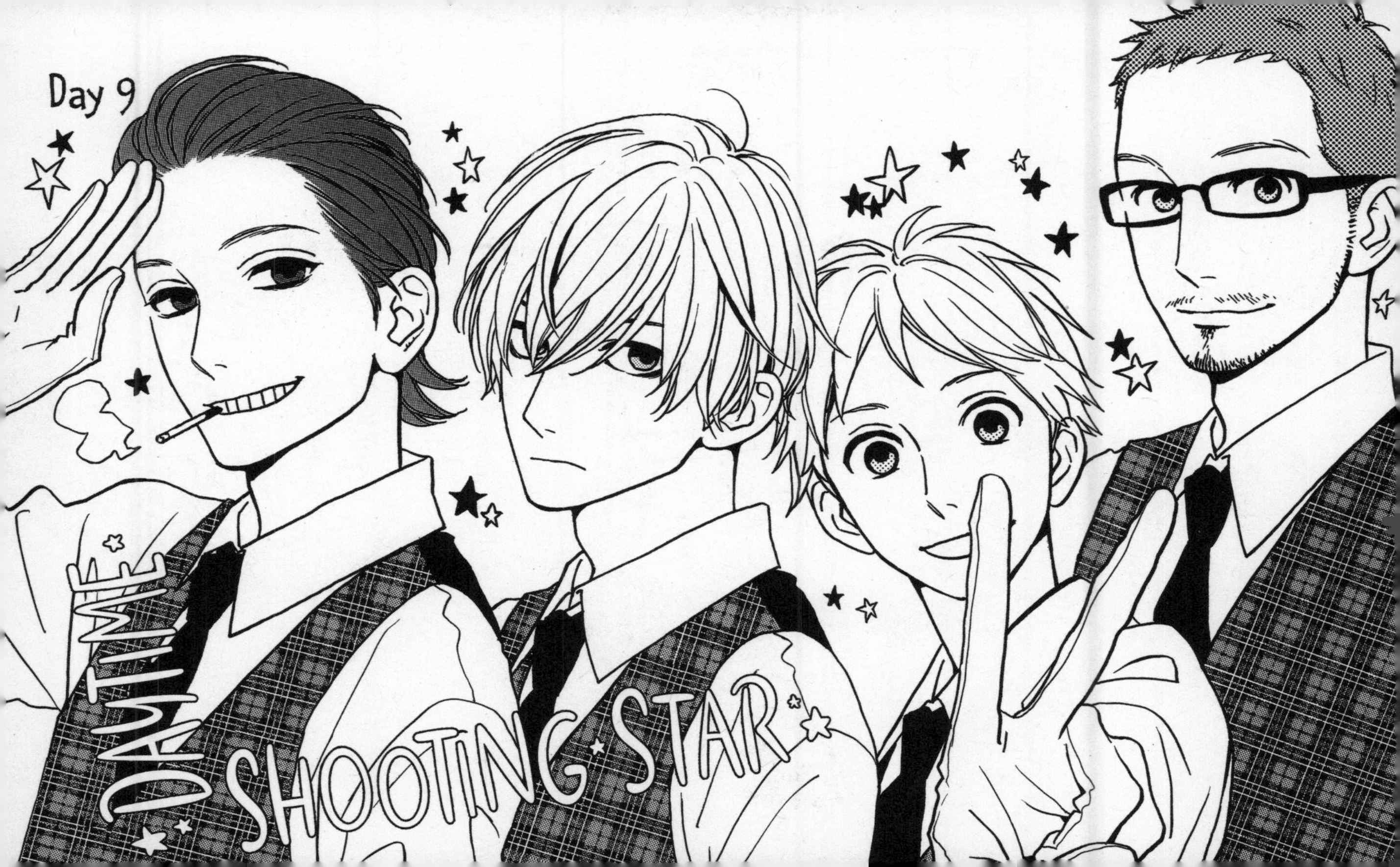
Day 9
DAYTIME SHOOTING STAR

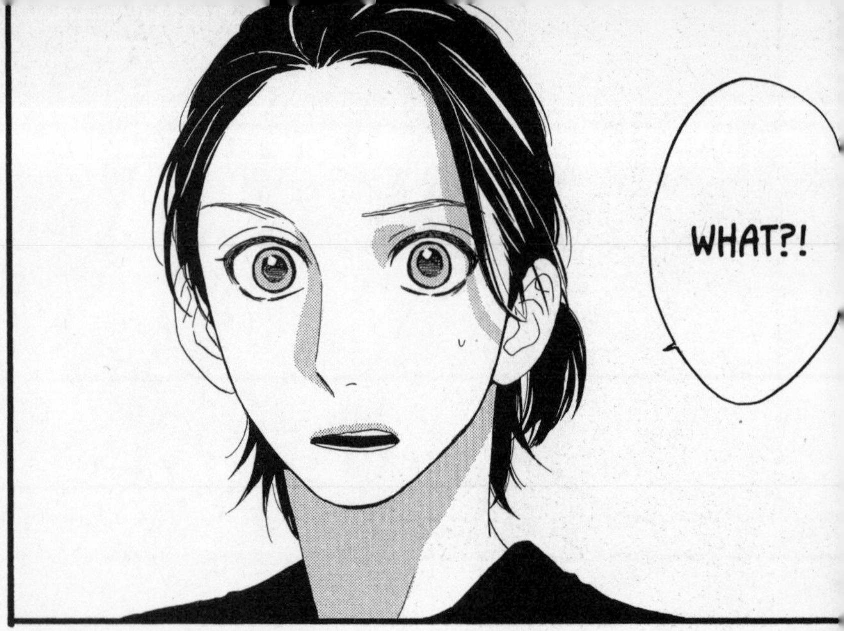
WHAT?!

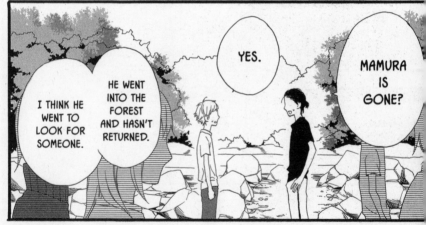

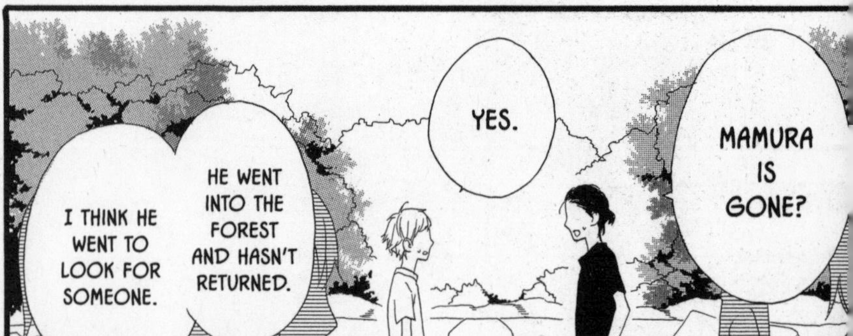
MAMURA IS GONE?
YES.
HE WENT INTO THE FOREST AND HASN'T RETURNED.
I THINK HE WENT TO LOOK FOR SOMEONE.

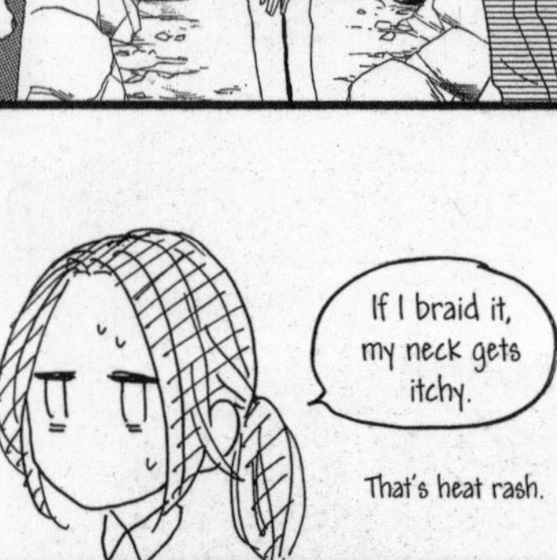
If I braid it, my neck gets itchy.
That's heat rash.

Suzume has her hair in a ponytail because it's been hot.

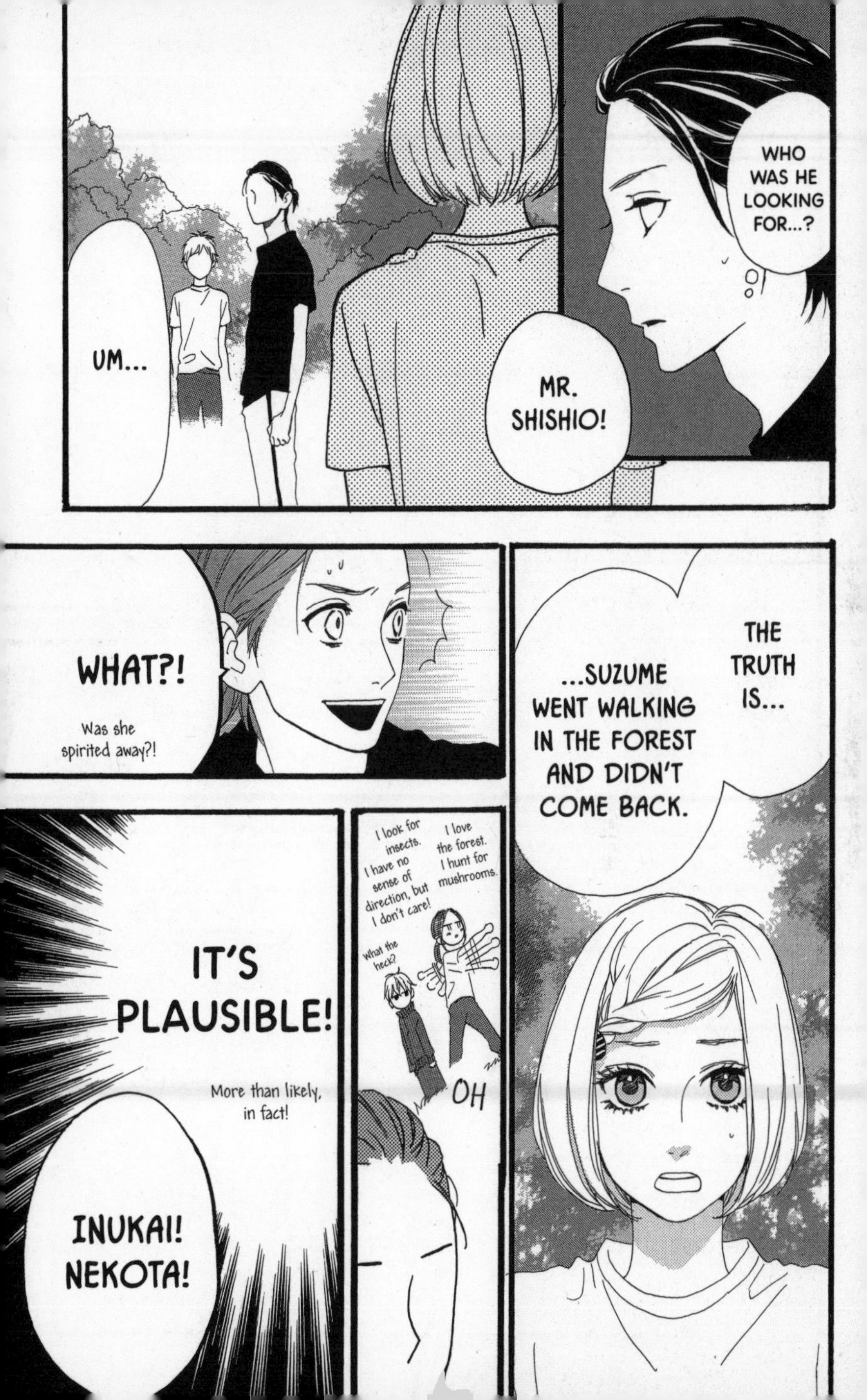
WHO WAS HE LOOKING FOR...?
MR. SHISHIO!
UM...
THE TRUTH IS...
...SUZUME WENT WALKING IN THE FOREST AND DIDN'T COME BACK.
WHAT?!
Was she spirited away?!
I love the forest. I hunt for mushrooms.
I look for insects. I have no sense of direction, but I don't care!
What the heck?
OH
IT'S PLAUSIBLE!
More than likely, in fact!
INUKAI! NEKOTA!

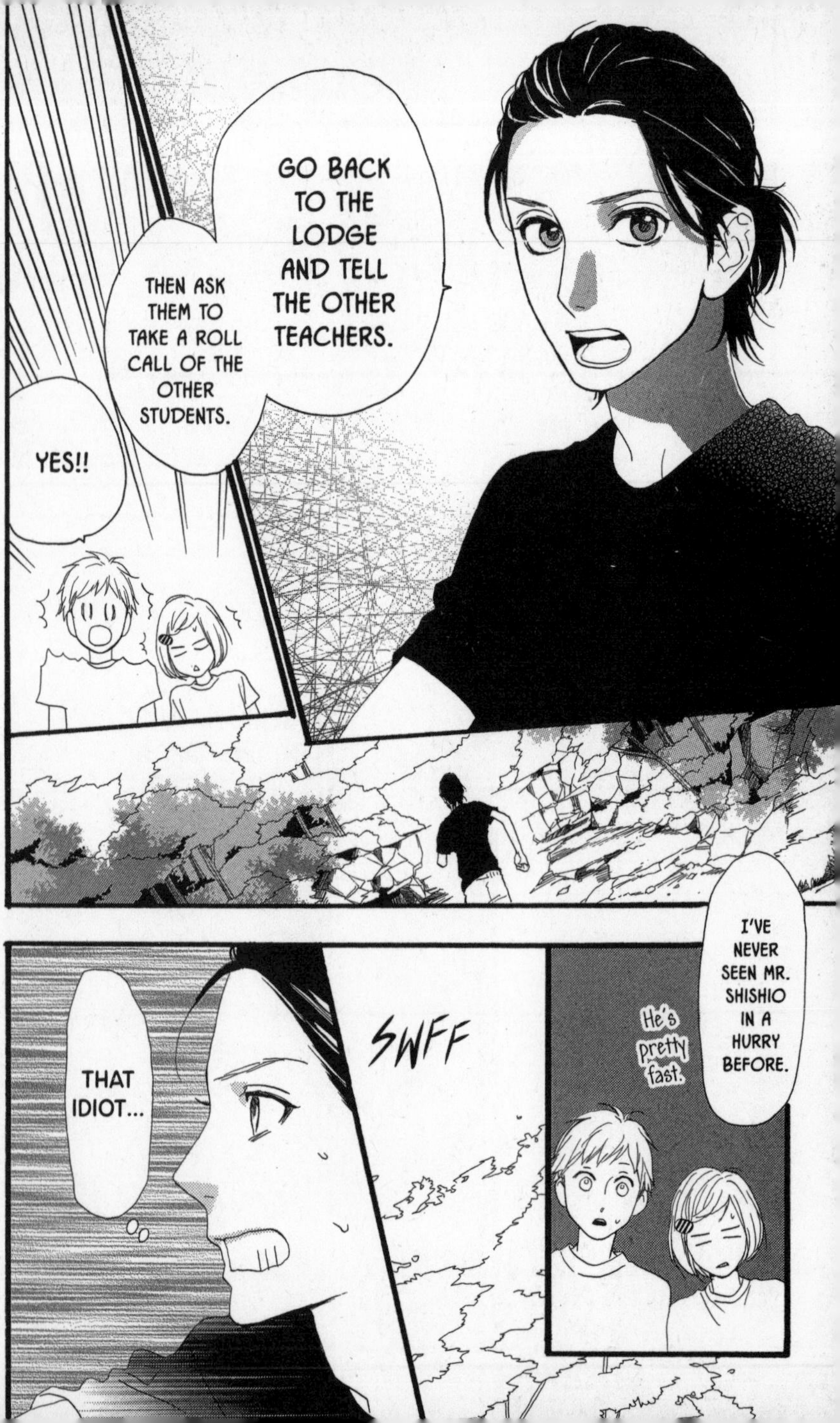
GO BACK TO THE LODGE AND TELL THE OTHER TEACHERS.
THEN ASK THEM TO TAKE A ROLL CALL OF THE OTHER STUDENTS.
YES!!
I'VE NEVER SEEN MR. SHISHIO IN A HURRY BEFORE.
He's pretty fast.
SWFF
THAT IDIOT...

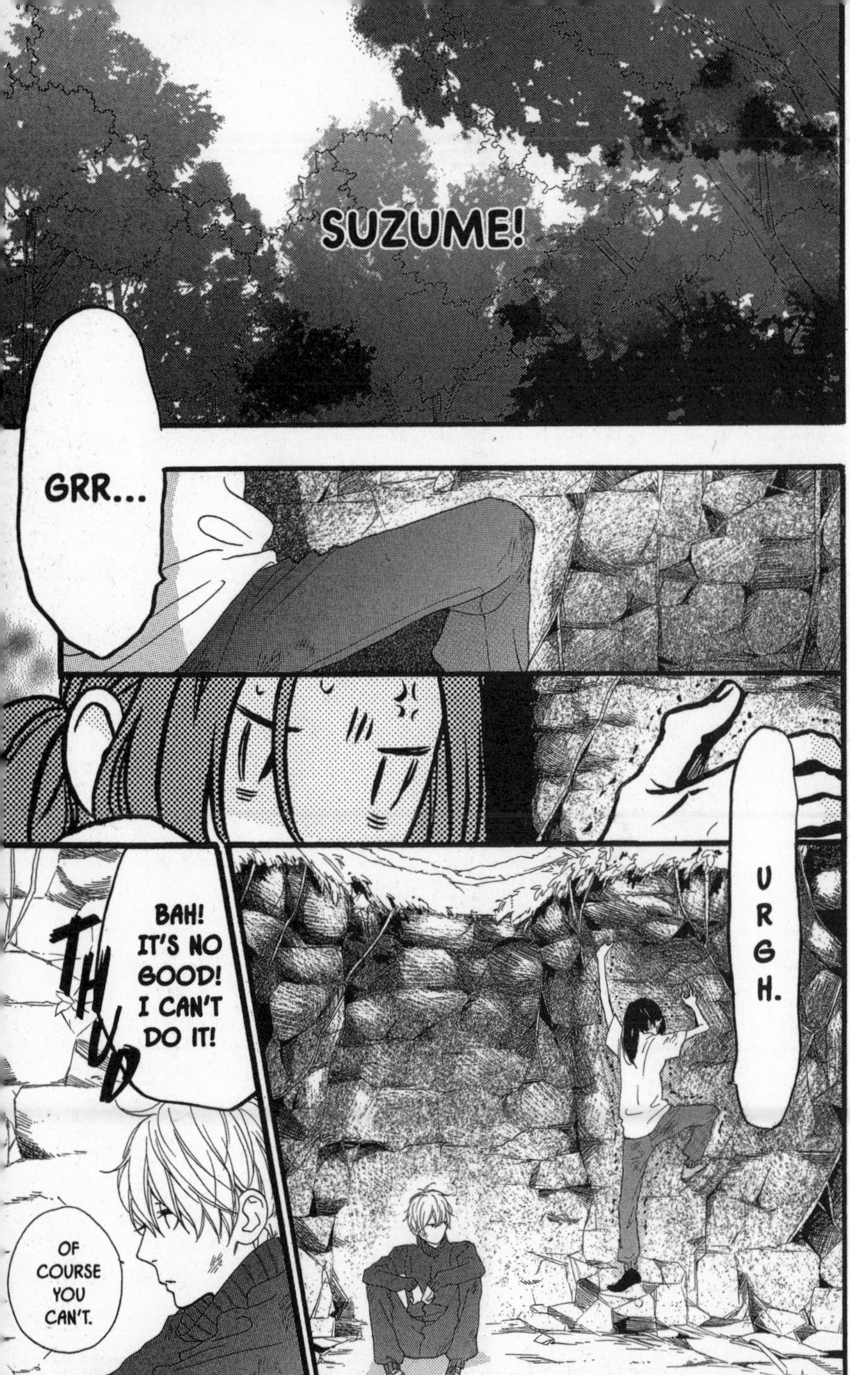
SUZUME!
GRR...
URGH.
THUD
BAH! IT'S NO GOOD! I CAN'T DO IT!
OF COURSE YOU CAN'T.

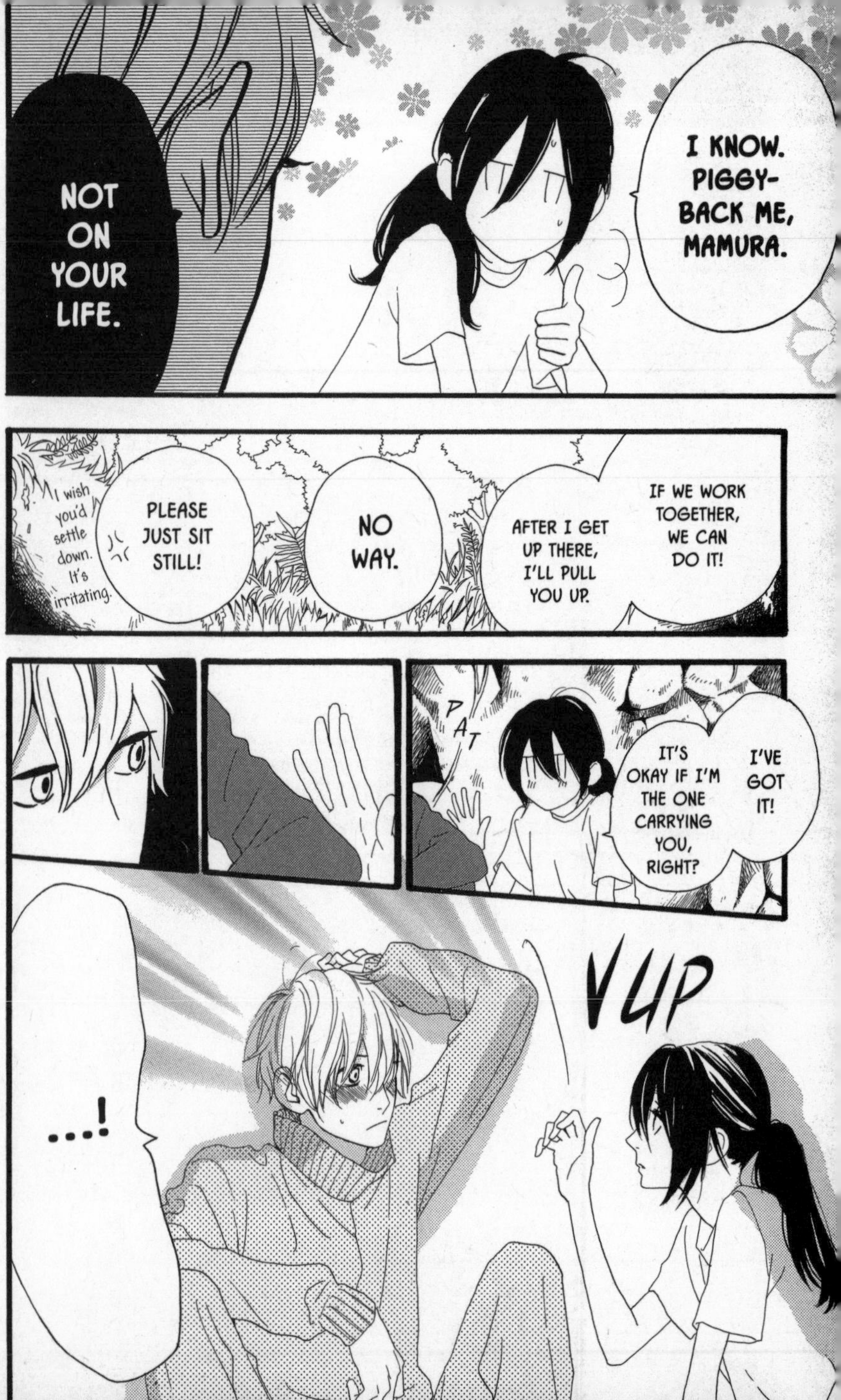
I KNOW. PIGGY-BACK ME, MAMURA.
NOT ON YOUR LIFE.
IF WE WORK TOGETHER, WE CAN DO IT!
AFTER I GET UP THERE, I'LL PULL YOU UP.
NO WAY.
PLEASE JUST SIT STILL!
I wish you'd settle down. It's irritating.
I'VE GOT IT!
IT'S OKAY IF I'M THE ONE CARRYING YOU, RIGHT?
PAT
VUP
...!

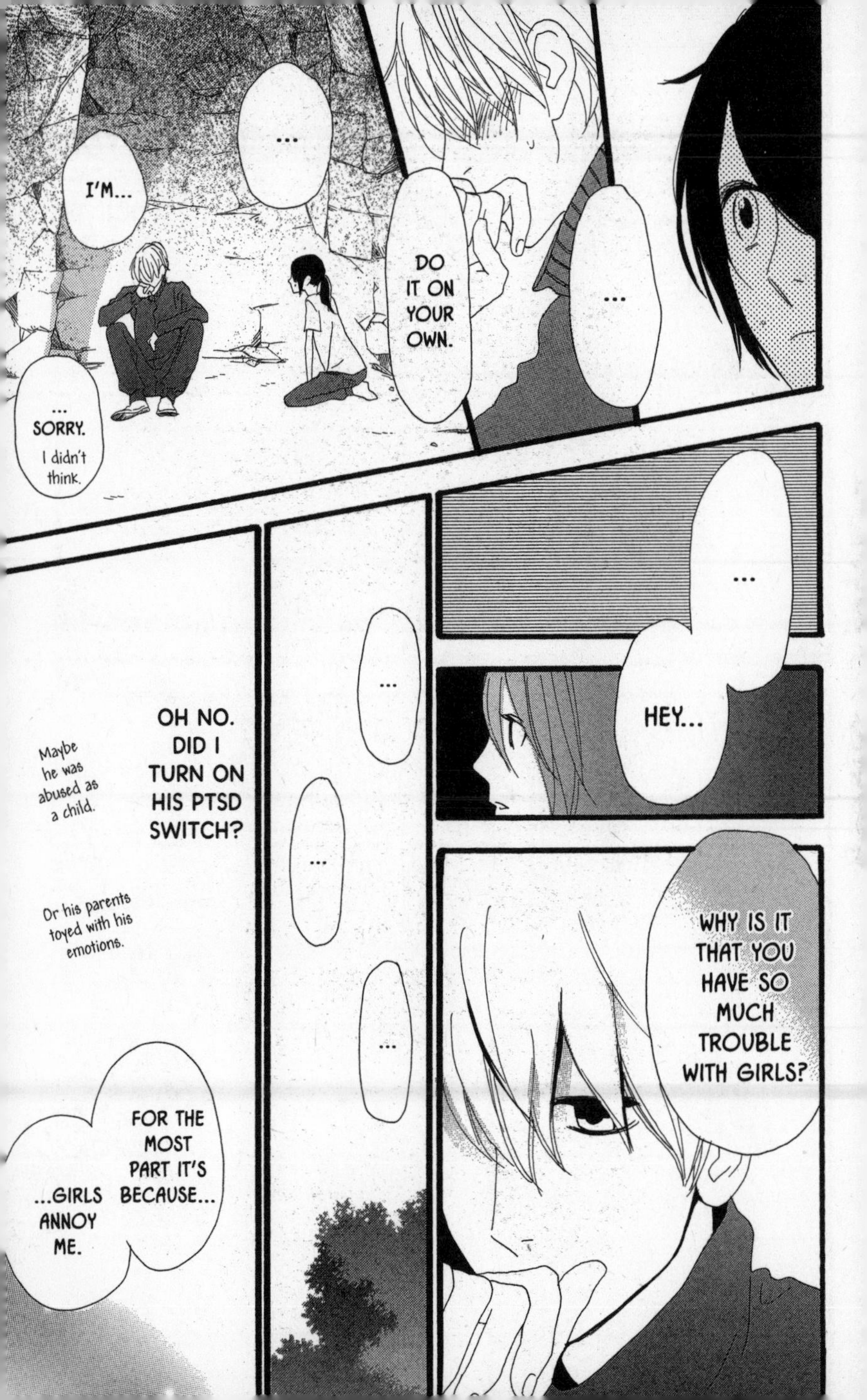

...
DO IT ON YOUR OWN.
...
I'M...
... SORRY. I didn't think.
...
HEY...
WHY IS IT THAT YOU HAVE SO MUCH TROUBLE WITH GIRLS?
...
...
...
OH NO. DID I TURN ON HIS PTSD SWITCH?
Maybe he was abused as a child.
Or his parents toyed with his emotions.
FOR THE MOST PART IT'S BECAUSE... ...GIRLS ANNOY ME.

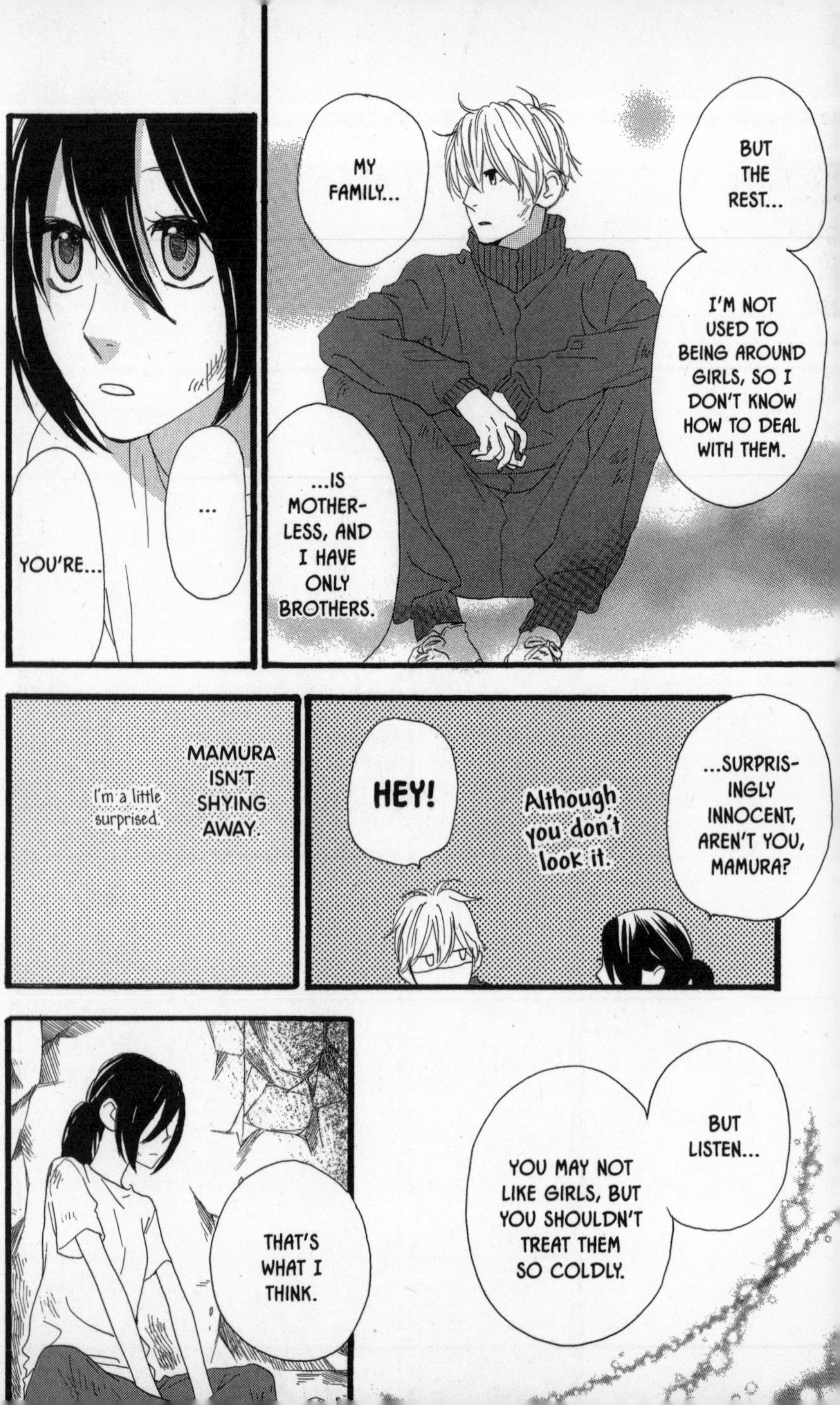
MY FAMILY...
...IS MOTHERLESS, AND I HAVE ONLY BROTHERS.
BUT THE REST...
I'M NOT USED TO BEING AROUND GIRLS, SO I DON'T KNOW HOW TO DEAL WITH THEM.
...
YOU'RE...
...SURPRISINGLY INNOCENT, AREN'T YOU, MAMURA?
Although you don't look it.
HEY!
MAMURA ISN'T SHYING AWAY.
I'm a little surprised.
BUT LISTEN...
YOU MAY NOT LIKE GIRLS, BUT YOU SHOULDN'T TREAT THEM SO COLDLY.
THAT'S WHAT I THINK.

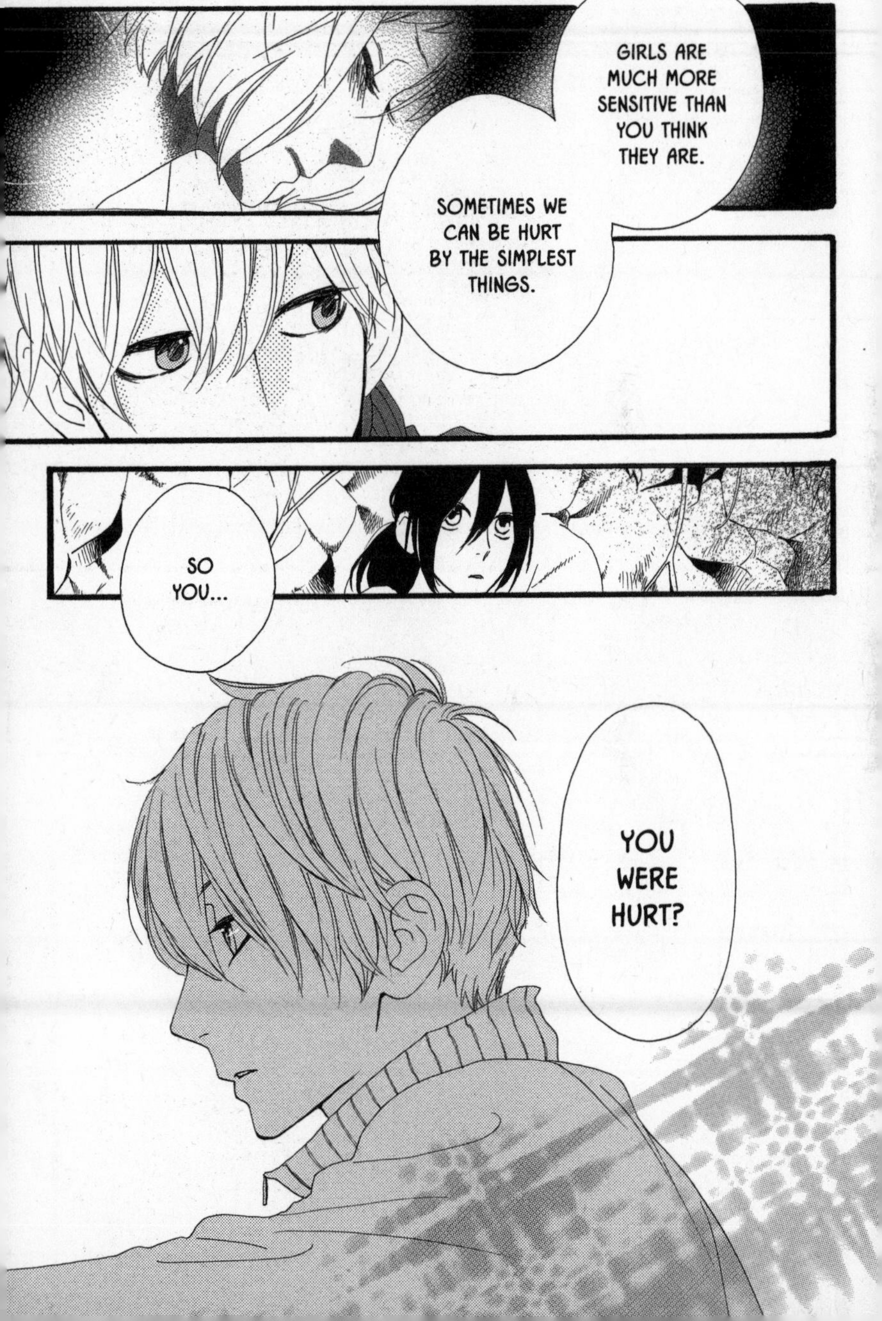
GIRLS ARE MUCH MORE SENSITIVE THAN YOU THINK THEY ARE.
SOMETIMES WE CAN BE HURT BY THE SIMPLEST THINGS.
SO YOU...
YOU WERE HURT?

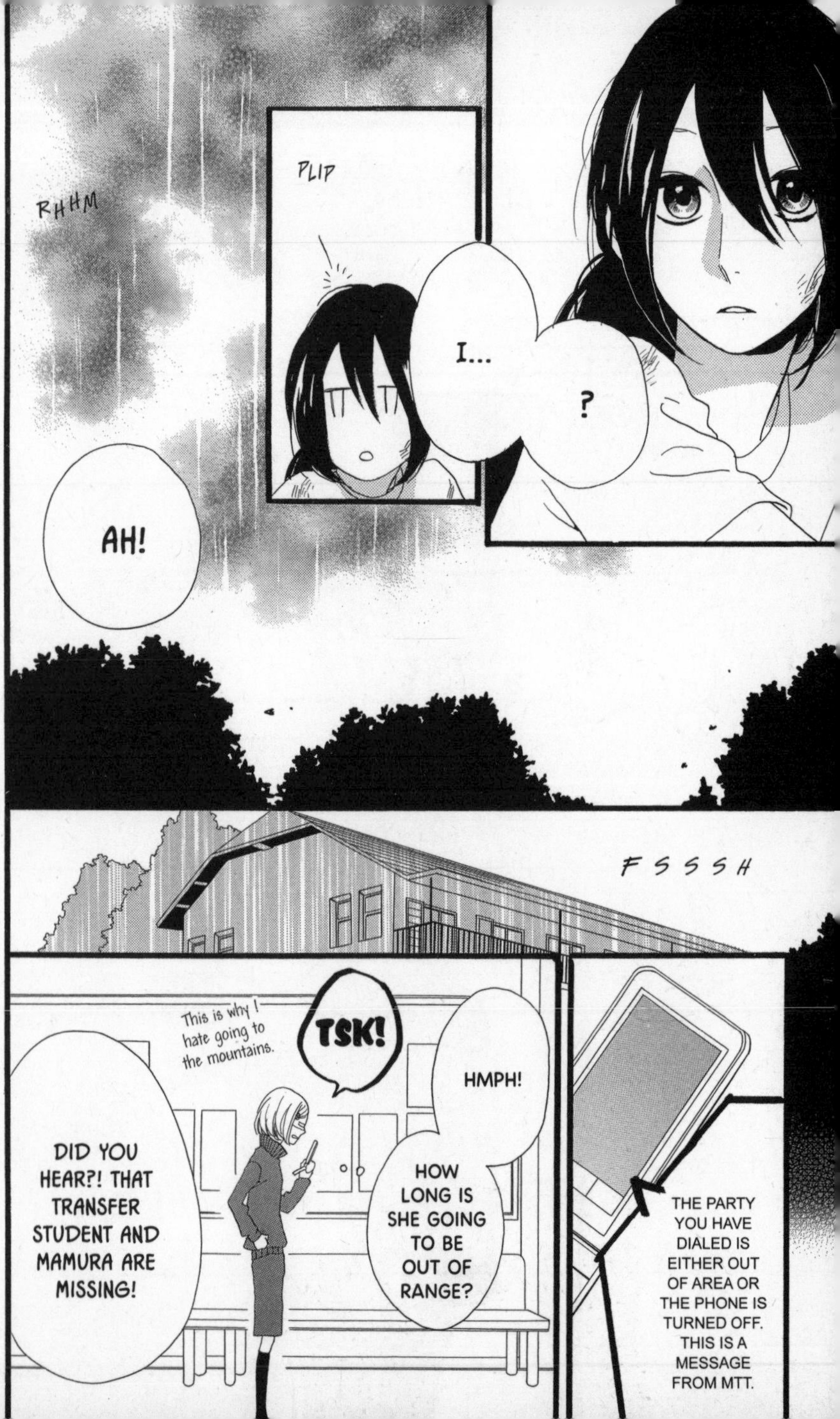
I...
?
PLIP
RHHM
AH!
FSSSH
THE PARTY YOU HAVE DIALED IS EITHER OUT OF AREA OR THE PHONE IS TURNED OFF. THIS IS A MESSAGE FROM MTT.
HMPH!
TSK!
HOW LONG IS SHE GOING TO BE OUT OF RANGE?
This is why I hate going to the mountains.
DID YOU HEAR?! THAT TRANSFER STUDENT AND MAMURA ARE MISSING!

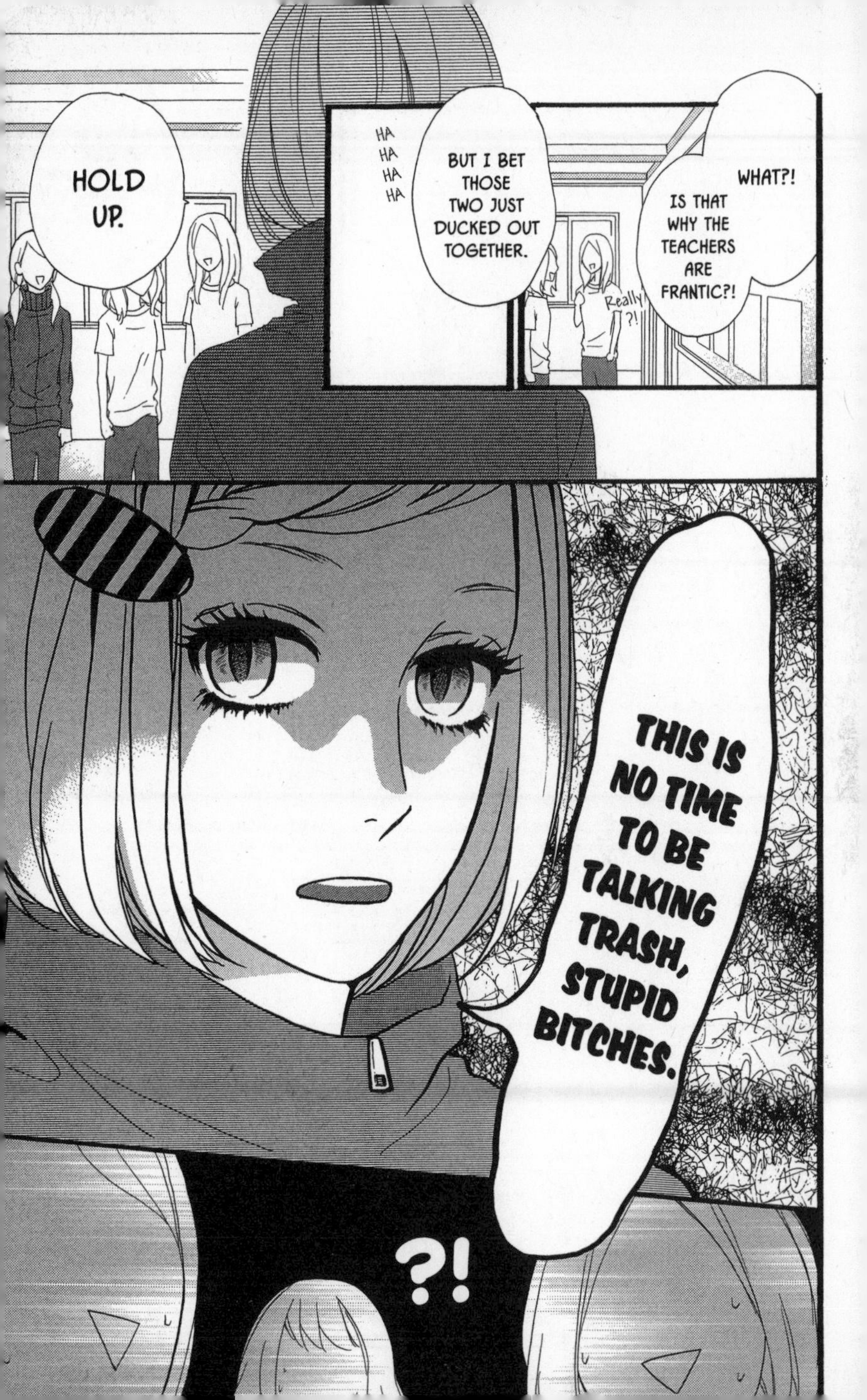
WHAT?! IS THAT WHY THE TEACHERS ARE FRANTIC?!
Really ?!
HA HA HA HA
BUT I BET THOSE TWO JUST DUCKED OUT TOGETHER.
HOLD UP.
THIS IS NO TIME TO BE TALKING TRASH, STUPID BITCHES.
?!

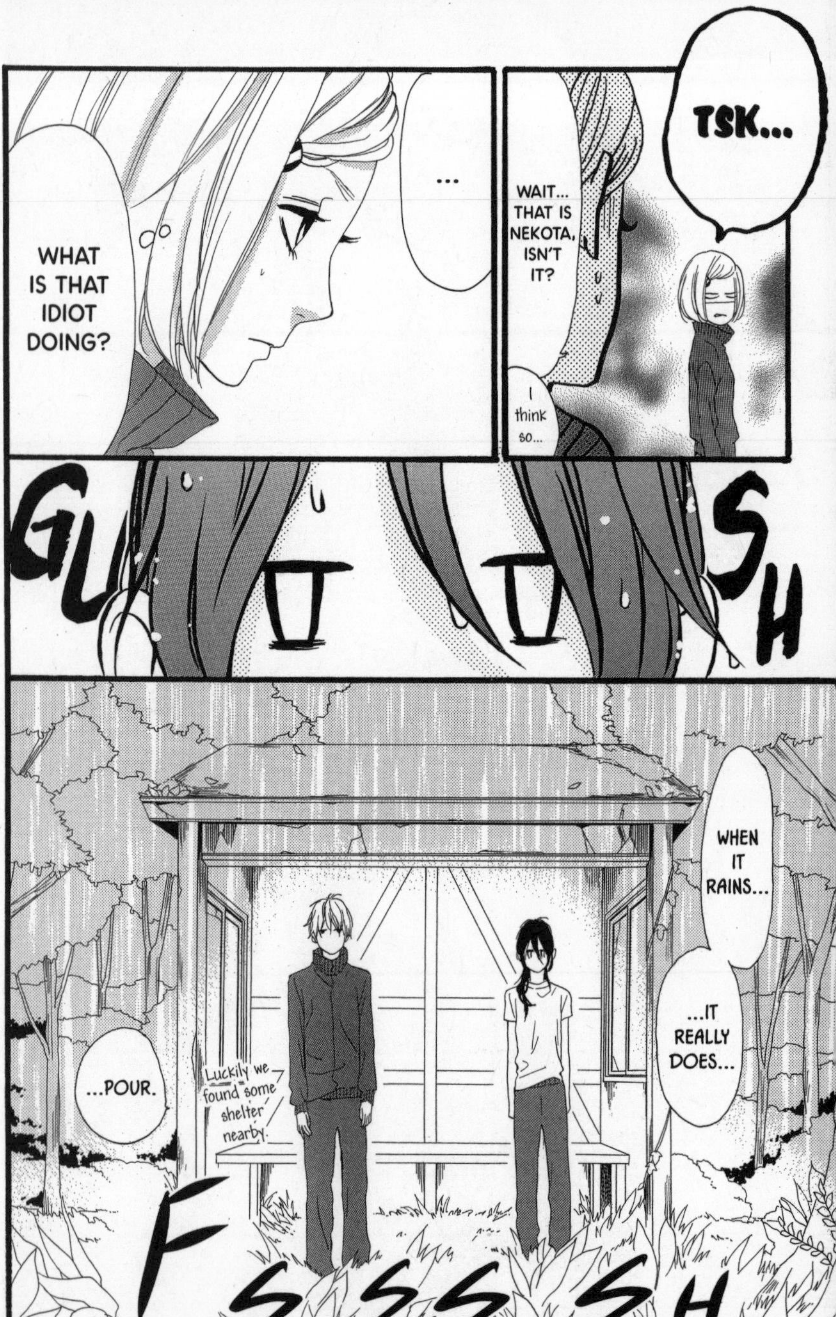
TSK...
WAIT... THAT IS NEKOTA, ISN'T IT?
I think so...
...
WHAT IS THAT IDIOT DOING?
GUSH
WHEN IT RAINS...
...IT REALLY DOES...
Luckily we found some shelter nearby.
...POUR.
FSSSSH

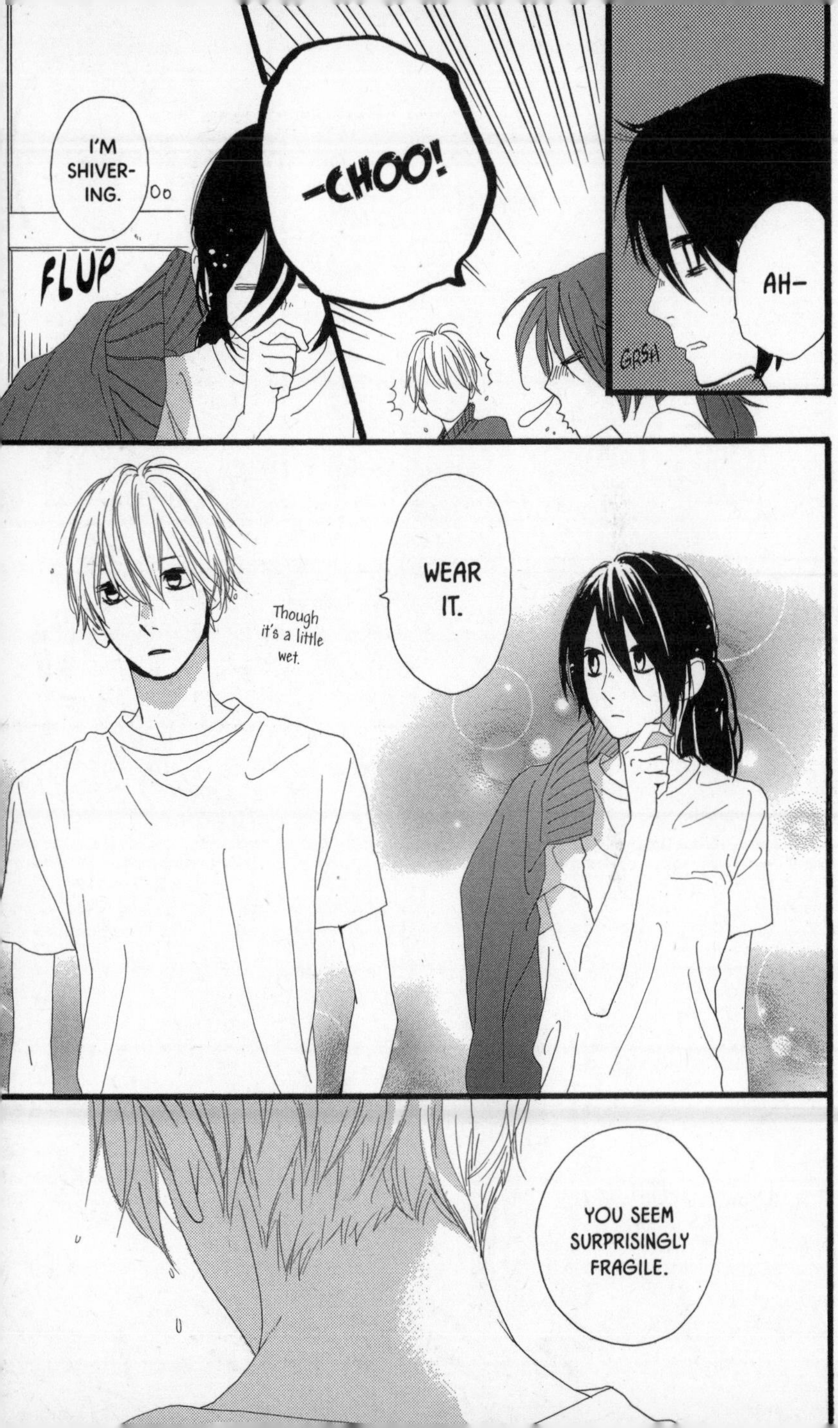
AH-
GRSH
-CHOO!
I'M SHIVER-ING.
FLUP
WEAR IT.
Though it's a little wet.
YOU SEEM SURPRISINGLY FRAGILE.

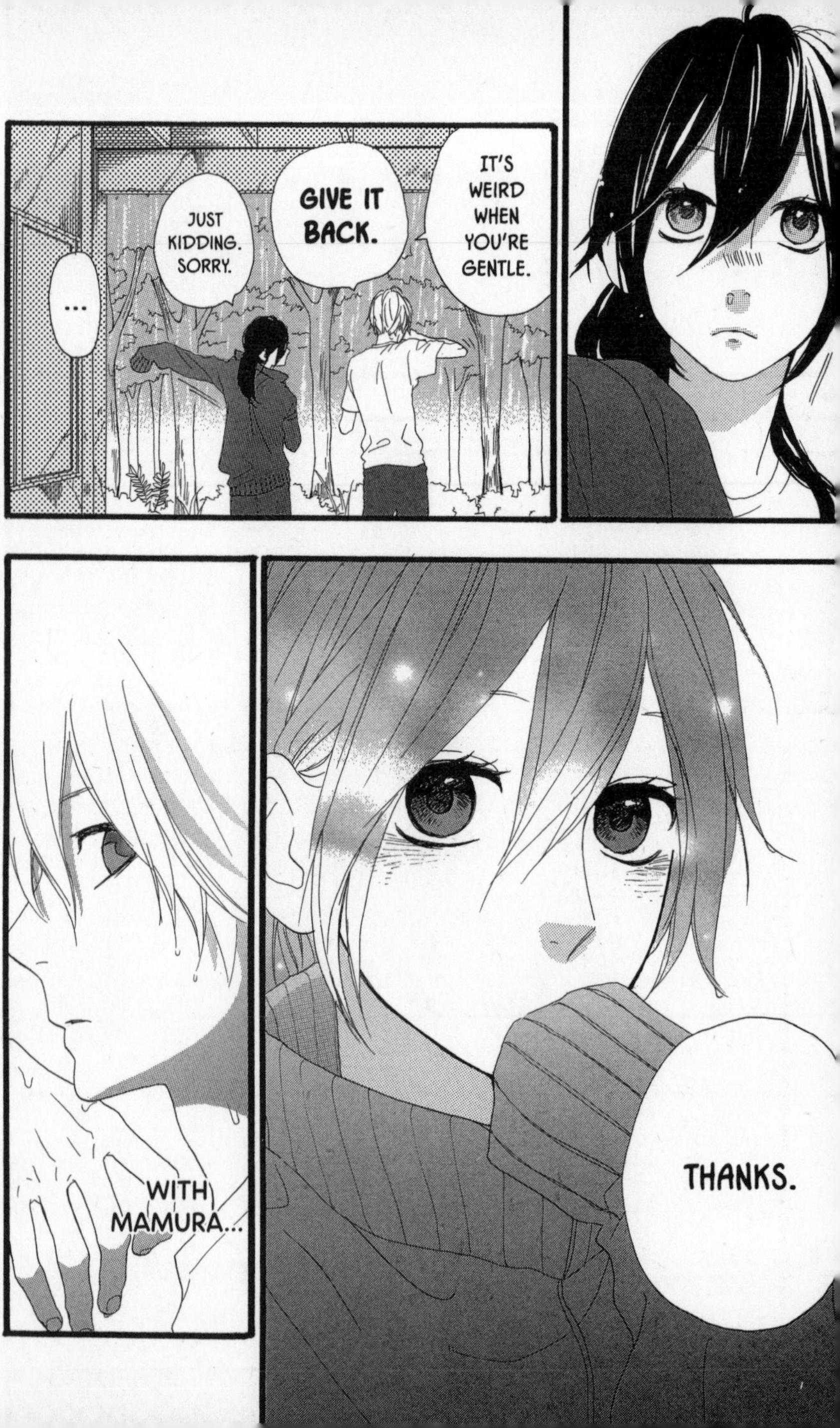
IT'S WEIRD WHEN YOU'RE GENTLE.
GIVE IT BACK.
JUST KIDDING. SORRY.
...
THANKS.
WITH MAMURA...

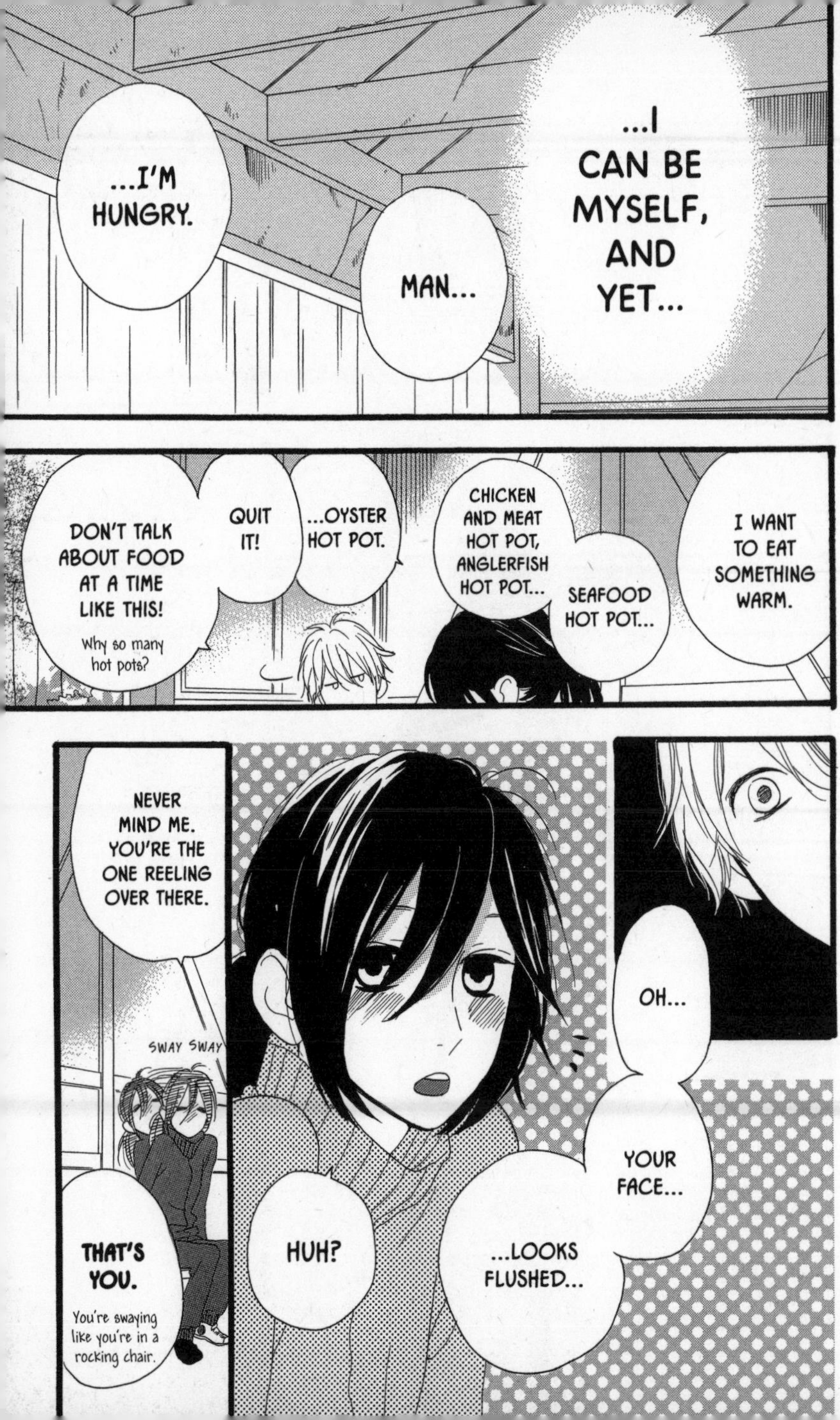
...I CAN BE MYSELF, AND YET...
MAN...
...I'M HUNGRY.
I WANT TO EAT SOMETHING WARM.
SEAFOOD HOT POT...
CHICKEN AND MEAT HOT POT, ANGLERFISH HOT POT...
...OYSTER HOT POT.
QUIT IT!
DON'T TALK ABOUT FOOD AT A TIME LIKE THIS!
Why so many hot pots?
OH...
YOUR FACE...
...LOOKS FLUSHED...
HUH?
NEVER MIND ME. YOU'RE THE ONE REELING OVER THERE.
SWAY SWAY
THAT'S YOU.
You're swaying like you're in a rocking chair.

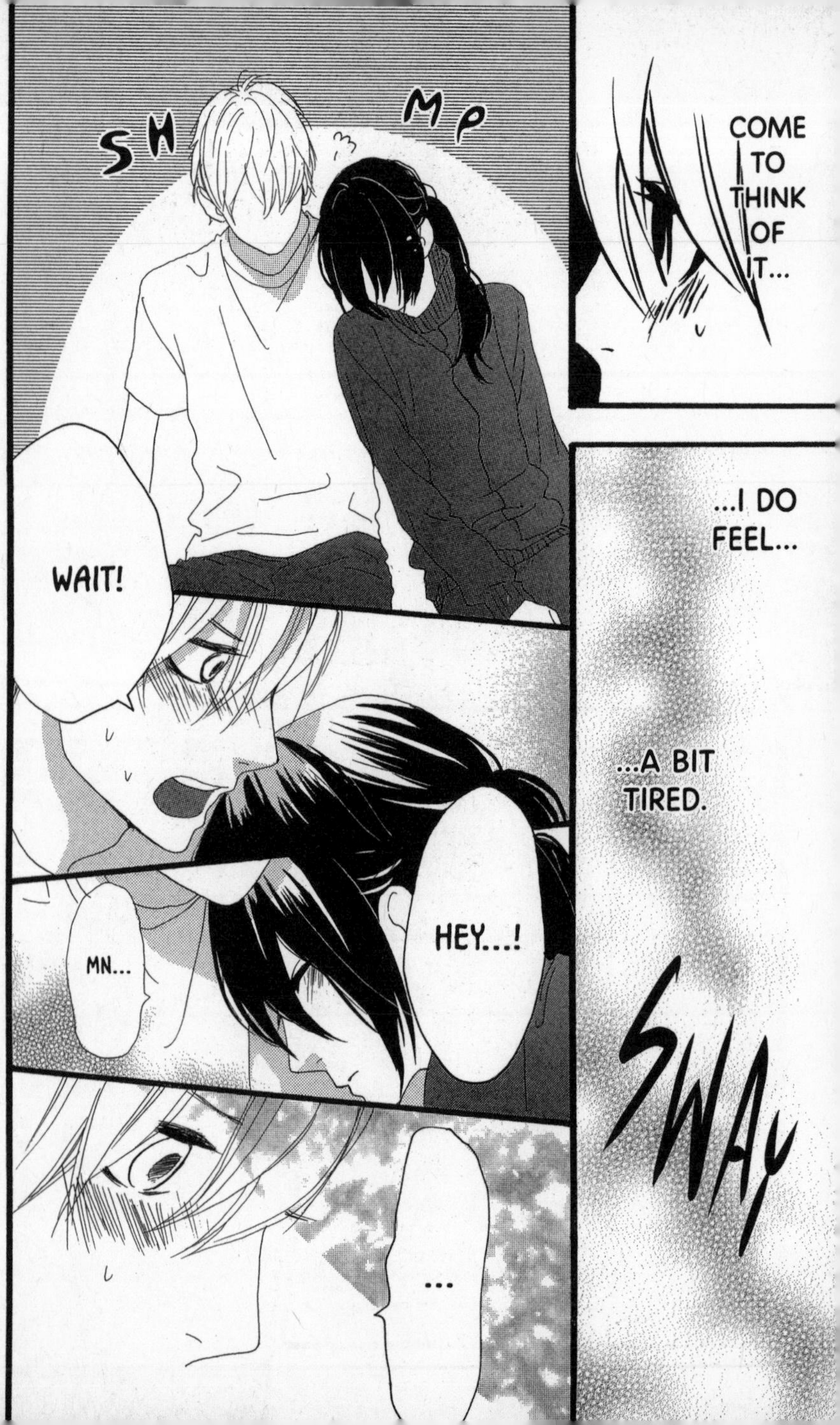
COME TO THINK OF IT...
...I DO FEEL...
...A BIT TIRED.
SWAY
SHMP
WAIT!
HEY...!
MN...
...

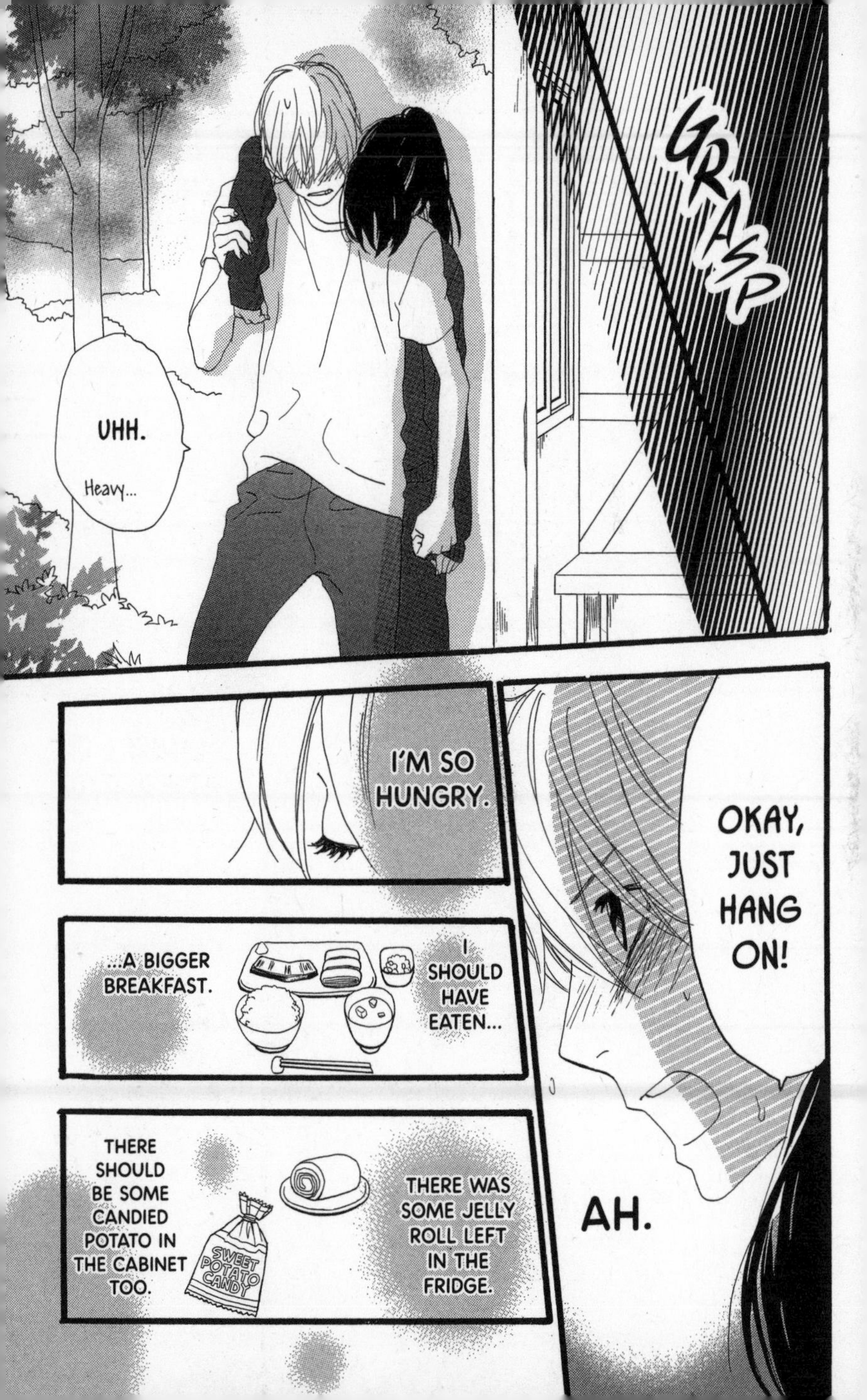
GRASP
UHH.
Heavy...
OKAY, JUST HANG ON!
AH.
I'M SO HUNGRY.
I SHOULD HAVE EATEN...
...A BIGGER BREAKFAST.
THERE WAS SOME JELLY ROLL LEFT IN THE FRIDGE.
THERE SHOULD BE SOME CANDIED POTATO IN THE CABINET TOO.
SWEET POTATO CANDY

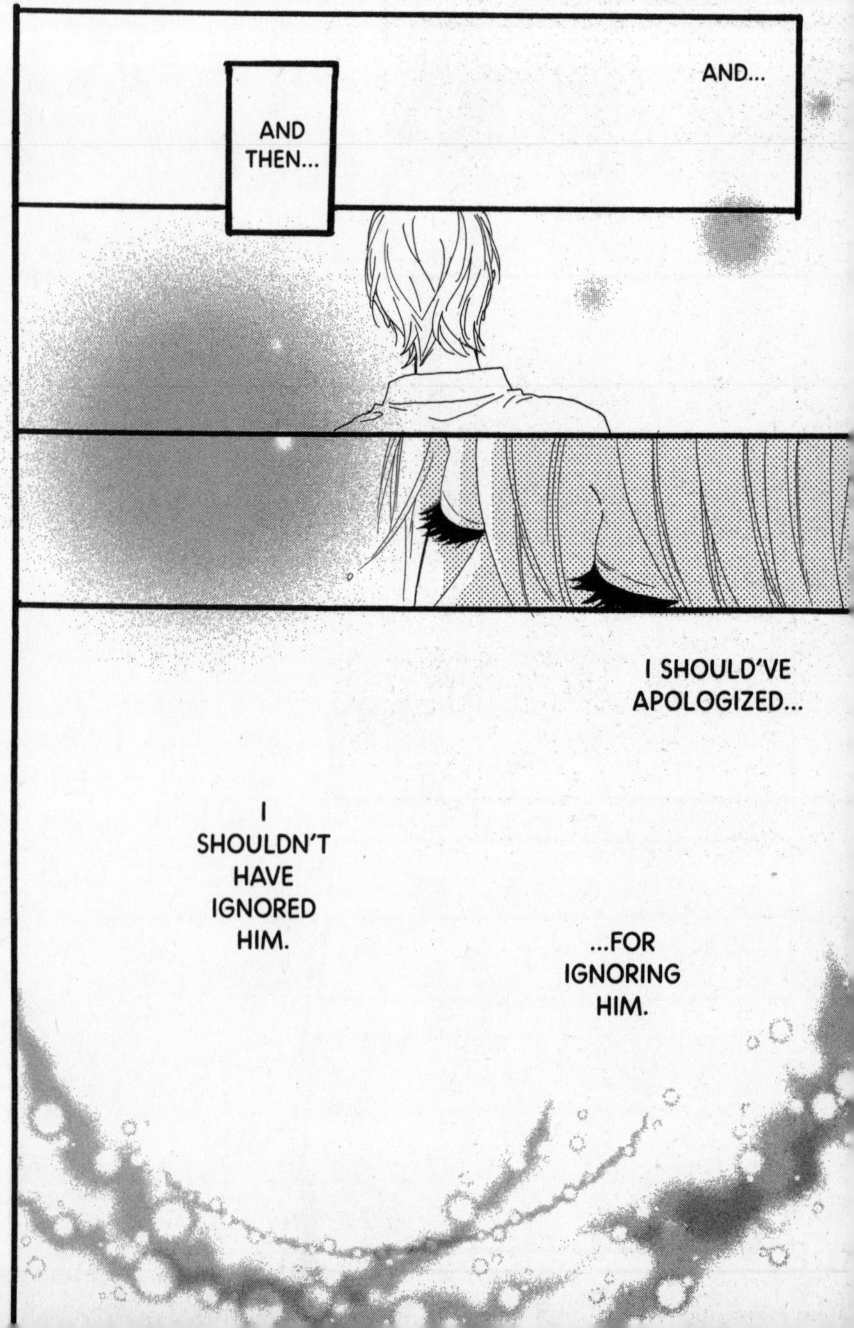
AND...
AND THEN...
I SHOULD'VE APOLOGIZED...
...FOR IGNORING HIM.
I SHOULDN'T HAVE IGNORED HIM.

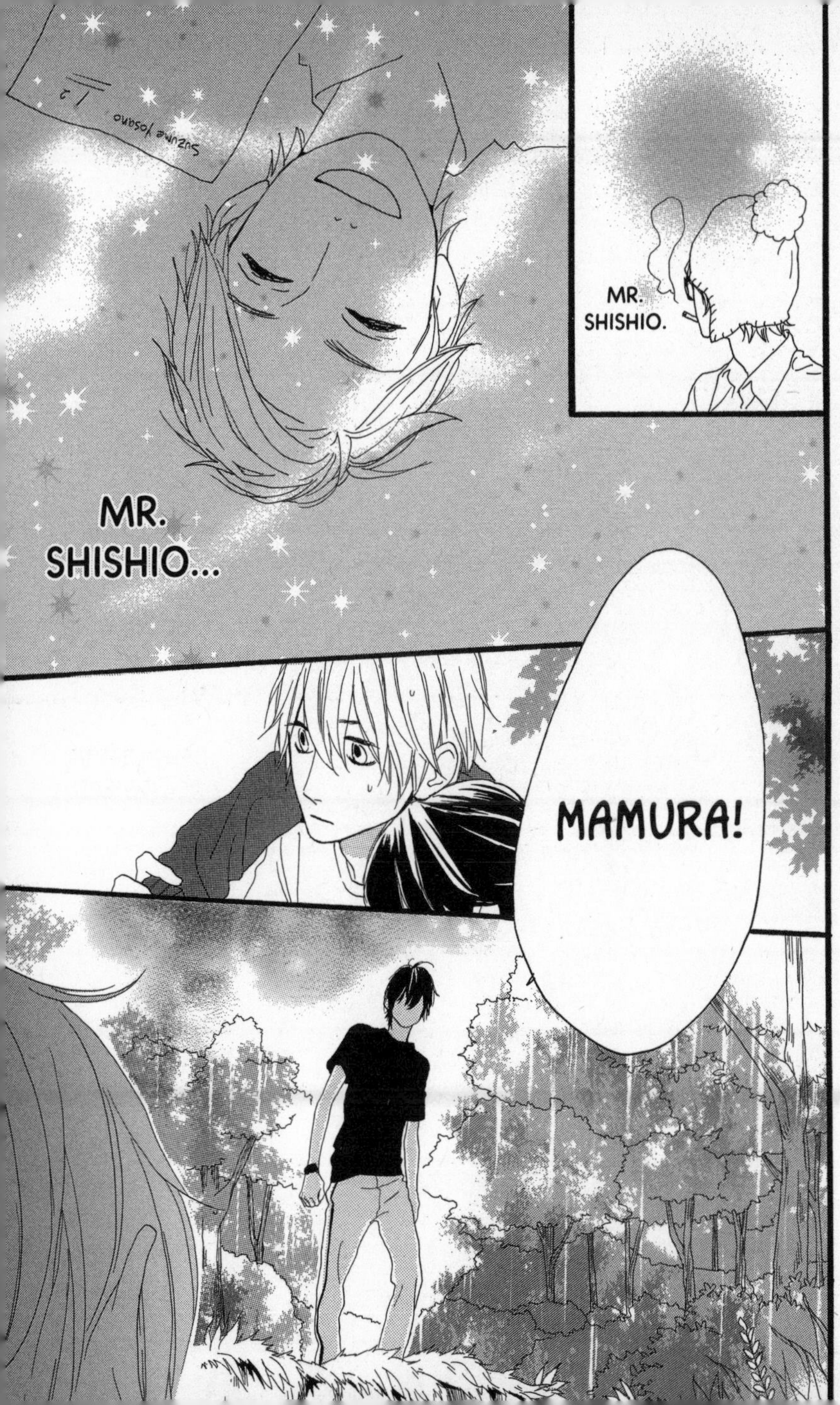
MR. SHISHIO.
MR. SHISHIO...
MAMURA!

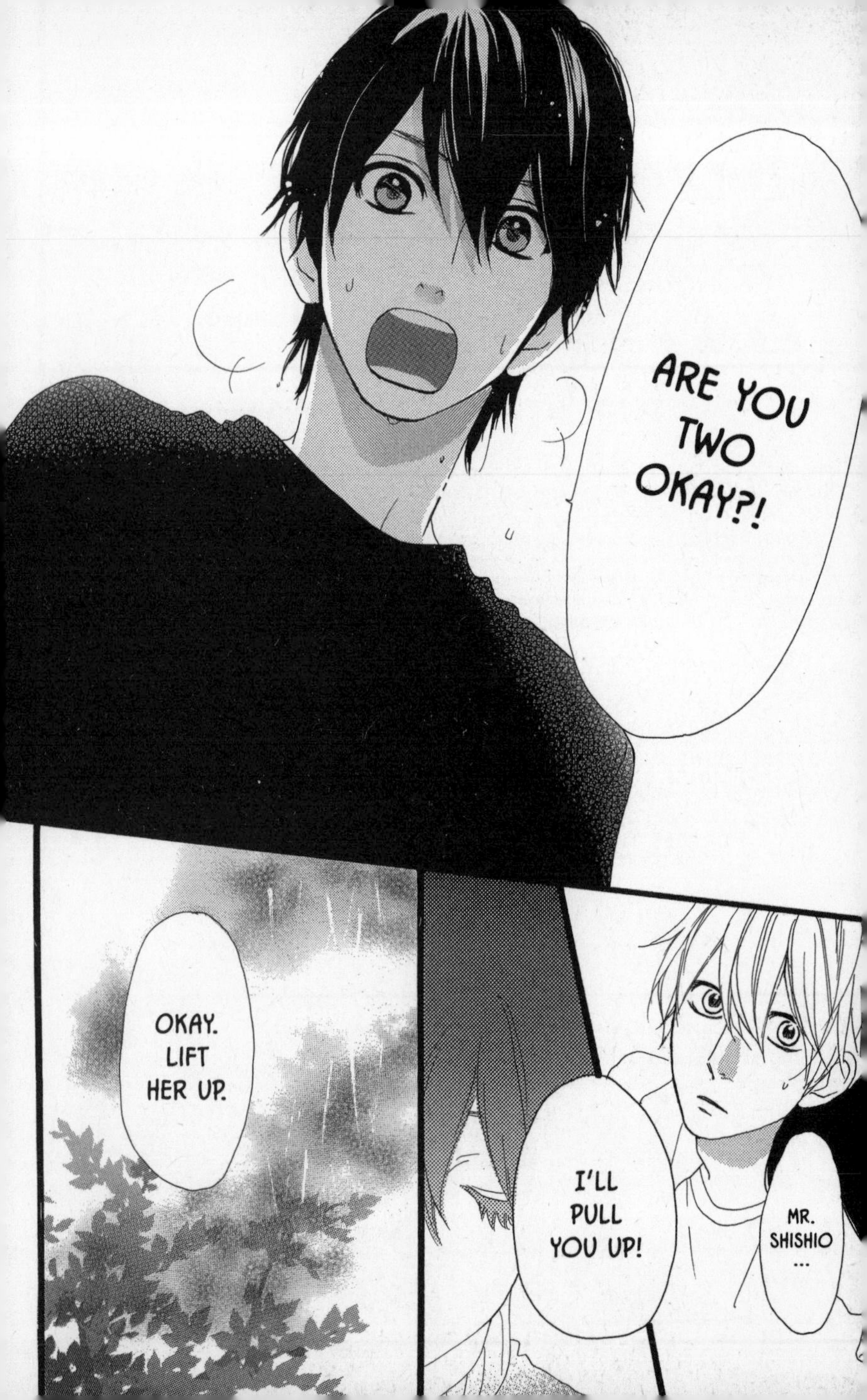
ARE YOU TWO OKAY?!
MR. SHISHIO ...
I'LL PULL YOU UP!
OKAY. LIFT HER UP.

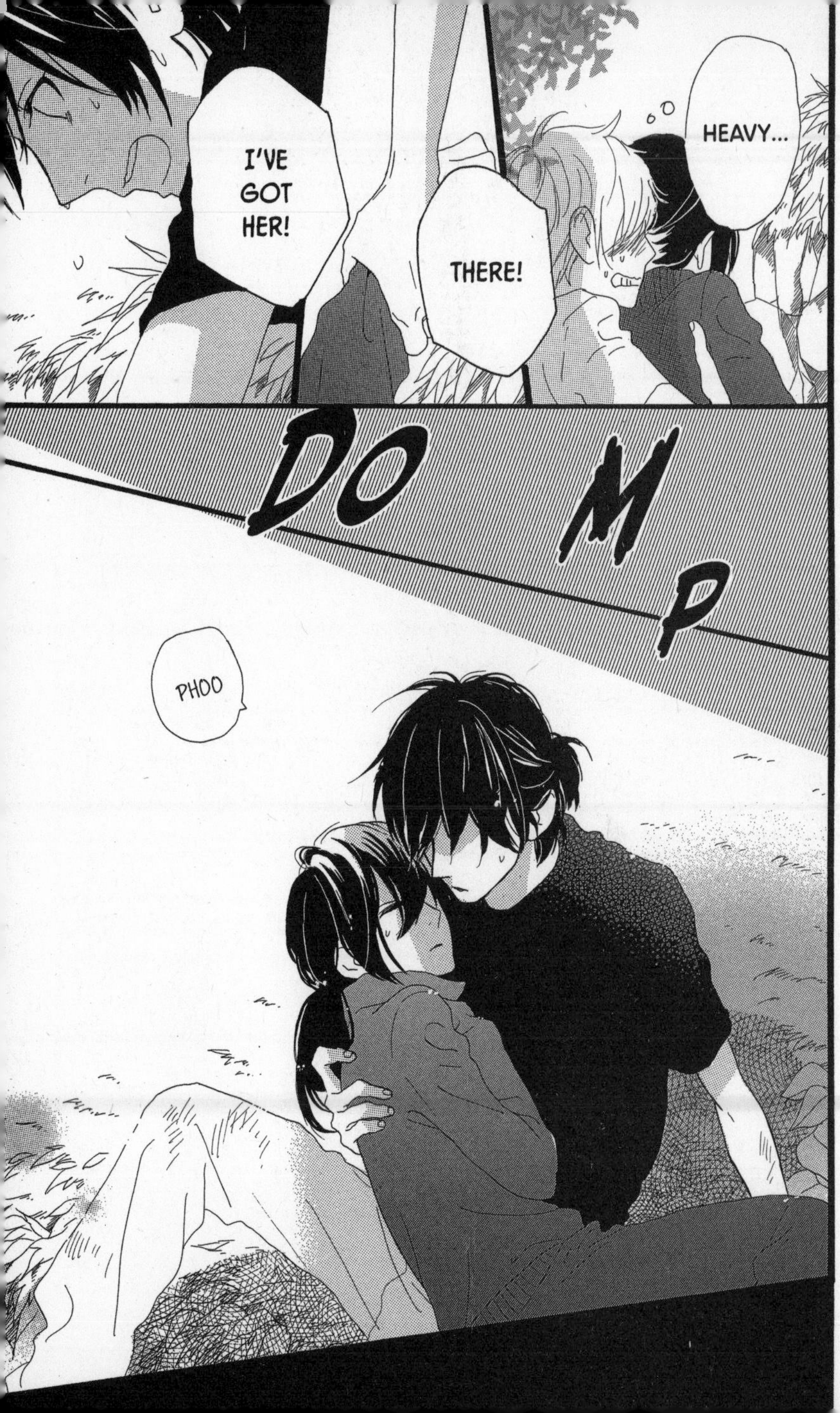
HEAVY...
THERE!
I'VE GOT HER!
DOMP
PHOO

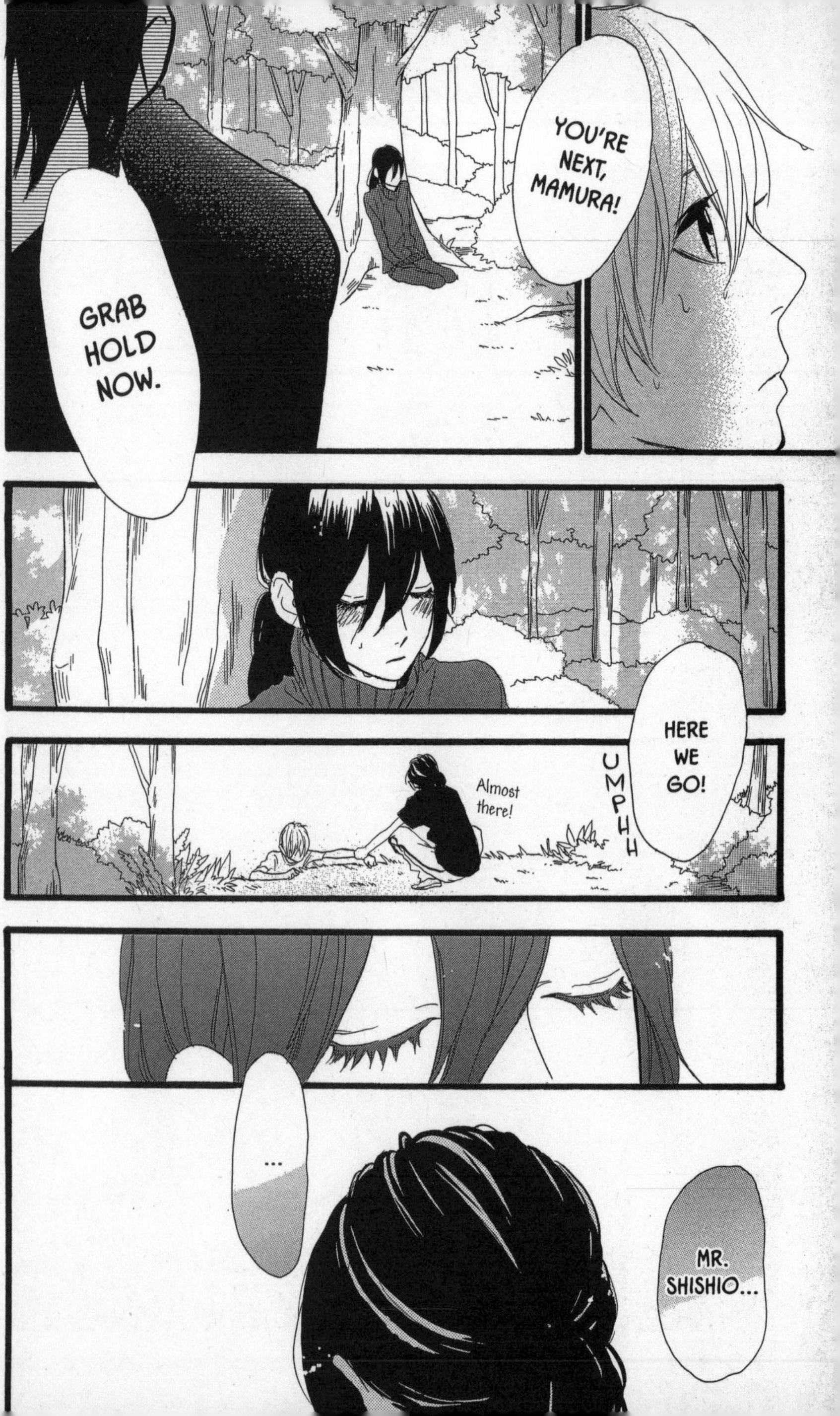
YOU'RE NEXT, MAMURA!
GRAB HOLD NOW.
HERE WE GO!
UMPHH
Almost there!
MR. SHISHIO...
...

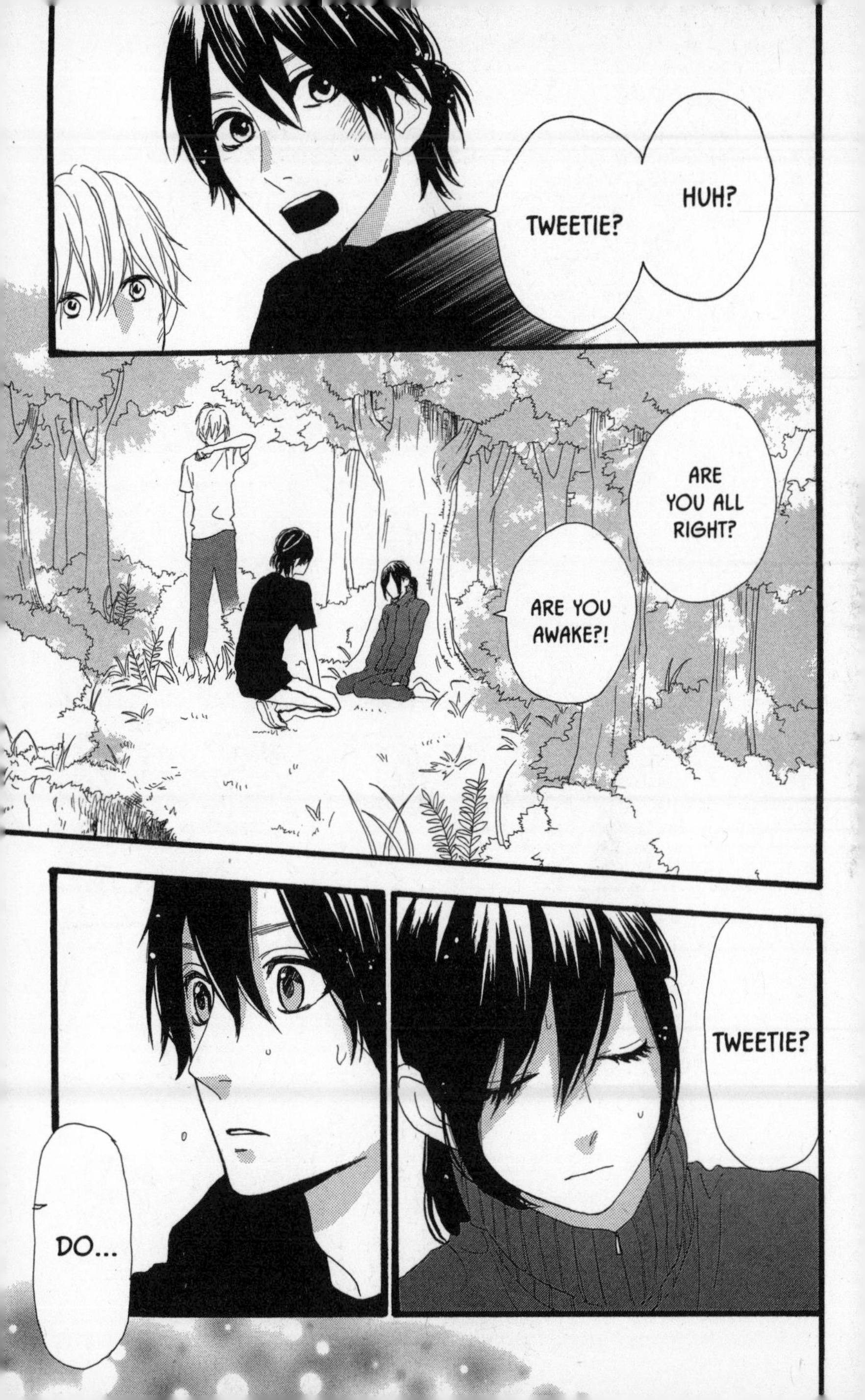
HUH?
TWEETIE?
ARE YOU ALL RIGHT?
ARE YOU AWAKE?!
A....
TWEETIE?
DO...

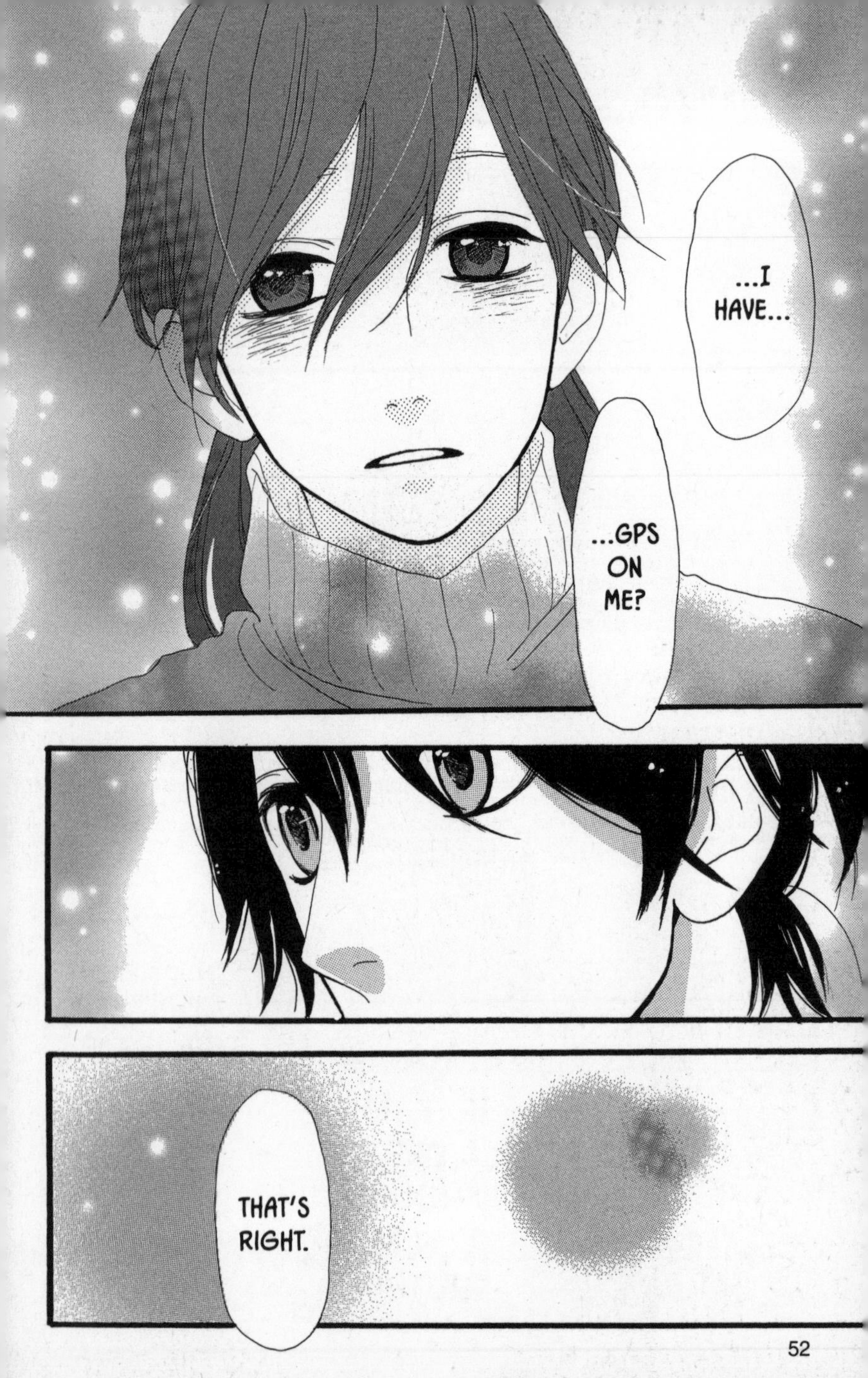
...I HAVE...
...GPS ON ME?
THAT'S RIGHT.

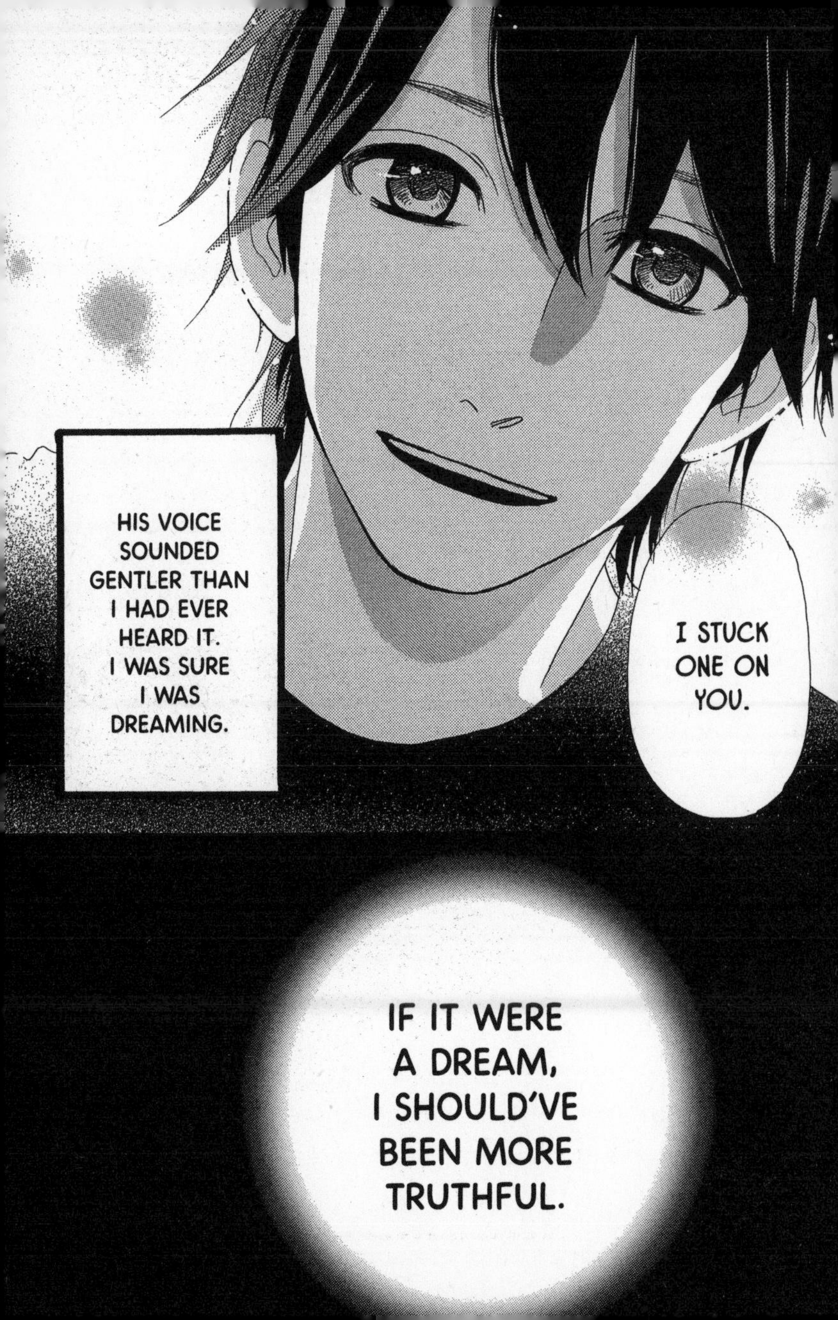
I STUCK ONE ON YOU.
HIS VOICE SOUNDED GENTLER THAN I HAD EVER HEARD IT. I WAS SURE I WAS DREAMING.
IF IT WERE A DREAM, I SHOULD'VE BEEN MORE TRUTHFUL.

Simple Scribbles ①

This is an unplanned page. I had nothing to write, so I decided to fill it with a scribble.

I just doodled this.

Why this hat?
Why the corn?
I do not know.

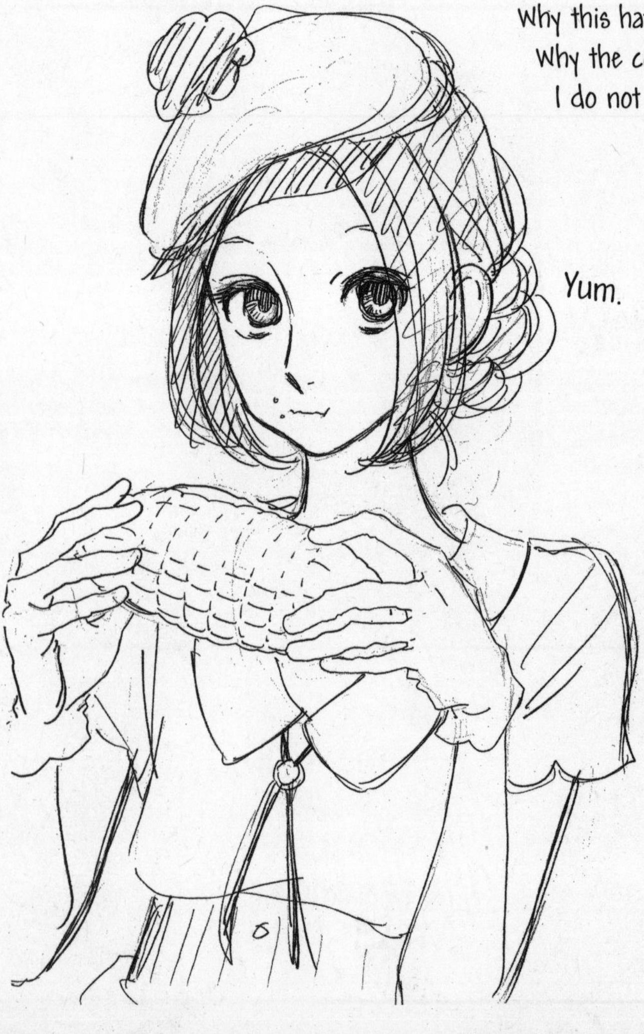

Yum.

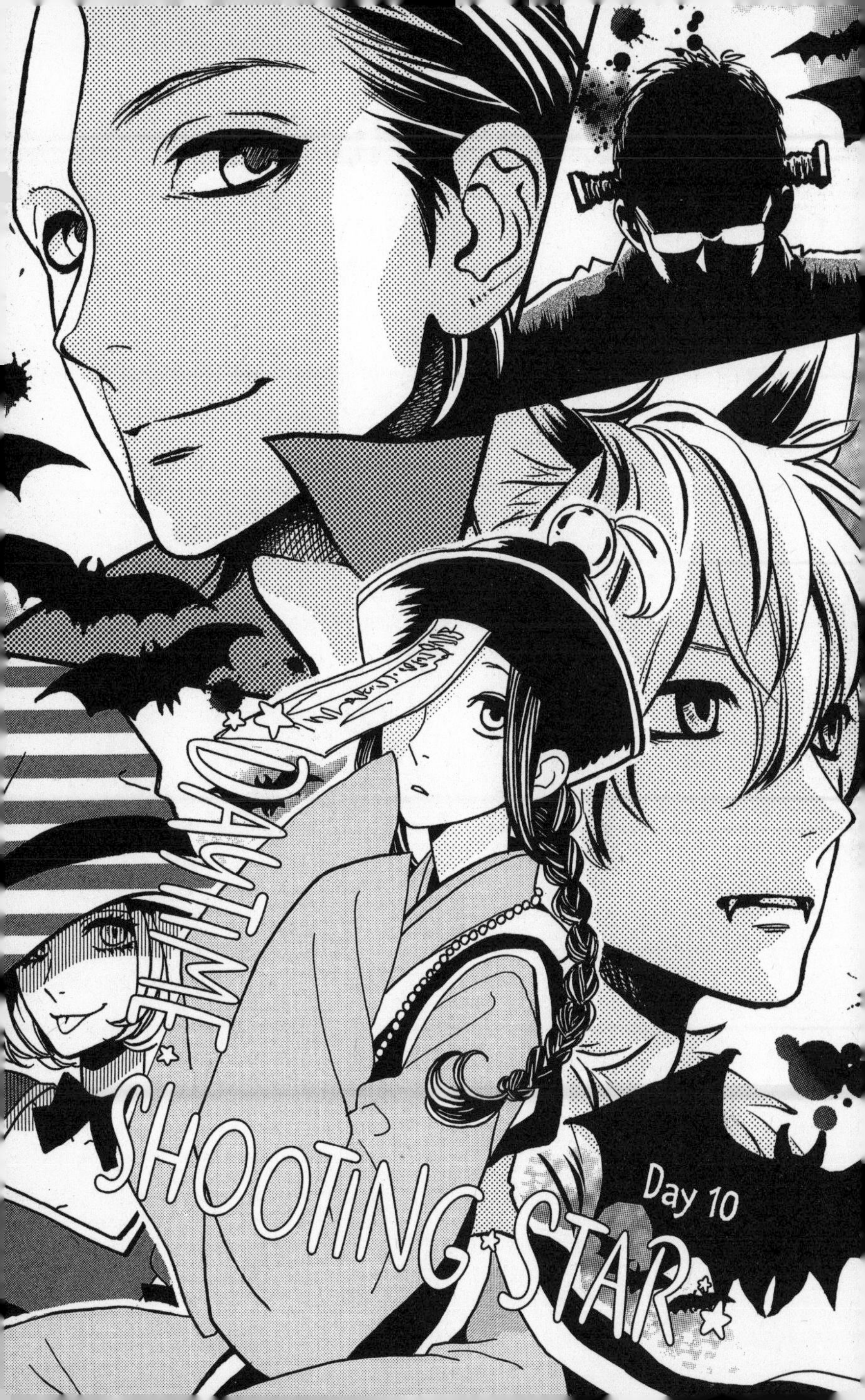
Daytime Shooting Star
Day 10

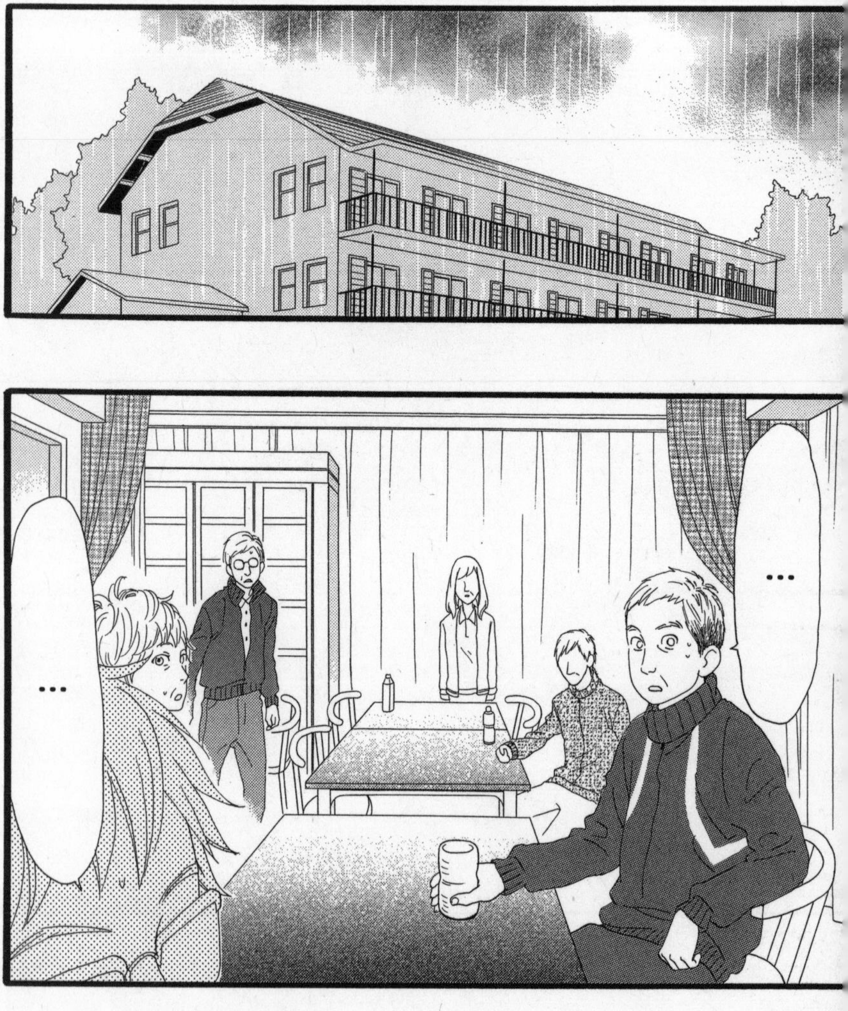
...
...

Monika Tsurutani

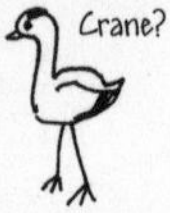
Crane?

Birthday: April 23
Height: 5'6"
Weight: 121 lbs

Blood Type: O

1. Any kind of hors d'oeuvres.
2. Gymnastics. Ballet.
3. My bust has grown and grown.

**Tsuru* means "crane."

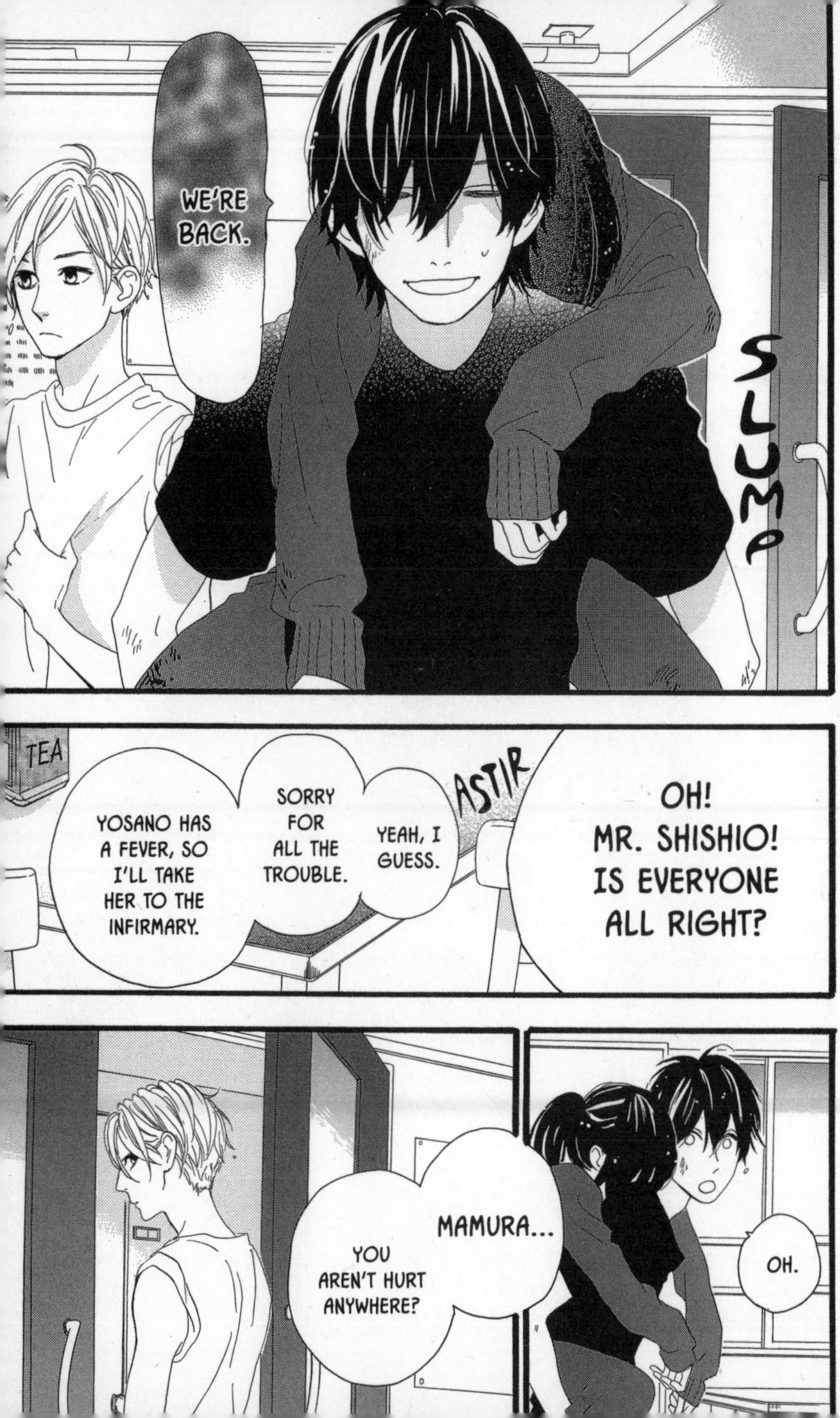
WE'RE BACK.
SLUMP
OH! MR. SHISHIO! IS EVERYONE ALL RIGHT?
ASTIR
YEAH, I GUESS.
SORRY FOR ALL THE TROUBLE.
YOSANO HAS A FEVER, SO I'LL TAKE HER TO THE INFIRMARY.
TEA
OH.
MAMURA...
YOU AREN'T HURT ANYWHERE?

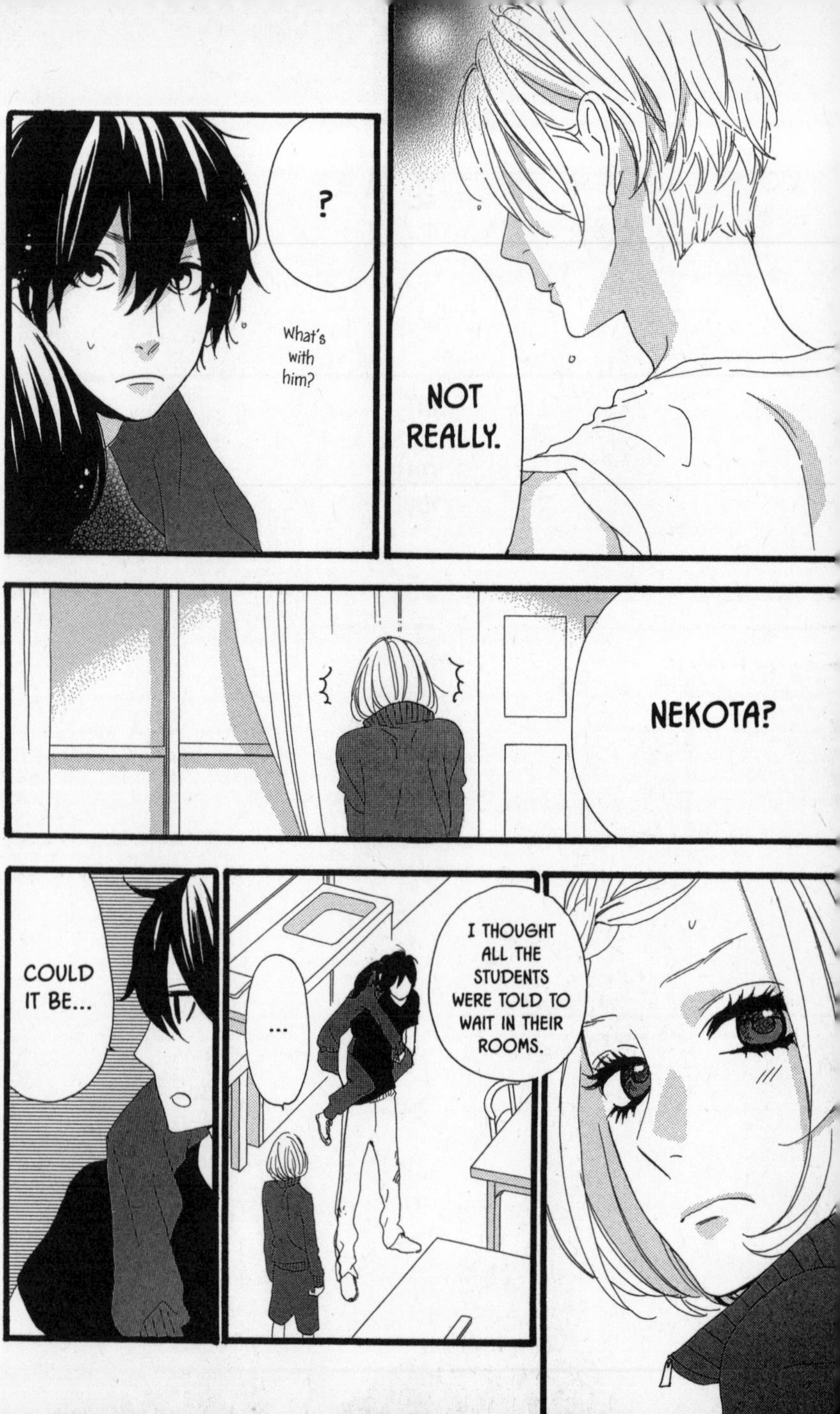
NOT REALLY.
?
What's with him?
NEKOTA?
I THOUGHT ALL THE STUDENTS WERE TOLD TO WAIT IN THEIR ROOMS.
...
COULD IT BE...

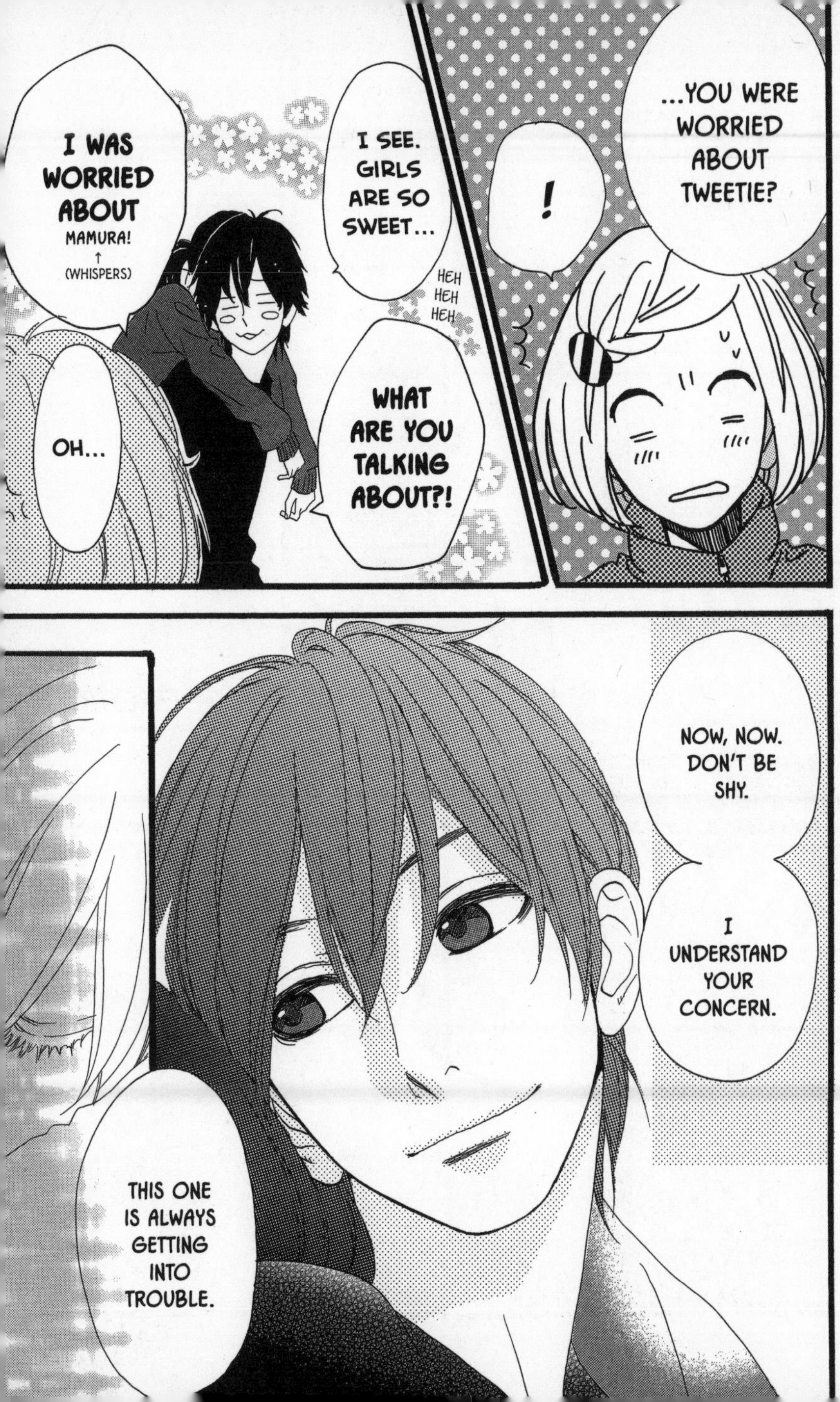
...YOU WERE WORRIED ABOUT TWEETIE?
!
I SEE. GIRLS ARE SO SWEET...
HEH HEH HEH
WHAT ARE YOU TALKING ABOUT?!
I WAS WORRIED ABOUT MAMURA!
↑ (WHISPERS)
OH...
NOW, NOW. DON'T BE SHY.
I UNDERSTAND YOUR CONCERN.
THIS ONE IS ALWAYS GETTING INTO TROUBLE.

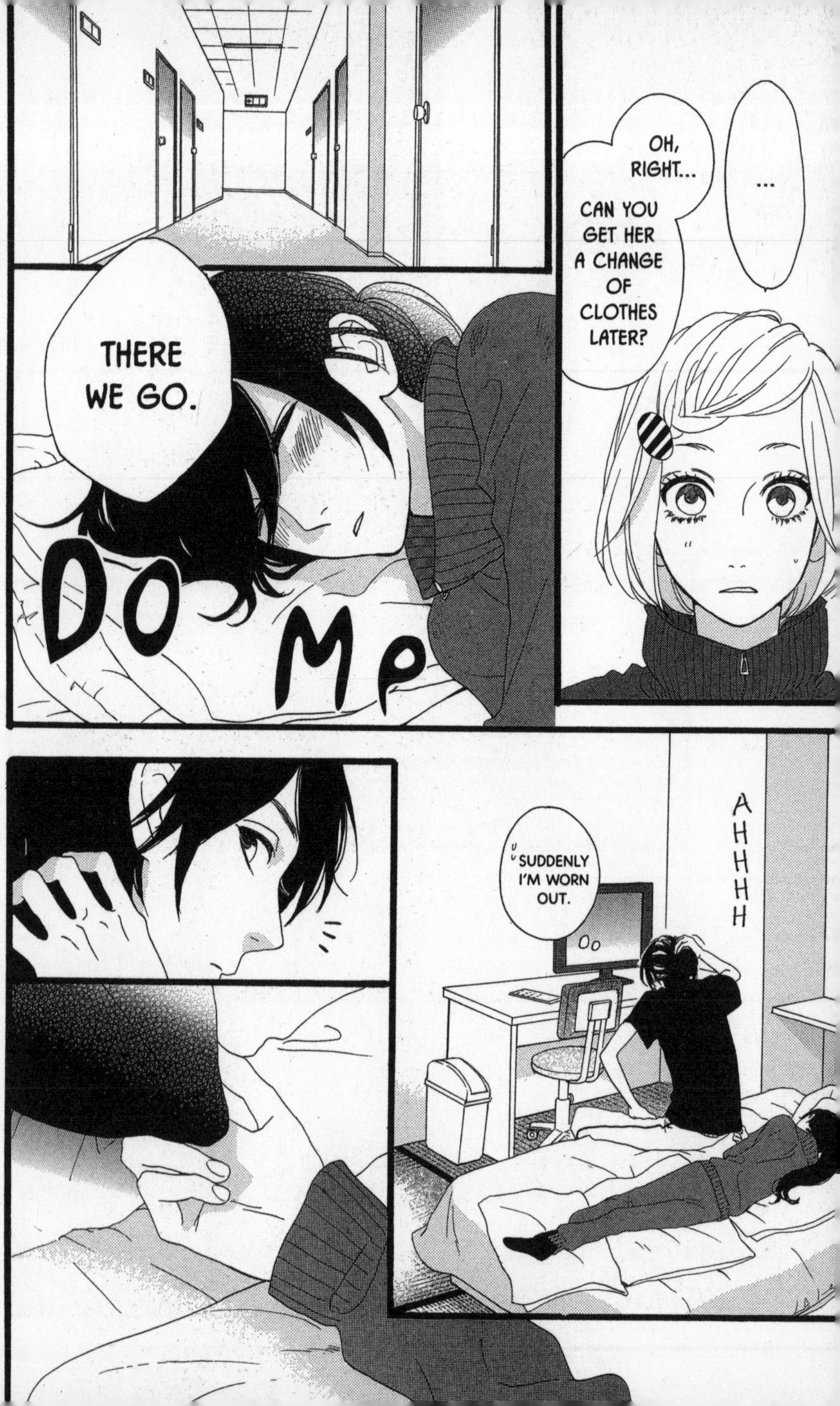
...
OH, RIGHT... CAN YOU GET HER A CHANGE OF CLOTHES LATER?
THERE WE GO.
DOMP
AHHHH
SUDDENLY I'M WORN OUT.

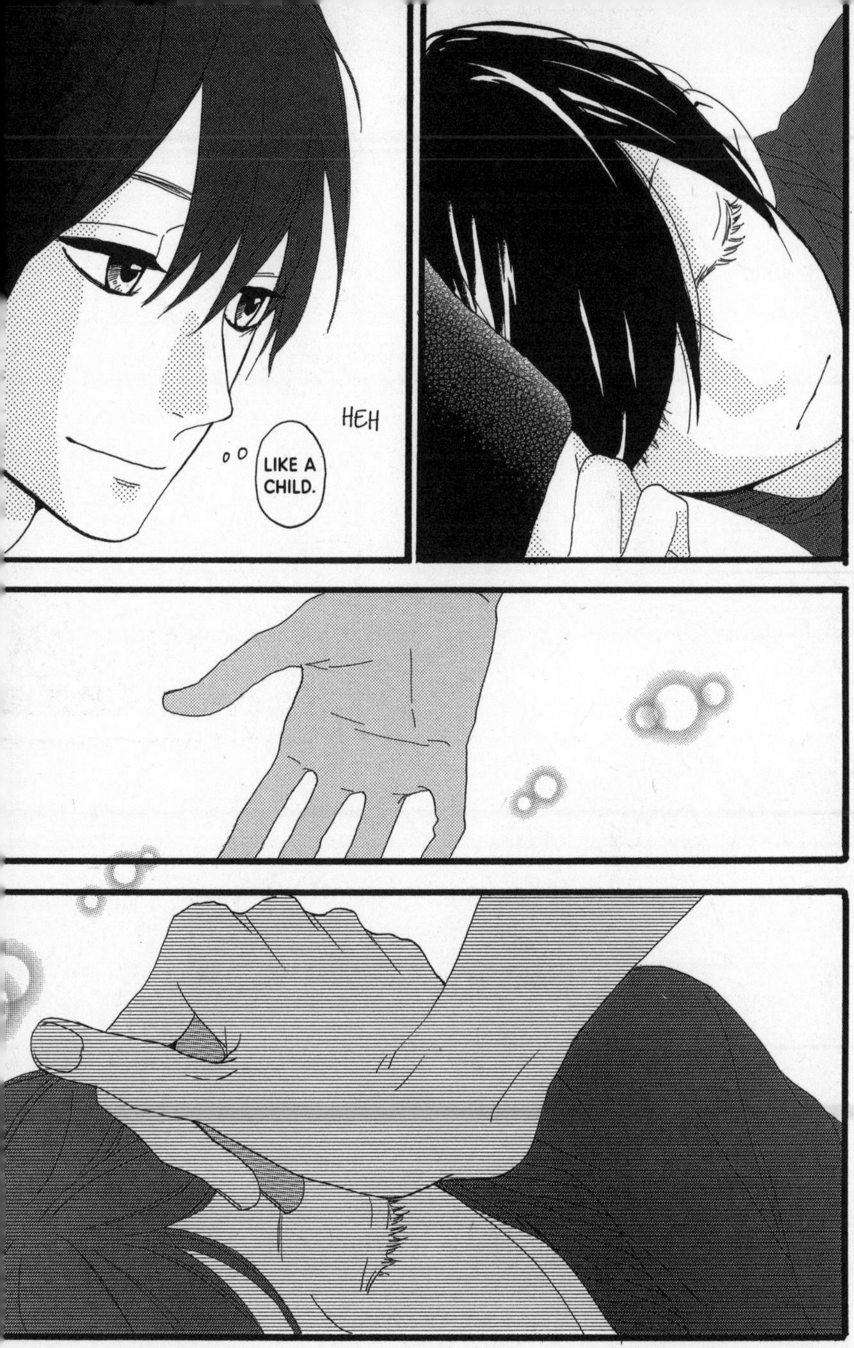
HEH
LIKE A CHILD.

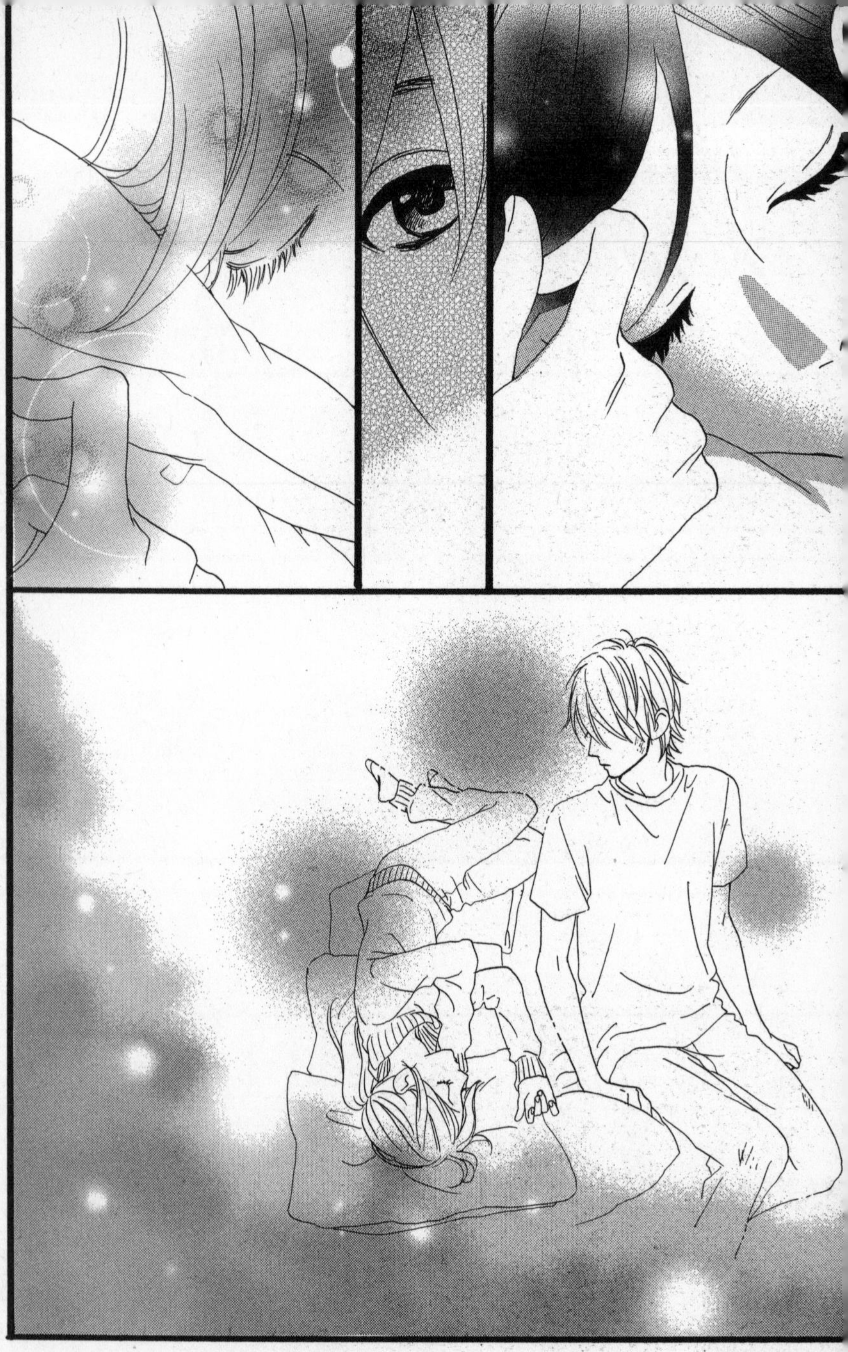

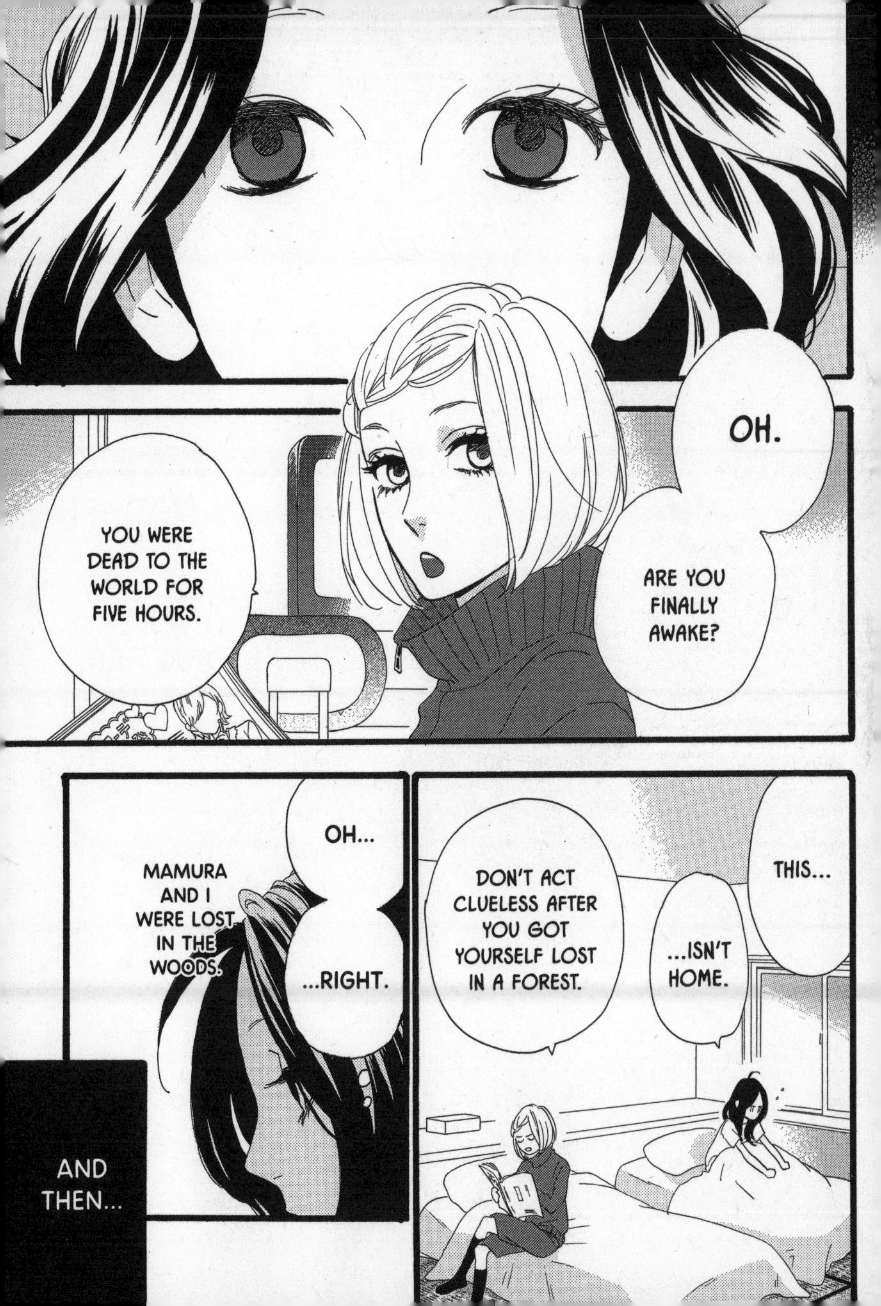

OH.
ARE YOU FINALLY AWAKE?
YOU WERE DEAD TO THE WORLD FOR FIVE HOURS.
THIS...
...ISN'T HOME.
DON'T ACT CLUELESS AFTER YOU GOT YOURSELF LOST IN A FOREST.
OH...
...RIGHT.
MAMURA AND I WERE LOST IN THE WOODS.
AND THEN...

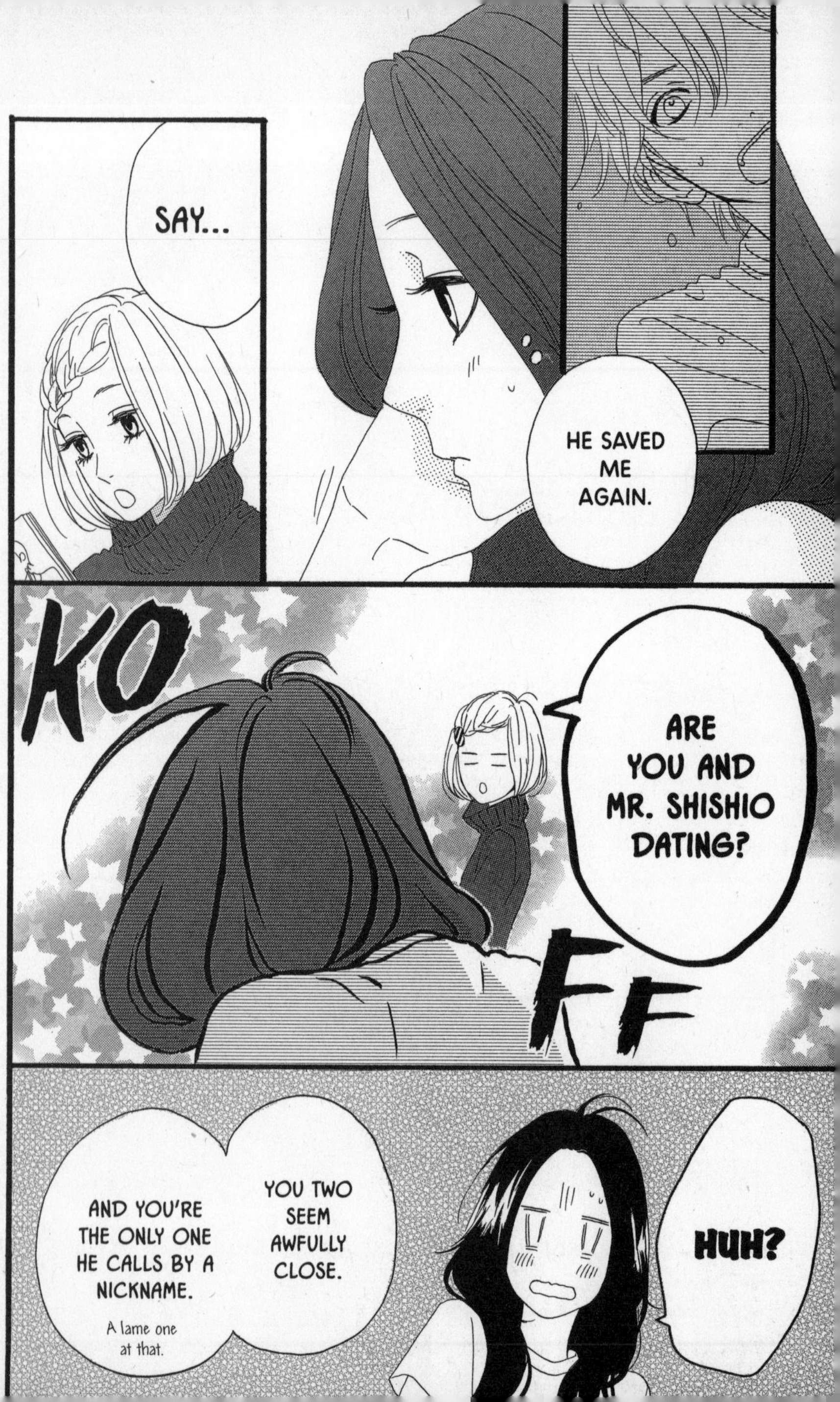
HE SAVED ME AGAIN.
SAY...
KOFF
ARE YOU AND MR. SHISHIO DATING?
HUH?
YOU TWO SEEM AWFULLY CLOSE.
AND YOU'RE THE ONLY ONE HE CALLS BY A NICKNAME.
A lame one at that.

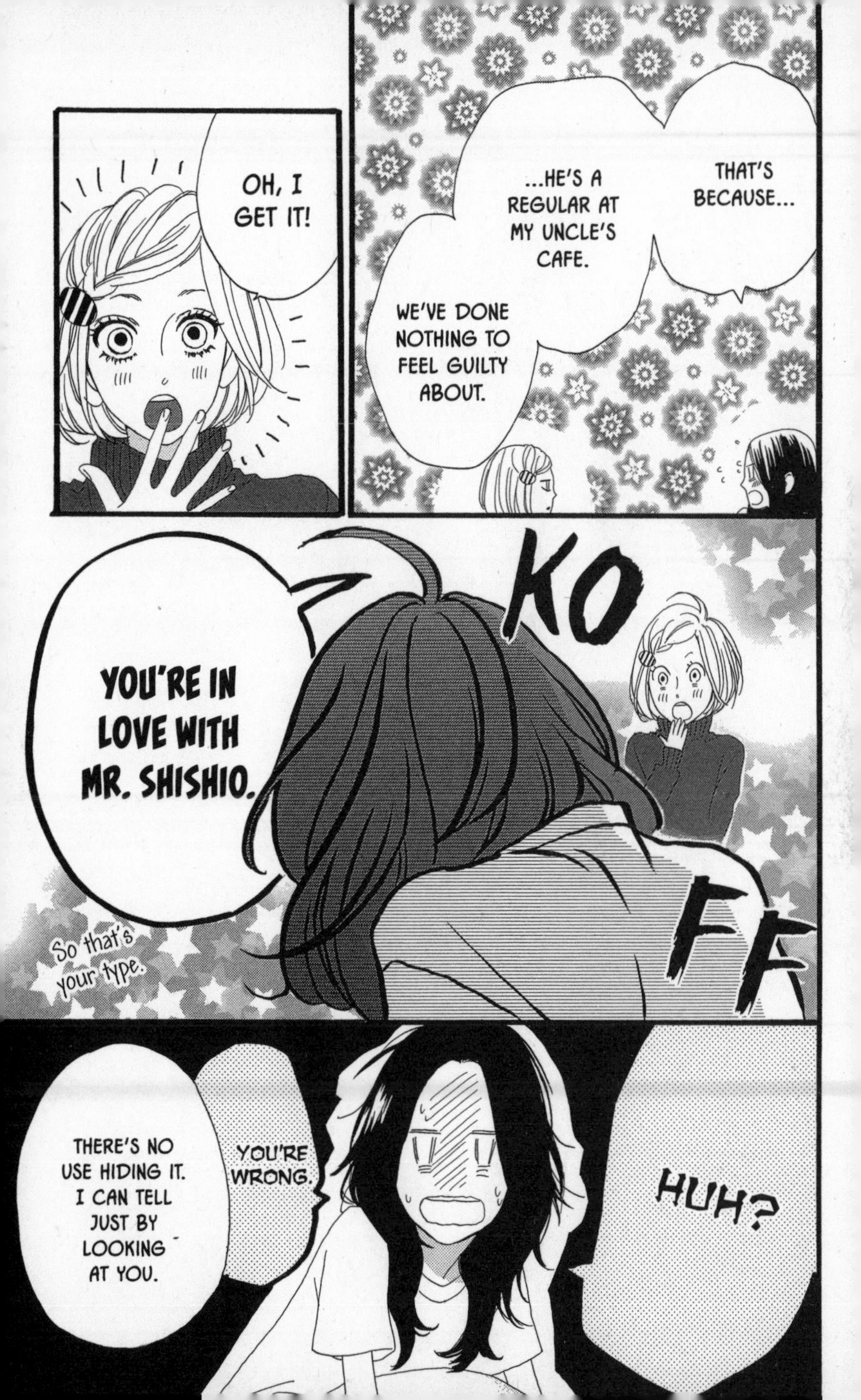
THAT'S BECAUSE...
...HE'S A REGULAR AT MY UNCLE'S CAFE.
WE'VE DONE NOTHING TO FEEL GUILTY ABOUT.
OH, I GET IT!
KOFF
YOU'RE IN LOVE WITH MR. SHISHIO.
So that's your type.
HUH?
YOU'RE WRONG.
THERE'S NO USE HIDING IT. I CAN TELL JUST BY LOOKING AT YOU.

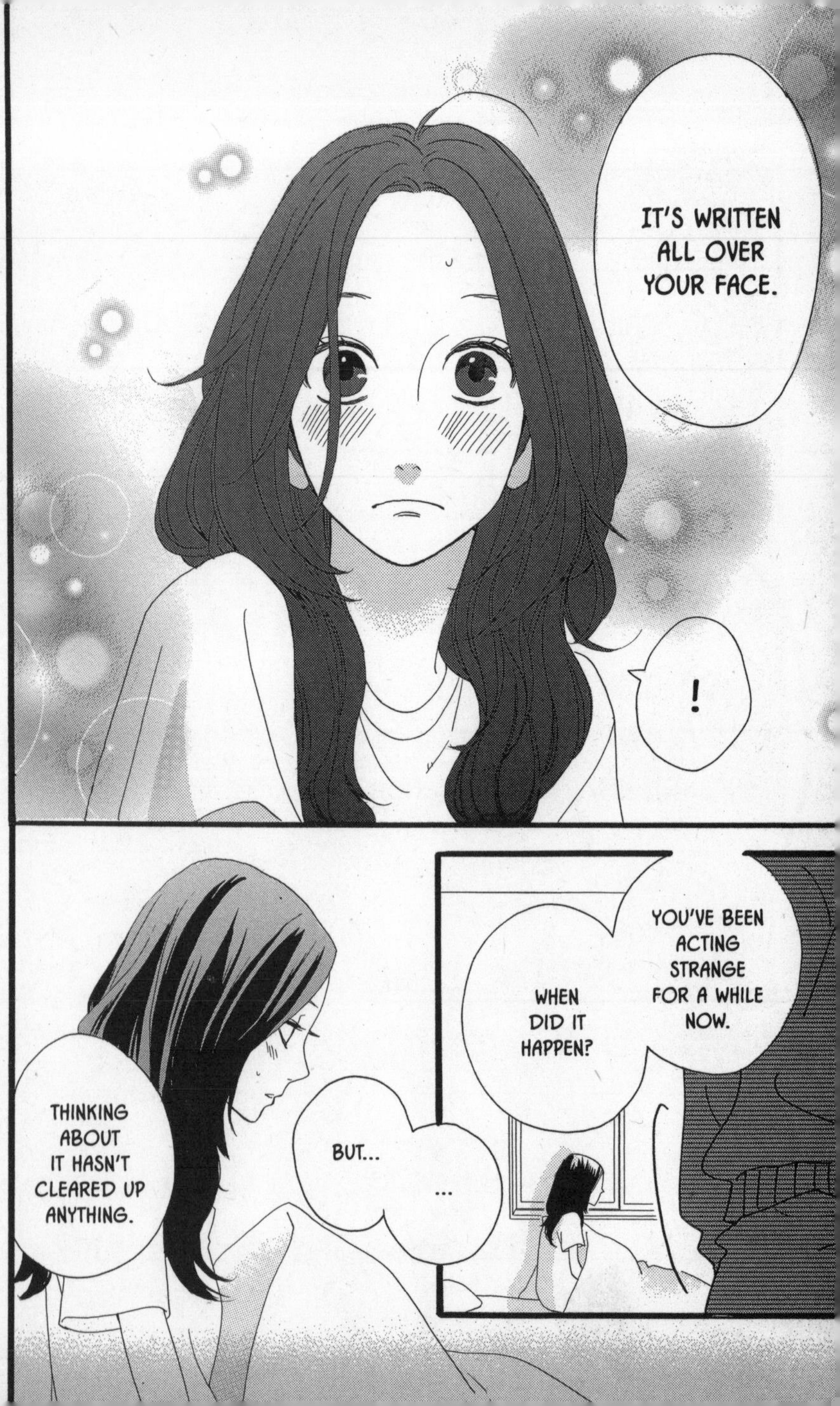
IT'S WRITTEN ALL OVER YOUR FACE.
!
YOU'VE BEEN ACTING STRANGE FOR A WHILE NOW.
WHEN DID IT HAPPEN?
BUT...
...
THINKING ABOUT IT HASN'T CLEARED UP ANYTHING.

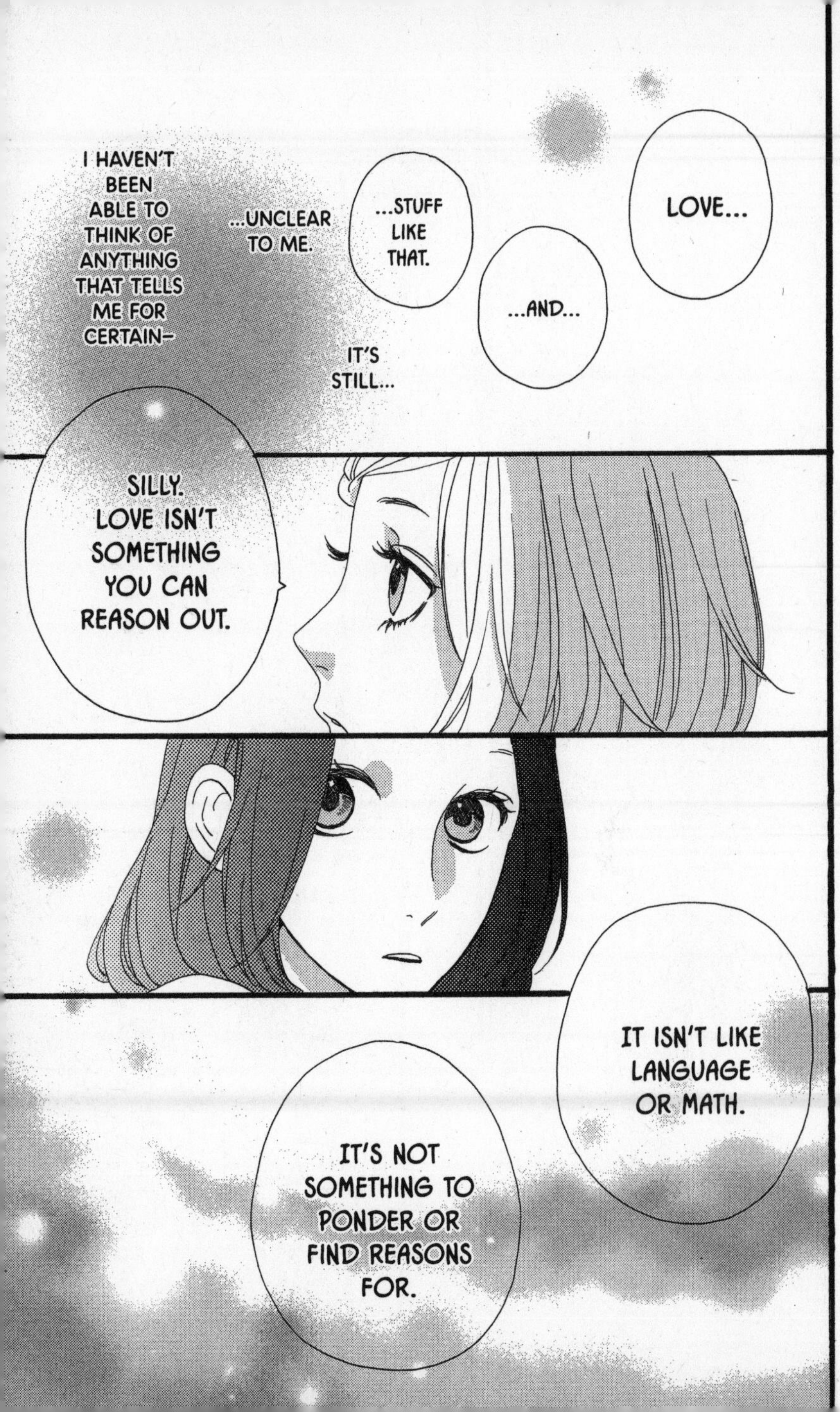
LOVE...
...AND...
...STUFF LIKE THAT.
IT'S STILL...
...UNCLEAR TO ME.
I HAVEN'T BEEN ABLE TO THINK OF ANYTHING THAT TELLS ME FOR CERTAIN–
SILLY. LOVE ISN'T SOMETHING YOU CAN REASON OUT.
IT ISN'T LIKE LANGUAGE OR MATH.
IT'S NOT SOMETHING TO PONDER OR FIND REASONS FOR.

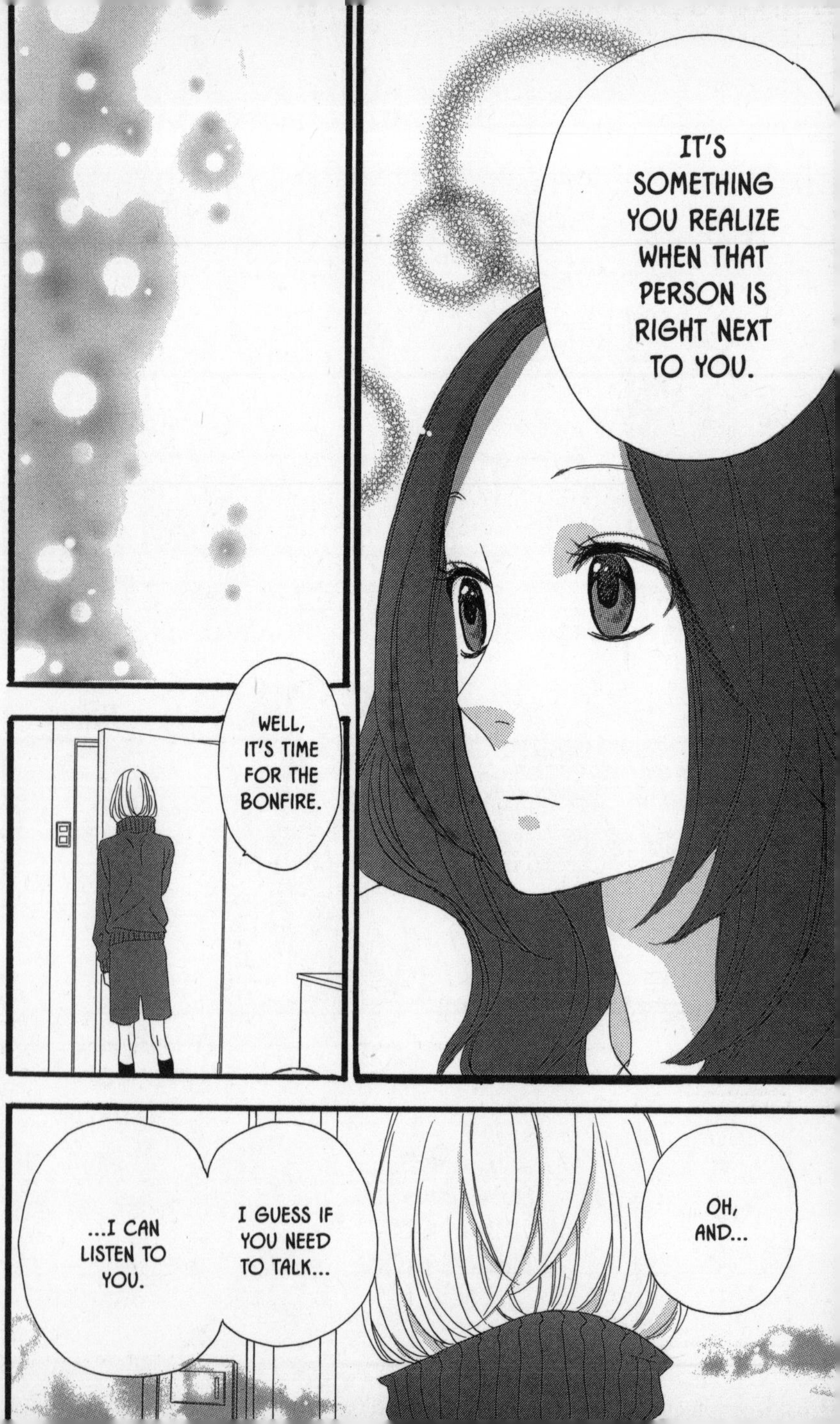

IT'S SOMETHING YOU REALIZE WHEN THAT PERSON IS RIGHT NEXT TO YOU.
WELL, IT'S TIME FOR THE BONFIRE.
OH, AND...
I GUESS IF YOU NEED TO TALK...
...I CAN LISTEN TO YOU.

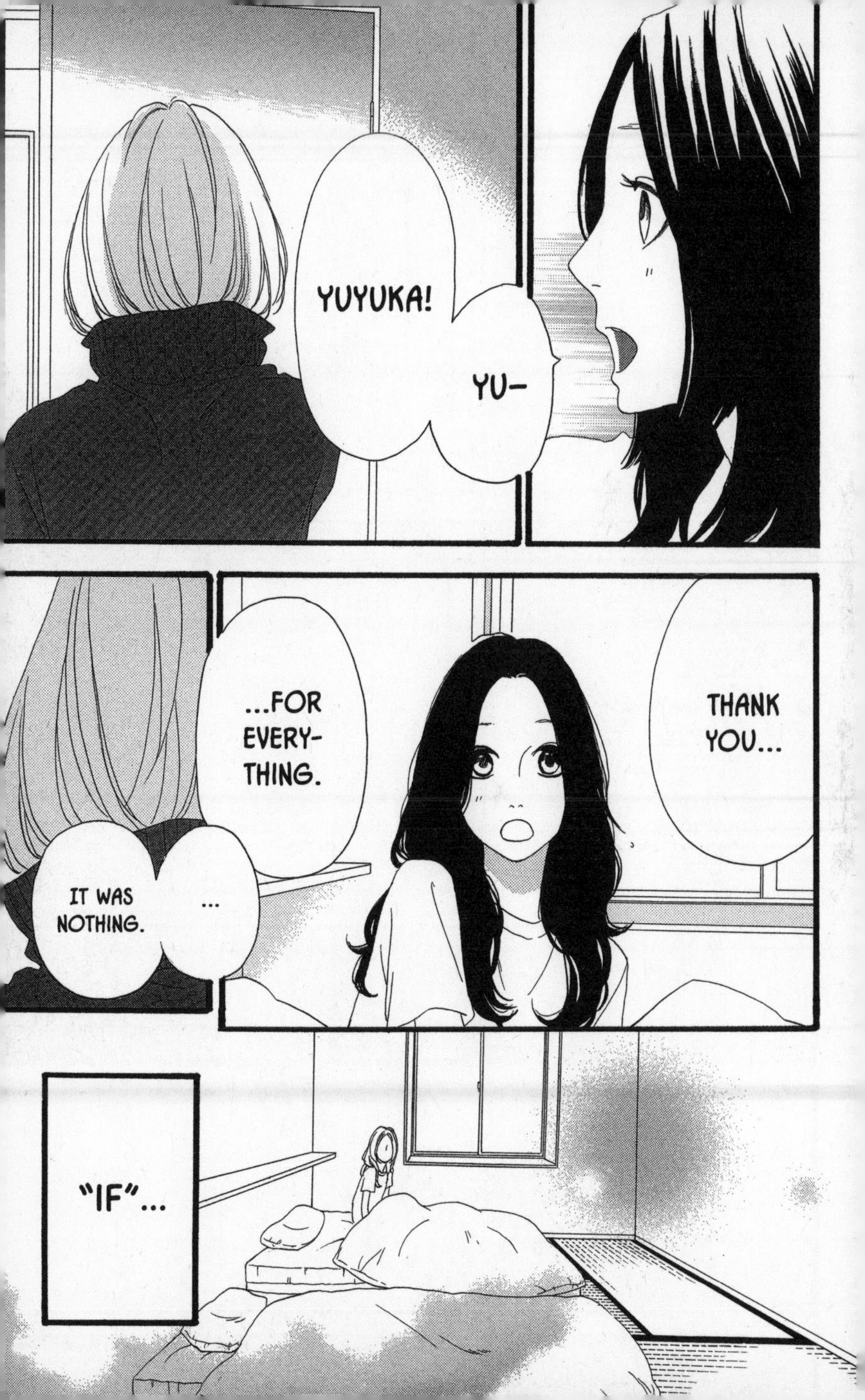
YU–
YUYUKA!
THANK YOU...
...FOR EVERYTHING.
...
IT WAS NOTHING.
"IF"...

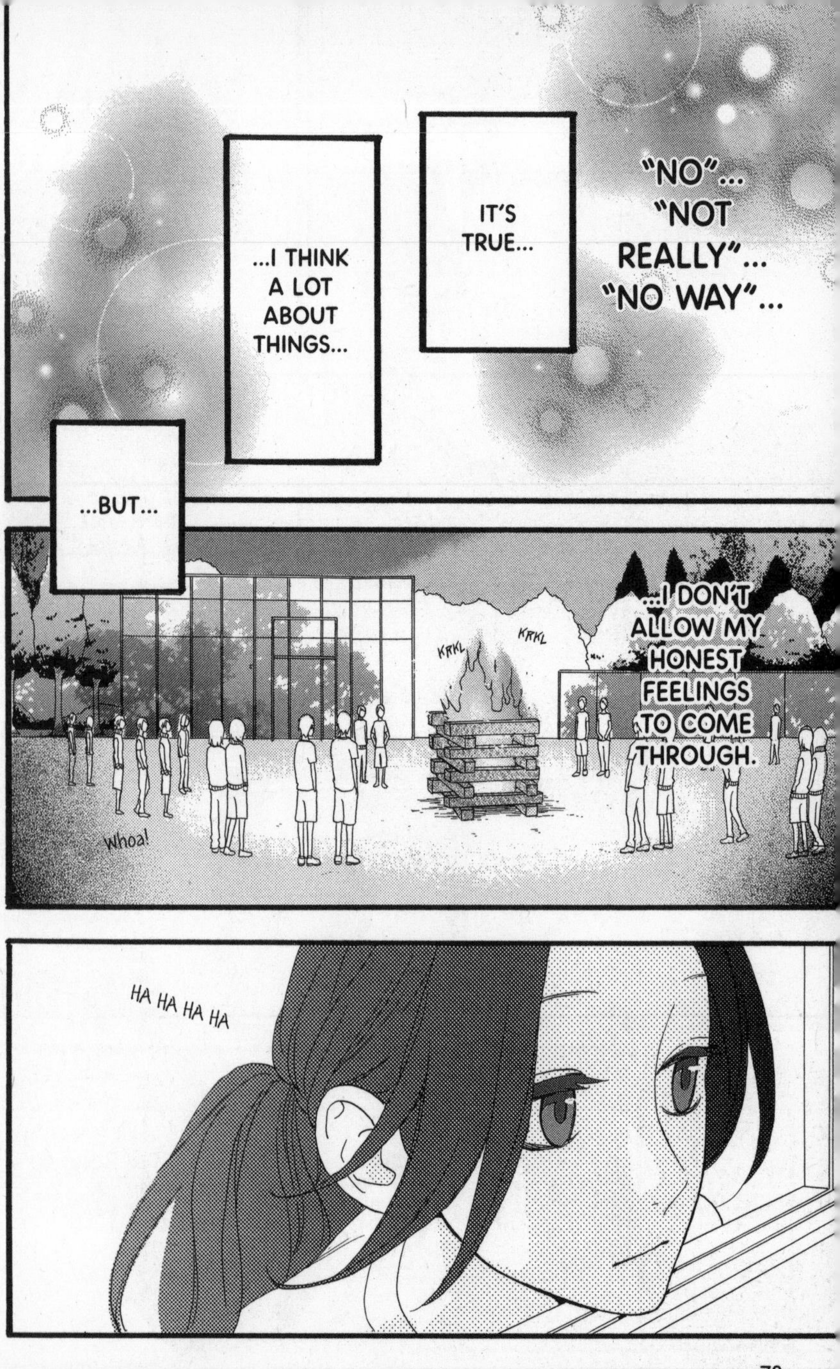
"NO"... "NOT REALLY"... "NO WAY"...
IT'S TRUE...
...I THINK A LOT ABOUT THINGS...
...BUT...
...I DON'T ALLOW MY HONEST FEELINGS TO COME THROUGH.
KRKL
KRKL
Whoa!
HA HA HA HA

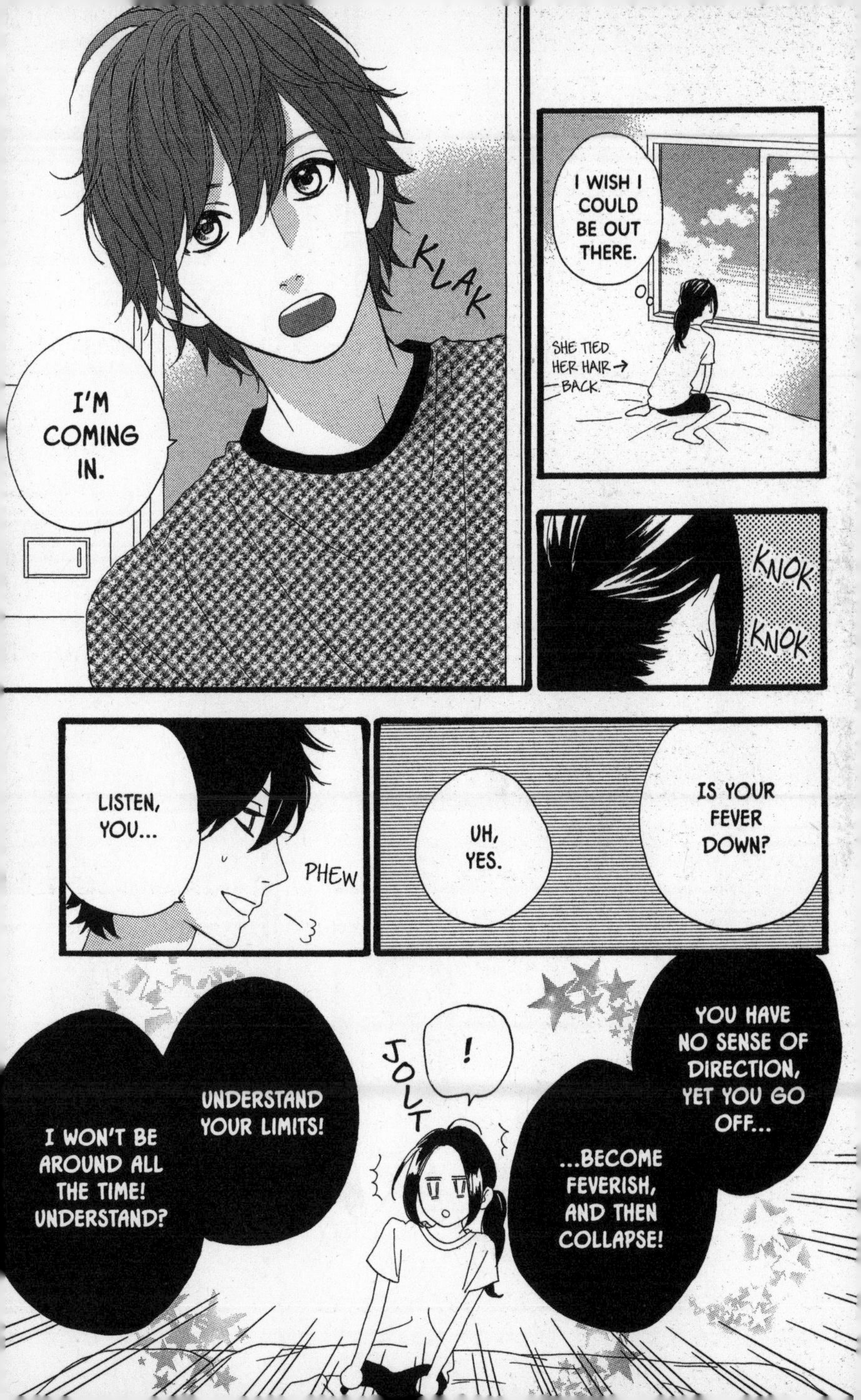
I WISH I COULD BE OUT THERE.
SHE TIED HER HAIR BACK.
KNOK KNOK
KLAK
I'M COMING IN.
IS YOUR FEVER DOWN?
UH, YES.
LISTEN, YOU...
PHEW
YOU HAVE NO SENSE OF DIRECTION, YET YOU GO OFF...
...BECOME FEVERISH, AND THEN COLLAPSE!
!
JOLT
UNDERSTAND YOUR LIMITS!
I WON'T BE AROUND ALL THE TIME! UNDERSTAND?

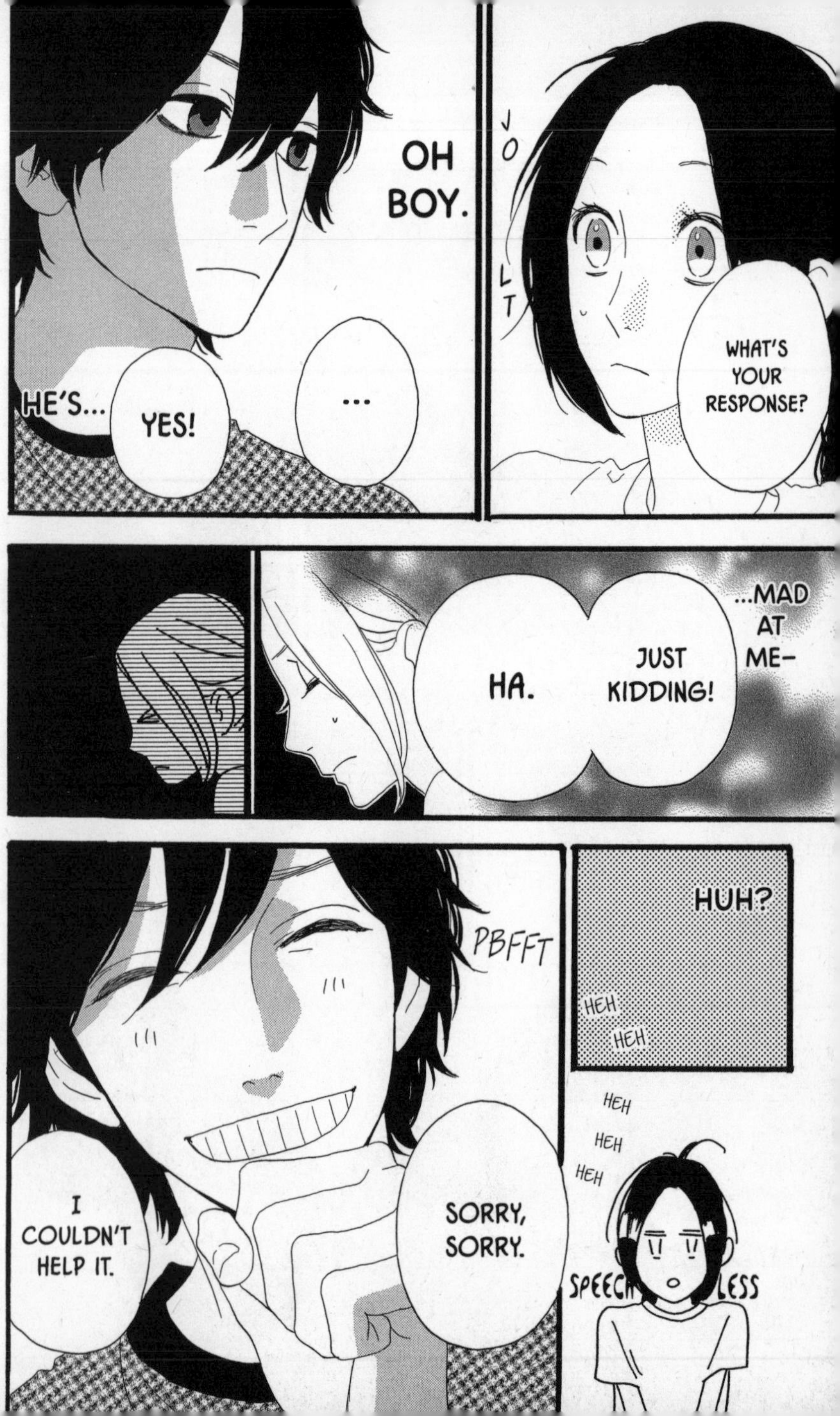
JOLT
WHAT'S YOUR RESPONSE?
OH BOY.
...
YES!
HE'S...
...MAD AT ME-
JUST KIDDING!
HA.
HUH?
HEH HEH
HEH HEH HEH
SPEECHLESS
PBFFT
SORRY, SORRY.
I COULDN'T HELP IT.

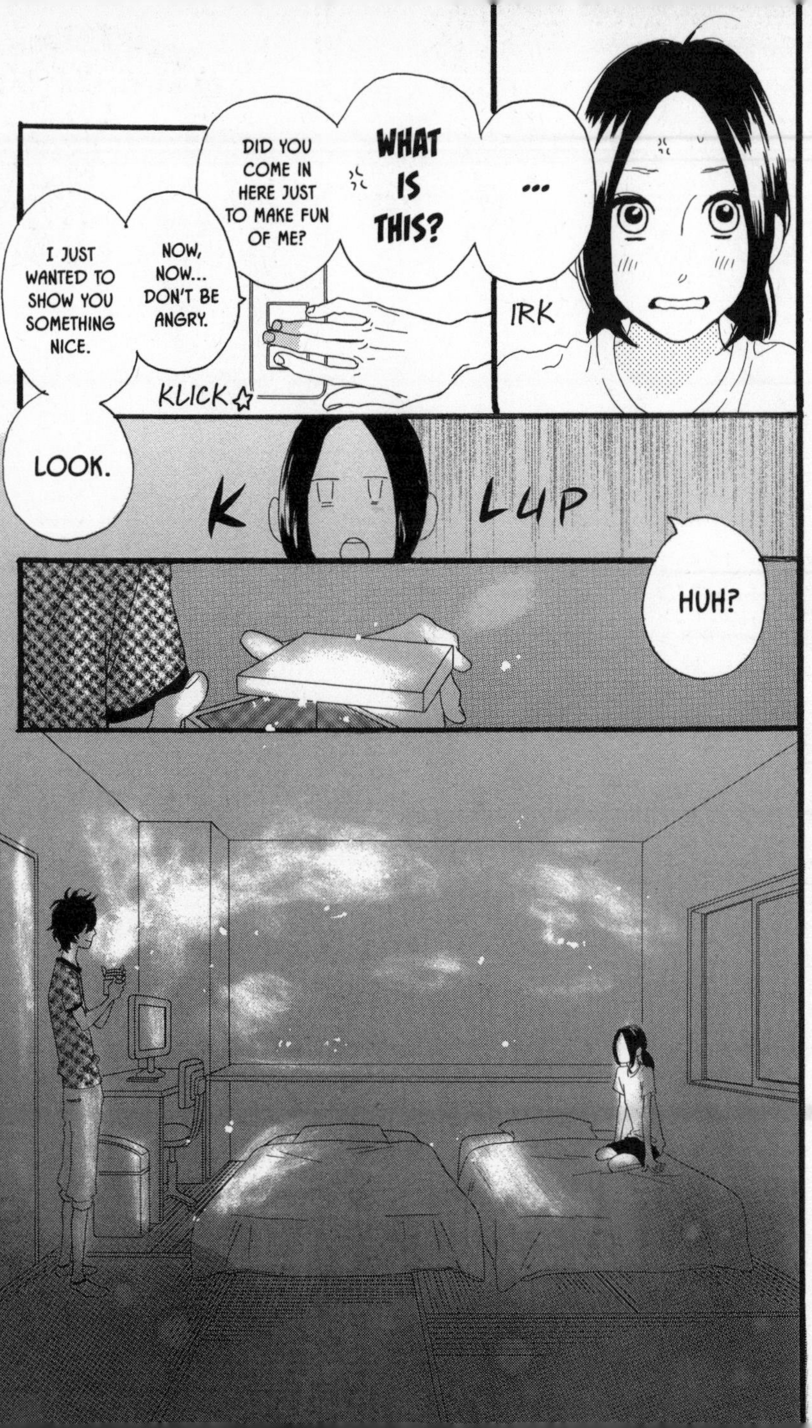
...
IRK
WHAT IS THIS?
DID YOU COME IN HERE JUST TO MAKE FUN OF ME?
NOW, NOW... DON'T BE ANGRY.
I JUST WANTED TO SHOW YOU SOMETHING NICE.
KLICK
LOOK.
K LUP
HUH?

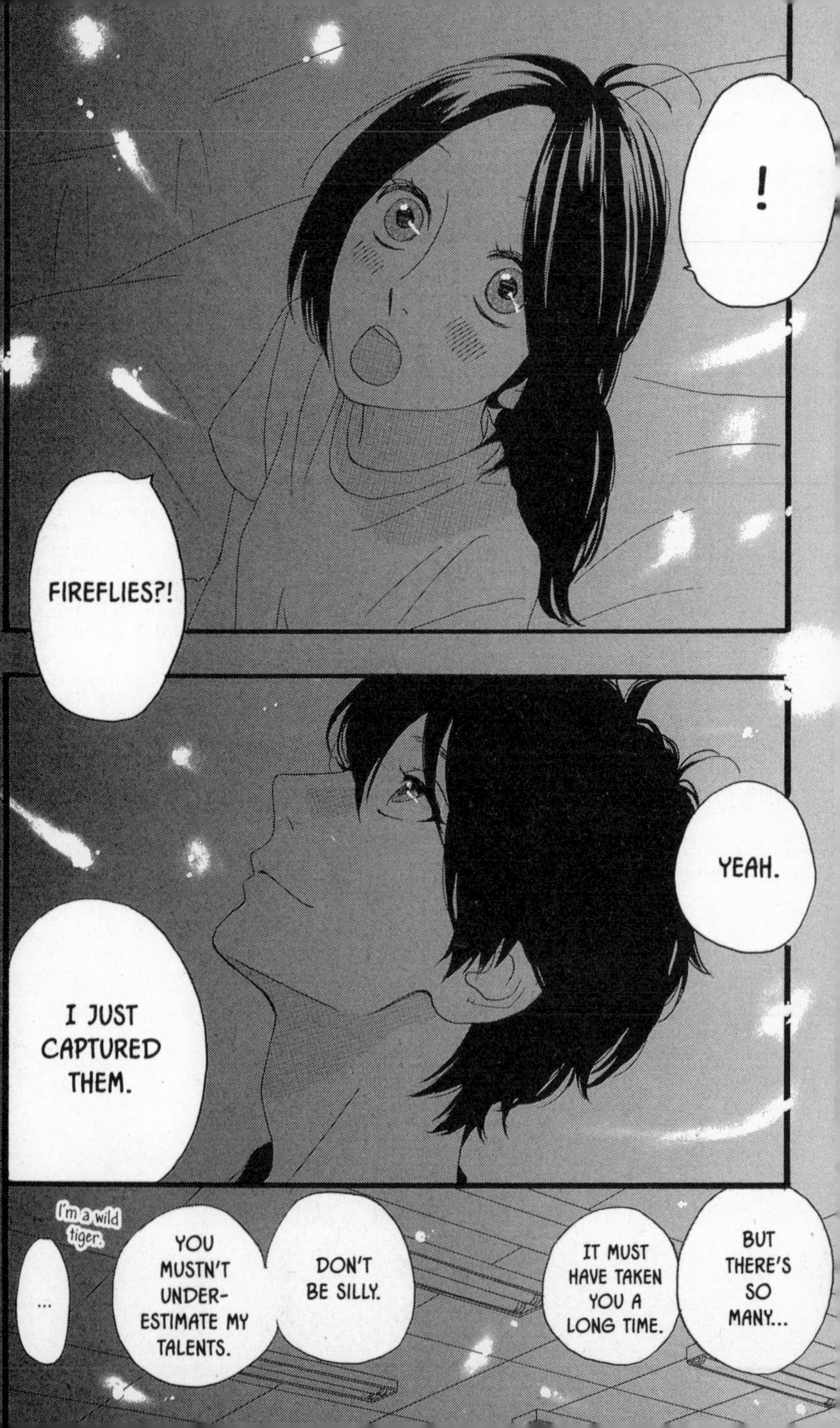
!
FIREFLIES?!
YEAH.
I JUST CAPTURED THEM.
BUT THERE'S SO MANY...
IT MUST HAVE TAKEN YOU A LONG TIME.
DON'T BE SILLY.
YOU MUSTN'T UNDER-ESTIMATE MY TALENTS.
I'm a wild tiger.
...

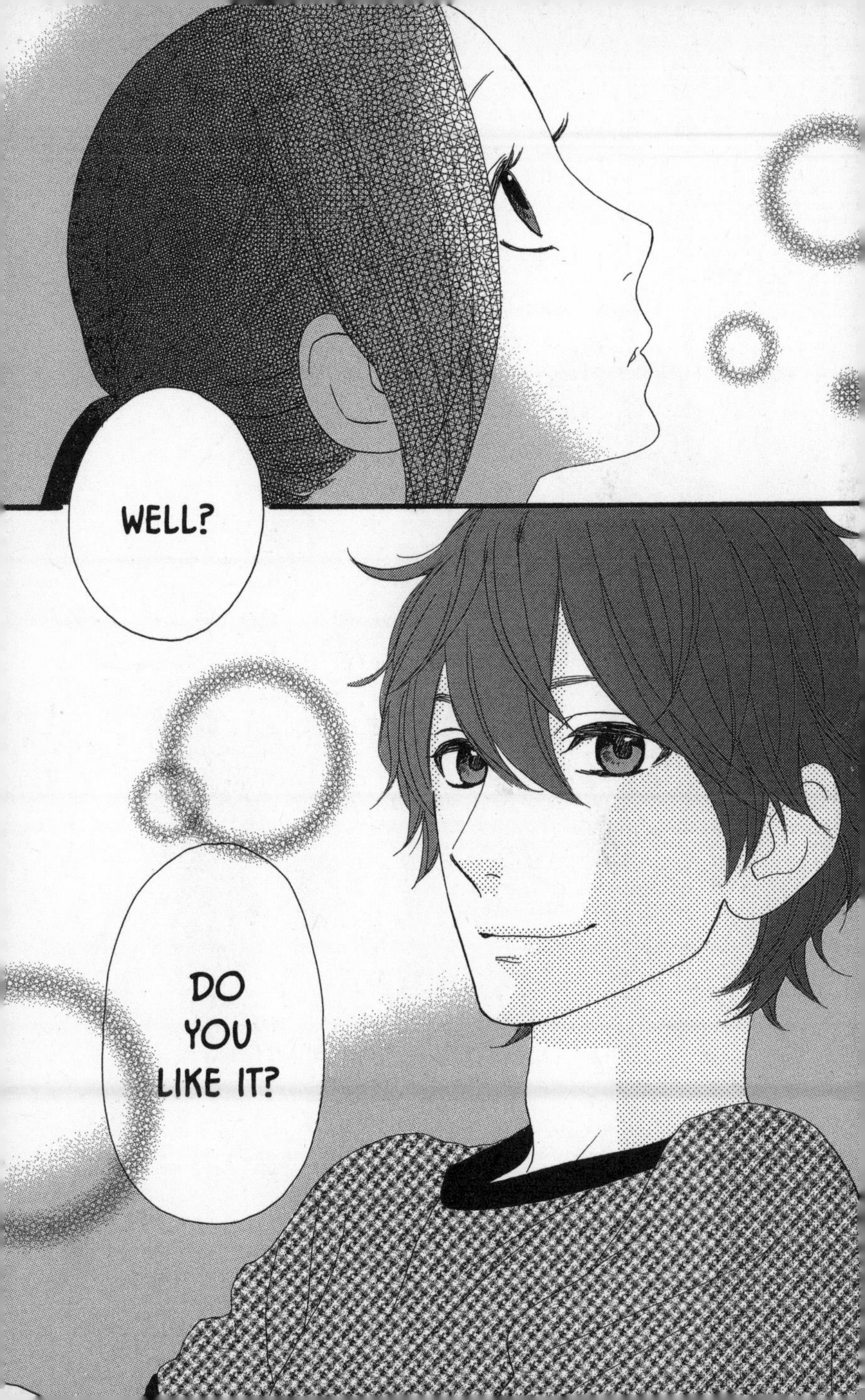
WELL?
DO YOU LIKE IT?

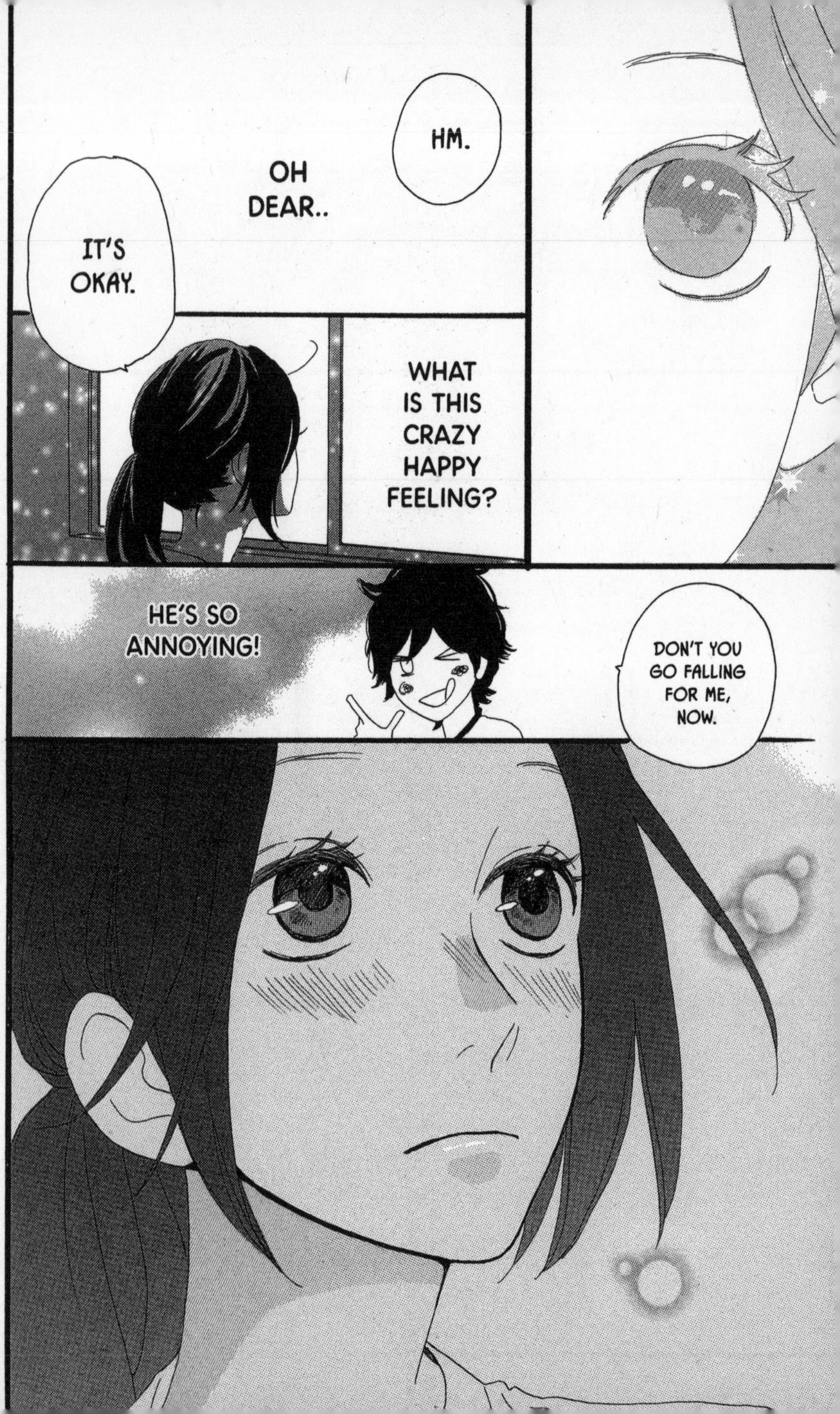
HM.
OH DEAR..
IT'S OKAY.
WHAT IS THIS CRAZY HAPPY FEELING?
DON'T YOU GO FALLING FOR ME, NOW.
HE'S SO ANNOYING!

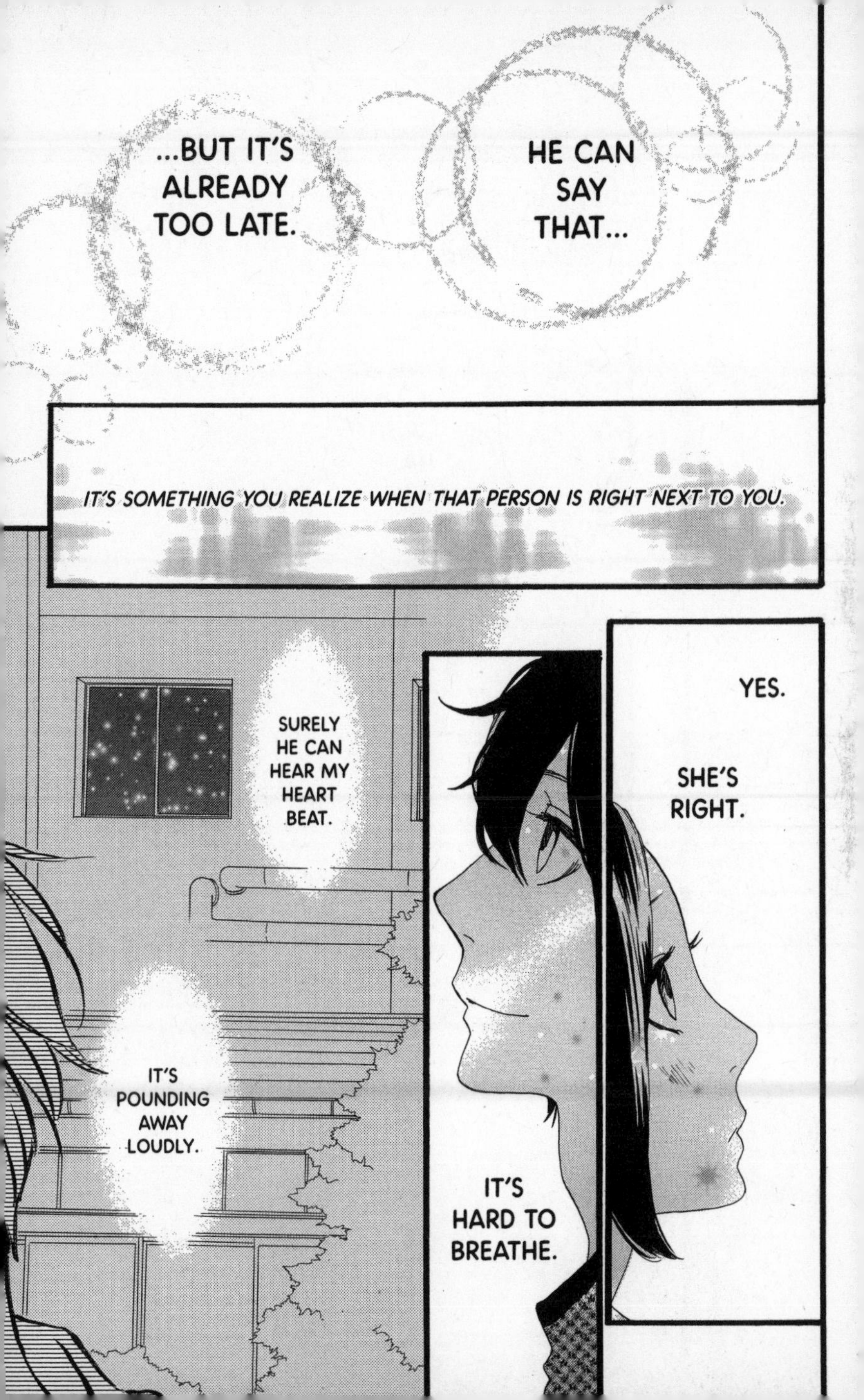
HE CAN SAY THAT...
...BUT IT'S ALREADY TOO LATE.
IT'S SOMETHING YOU REALIZE WHEN THAT PERSON IS RIGHT NEXT TO YOU.
YES.
SHE'S RIGHT.
IT'S HARD TO BREATHE.
SURELY HE CAN HEAR MY HEART BEAT.
IT'S POUNDING AWAY LOUDLY.

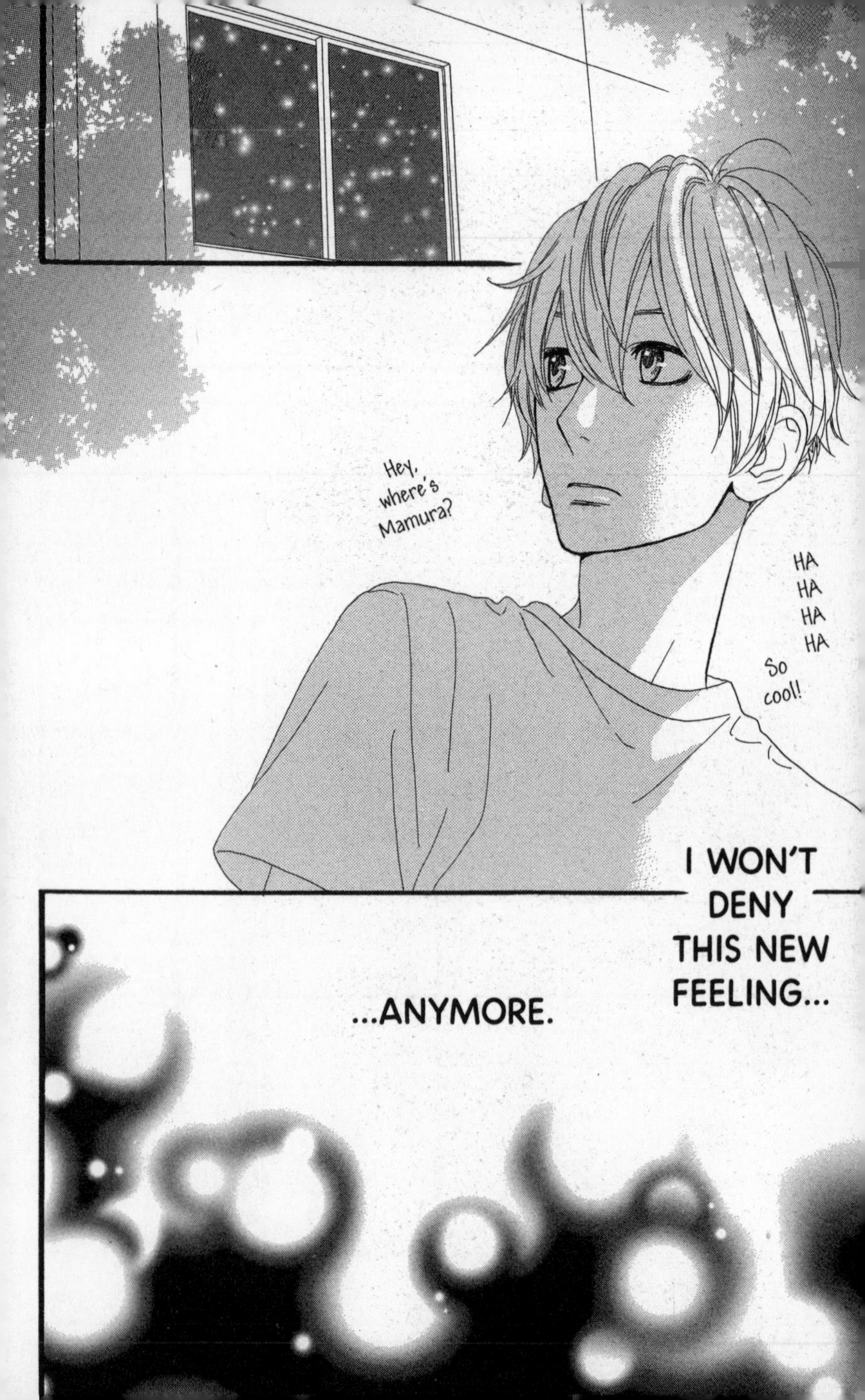
HA HA HA HA
So cool!
Hey, where's Mamura?
I WON'T DENY THIS NEW FEELING...
...ANYMORE.

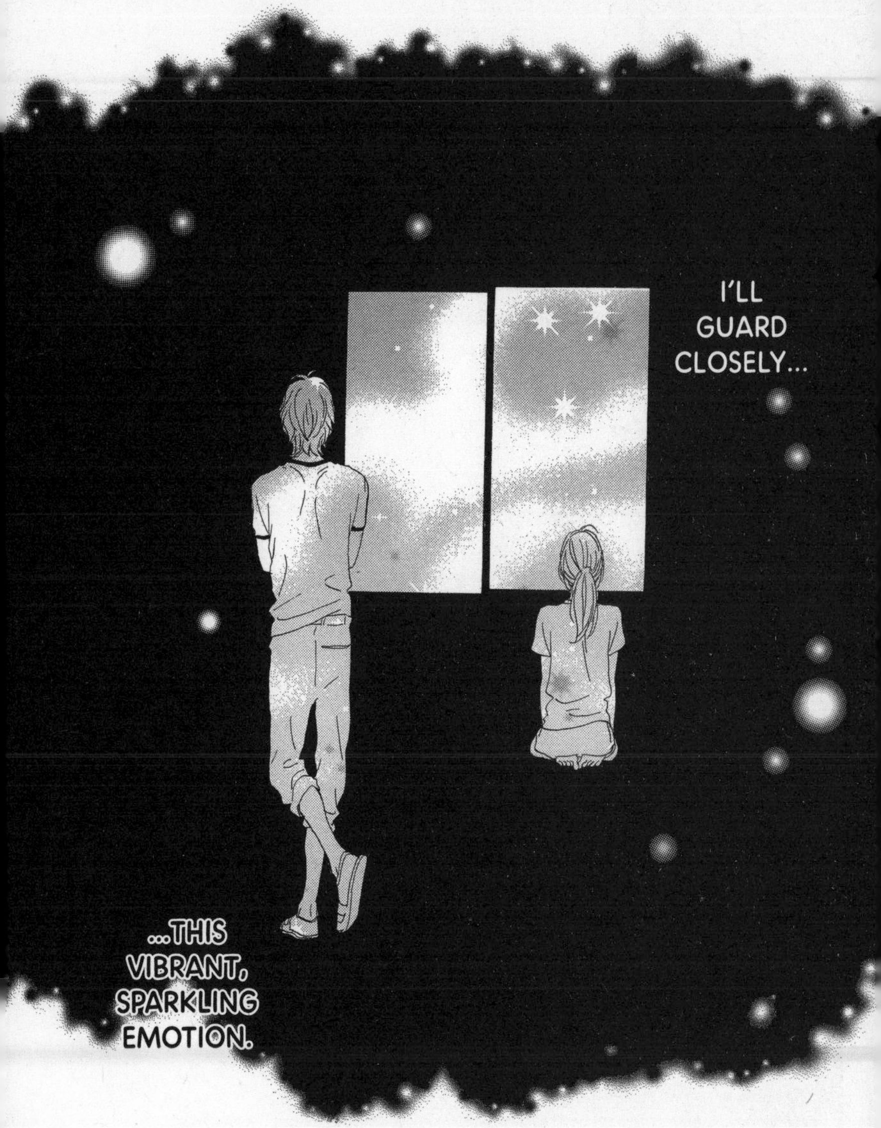
I'LL GUARD CLOSELY...
...THIS VIBRANT, SPARKLING EMOTION.

Simple Scribbles ②

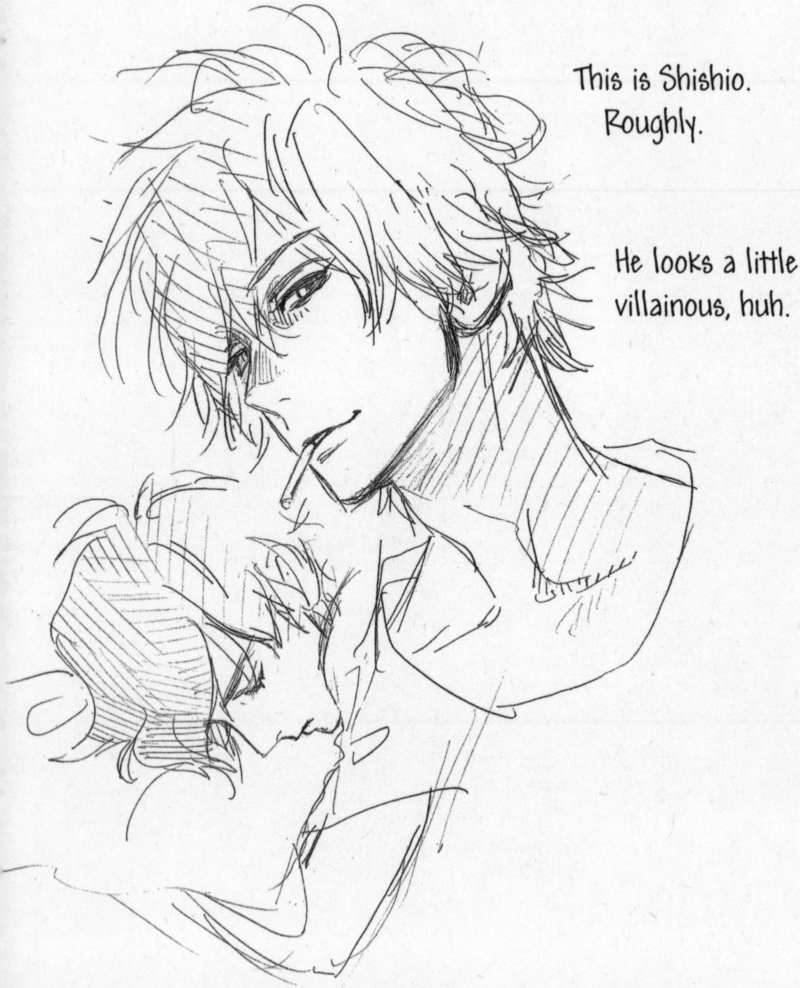
This is Shishio.
Roughly.
He looks a little villainous, huh.

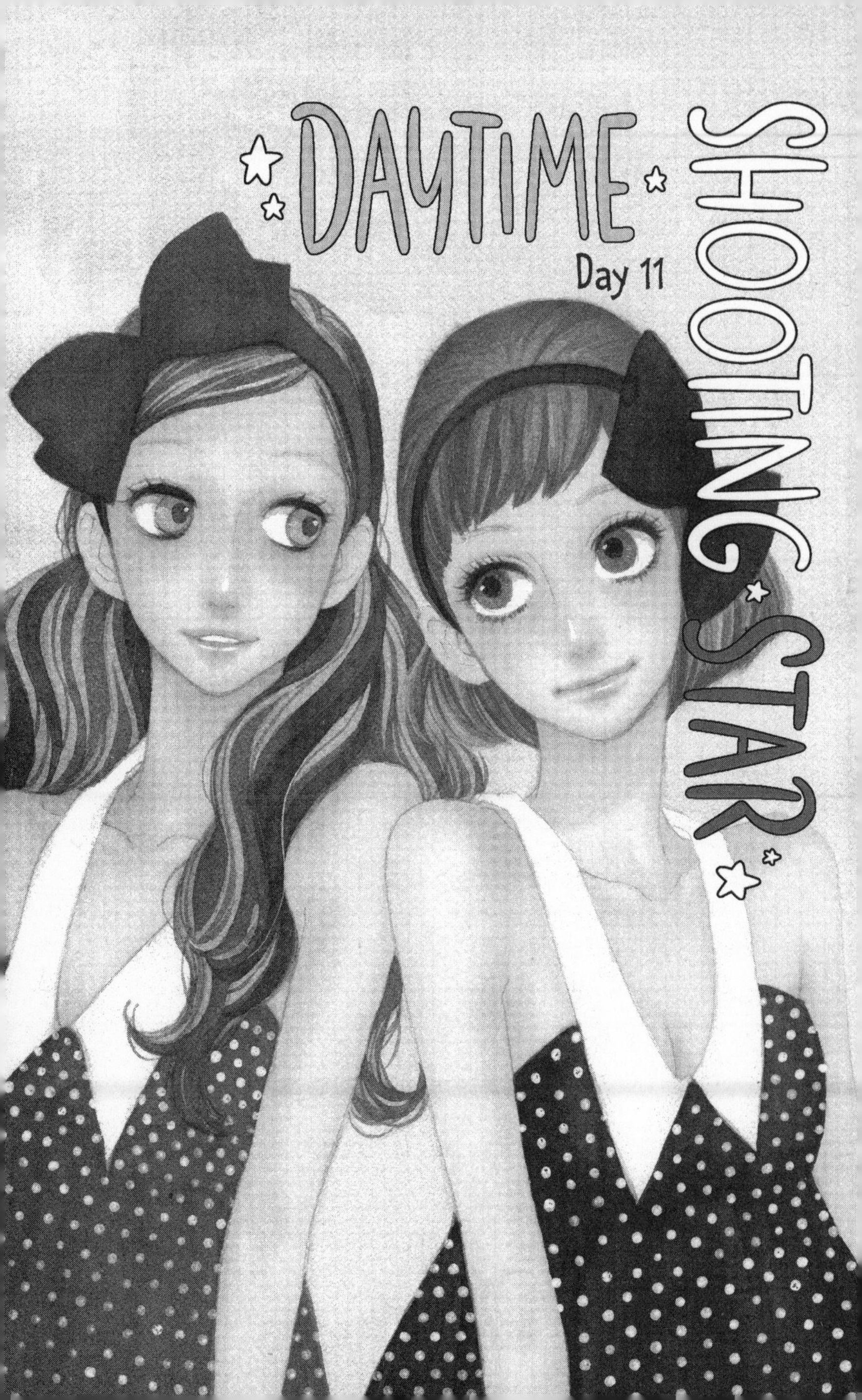
DAYTIME
SHOOTING STAR
Day 11

Daytime Theater

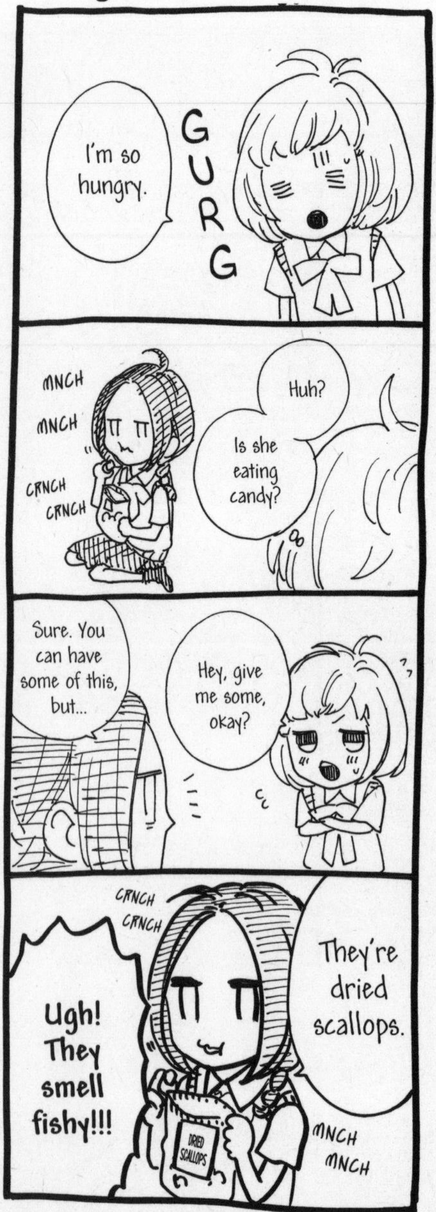
GURG
I'm so hungry.
Huh?
Is she eating candy?
MNCH
MNCH
CRNCH
CRNCH
Hey, give me some, okay?
Sure. You can have some of this, but...
They're dried scallops.
CRNCH
CRNCH
MNCH
MNCH
DRIED SCALLOPS
Ugh! They smell fishy!!!

The End

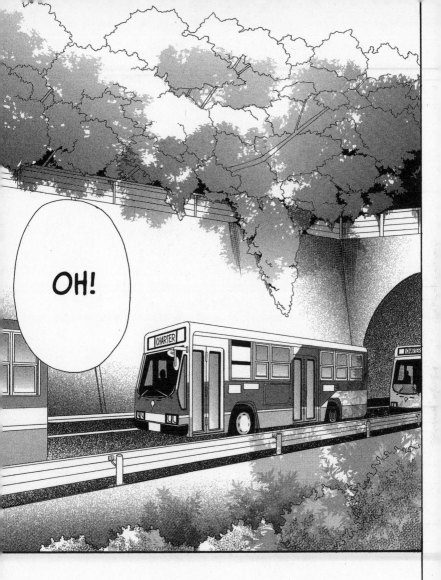

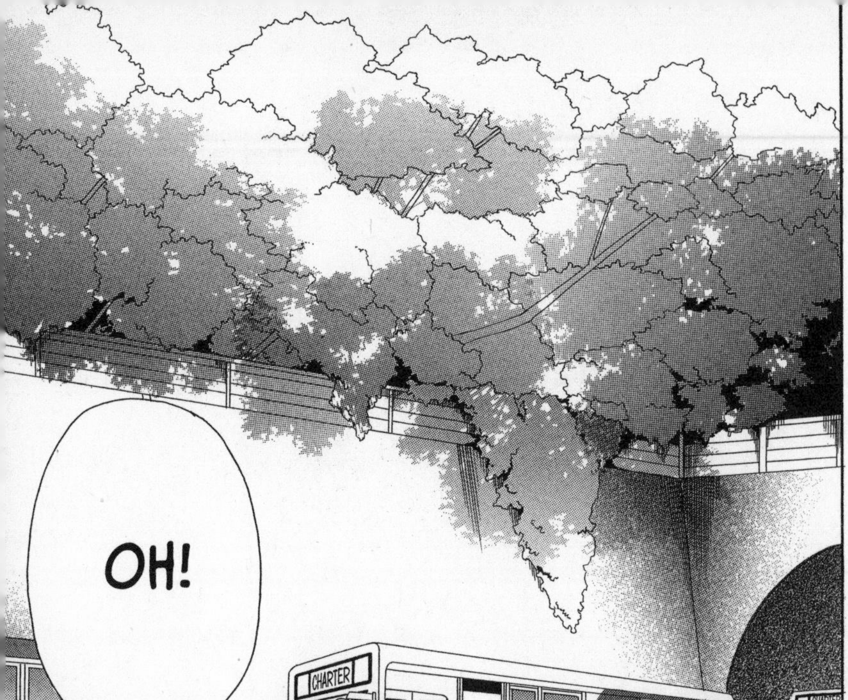
OH!
CHARTER
CHARTER

Nana Kameyoshi 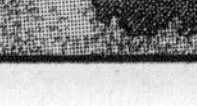
Yo!

Birthday: November 1

Height: 5'1"

Weight: 95 lbs

Blood Type: B

1. Carbonated drinks.
2. Bass. Karaoke.
3. I want to try body piercing, but I'm too scared to go by myself.

*Kame means "turtle."

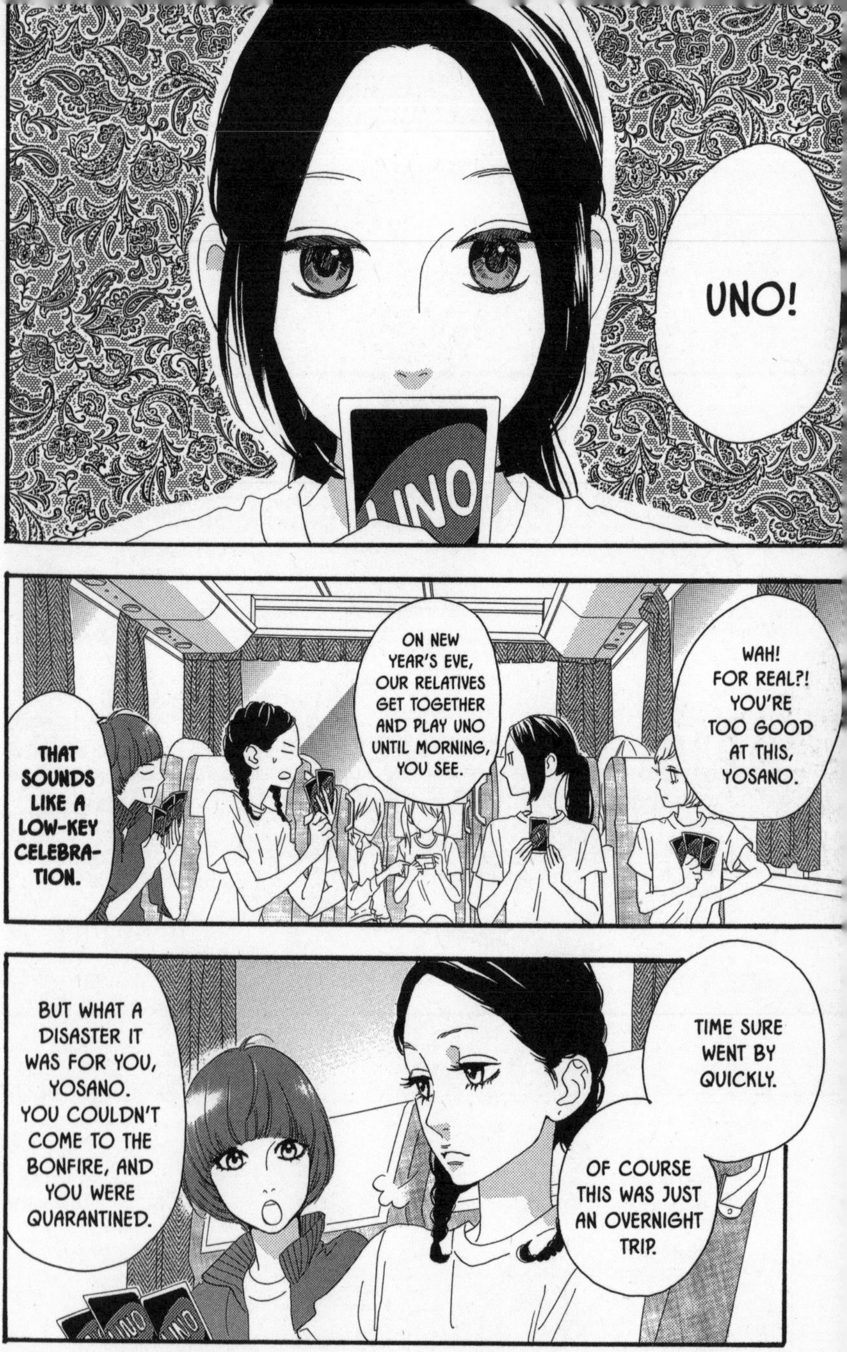
UNO!
UNO
WAH! FOR REAL?! YOU'RE TOO GOOD AT THIS, YOSANO.
ON NEW YEAR'S EVE, OUR RELATIVES GET TOGETHER AND PLAY UNO UNTIL MORNING, YOU SEE.
THAT SOUNDS LIKE A LOW-KEY CELEBRATION.
TIME SURE WENT BY QUICKLY.
OF COURSE THIS WAS JUST AN OVERNIGHT TRIP.
BUT WHAT A DISASTER IT WAS FOR YOU, YOSANO. YOU COULDN'T COME TO THE BONFIRE, AND YOU WERE QUARANTINED.
UNO

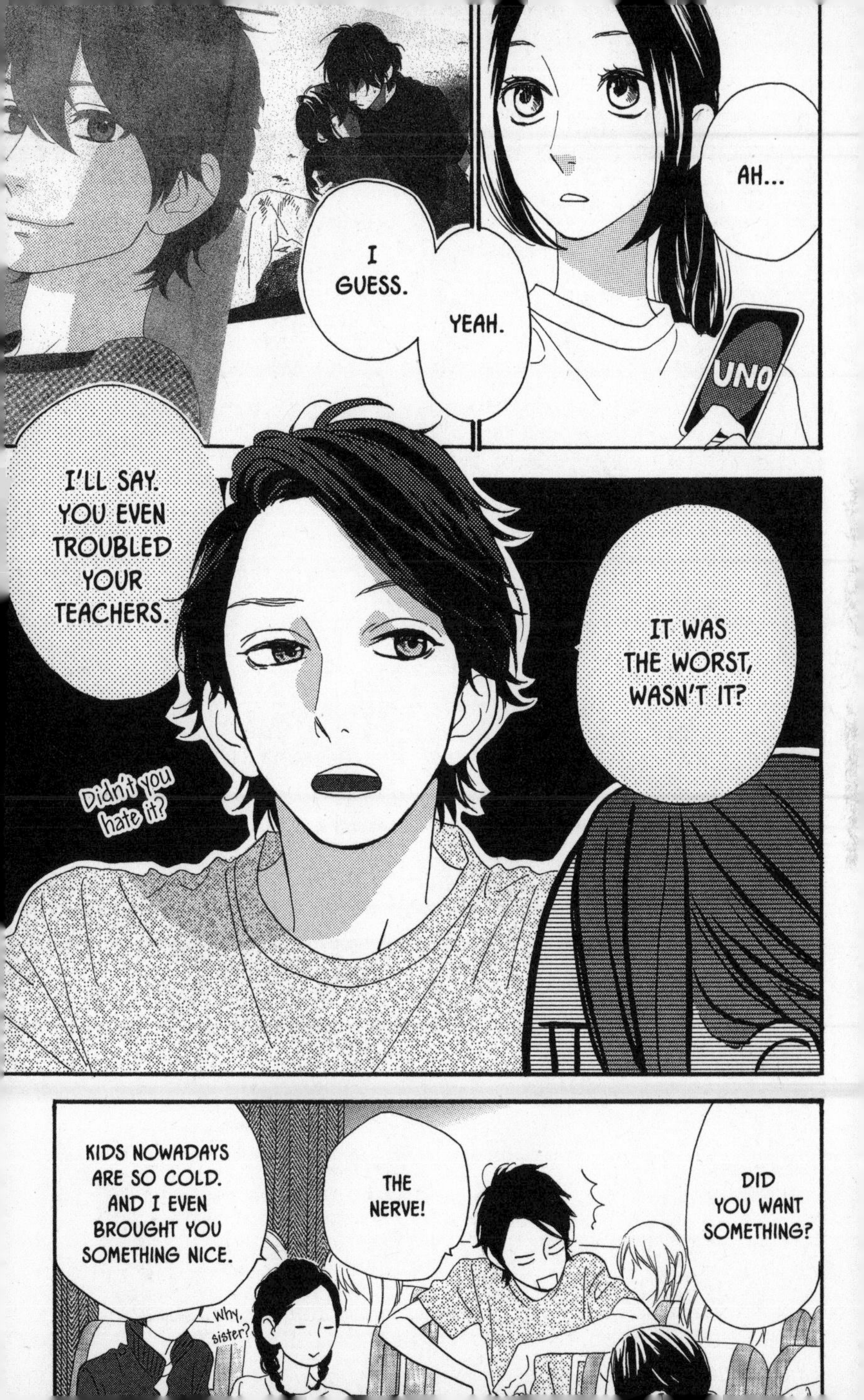
AH...
I GUESS.
YEAH.
IT WAS THE WORST, WASN'T IT?
I'LL SAY. YOU EVEN TROUBLED YOUR TEACHERS.
Didn't you hate it?
DID YOU WANT SOMETHING?
THE NERVE!
KIDS NOWADAYS ARE SO COLD. AND I EVEN BROUGHT YOU SOMETHING NICE.
Why, sister?

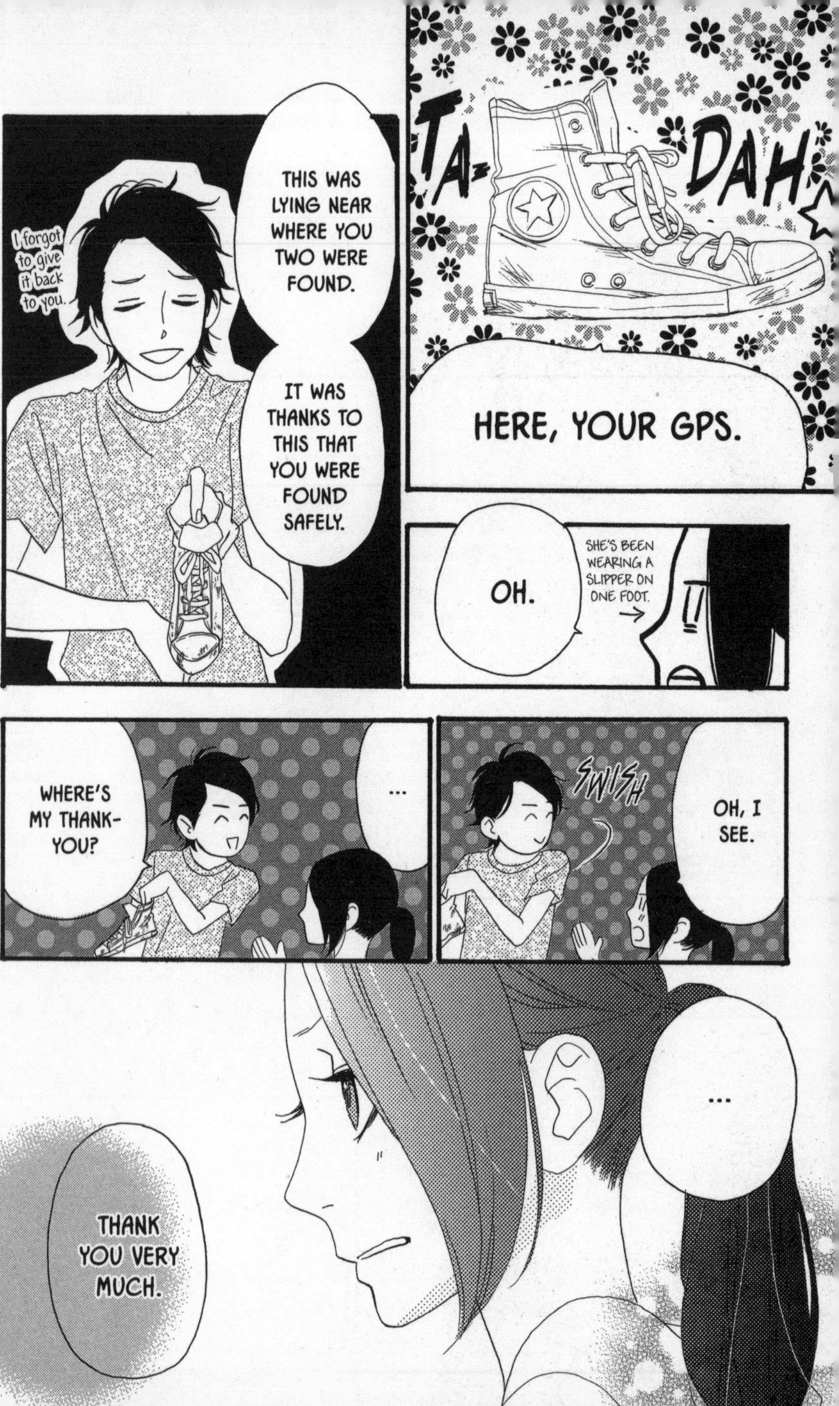
TA-DAH
HERE, YOUR GPS.
THIS WAS LYING NEAR WHERE YOU TWO WERE FOUND.
IT WAS THANKS TO THIS THAT YOU WERE FOUND SAFELY.
I forgot to give it back to you.
OH.
SHE'S BEEN WEARING A SLIPPER ON ONE FOOT.
SWISH
OH, I SEE.
...
WHERE'S MY THANK-YOU?
...
THANK YOU VERY MUCH.

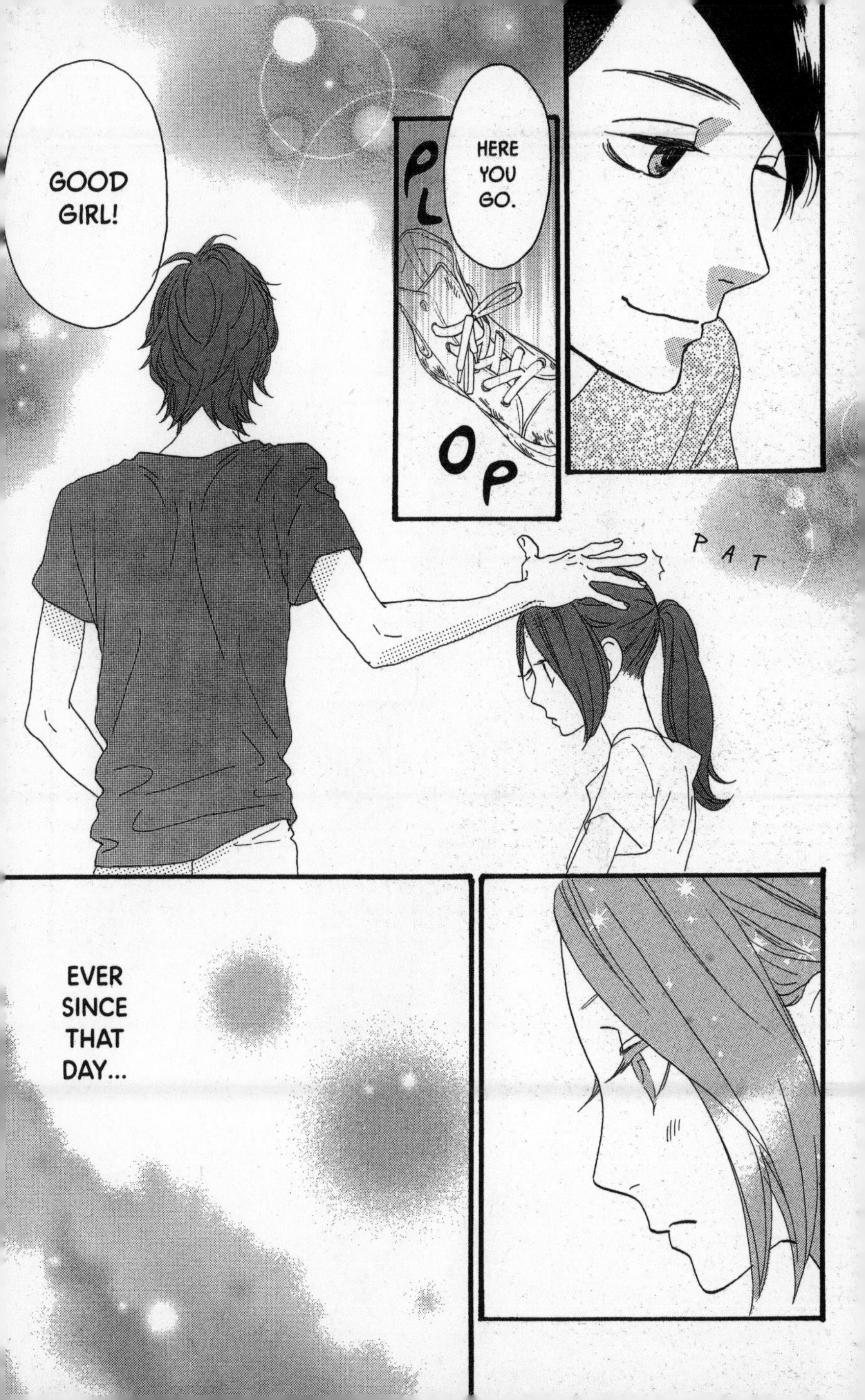
HERE YOU GO.
PLOP
GOOD GIRL!
PAT
EVER SINCE THAT DAY...

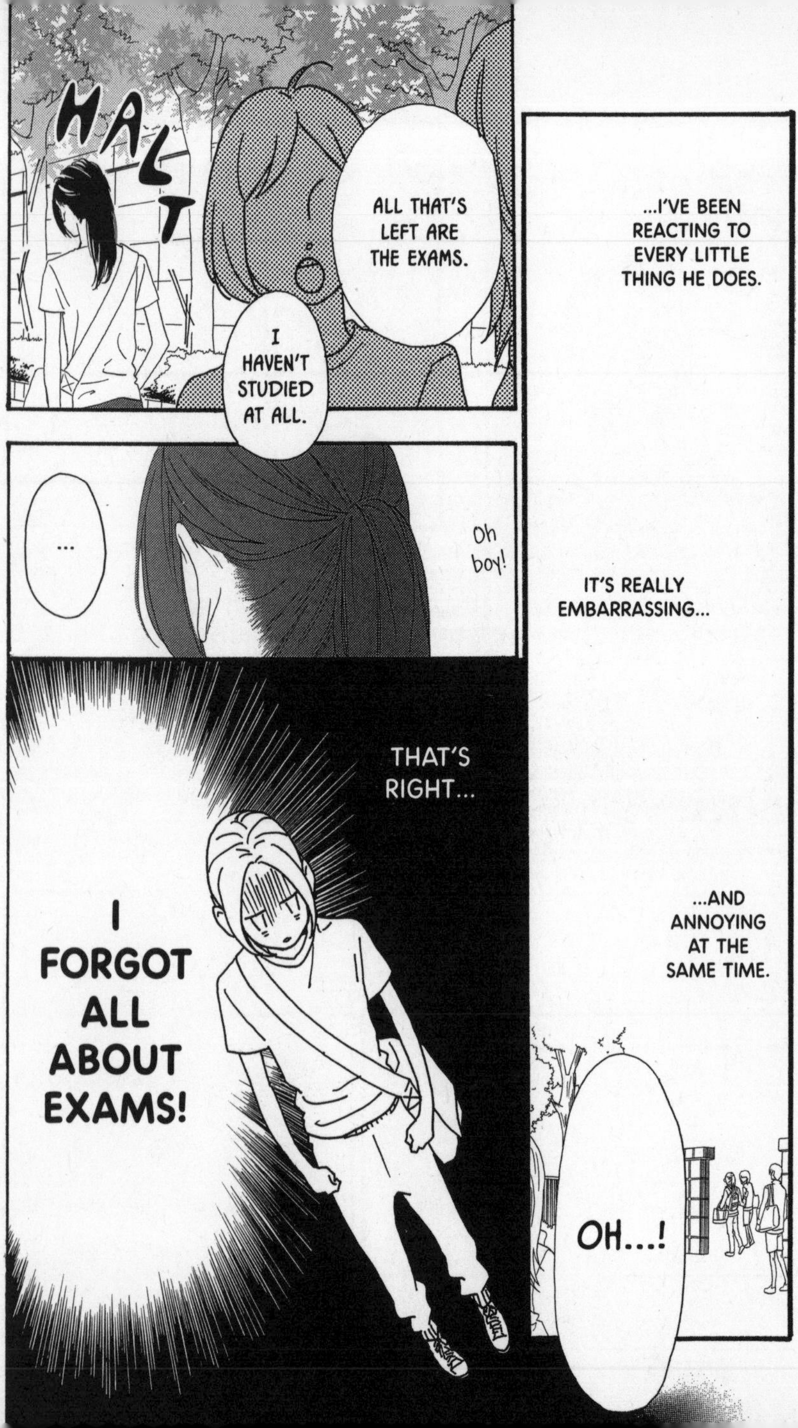
...I'VE BEEN REACTING TO EVERY LITTLE THING HE DOES.
IT'S REALLY EMBARRASSING...
...AND ANNOYING AT THE SAME TIME.
OH...!
HALT
ALL THAT'S LEFT ARE THE EXAMS.
I HAVEN'T STUDIED AT ALL.
Oh boy!
...
THAT'S RIGHT...
I FORGOT ALL ABOUT EXAMS!

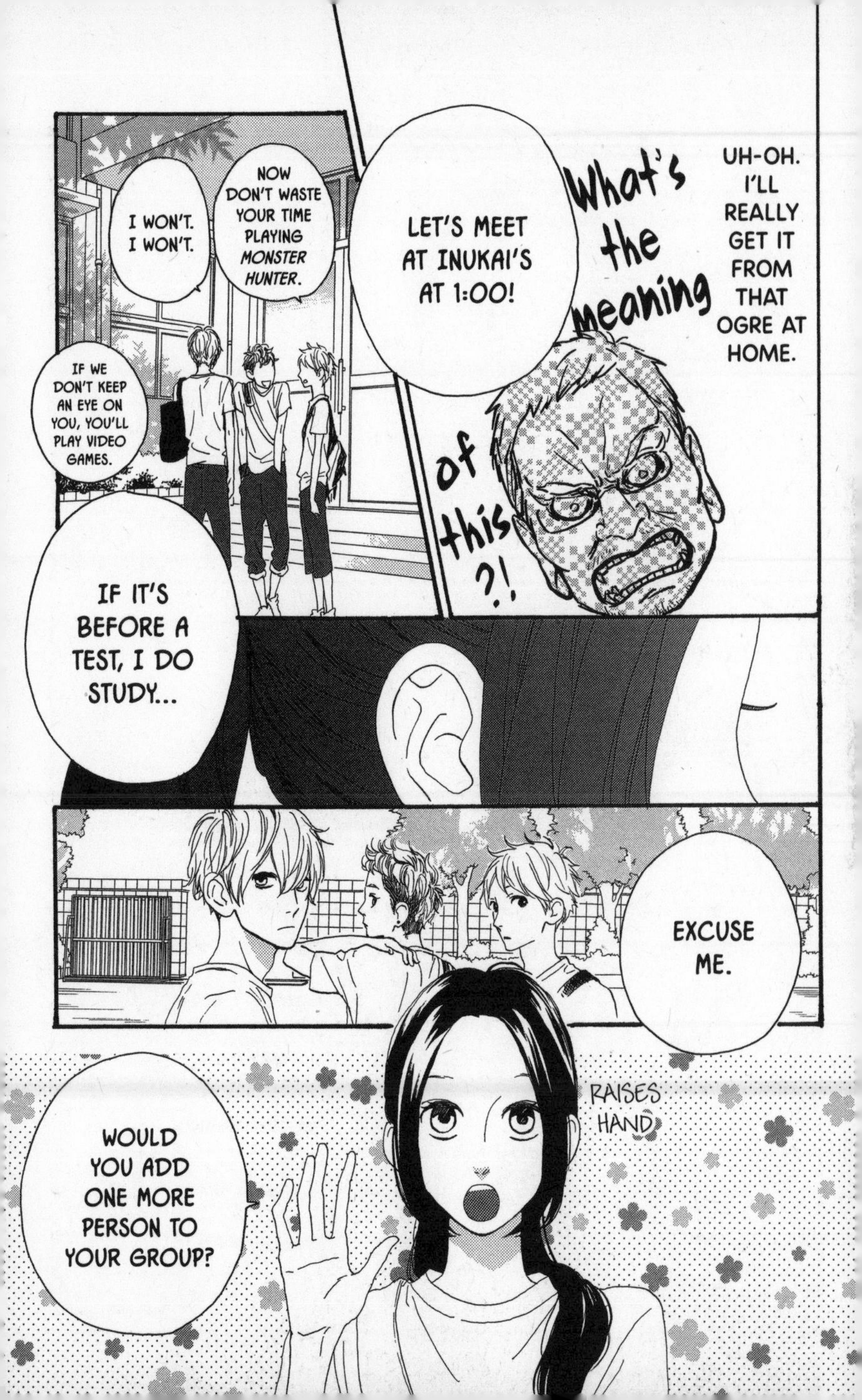
LET'S MEET AT INUKAI'S AT 1:00!
UH-OH. I'LL REALLY GET IT FROM THAT OGRE AT HOME.
What's the meaning of this?!
NOW DON'T WASTE YOUR TIME PLAYING MONSTER HUNTER.
I WON'T. I WON'T.
IF WE DON'T KEEP AN EYE ON YOU, YOU'LL PLAY VIDEO GAMES.
IF IT'S BEFORE A TEST, I DO STUDY...
EXCUSE ME.
RAISES HAND
WOULD YOU ADD ONE MORE PERSON TO YOUR GROUP?

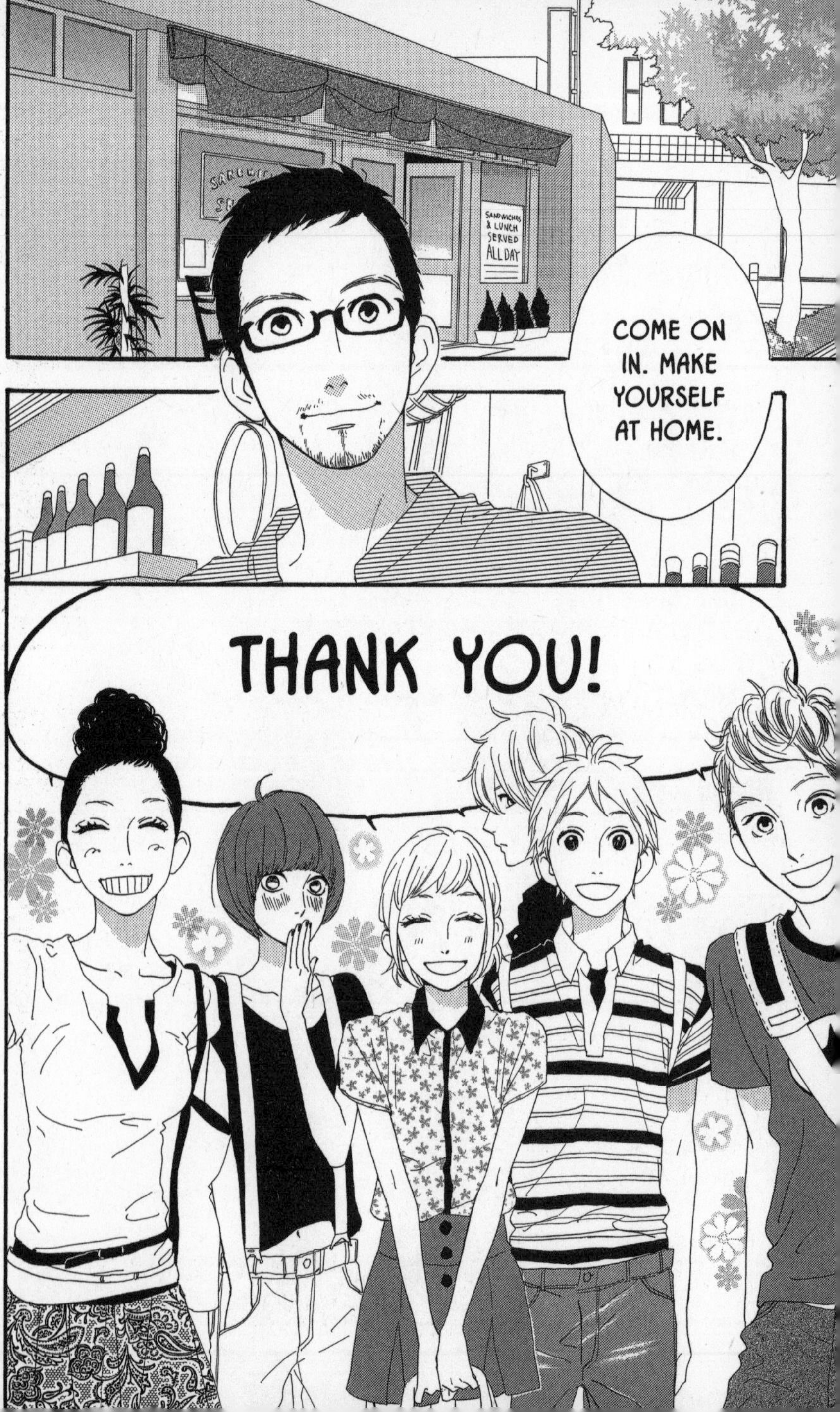
SANDWICHES & LUNCH SERVED ALL DAY
COME ON IN. MAKE YOURSELF AT HOME.
THANK YOU!

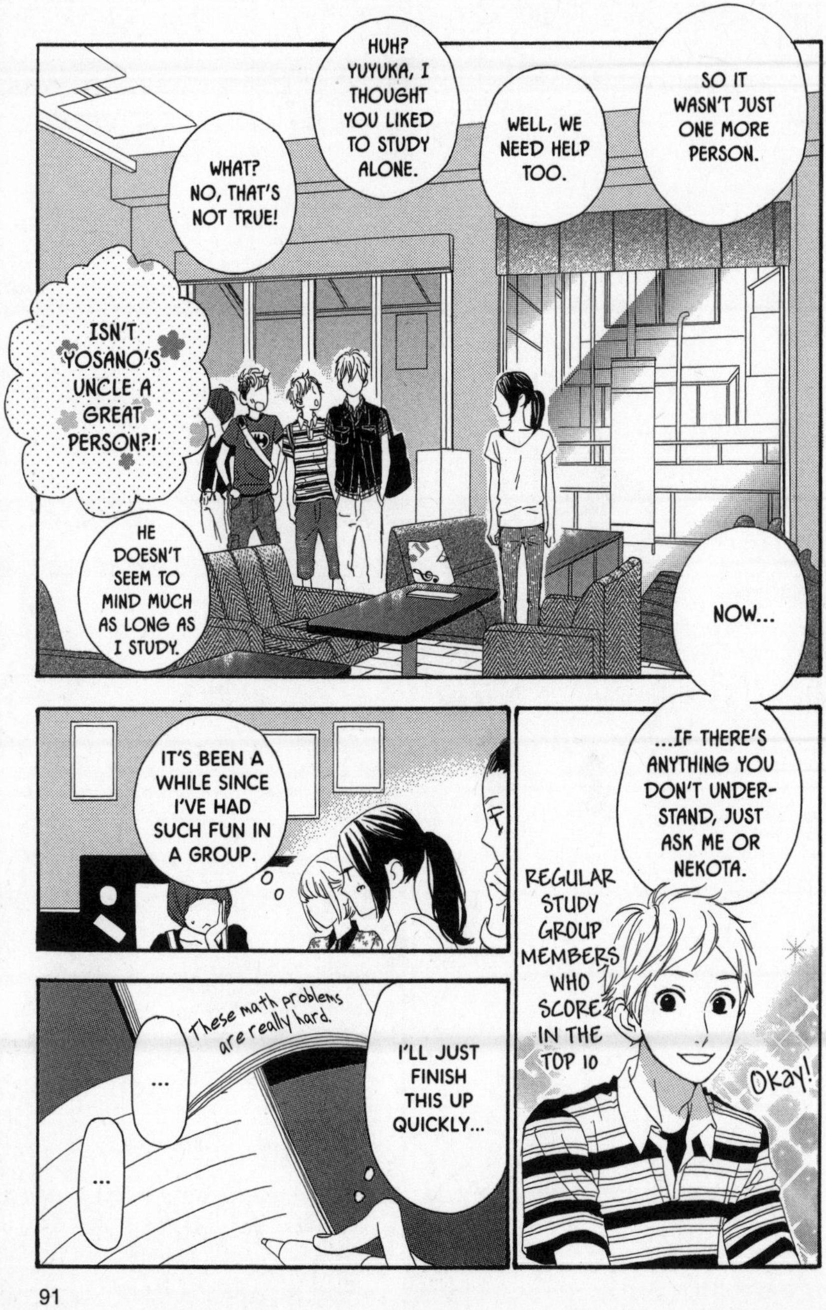
SO IT WASN'T JUST ONE MORE PERSON.
WELL, WE NEED HELP TOO.
HUH? YUYUKA, I THOUGHT YOU LIKED TO STUDY ALONE.
WHAT? NO, THAT'S NOT TRUE!
ISN'T YOSANO'S UNCLE A GREAT PERSON?!
HE DOESN'T SEEM TO MIND MUCH AS LONG AS I STUDY.
NOW...
...IF THERE'S ANYTHING YOU DON'T UNDER-STAND, JUST ASK ME OR NEKOTA.
REGULAR STUDY GROUP MEMBERS WHO SCORE IN THE TOP 10
Okay!
IT'S BEEN A WHILE SINCE I'VE HAD SUCH FUN IN A GROUP.
I'LL JUST FINISH THIS UP QUICKLY...
These math problems are really hard.
...
...

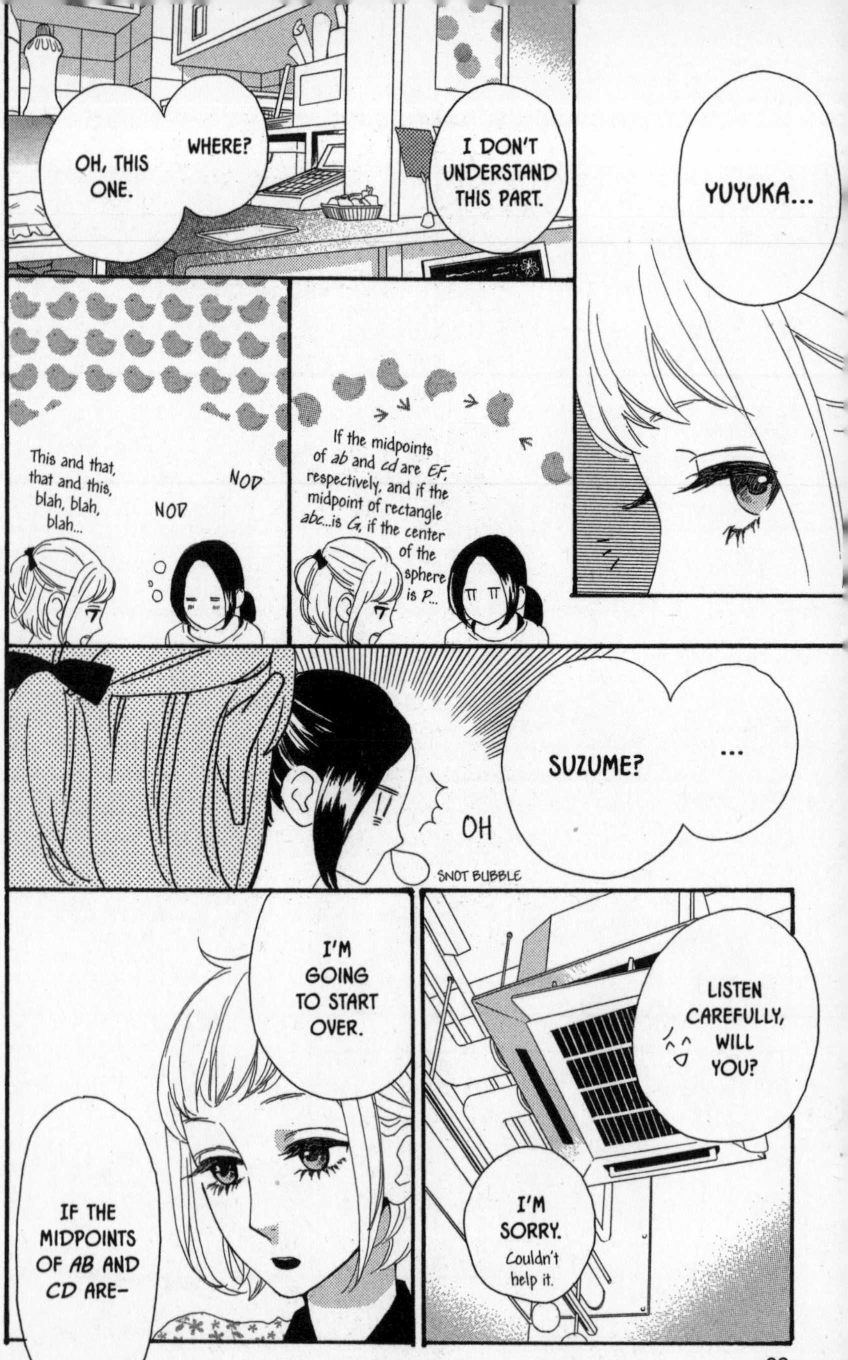
YUYUKA...
I DON'T UNDERSTAND THIS PART.
WHERE?
OH, THIS ONE.
If the midpoints of ab and cd are EF, respectively, and if the midpoint of rectangle abc...is G, if the center of the sphere is P...
NOD
NOD
This and that, that and this, blah, blah, blah...
...
SUZUME?
OH
SNOT BUBBLE
LISTEN CAREFULLY, WILL YOU?
I'M SORRY.
Couldn't help it.
I'M GOING TO START OVER.
IF THE MIDPOINTS OF AB AND CD ARE–

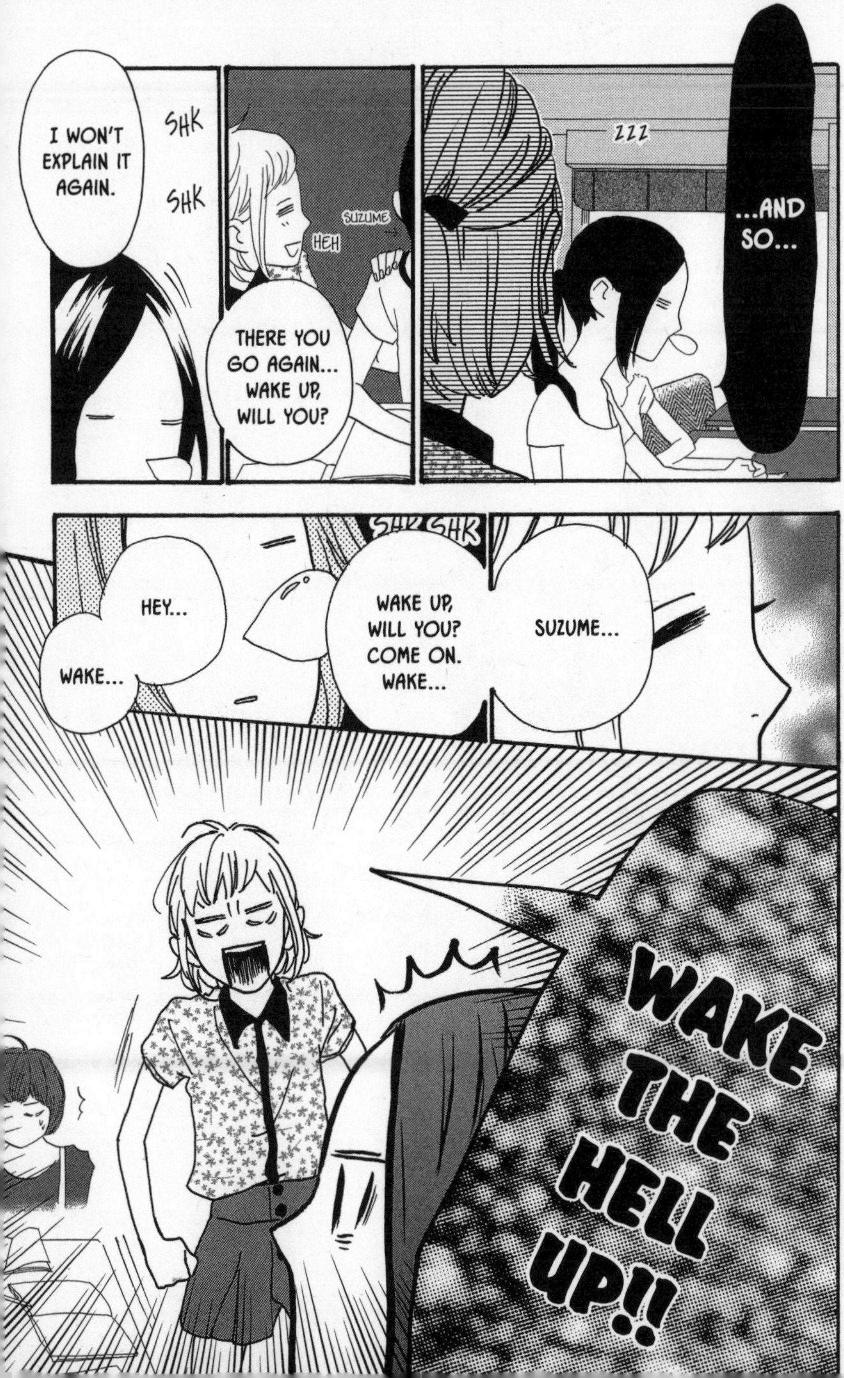
...AND SO...
ZZZ
SUZUME
HEH
THERE YOU GO AGAIN... WAKE UP, WILL YOU?
I WON'T EXPLAIN IT AGAIN.
SHK
SHK
SHK SHK
SUZUME...
WAKE UP, WILL YOU? COME ON. WAKE...
HEY...
WAKE...
WAKE THE HELL UP!!

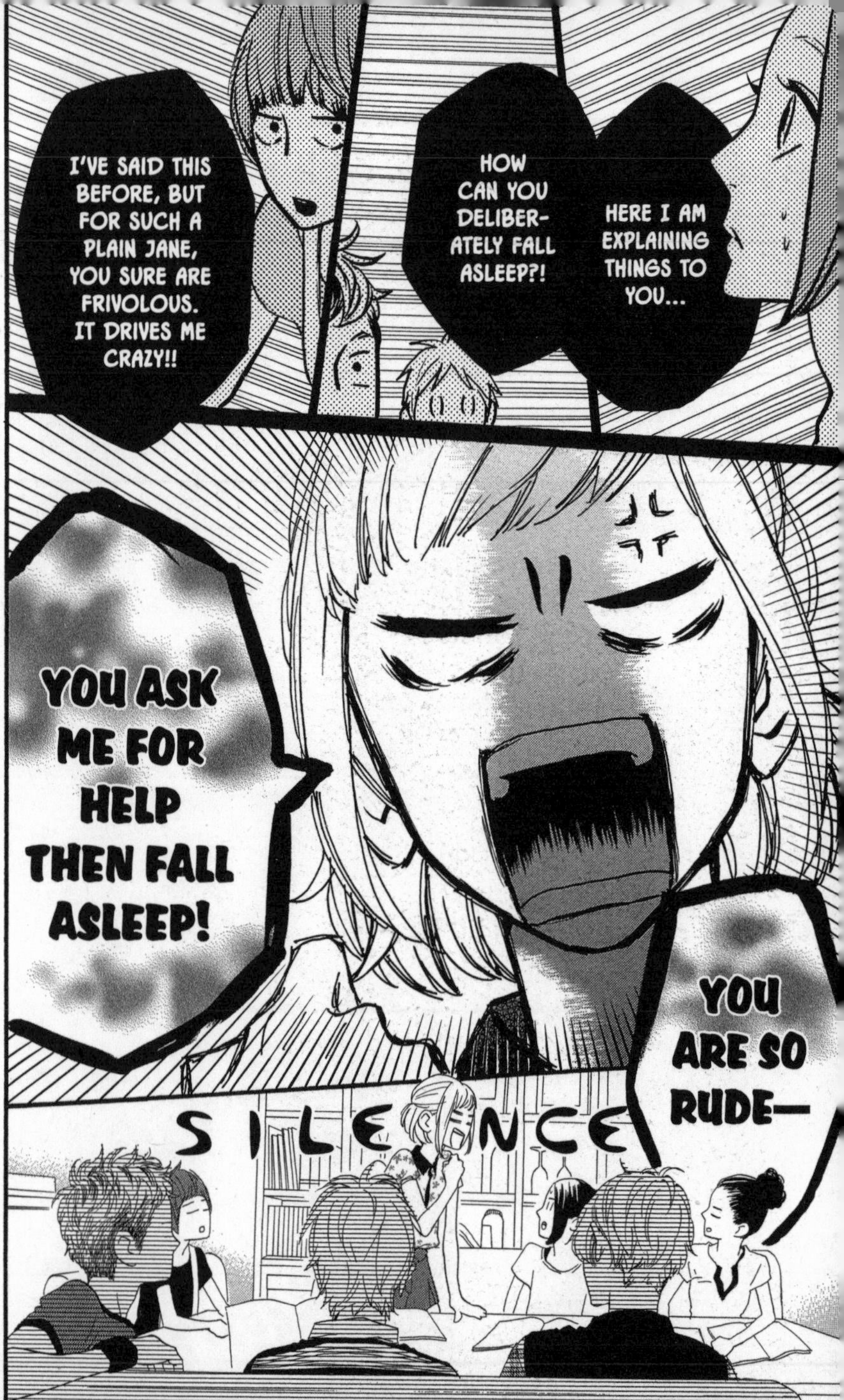
HERE I AM EXPLAINING THINGS TO YOU...
HOW CAN YOU DELIBER-ATELY FALL ASLEEP?!
I'VE SAID THIS BEFORE, BUT FOR SUCH A PLAIN JANE, YOU SURE ARE FRIVOLOUS. IT DRIVES ME CRAZY!!
YOU ASK ME FOR HELP THEN FALL ASLEEP!
YOU ARE SO RUDE—
SILENCE

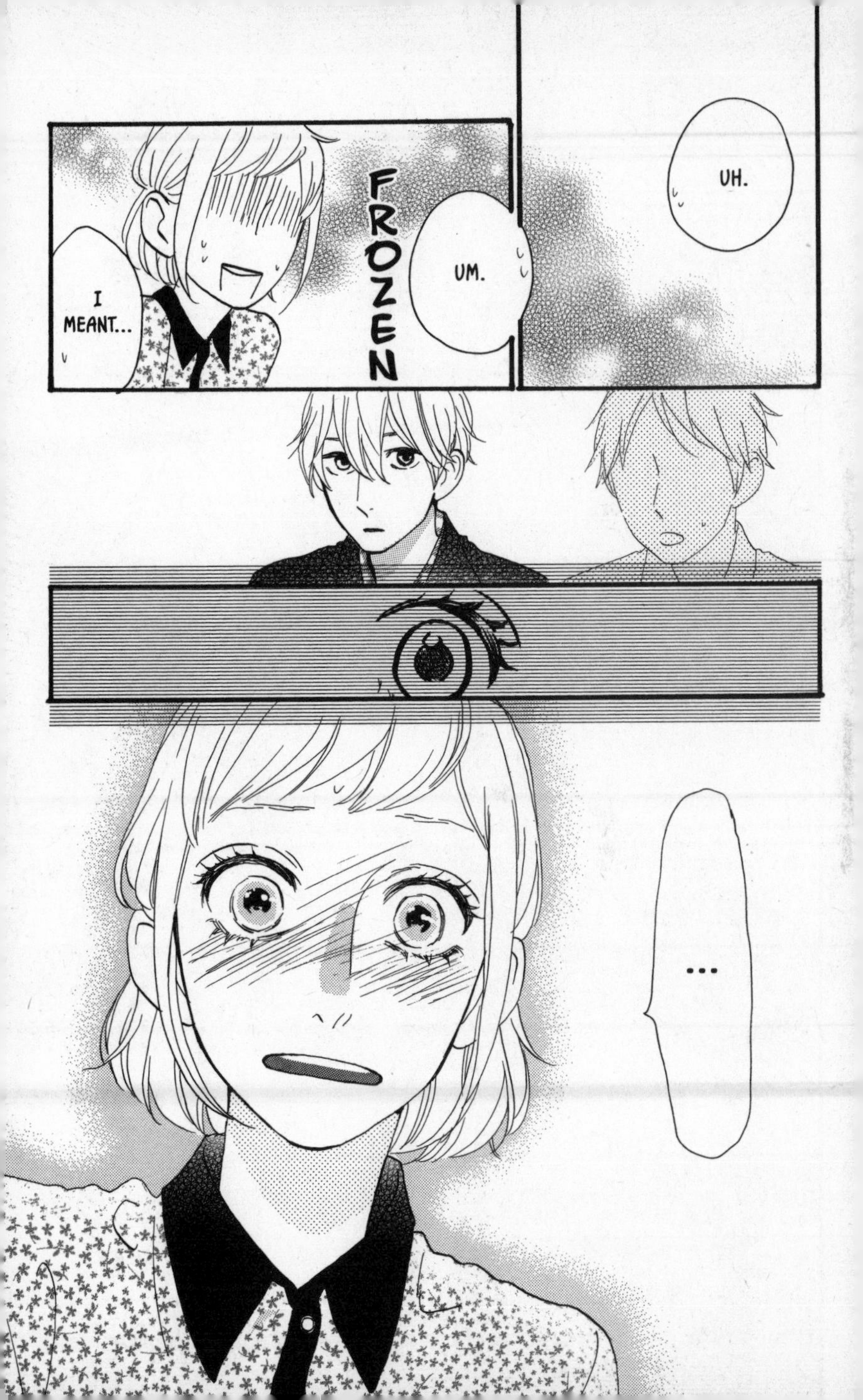
UH.
UM.
FROZEN
I MEANT...
...

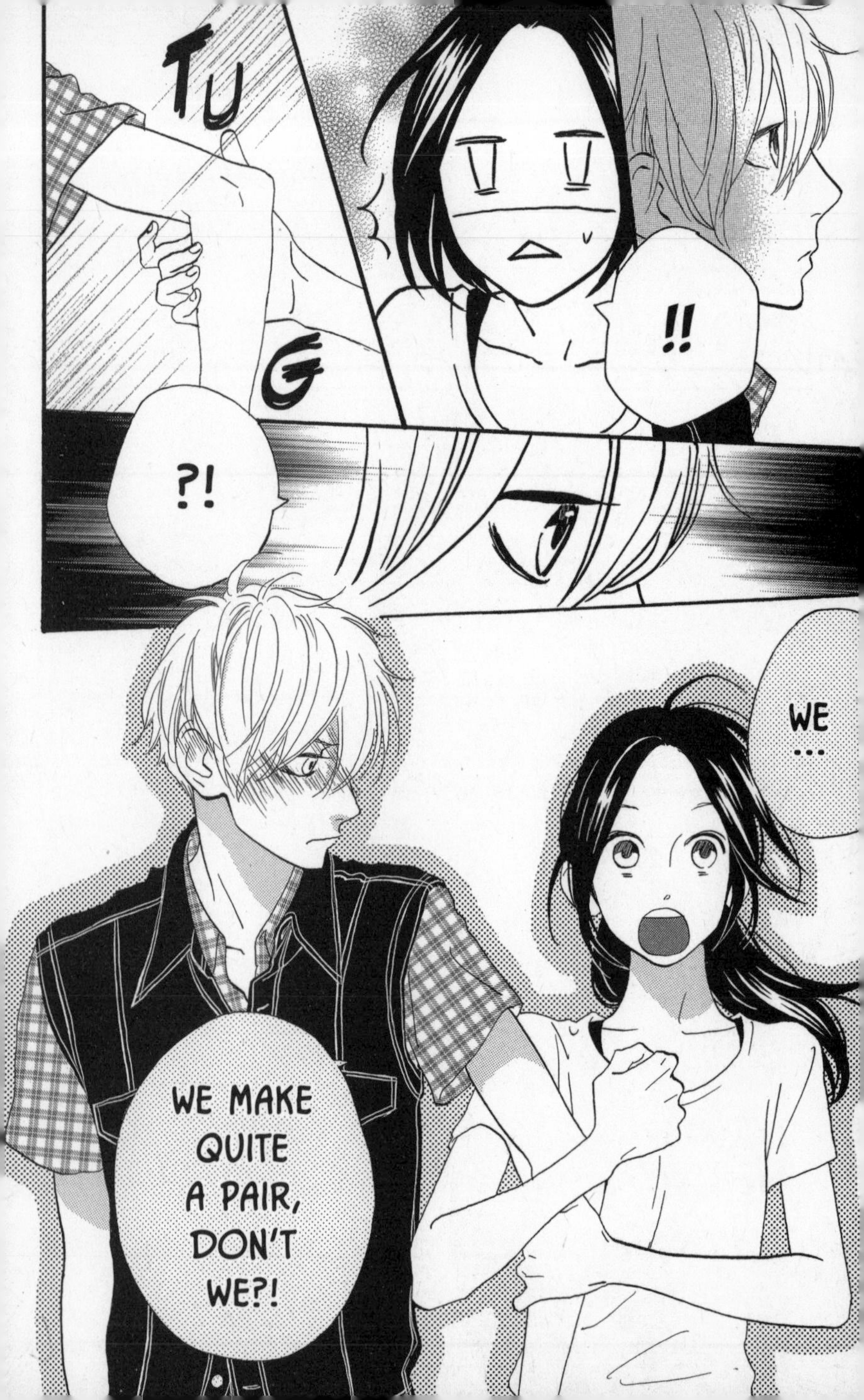
!!
TUG
?!
WE...
WE MAKE QUITE A PAIR, DON'T WE?!

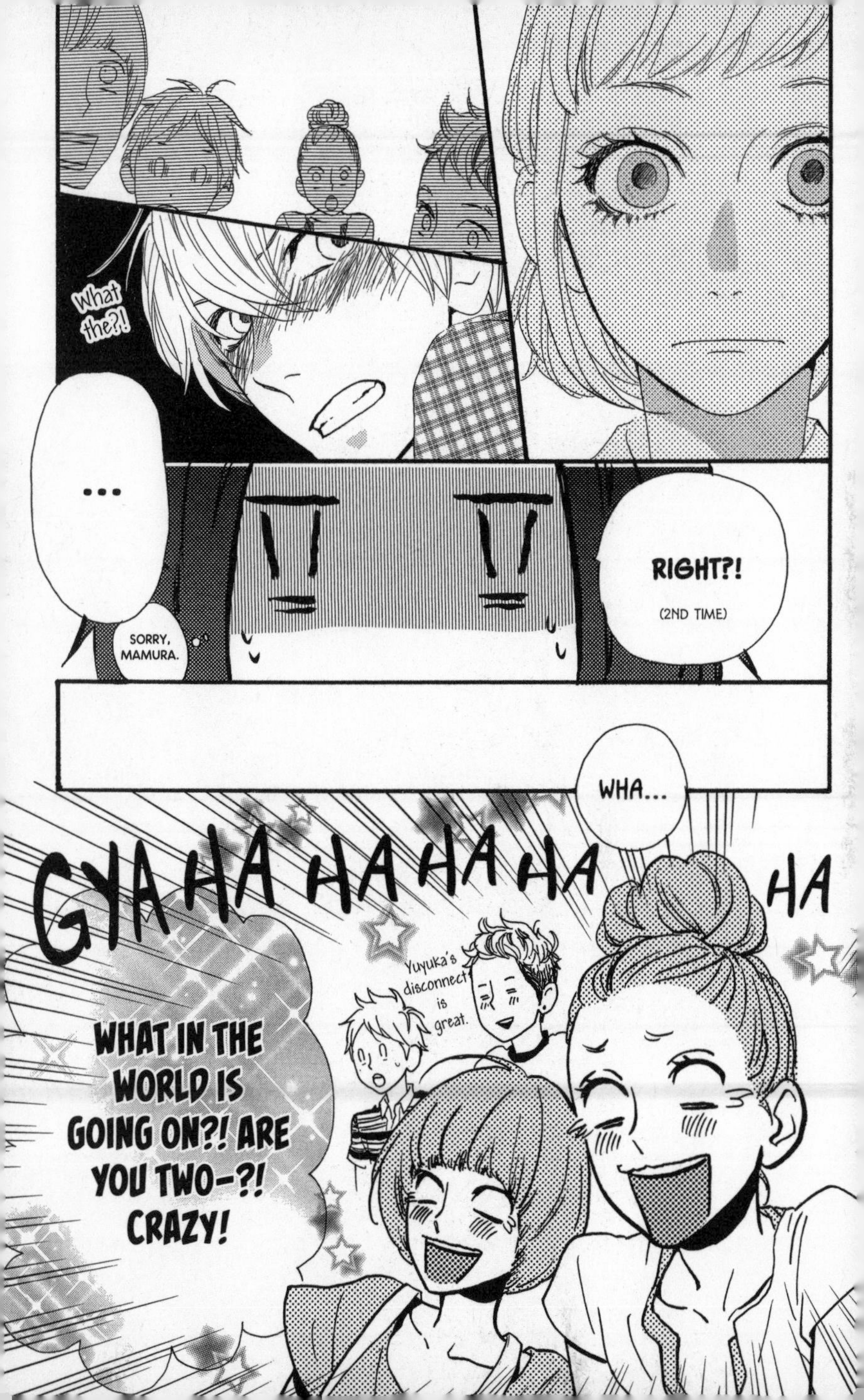
What the?!
RIGHT?!
(2ND TIME)
...
SORRY, MAMURA.
WHA...
GYAHA HA HA HA HA HA
Yuyuka's disconnect is great.
WHAT IN THE WORLD IS GOING ON?! ARE YOU TWO-?! CRAZY!

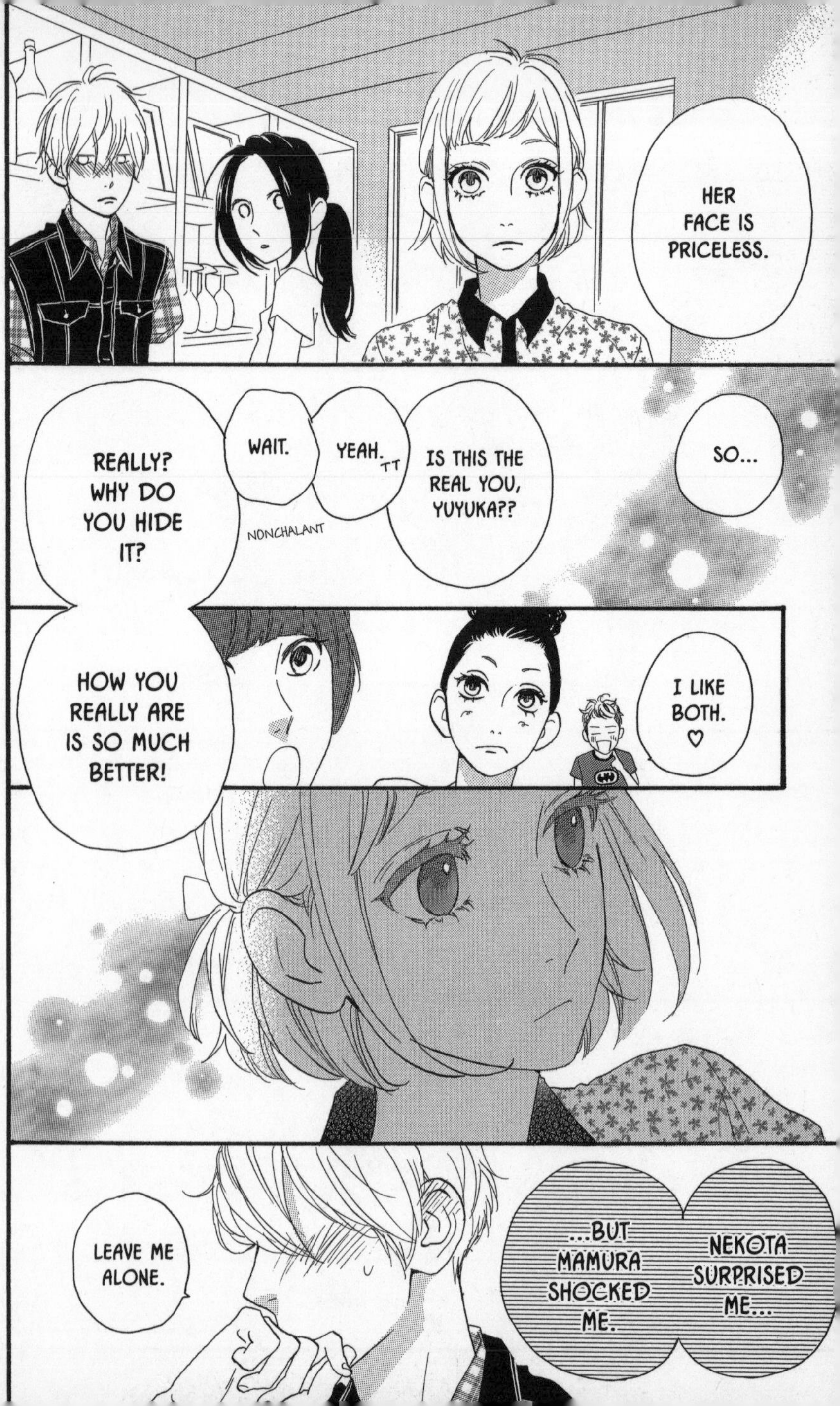
HER FACE IS PRICELESS.
SO...
IS THIS THE REAL YOU, YUYUKA??
YEAH.
WAIT.
NONCHALANT
REALLY? WHY DO YOU HIDE IT?
I LIKE BOTH. ♡
HOW YOU REALLY ARE IS SO MUCH BETTER!
NEKOTA SURPRISED ME...
...BUT MAMURA SHOCKED ME.
LEAVE ME ALONE.

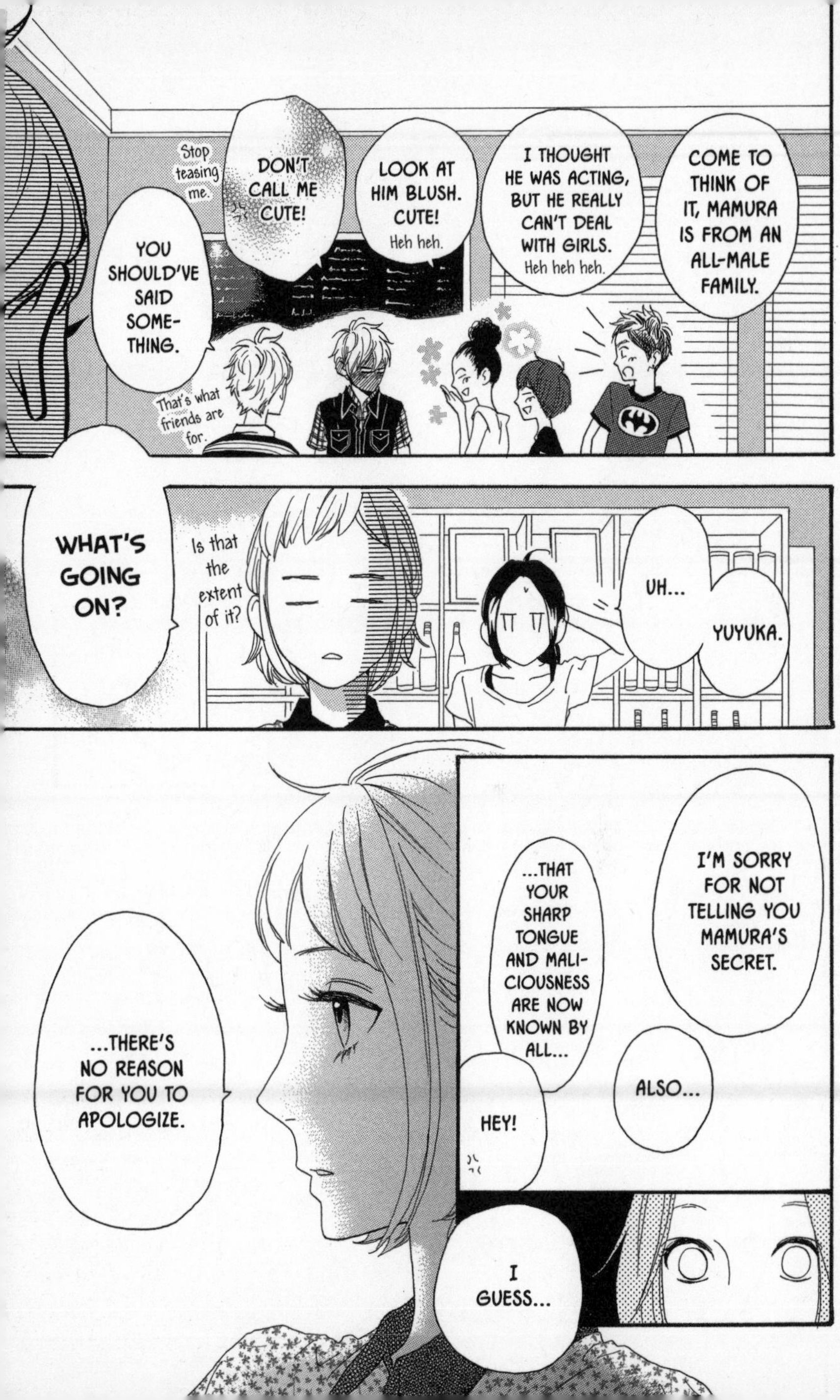
COME TO THINK OF IT, MAMURA IS FROM AN ALL-MALE FAMILY.
I THOUGHT HE WAS ACTING, BUT HE REALLY CAN'T DEAL WITH GIRLS.
Heh heh heh.
LOOK AT HIM BLUSH. CUTE!
Heh heh.
DON'T CALL ME CUTE!
Stop teasing me.
YOU SHOULD'VE SAID SOME-THING.
That's what friends are for.
UH...
YUYUKA.
Is that the extent of it?
WHAT'S GOING ON?
I'M SORRY FOR NOT TELLING YOU MAMURA'S SECRET.
ALSO...
...THAT YOUR SHARP TONGUE AND MALI-CIOUSNESS ARE NOW KNOWN BY ALL...
HEY!
I GUESS...
...THERE'S NO REASON FOR YOU TO APOLOGIZE.

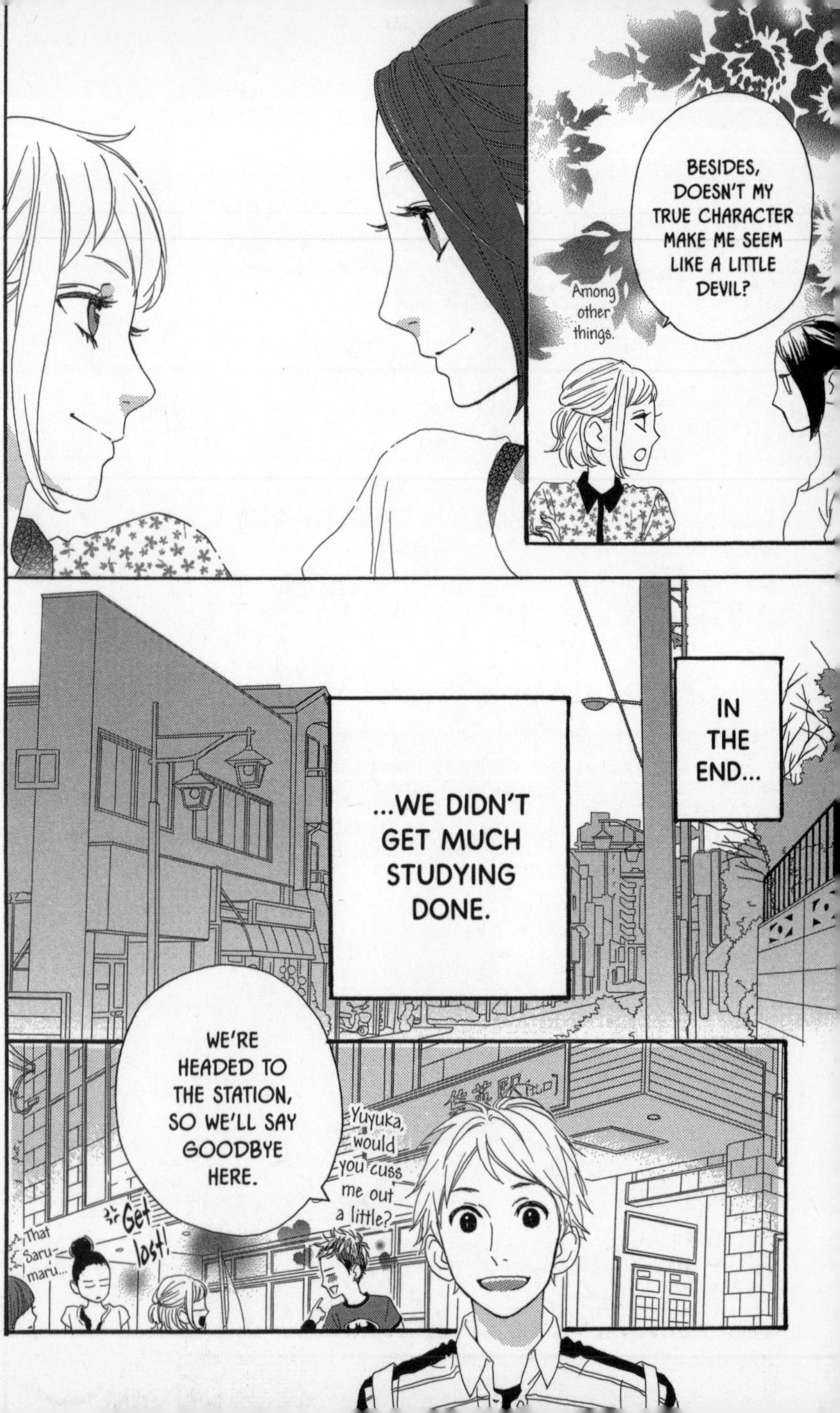
BESIDES, DOESN'T MY TRUE CHARACTER MAKE ME SEEM LIKE A LITTLE DEVIL?
Among other things.
IN THE END...
...WE DIDN'T GET MUCH STUDYING DONE.
WE'RE HEADED TO THE STATION, SO WE'LL SAY GOODBYE HERE.
Yuyuka, would you cuss me out a little?
Get lost!
That Saru-maru...

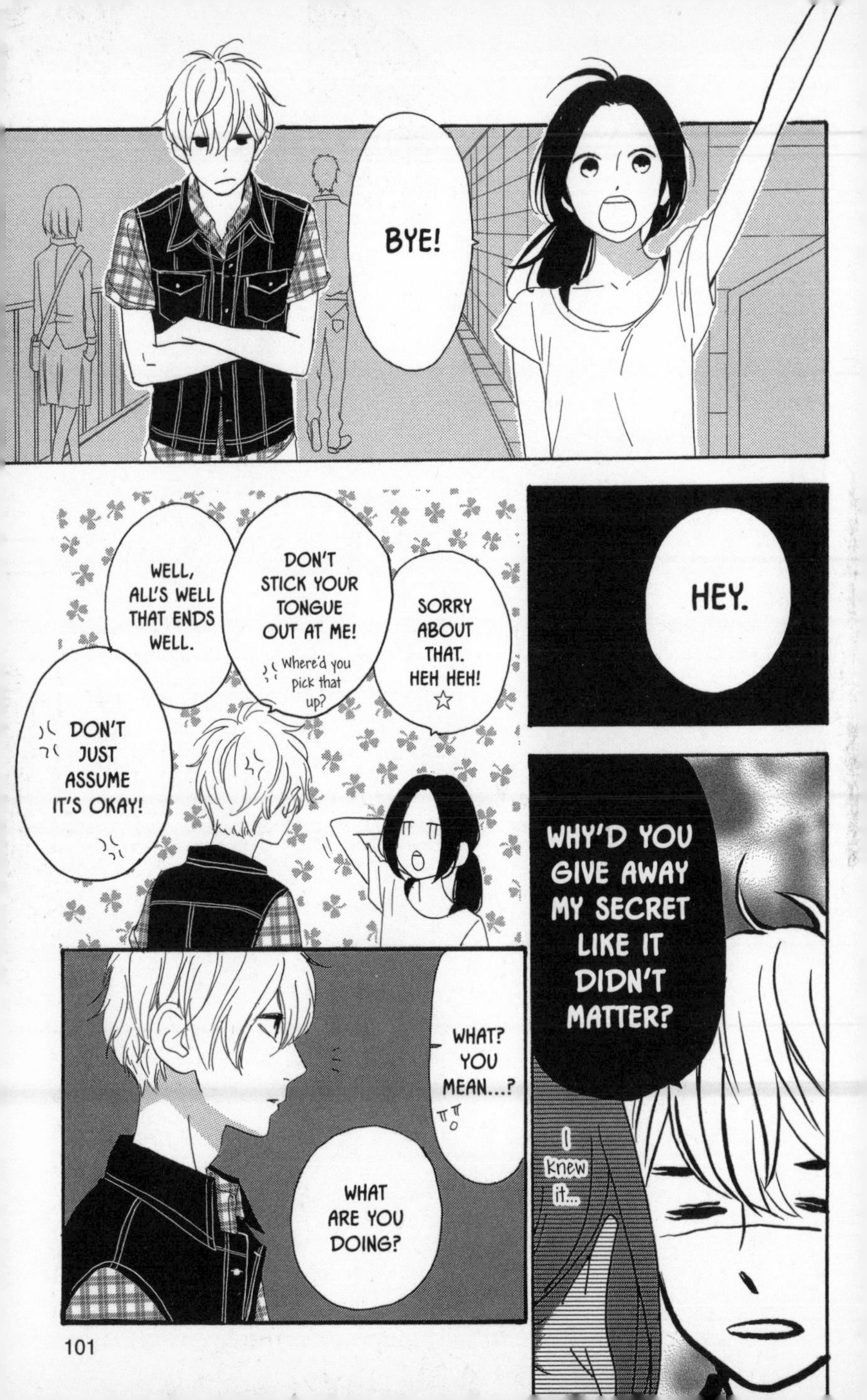

BYE!
HEY.
SORRY ABOUT THAT. HEH HEH! ☆
DON'T STICK YOUR TONGUE OUT AT ME!
Where'd you pick that up?
WELL, ALL'S WELL THAT ENDS WELL.
DON'T JUST ASSUME IT'S OKAY!
WHAT ARE YOU DOING?
WHAT? YOU MEAN...?
WHY'D YOU GIVE AWAY MY SECRET LIKE IT DIDN'T MATTER?
I knew it...

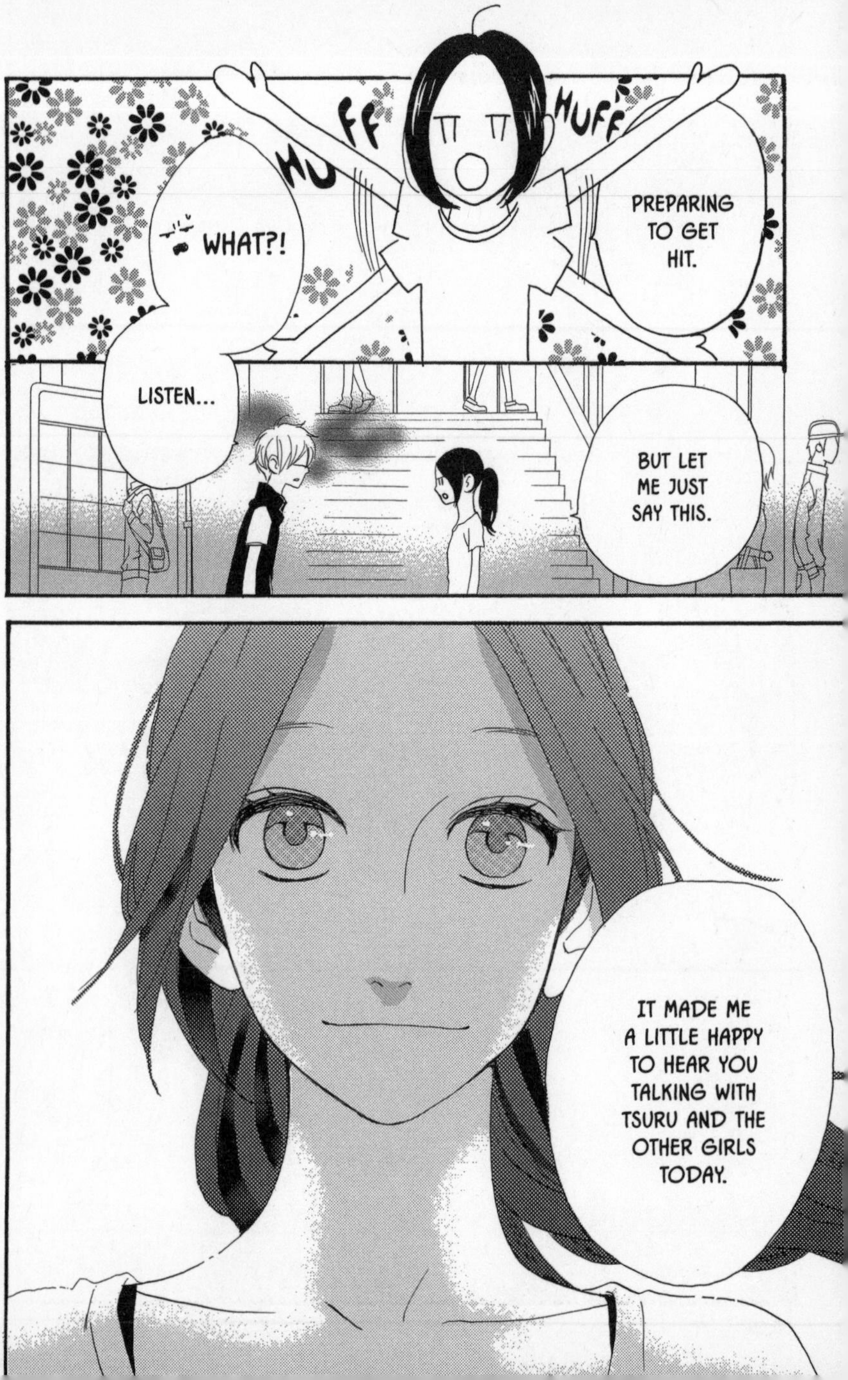
HUFF
PREPARING TO GET HIT.
HUFF
WHAT?!
LISTEN...
BUT LET ME JUST SAY THIS.
IT MADE ME A LITTLE HAPPY TO HEAR YOU TALKING WITH TSURU AND THE OTHER GIRLS TODAY.

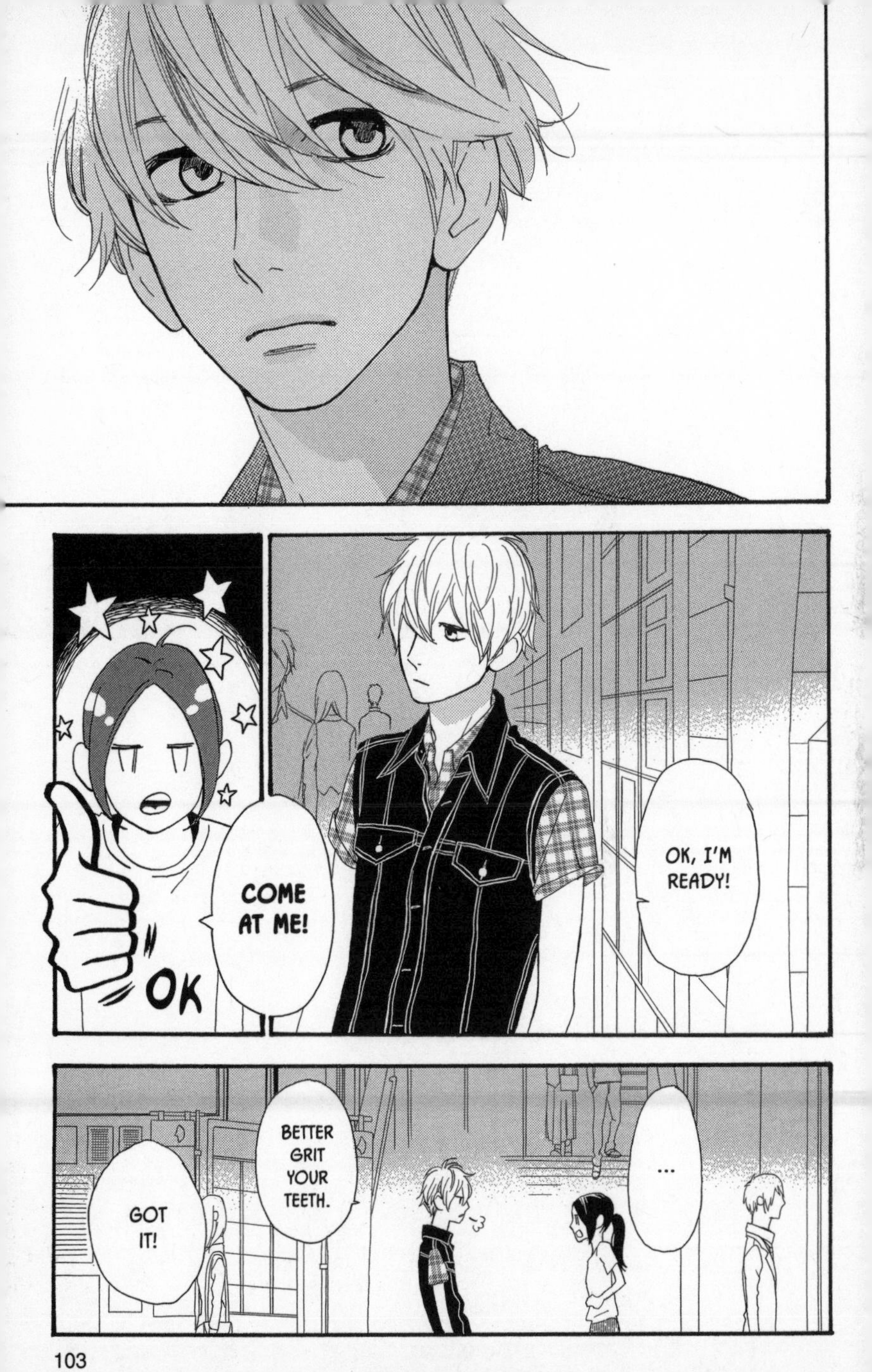
OK, I'M READY!
COME AT ME!
OK
...
BETTER GRIT YOUR TEETH.
GOT IT!

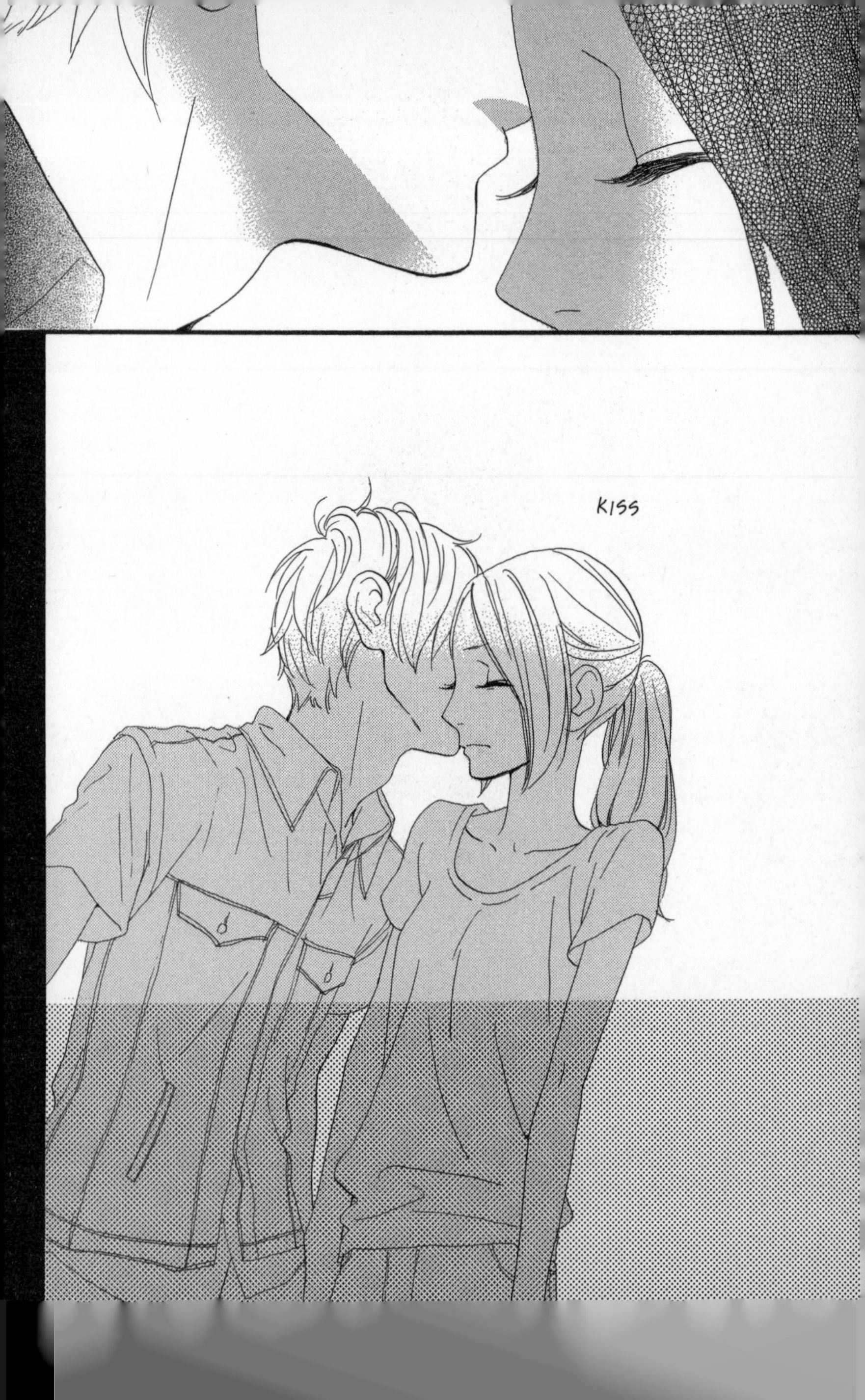
KISS

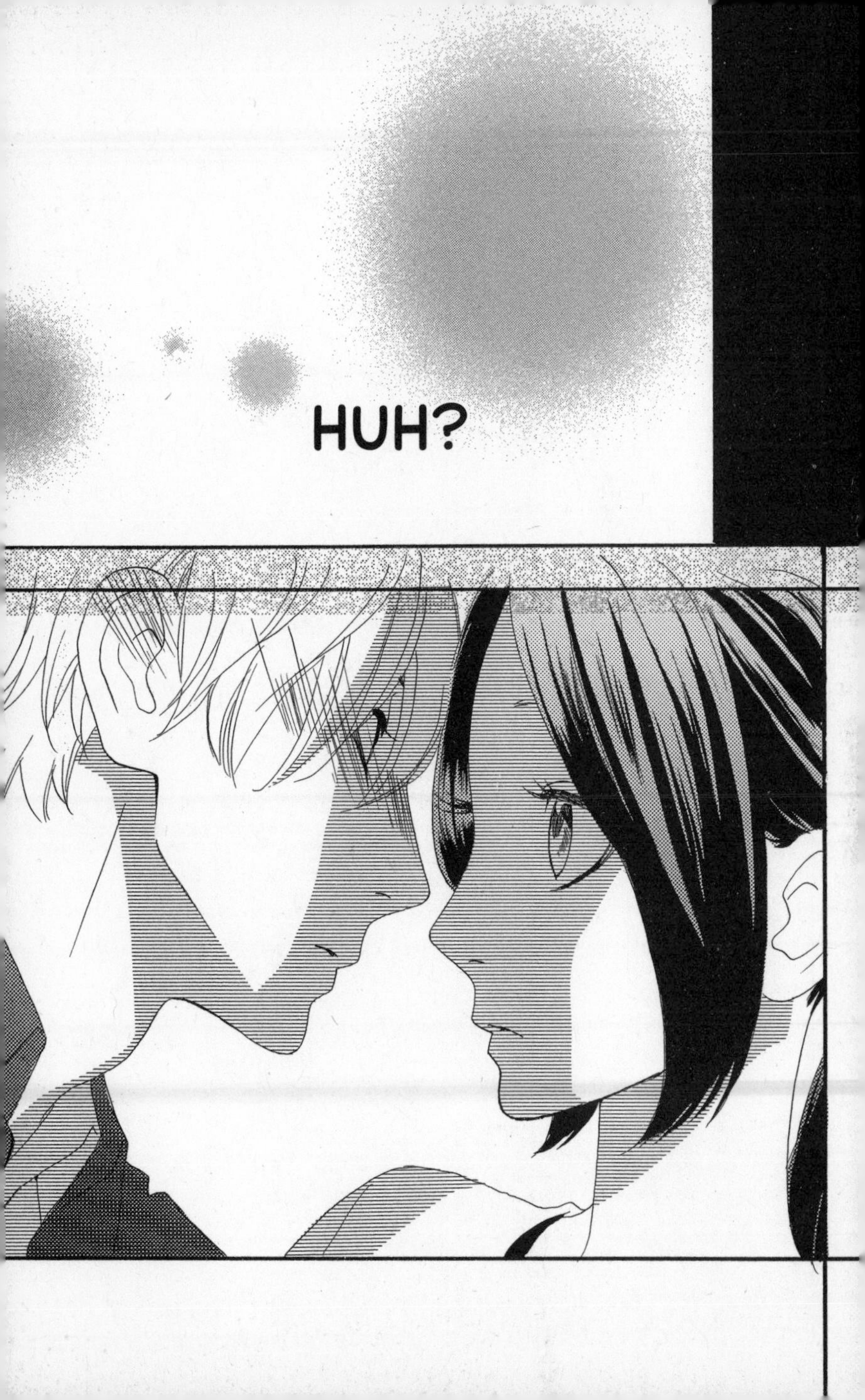
HUH?

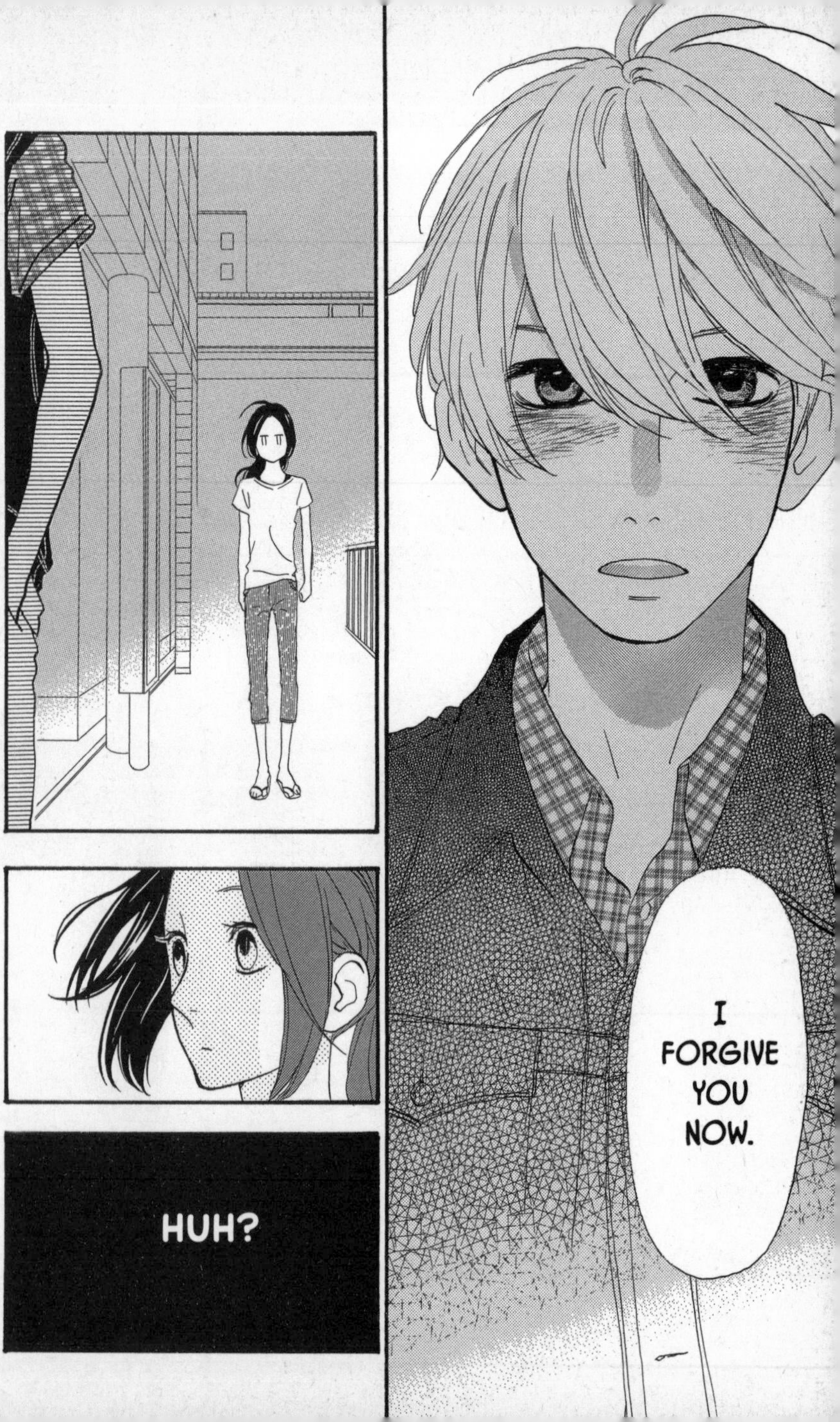

I FORGIVE YOU NOW.
HUH?

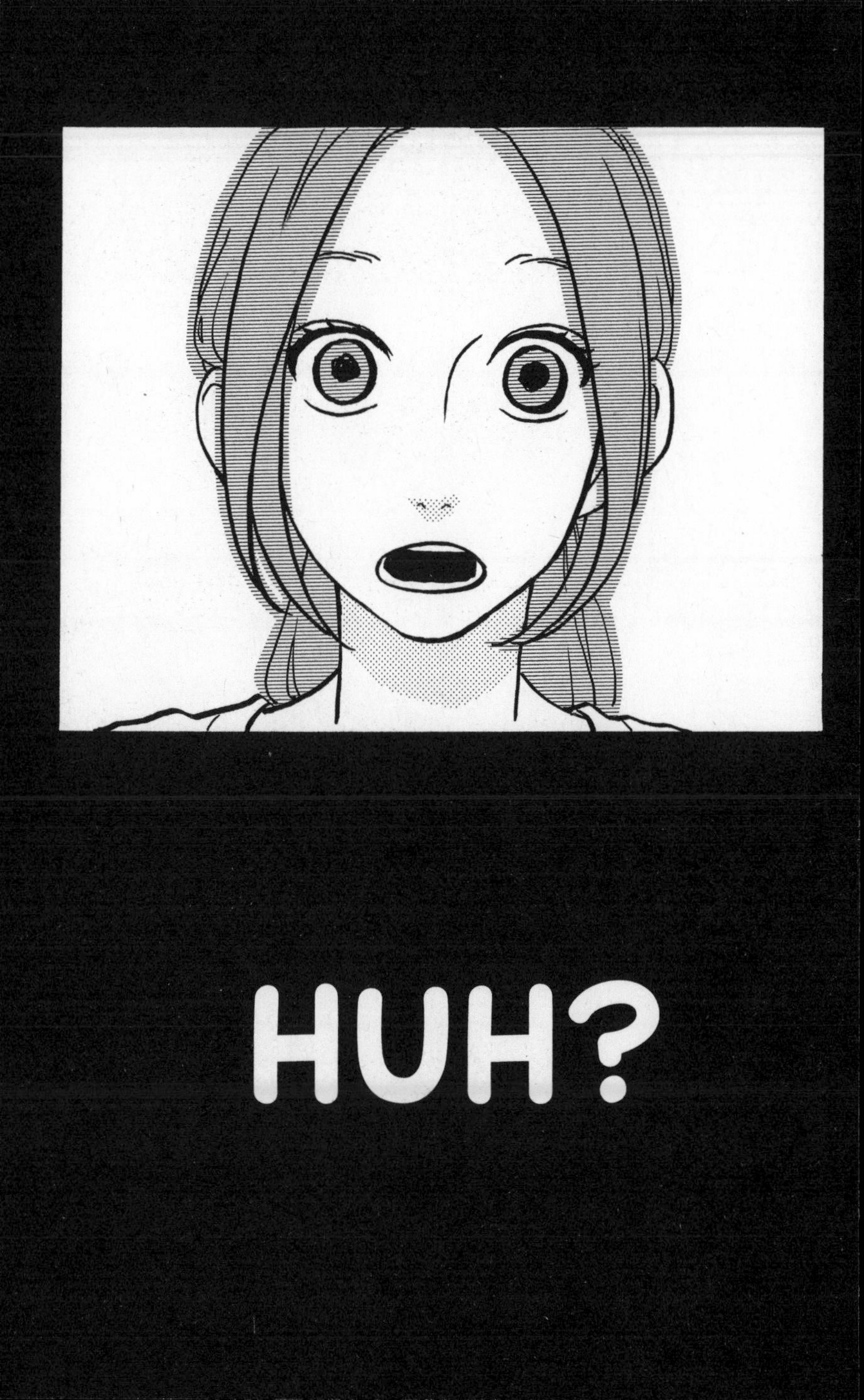
HUH?

Simple Scribbles③

• Mamura

Staid Man Version

Come to think of it, I said on Twitter that I would be doing staid versions of Mamura and Shishio.

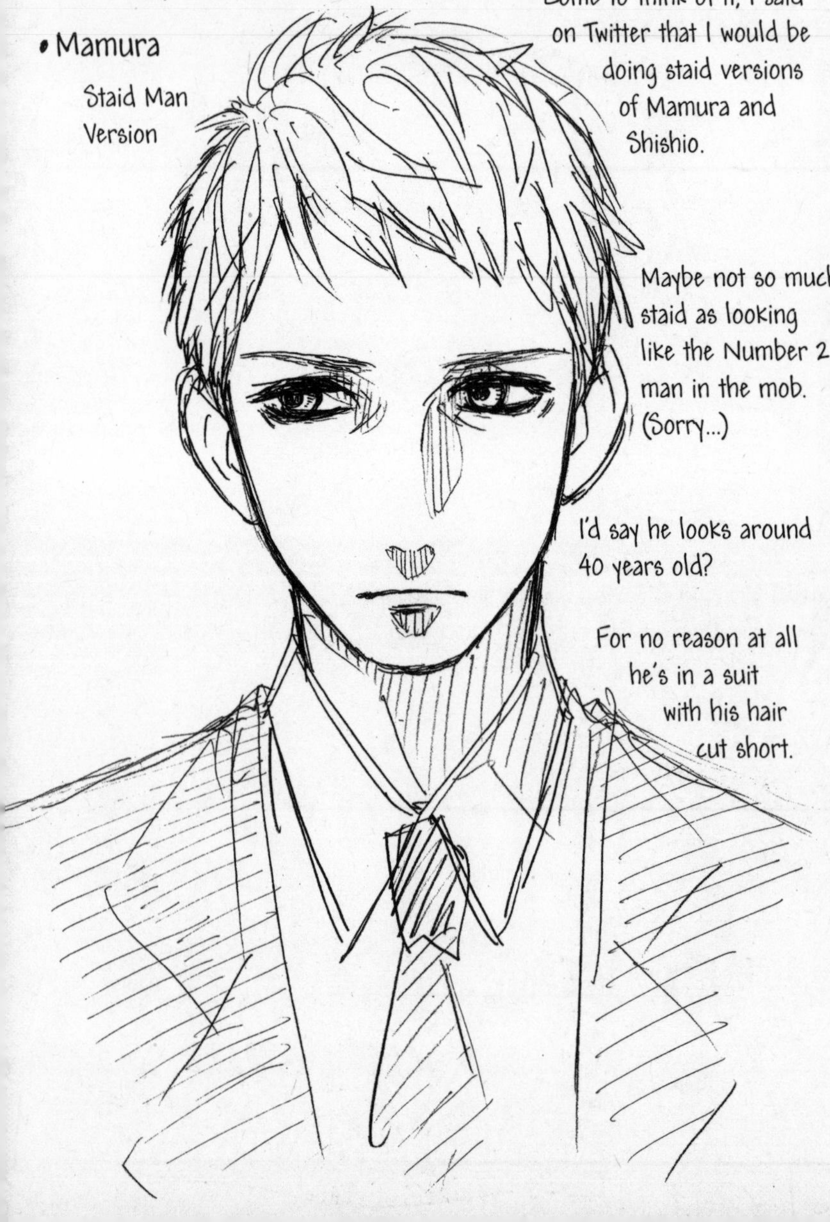

Maybe not so much staid as looking like the Number 2 man in the mob. (Sorry...)

I'd say he looks around 40 years old?

For no reason at all he's in a suit with his hair cut short.

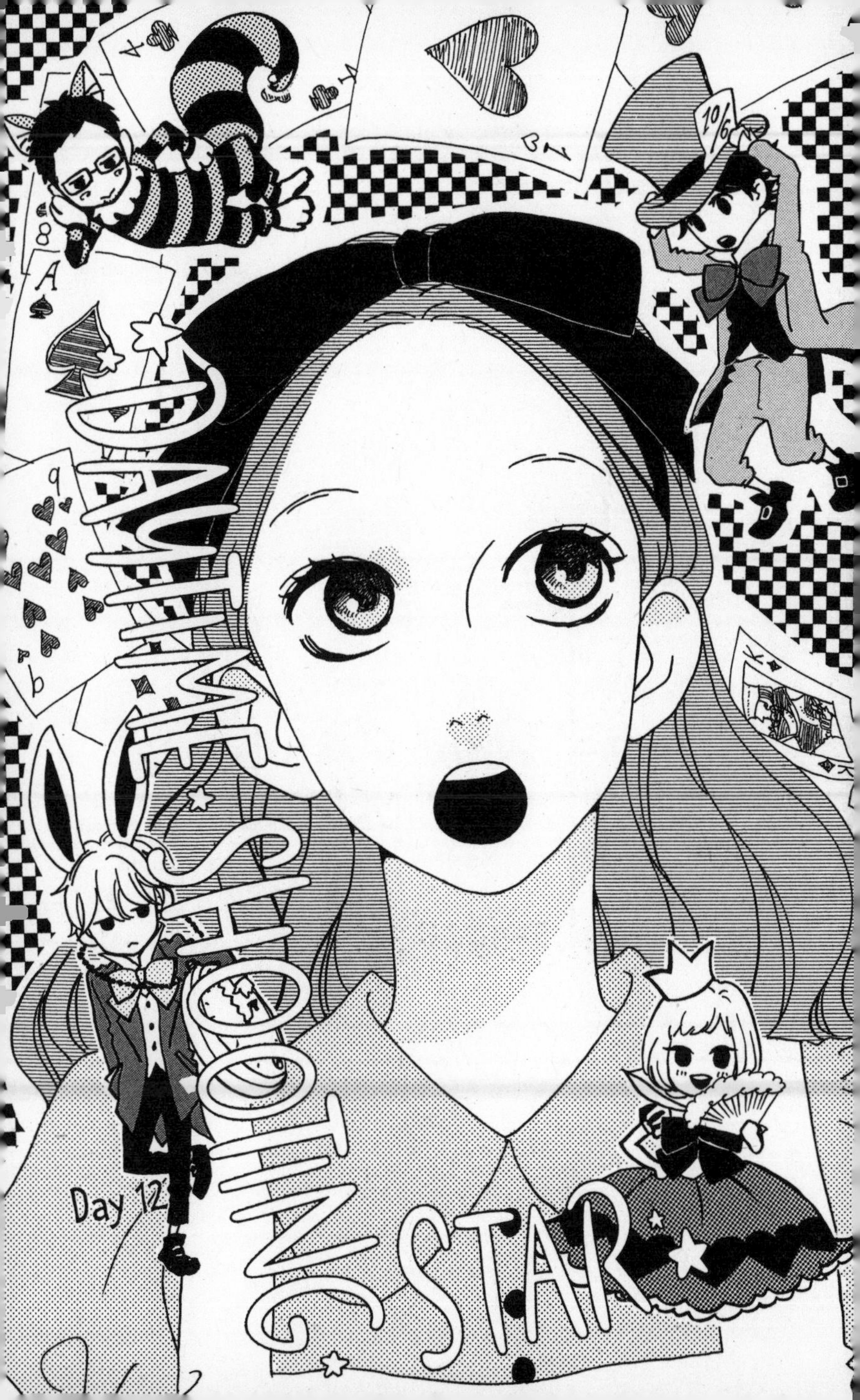
DAYTIME SHOOTING STAR
Day 12

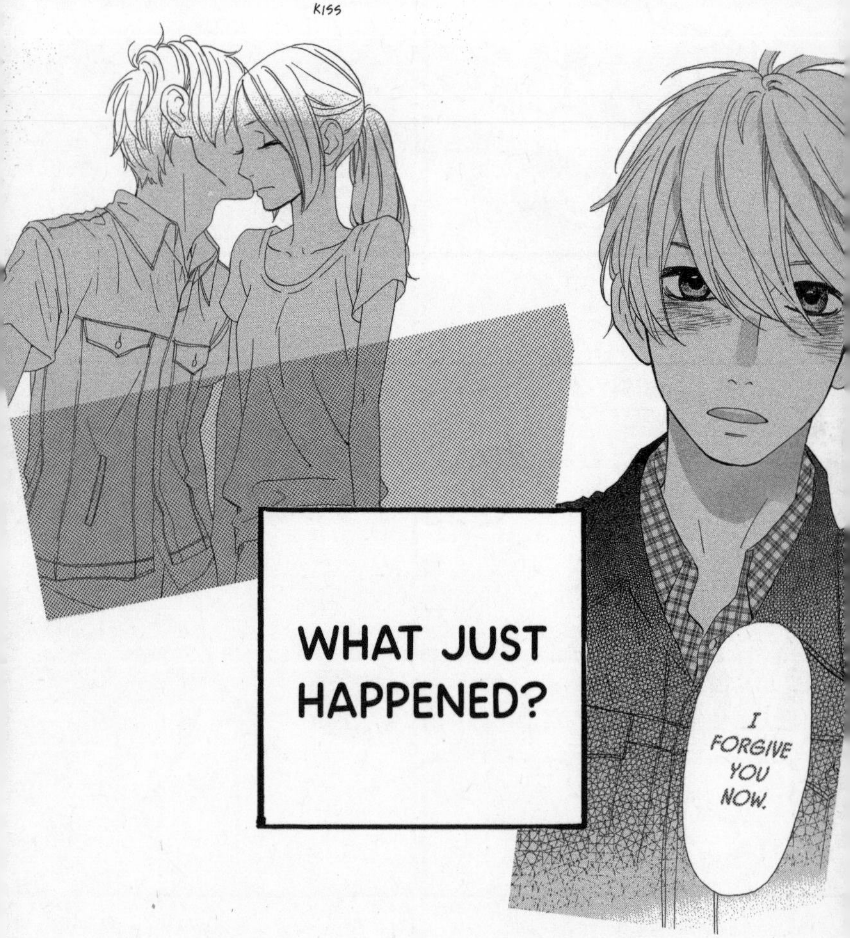
KISS
I FORGIVE YOU NOW.
WHAT JUST HAPPENED?

Manabu Inukai Bow wow

Birthday: July 13

Blood Type: O

Height: 5'6"

Weight: 132 lbs

1. Train station lunches.
2. Spectator sports.
3. I've stopped growing taller.

Inu means "dog."

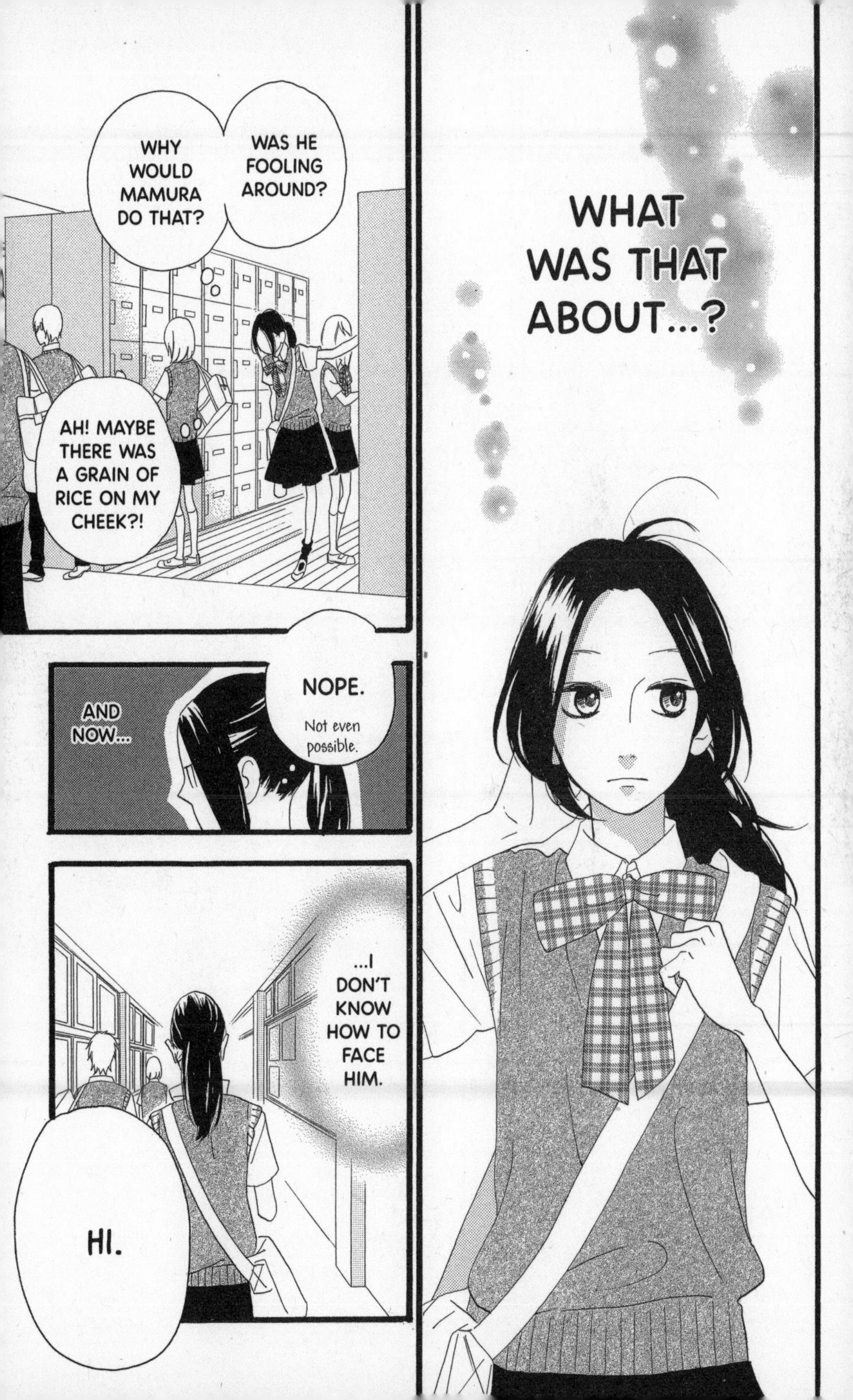
WHAT WAS THAT ABOUT...?
WAS HE FOOLING AROUND?
WHY WOULD MAMURA DO THAT?
AH! MAYBE THERE WAS A GRAIN OF RICE ON MY CHEEK?!
NOPE.
Not even possible.
AND NOW...
...I DON'T KNOW HOW TO FACE HIM.
HI.

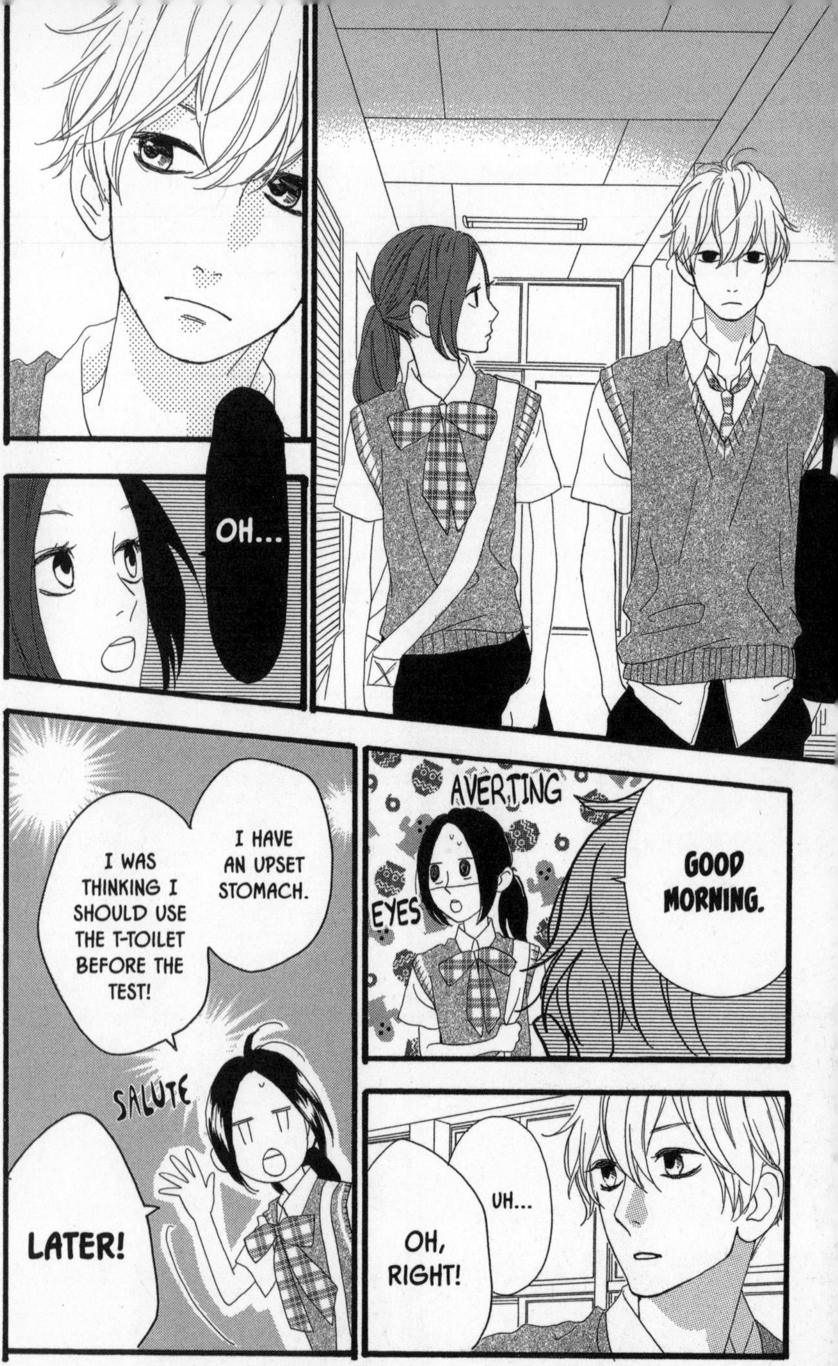
OH...
GOOD MORNING.
AVERTING EYES
UH...
OH, RIGHT!
I HAVE AN UPSET STOMACH.
I WAS THINKING I SHOULD USE THE T-TOILET BEFORE THE TEST!
SALUTE
LATER!

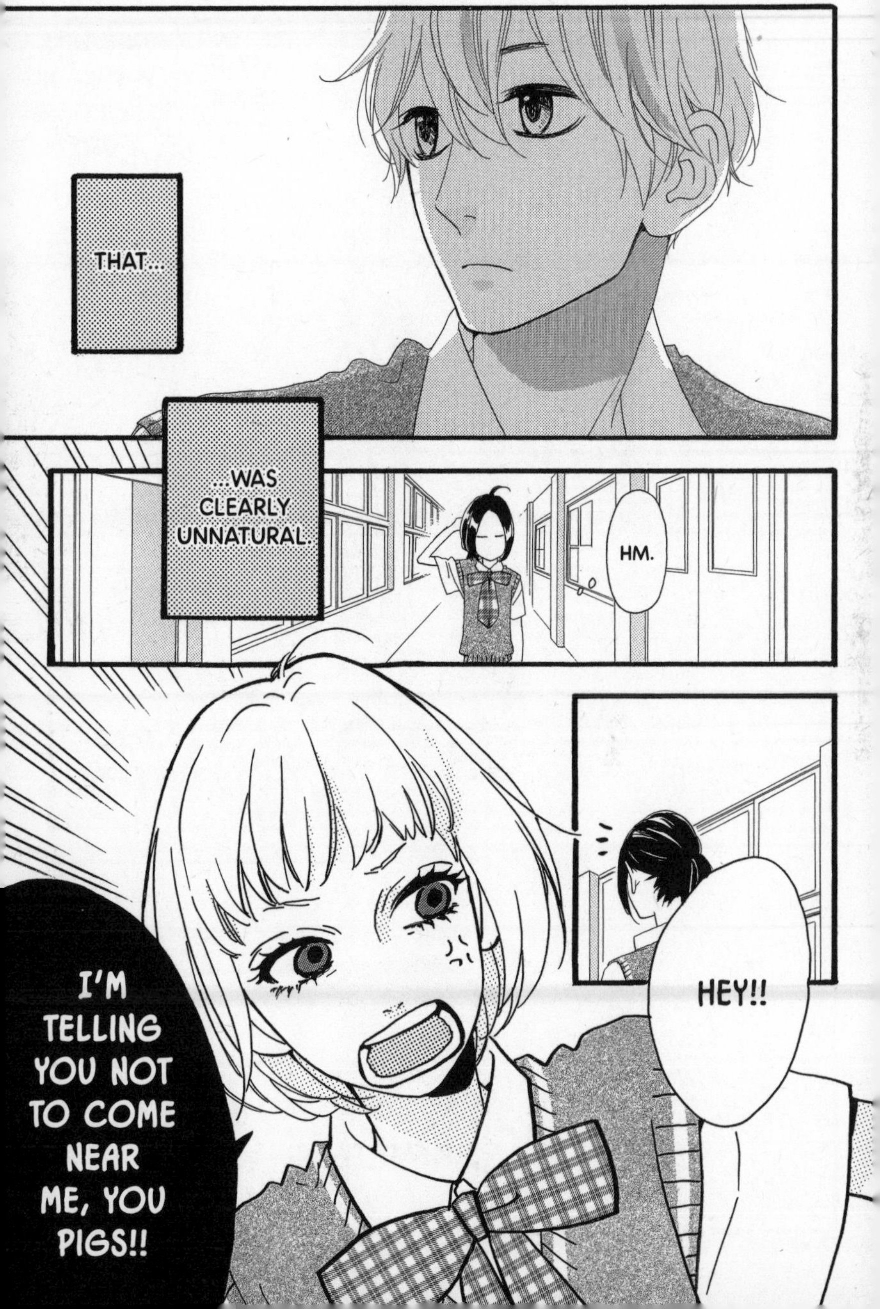
THAT...
...WAS CLEARLY UNNATURAL.
HM.
HEY!!
I'M TELLING YOU NOT TO COME NEAR ME, YOU PIGS!!

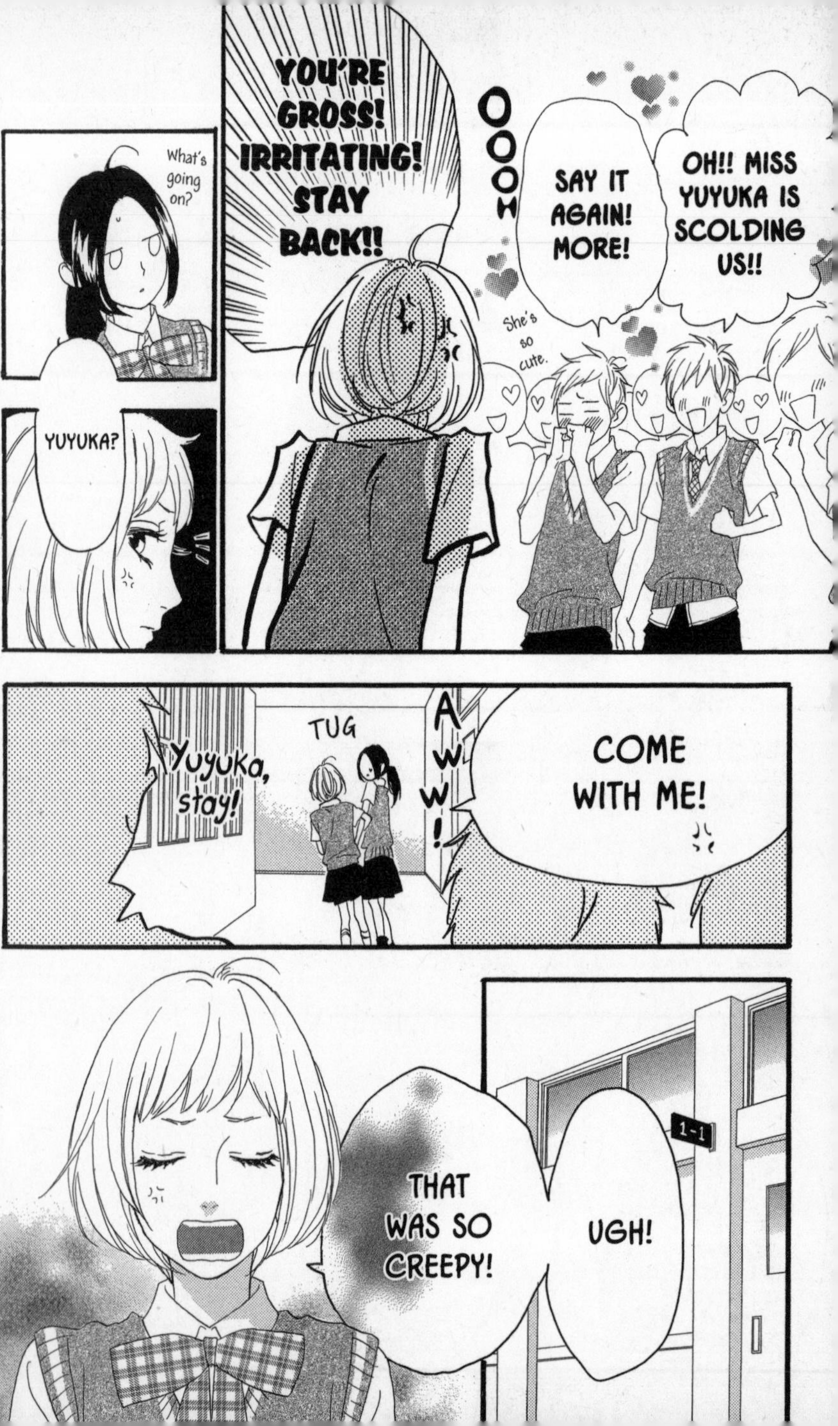
OH!! MISS YUYUKA IS SCOLDING US!!
SAY IT AGAIN! MORE!
OOOH
She's so cute.
YOU'RE GROSS! IRRITATING! STAY BACK!!
What's going on?
YUYUKA?
COME WITH ME!
AWW!
TUG
Yuyuka, stay!
UGH!
THAT WAS SO CREEPY!

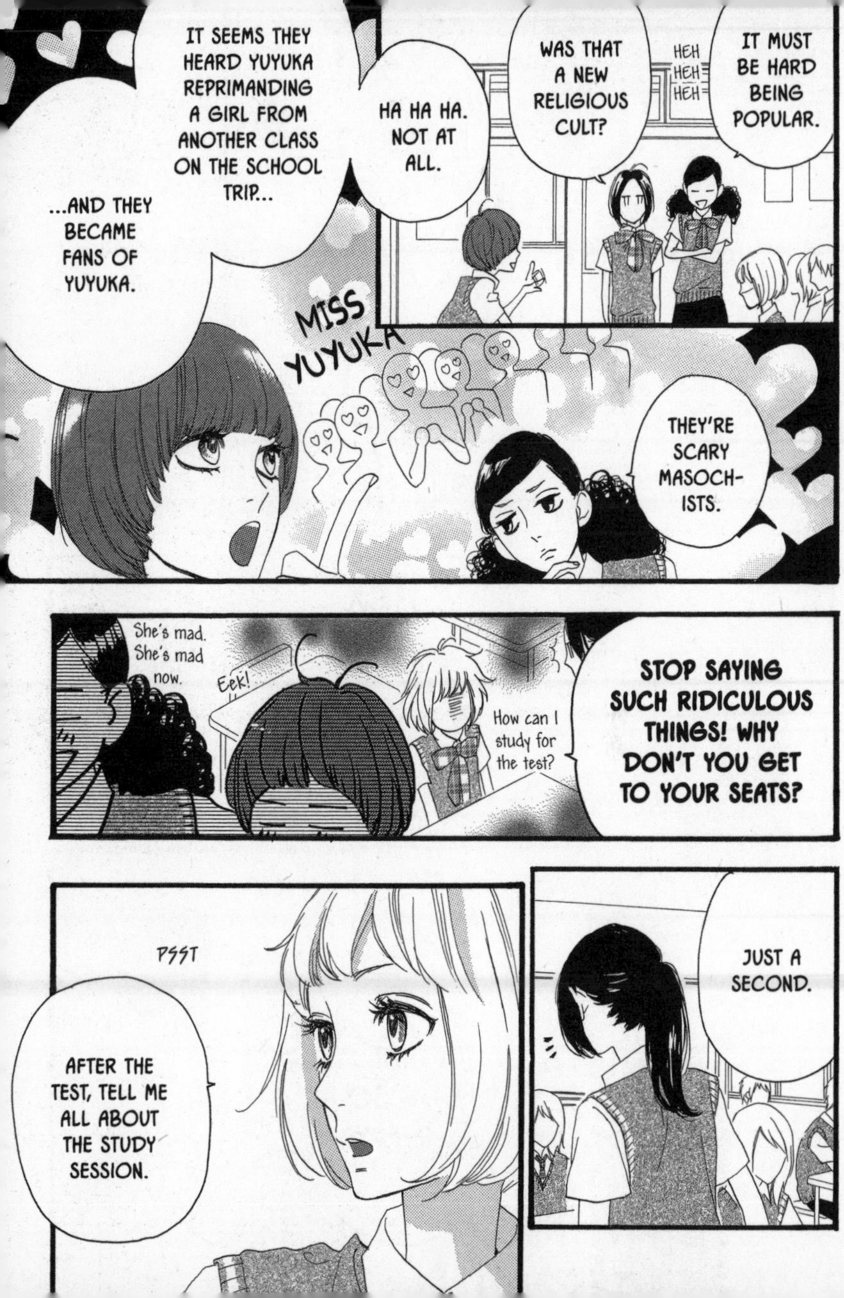
IT MUST BE HARD BEING POPULAR.
HEH HEH HEH
WAS THAT A NEW RELIGIOUS CULT?
HA HA HA. NOT AT ALL.
IT SEEMS THEY HEARD YUYUKA REPRIMANDING A GIRL FROM ANOTHER CLASS ON THE SCHOOL TRIP...
...AND THEY BECAME FANS OF YUYUKA.
MISS YUYUKA
THEY'RE SCARY MASOCH-ISTS.
STOP SAYING SUCH RIDICULOUS THINGS! WHY DON'T YOU GET TO YOUR SEATS?
How can I study for the test?
Eek!
She's mad. She's mad now.
JUST A SECOND.
PSST
AFTER THE TEST, TELL ME ALL ABOUT THE STUDY SESSION.

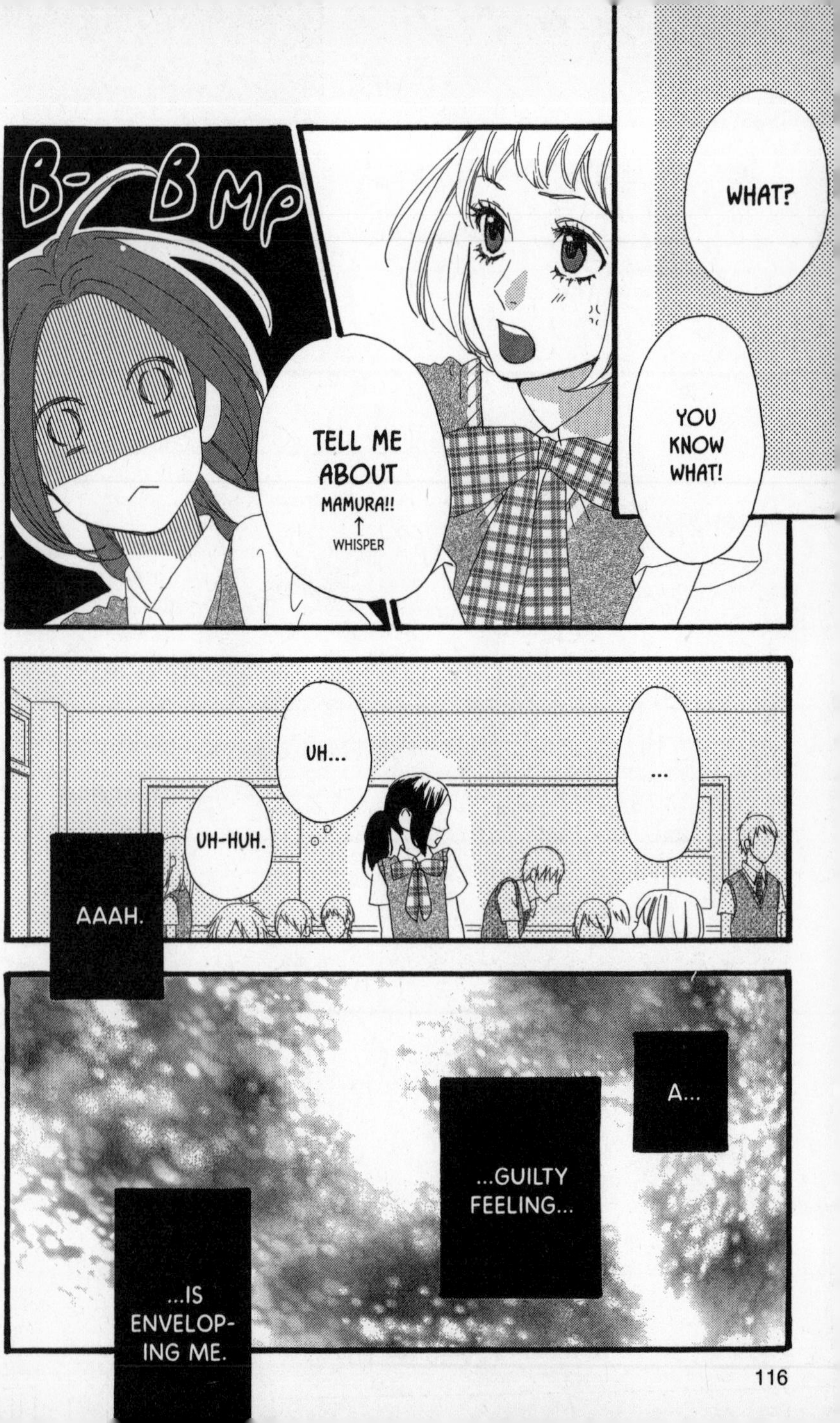
WHAT?
YOU KNOW WHAT!
TELL ME ABOUT MAMURA!!
↑
WHISPER
B-BMP
...
UH...
UH-HUH.
AAAH.
A...
...GUILTY FEELING...
...IS ENVELOP-ING ME.

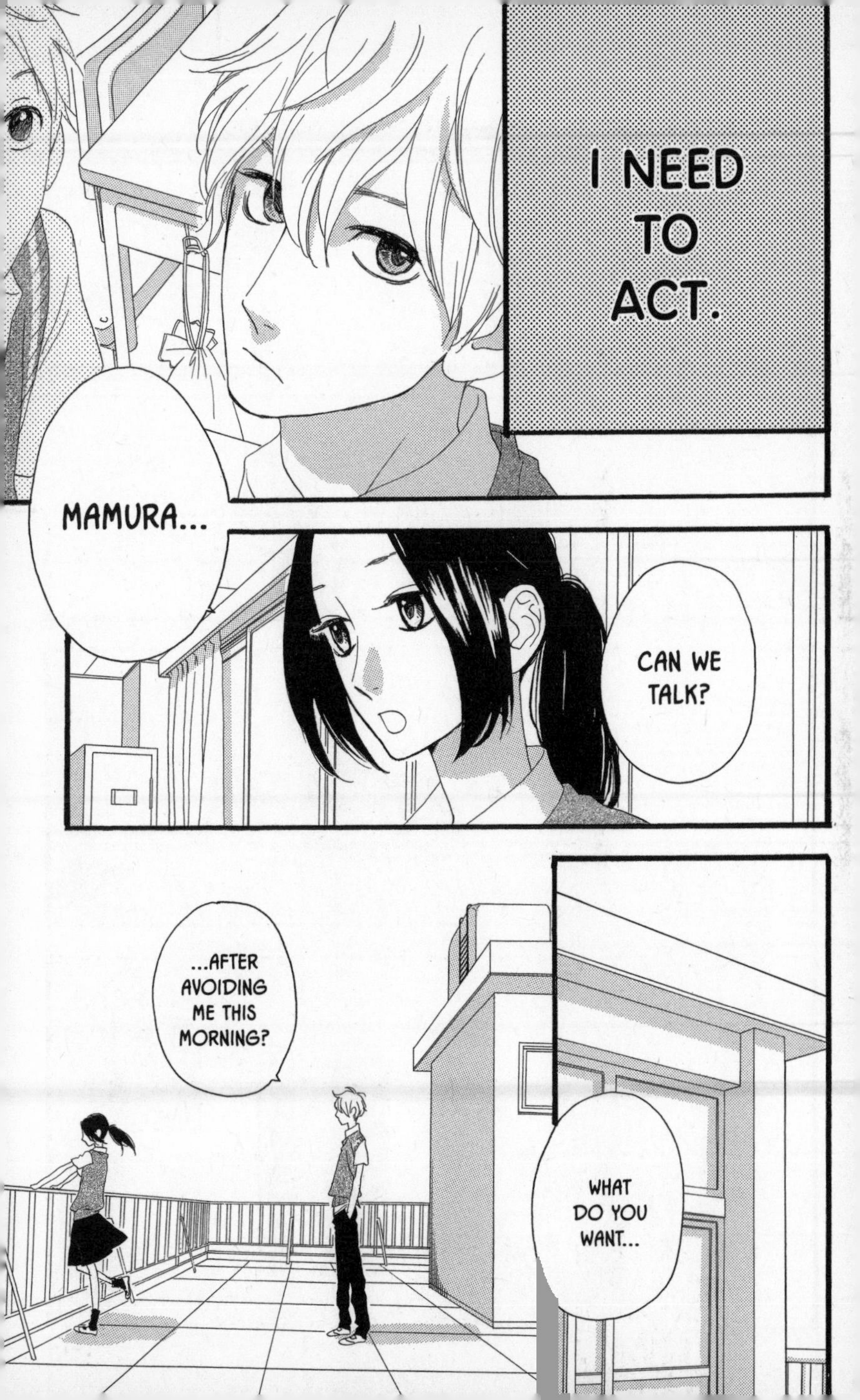
I NEED TO ACT.
MAMURA...
CAN WE TALK?
WHAT DO YOU WANT...
...AFTER AVOIDING ME THIS MORNING?

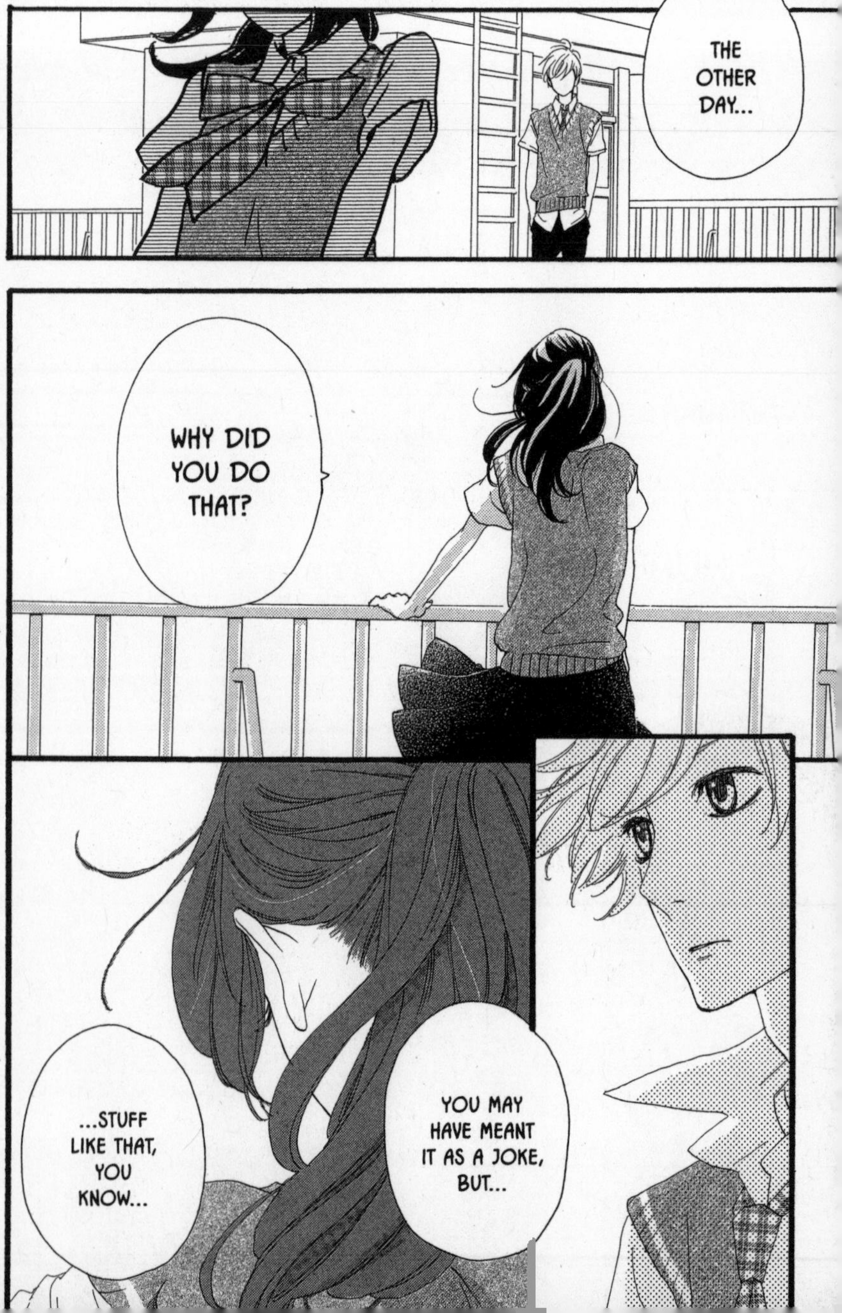
THE OTHER DAY...
WHY DID YOU DO THAT?
YOU MAY HAVE MEANT IT AS A JOKE, BUT...
...STUFF LIKE THAT, YOU KNOW...

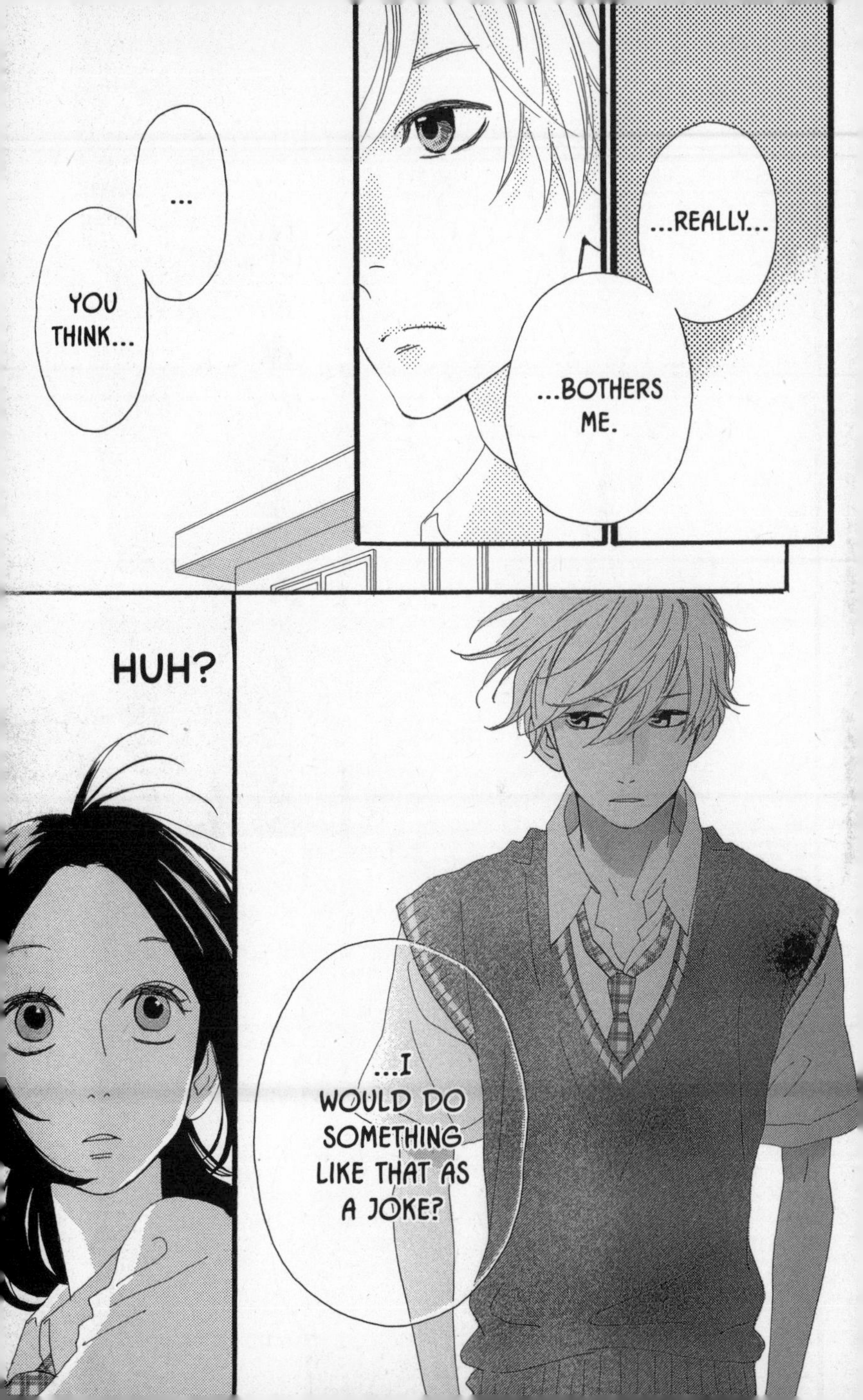
...REALLY...
...BOTHERS ME.
...
YOU THINK...
...I WOULD DO SOMETHING LIKE THAT AS A JOKE?
HUH?

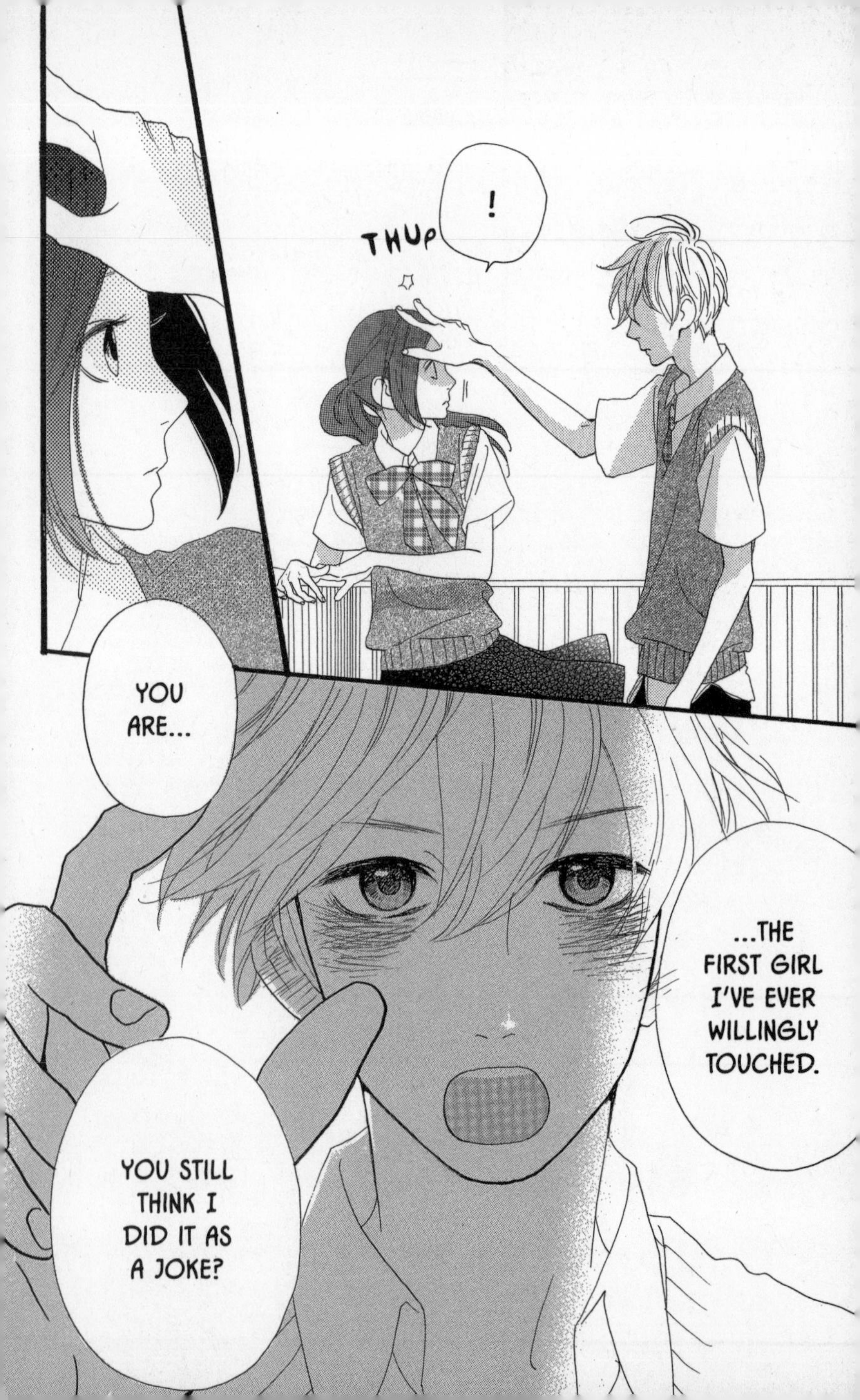
THUP
!
YOU ARE...
...THE FIRST GIRL I'VE EVER WILLINGLY TOUCHED.
YOU STILL THINK I DID IT AS A JOKE?

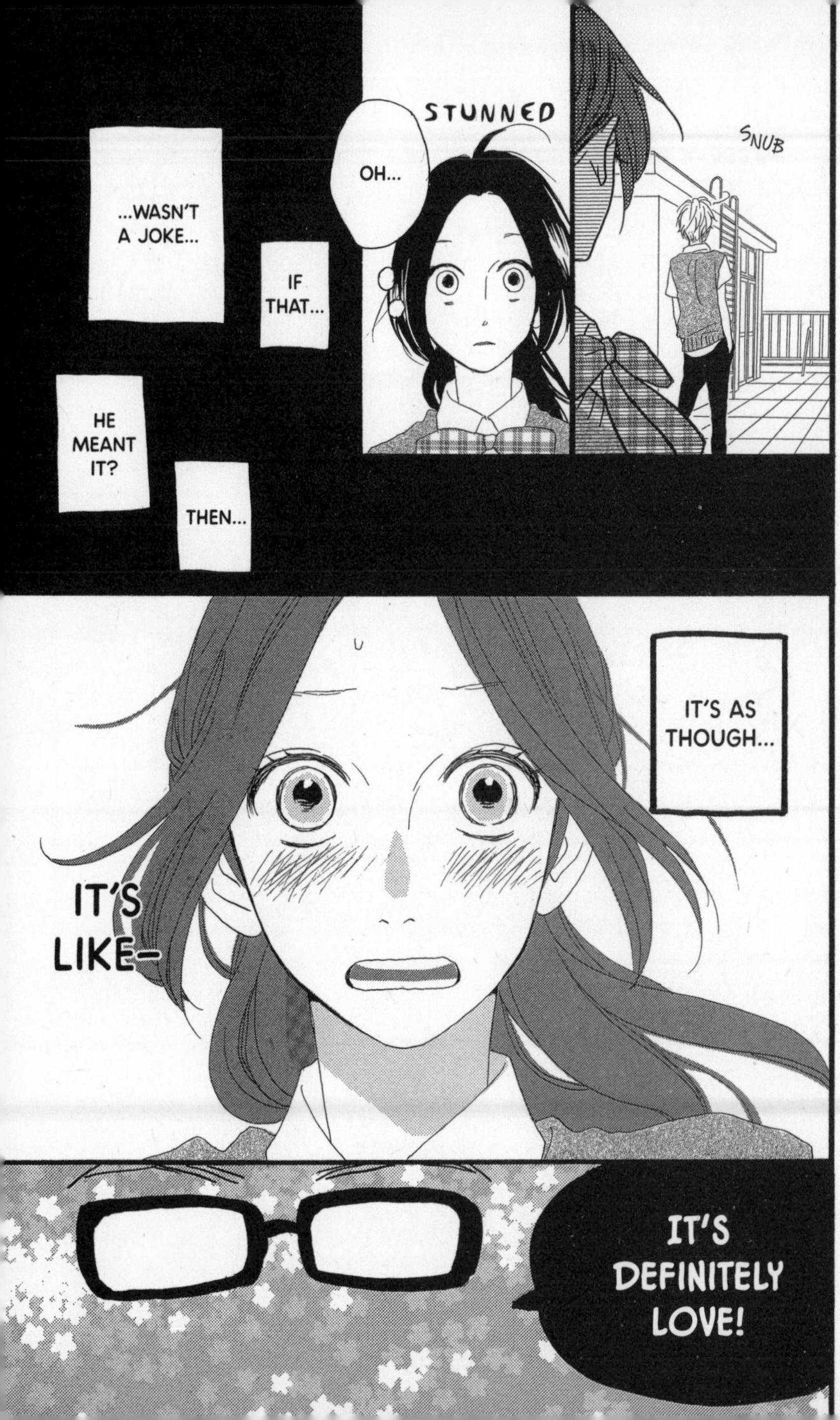
SNUB
STUNNED
OH...
IF THAT...
...WASN'T A JOKE...
HE MEANT IT?
THEN...
IT'S AS THOUGH...
IT'S LIKE—
IT'S DEFINITELY LOVE!

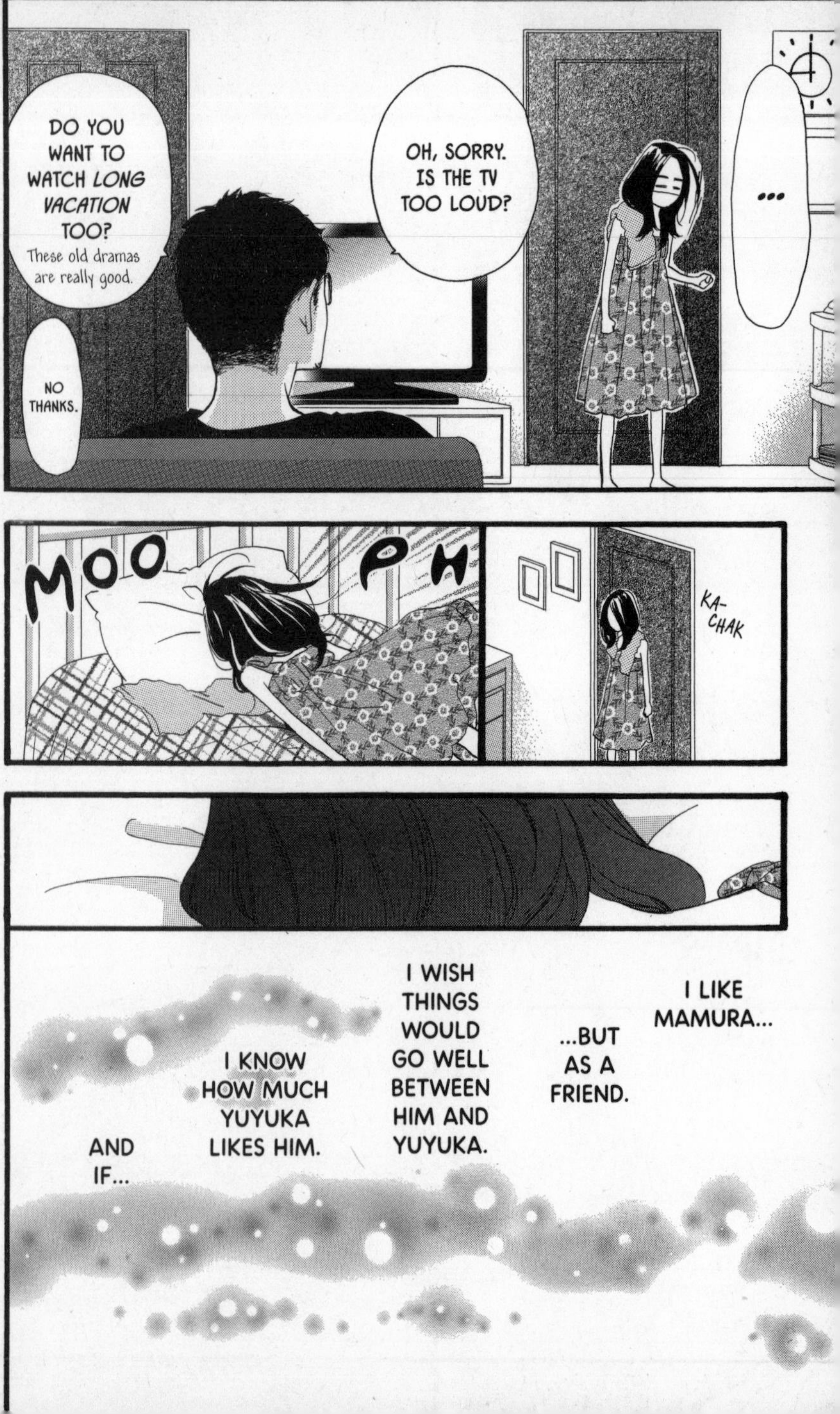
...
OH, SORRY. IS THE TV TOO LOUD?
DO YOU WANT TO WATCH *LONG VACATION* TOO? These old dramas are really good.
NO THANKS.
KA-CHAK
MOOPH
I LIKE MAMURA...
...BUT AS A FRIEND.
I WISH THINGS WOULD GO WELL BETWEEN HIM AND YUYUKA.
I KNOW HOW MUCH YUYUKA LIKES HIM.
AND IF...

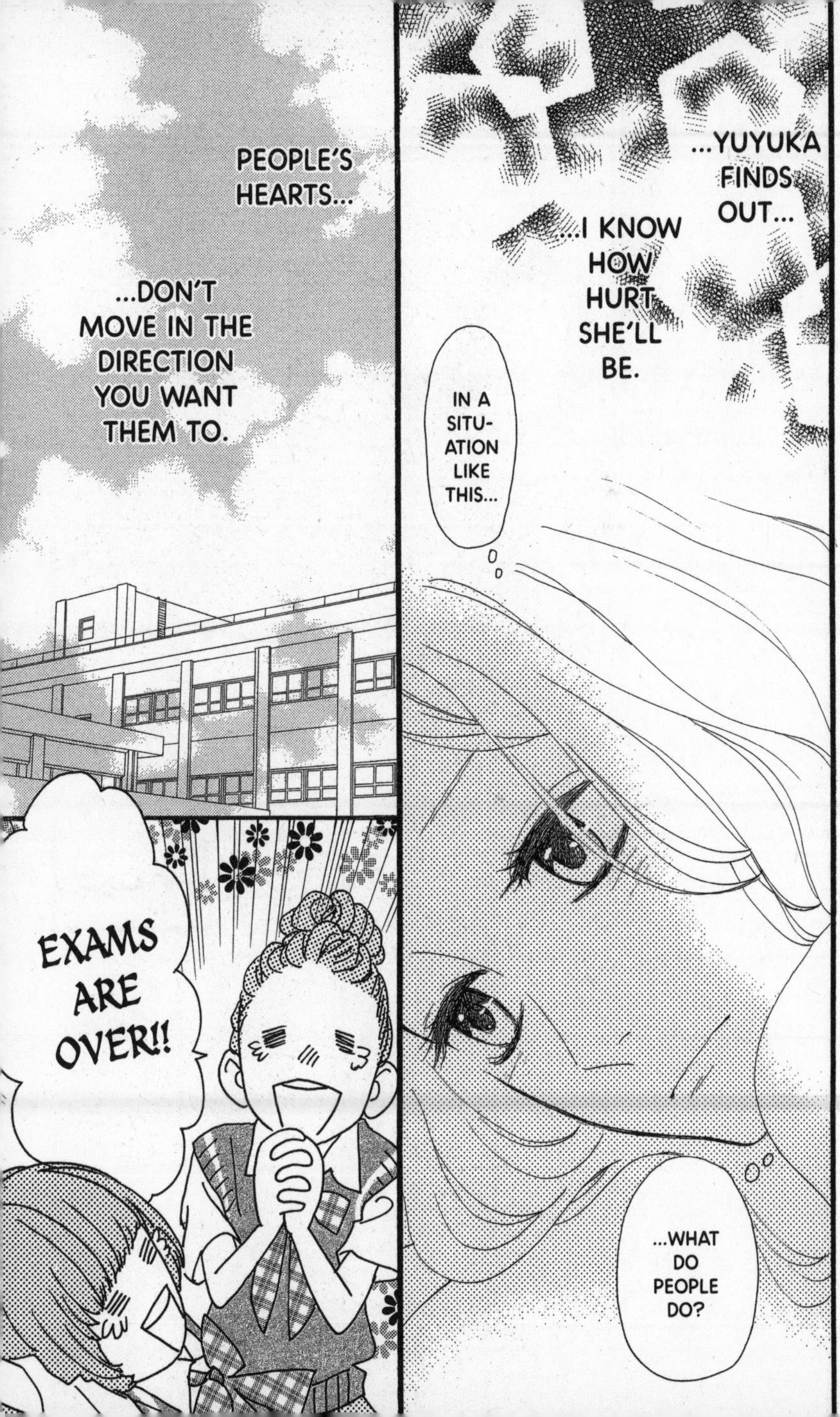
...YUYUKA FINDS OUT...
...I KNOW HOW HURT SHE'LL BE.
IN A SITUATION LIKE THIS...
...WHAT DO PEOPLE DO?
PEOPLE'S HEARTS...
...DON'T MOVE IN THE DIRECTION YOU WANT THEM TO.
EXAMS ARE OVER!!

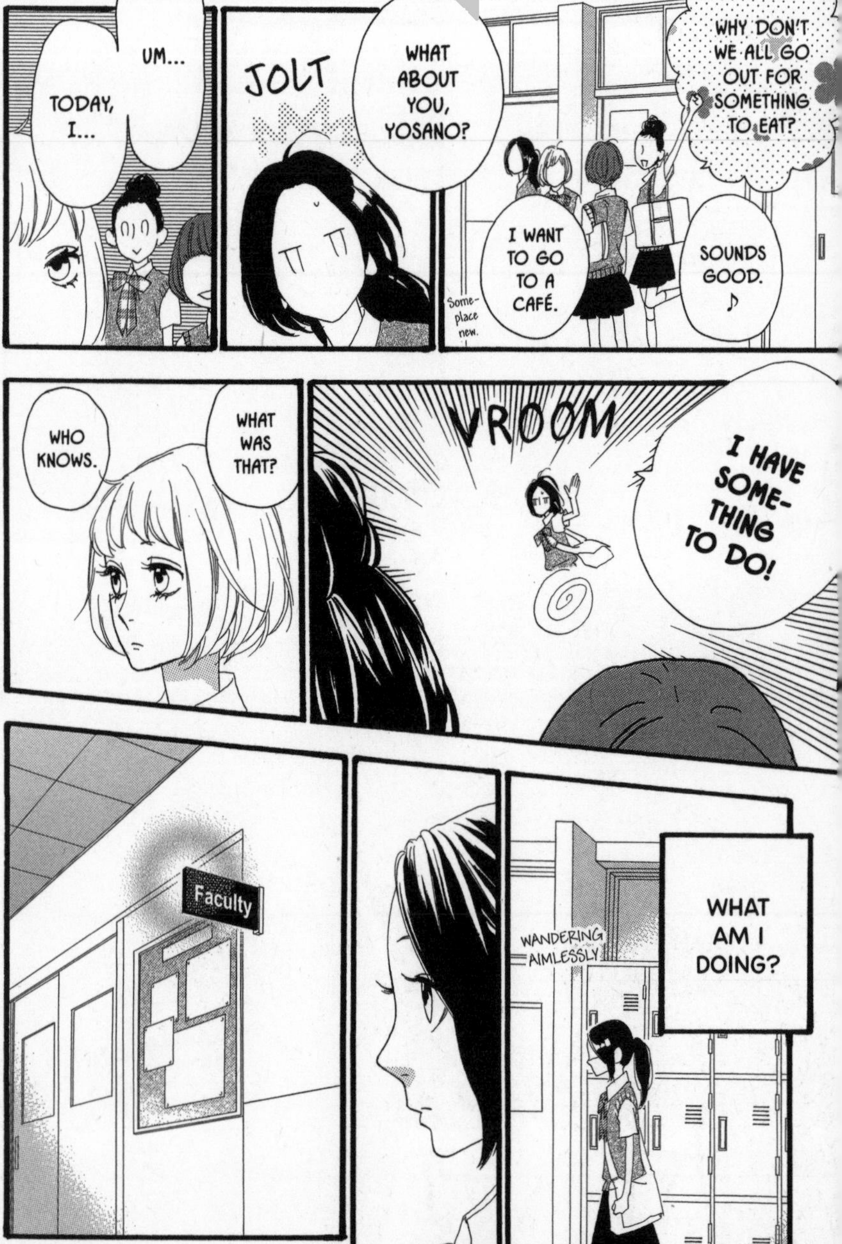
WHY DON'T WE ALL GO OUT FOR SOMETHING TO EAT?
SOUNDS GOOD. ♪
I WANT TO GO TO A CAFÉ.
Someplace new.
JOLT
WHAT ABOUT YOU, YOSANO?
UM...
TODAY, I...
VROOM
I HAVE SOMETHING TO DO!
WHAT WAS THAT?
WHO KNOWS.
WHAT AM I DOING?
WANDERING AIMLESSLY
Faculty

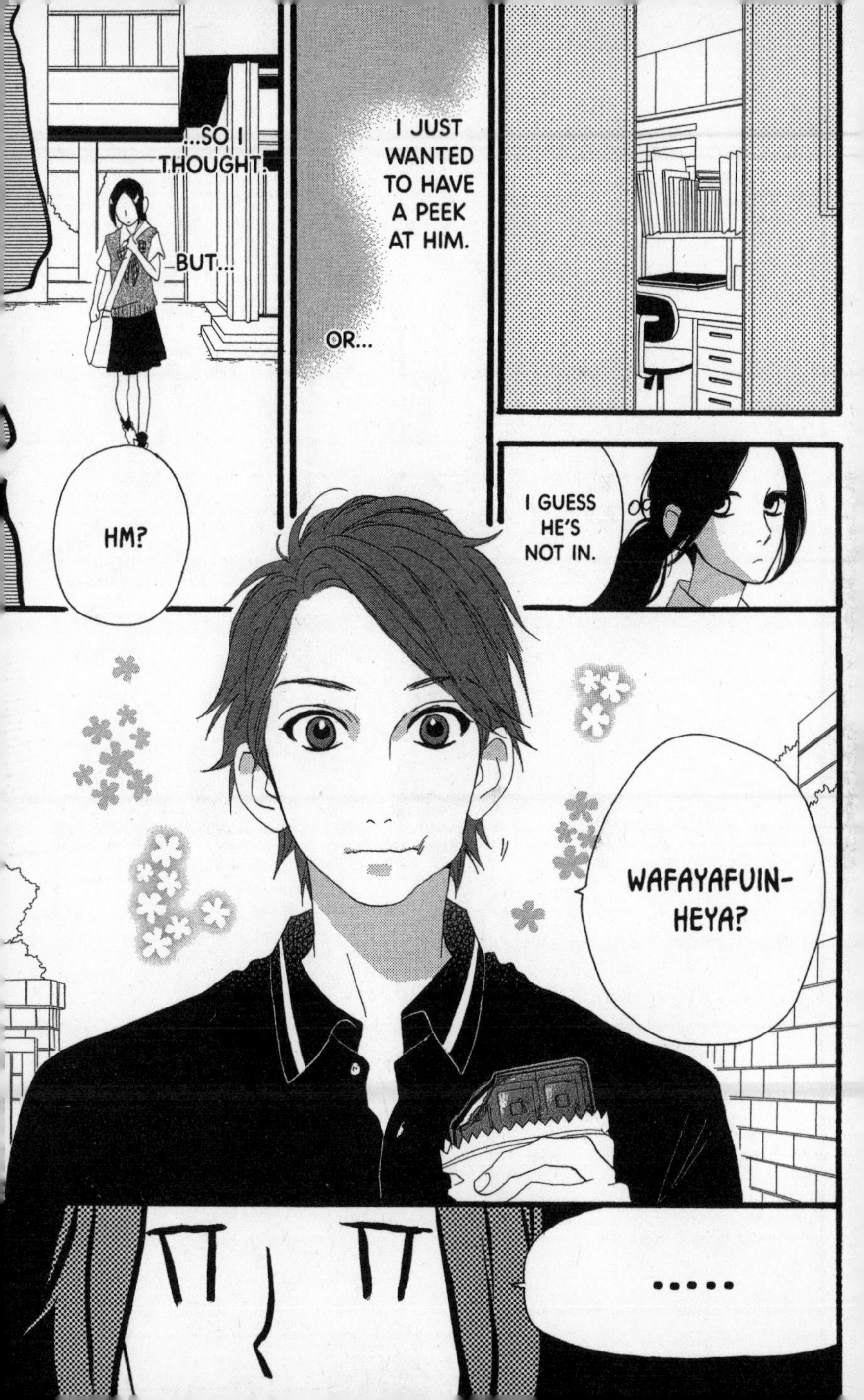
I GUESS HE'S NOT IN.
I JUST WANTED TO HAVE A PEEK AT HIM.
OR...
...SO I THOUGHT.
BUT...
HM?
WAFAYAFUIN-HEYA?
.....

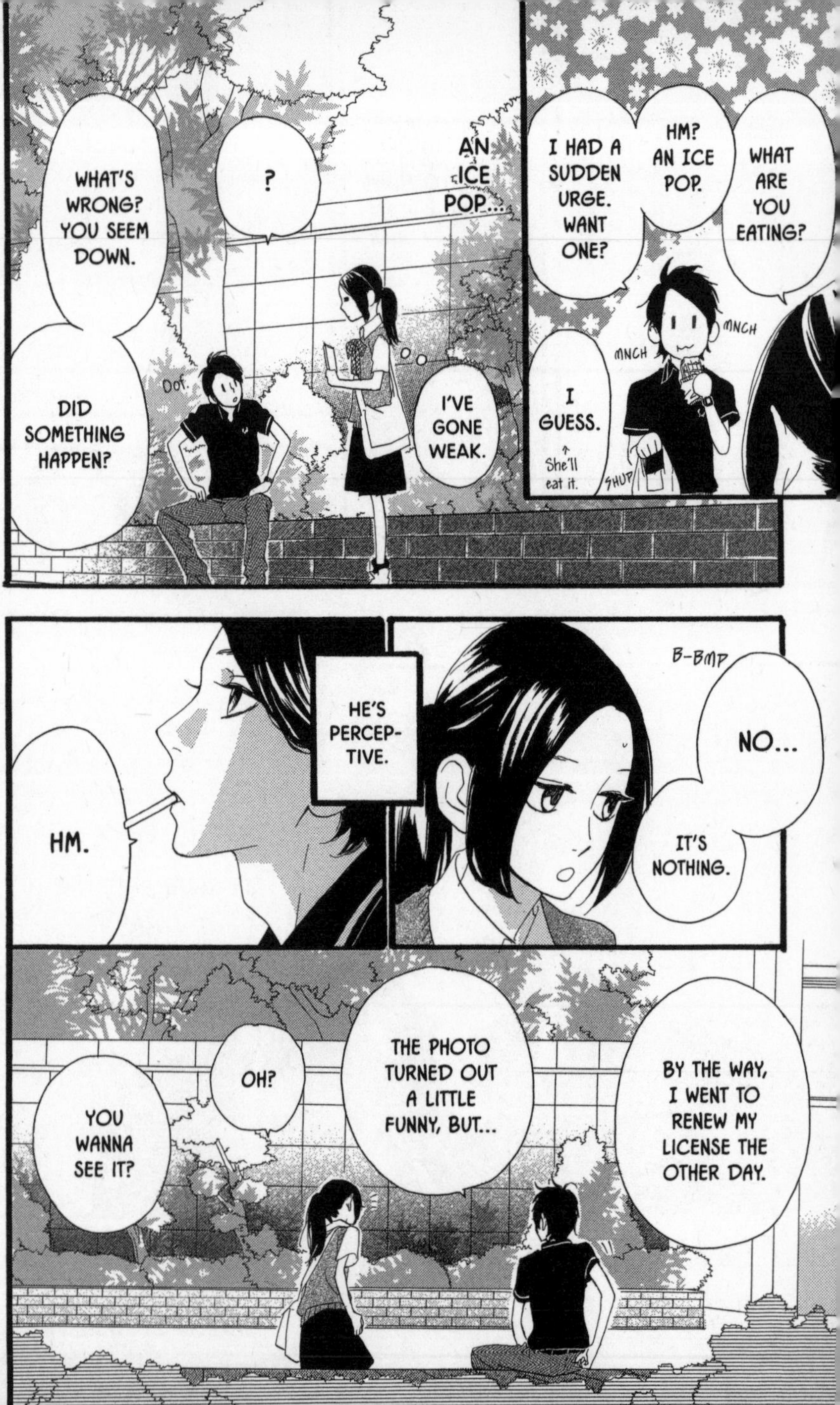
WHAT ARE YOU EATING?
HM? AN ICE POP.
I HAD A SUDDEN URGE. WANT ONE?
MNCH
MNCH
I GUESS.
She'll eat it.
SHUP
AN ICE POP...
I'VE GONE WEAK.
?
WHAT'S WRONG? YOU SEEM DOWN.
Dof
DID SOMETHING HAPPEN?
B-BMP
NO...
IT'S NOTHING.
HE'S PERCEPTIVE.
HM.
BY THE WAY, I WENT TO RENEW MY LICENSE THE OTHER DAY.
THE PHOTO TURNED OUT A LITTLE FUNNY, BUT...
OH?
YOU WANNA SEE IT?

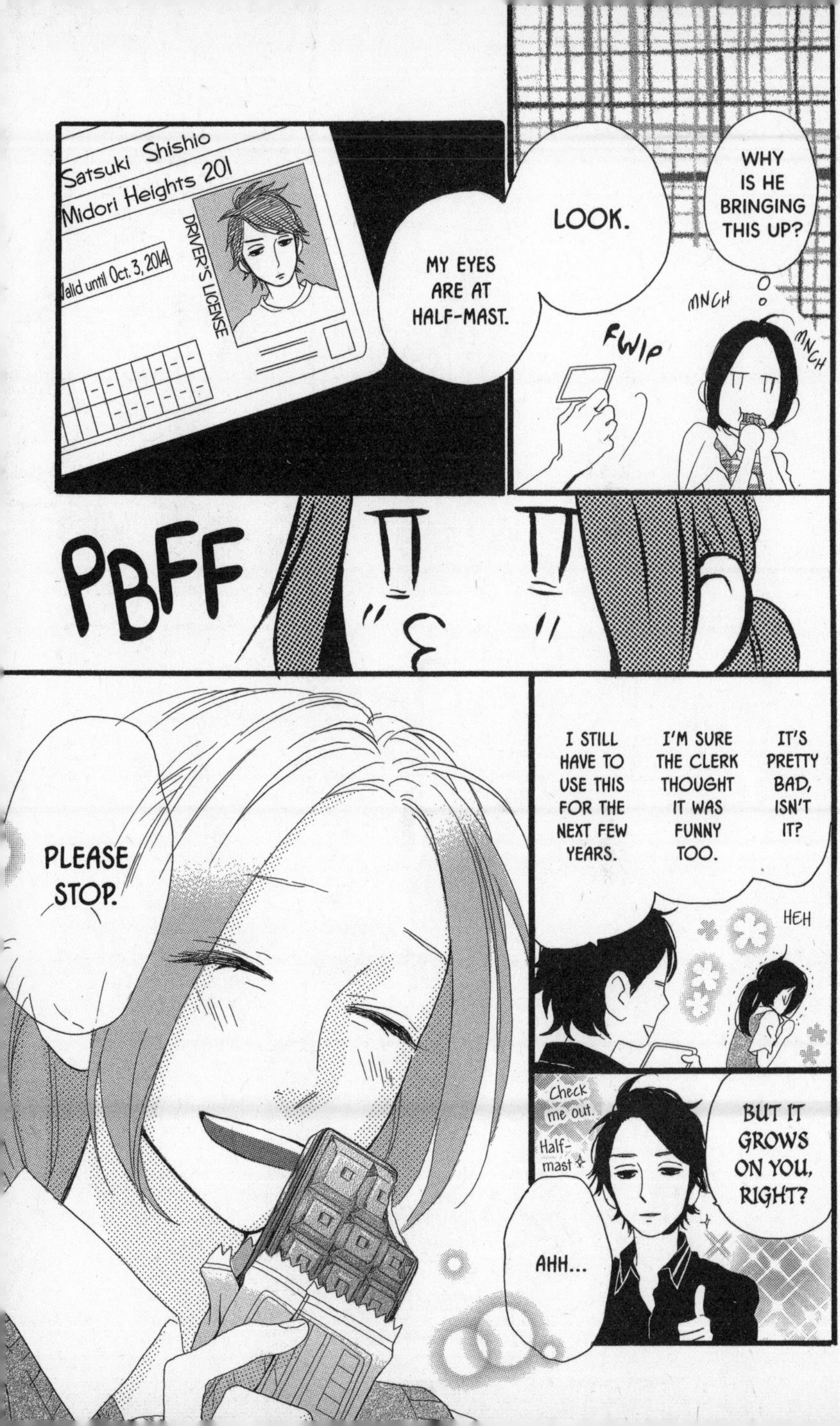
WHY IS HE BRINGING THIS UP?
MNCH
MNCH
FWIP
LOOK.
MY EYES ARE AT HALF-MAST.
Satsuki Shishio
Midori Heights 201
Valid until Oct. 3, 2014
DRIVER'S LICENSE
PBFF
IT'S PRETTY BAD, ISN'T IT?
I'M SURE THE CLERK THOUGHT IT WAS FUNNY TOO.
I STILL HAVE TO USE THIS FOR THE NEXT FEW YEARS.
HEH
BUT IT GROWS ON YOU, RIGHT?
Check me out.
Half-mast
AHH...
PLEASE STOP.

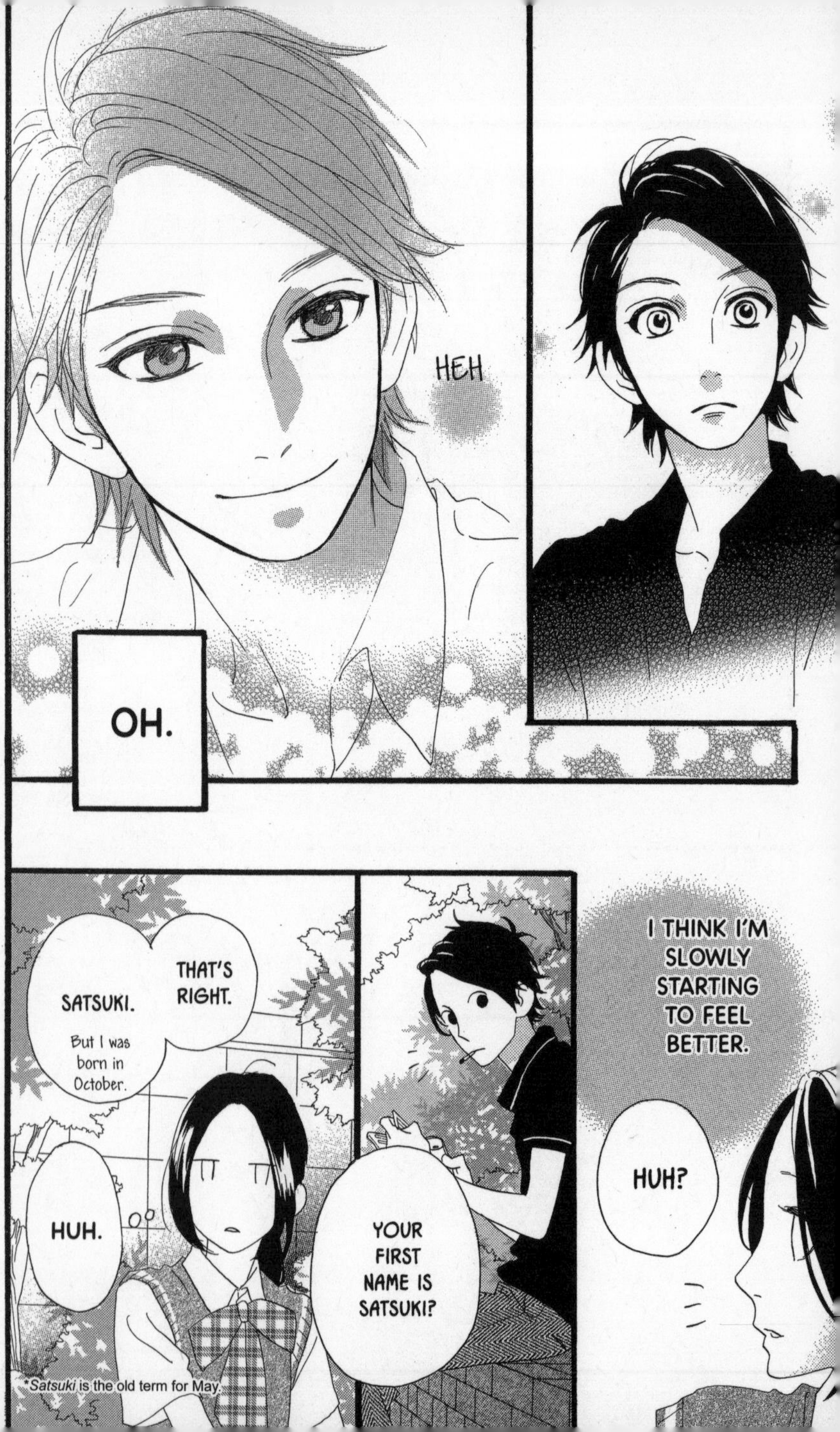
HEH
OH.
I THINK I'M SLOWLY STARTING TO FEEL BETTER.
HUH?
YOUR FIRST NAME IS SATSUKI?
THAT'S RIGHT.
SATSUKI.
But I was born in October.
HUH.

**Satsuki* is the old term for May.

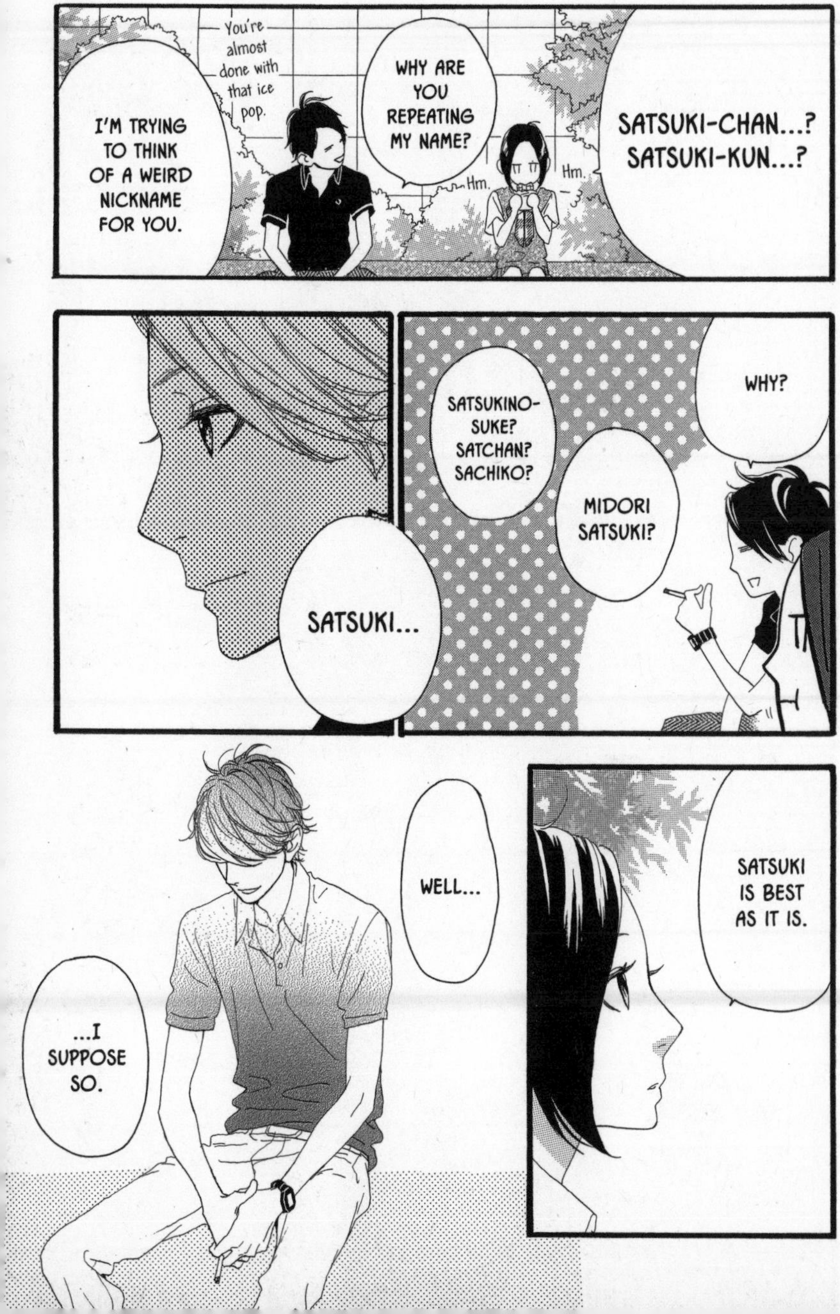
SATSUKI-CHAN...? SATSUKI-KUN...?
Hm.
Hm.
WHY ARE YOU REPEATING MY NAME?
You're almost done with that ice pop.
I'M TRYING TO THINK OF A WEIRD NICKNAME FOR YOU.
WHY?
MIDORI SATSUKI?
SATSUKINO-SUKE? SATCHAN? SACHIKO?
SATSUKI...
SATSUKI IS BEST AS IT IS.
WELL...
...I SUPPOSE SO.

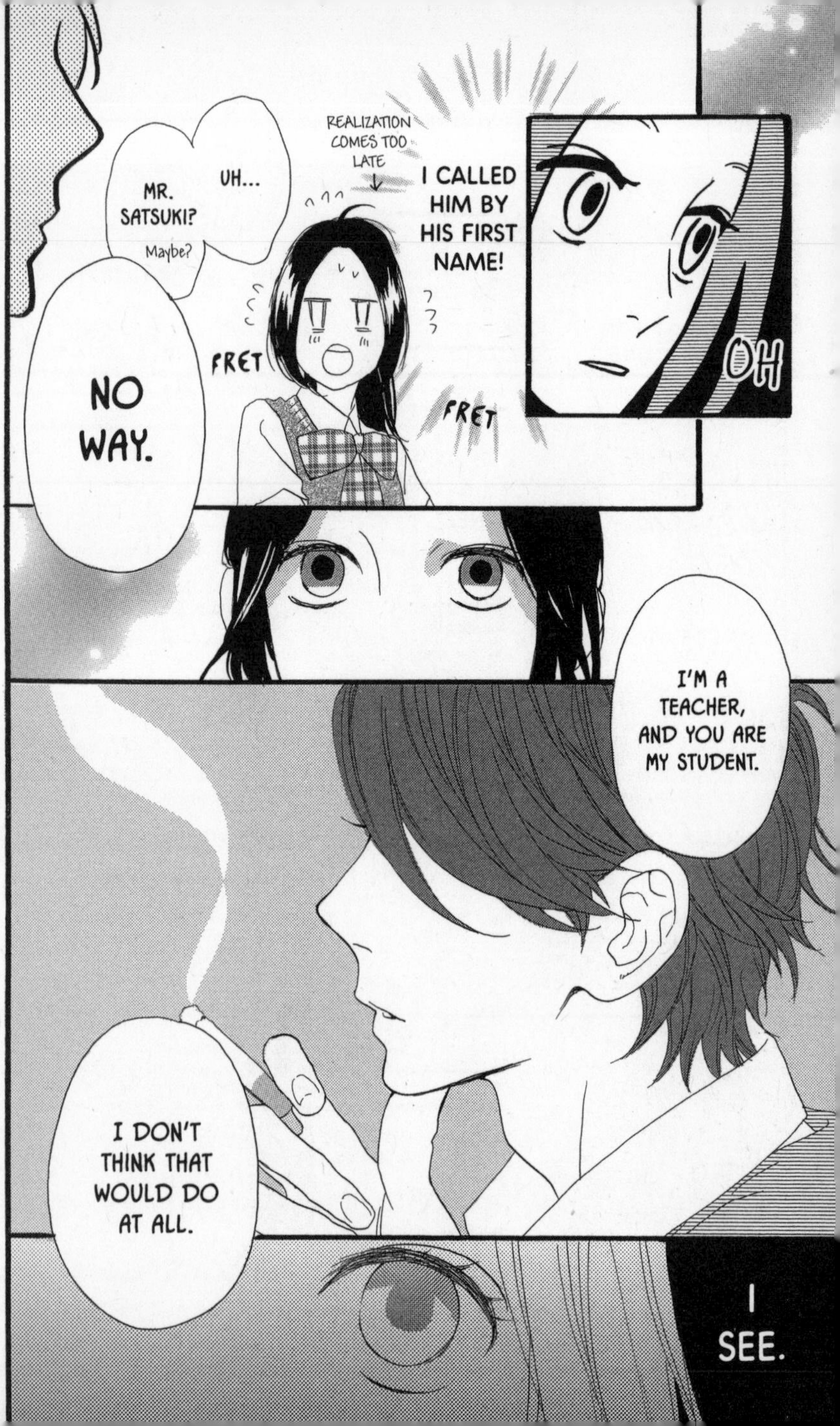
OH
I CALLED HIM BY HIS FIRST NAME!
REALIZATION COMES TOO LATE
FRET
FRET
UH... MR. SATSUKI?
Maybe?
NO WAY.
I'M A TEACHER, AND YOU ARE MY STUDENT.
I DON'T THINK THAT WOULD DO AT ALL.
I SEE.

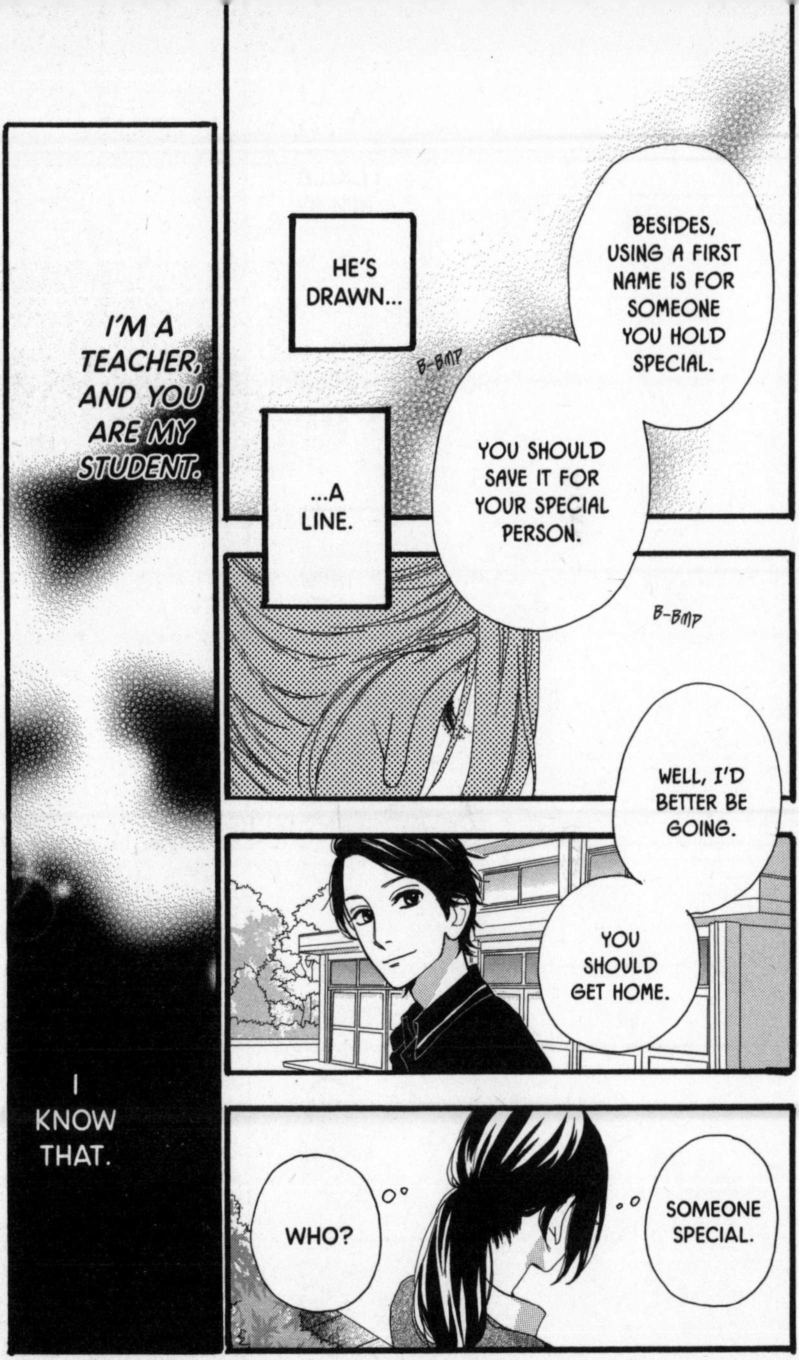
BESIDES, USING A FIRST NAME IS FOR SOMEONE YOU HOLD SPECIAL.
HE'S DRAWN...
B-BMP
YOU SHOULD SAVE IT FOR YOUR SPECIAL PERSON.
...A LINE.
B-BMP
WELL, I'D BETTER BE GOING.
YOU SHOULD GET HOME.
SOMEONE SPECIAL.
WHO?
I'M A TEACHER, AND YOU ARE MY STUDENT.
I KNOW THAT.

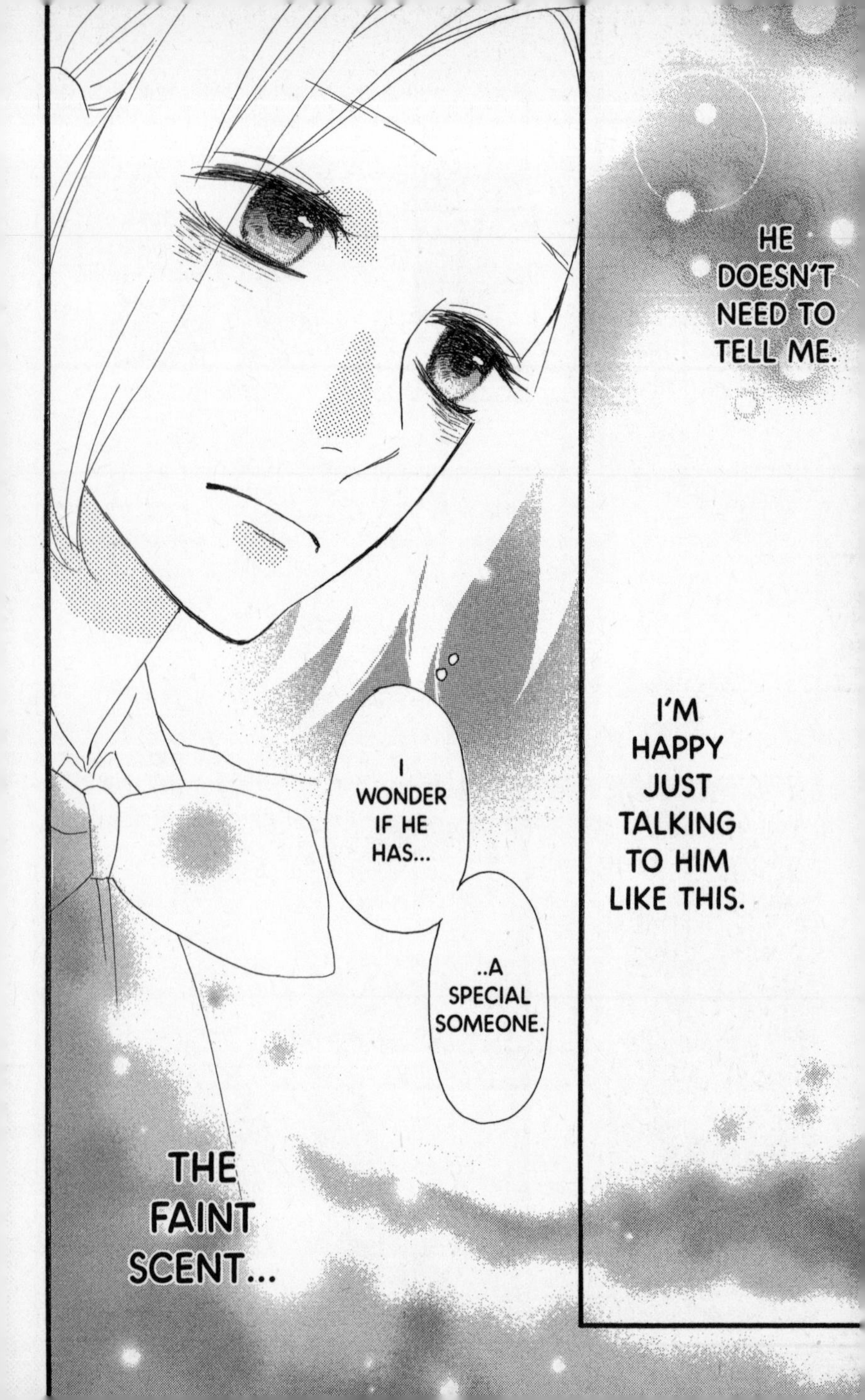
HE DOESN'T NEED TO TELL ME.
I'M HAPPY JUST TALKING TO HIM LIKE THIS.
I WONDER IF HE HAS...
..A SPECIAL SOMEONE.
THE FAINT SCENT...

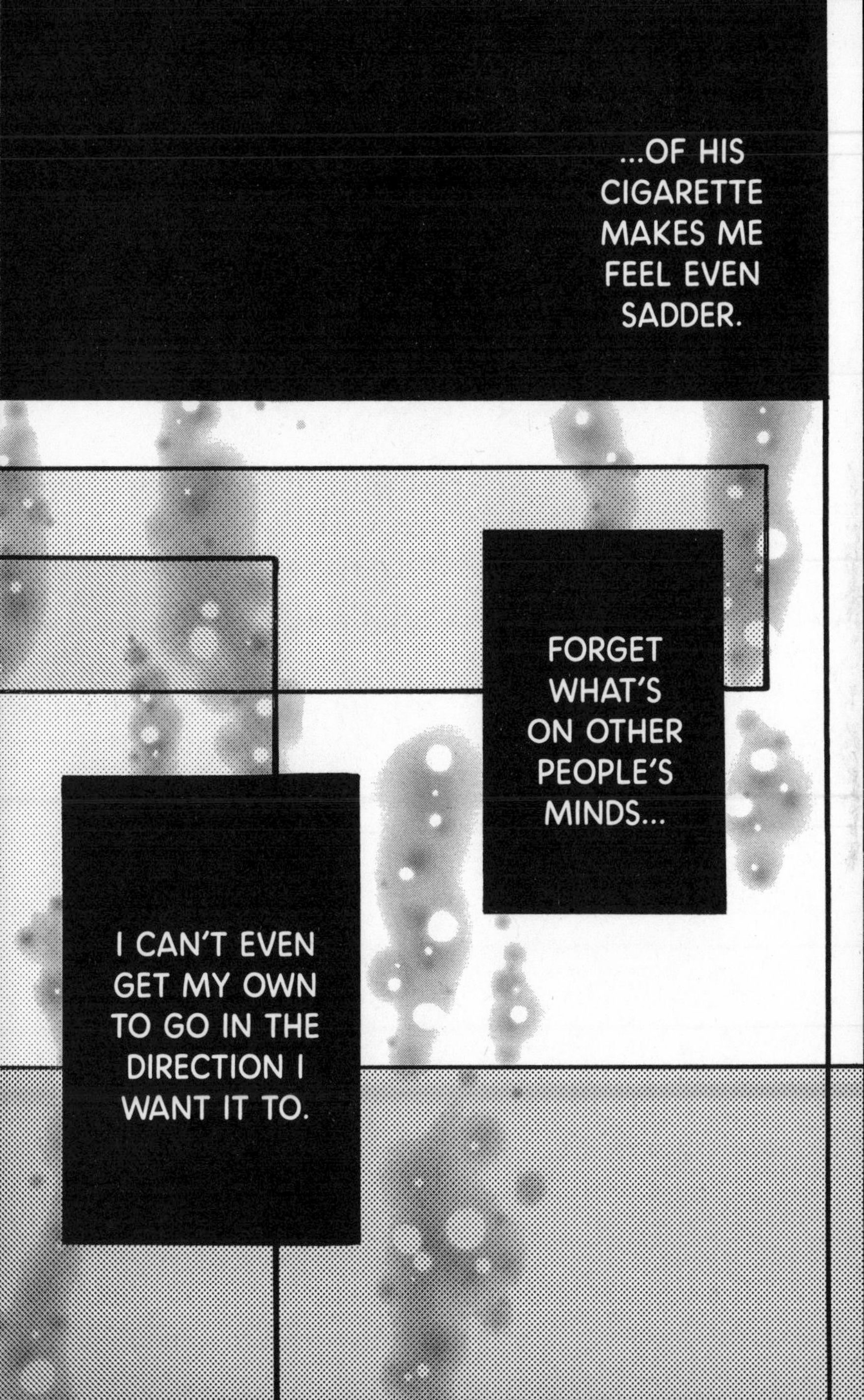
...OF HIS CIGARETTE MAKES ME FEEL EVEN SADDER.
FORGET WHAT'S ON OTHER PEOPLE'S MINDS...
I CAN'T EVEN GET MY OWN TO GO IN THE DIRECTION I WANT IT TO.

Simple Scribbles ④

• Shishio

Staid Man Version

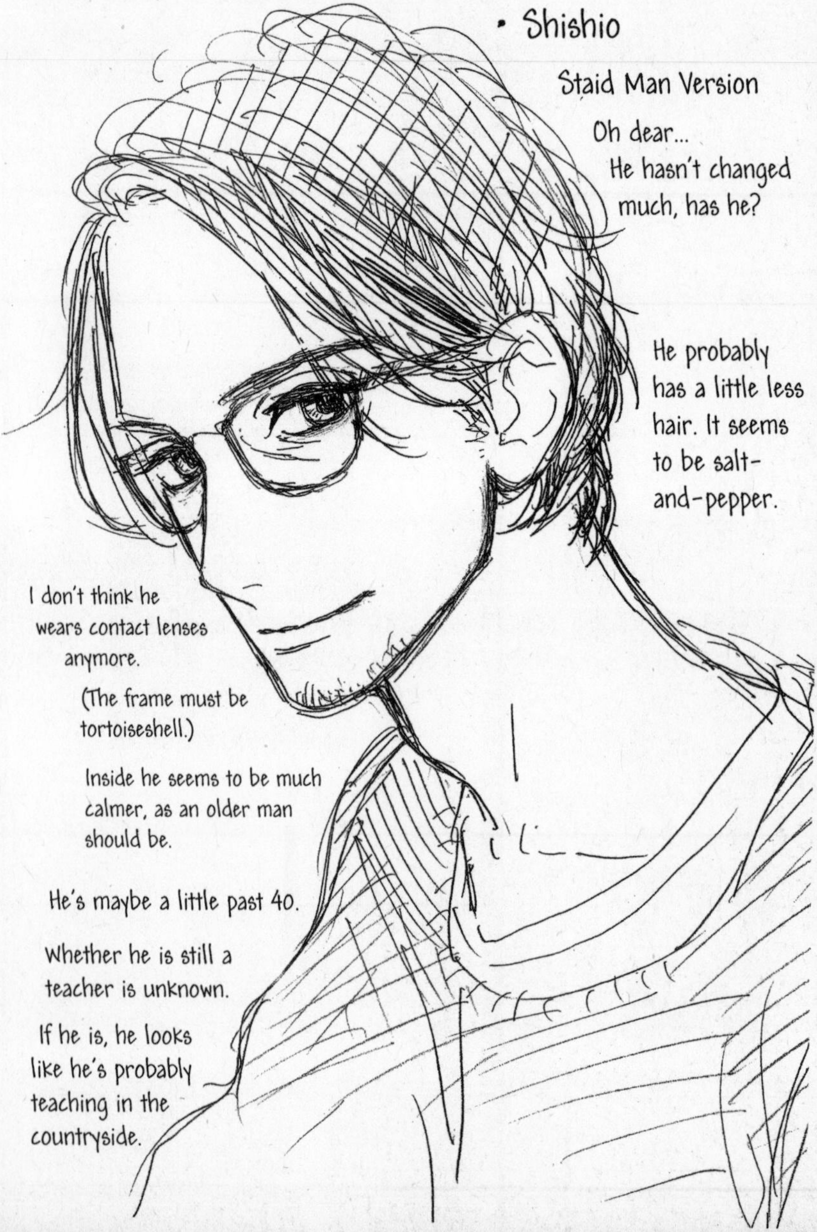

Oh dear... He hasn't changed much, has he?

He probably has a little less hair. It seems to be salt-and-pepper.

I don't think he wears contact lenses anymore.

(The frame must be tortoiseshell.)

Inside he seems to be much calmer, as an older man should be.

He's maybe a little past 40.

Whether he is still a teacher is unknown.

If he is, he looks like he's probably teaching in the countryside.

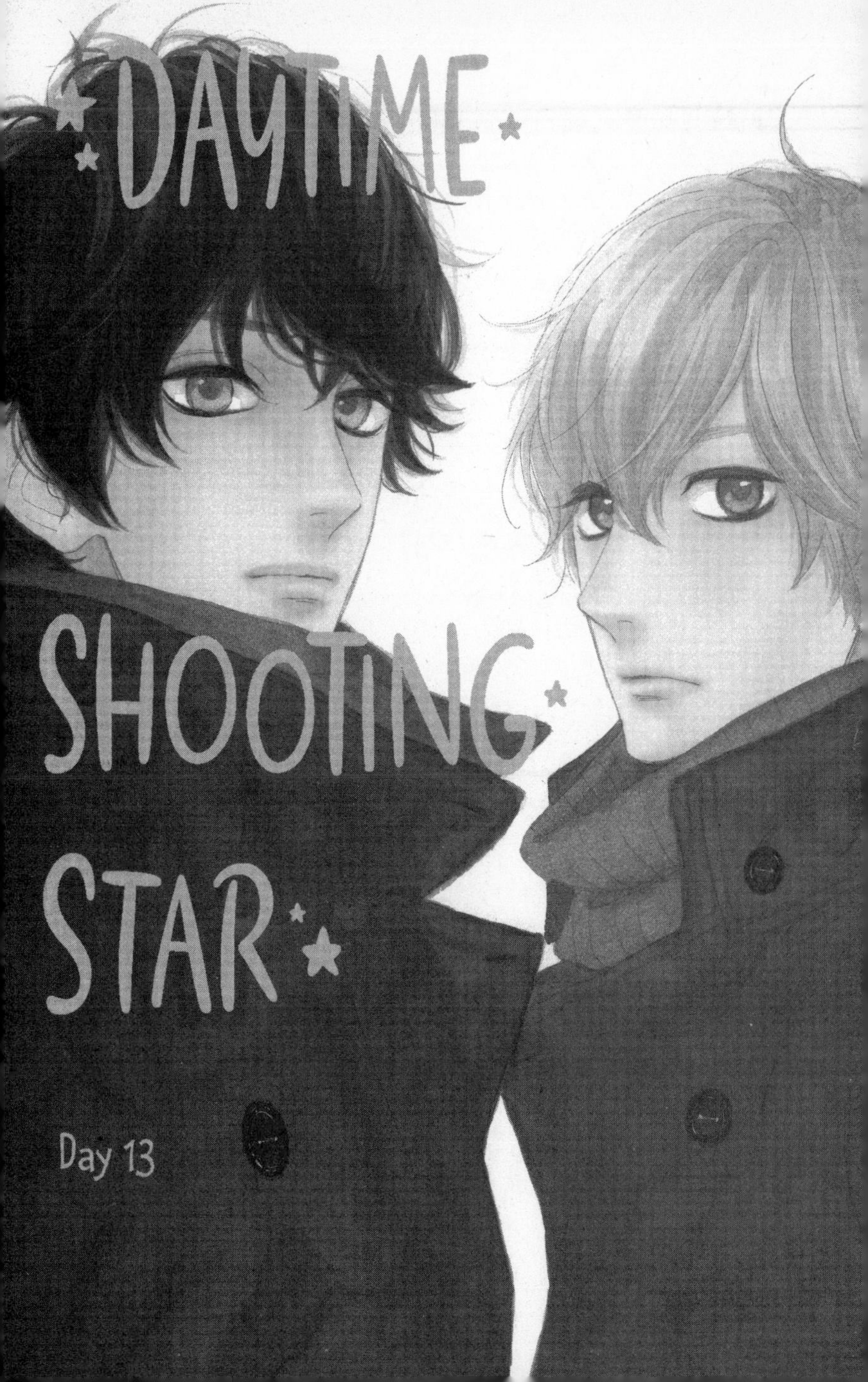
DAYTIME
SHOOTING
STAR
Day 13

Normal Style
(School)

Days-Off Style
(Weekend)
Total Bedhead

FWAH

FWAH

After-Bath Style
(A Bit Calmer)

Shishio's Hairstyles

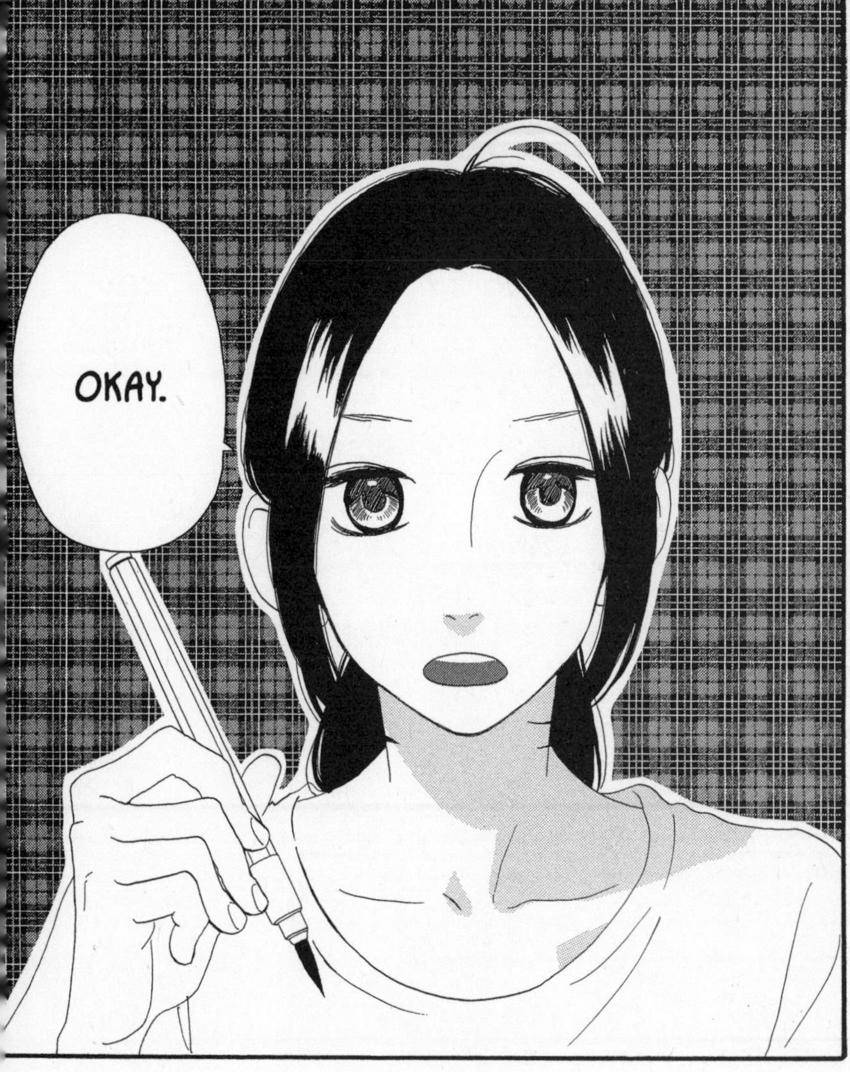
OKAY.

Kotetsu Sarumaru 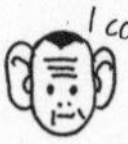
The drawing is so bad I could cry.

Birthday: September 20
Height: 5'8"
Weight: 130 lbs

Blood Type: B

1. Ginger pork.
2. Video games.
3. My mom caught me buying a porn magazine.

**Saru* means "monkey."

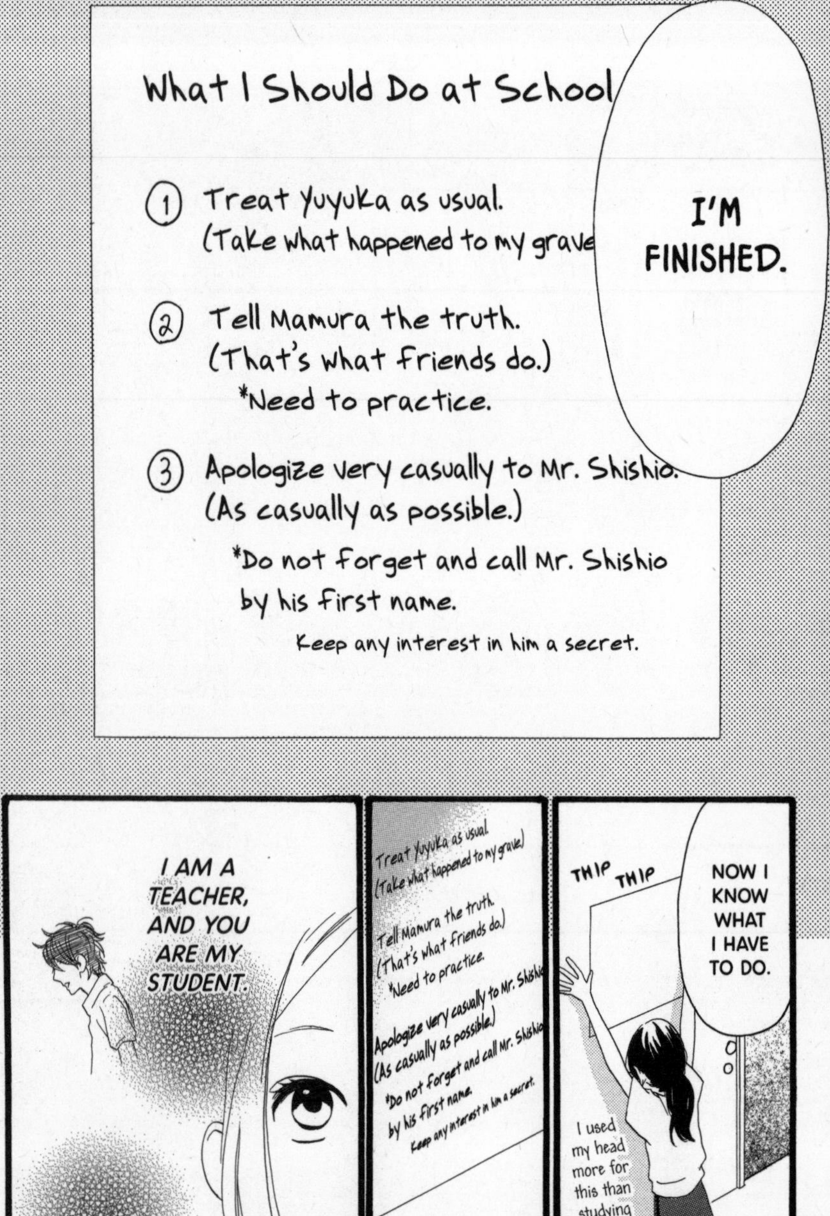
What I Should Do at School
① Treat Yuyuka as usual.
(Take what happened to my grave
② Tell Mamura the truth.
(That's what friends do.)
*Need to practice.
③ Apologize very casually to Mr. Shishio.
(As casually as possible.)
*Do not forget and call Mr. Shishio by his first name.
Keep any interest in him a secret.
I'M FINISHED.
NOW I KNOW WHAT I HAVE TO DO.
THIP THIP
I used my head more for this than studying for exams.
Treat Yuyuka as usual.
(Take what happened to my grave.)
Tell Mamura the truth.
(That's what friends do.)
*Need to practice.
Apologize very casually to Mr. Shishio
(As casually as possible.)
*Do not forget and call Mr. Shishio
by his first name.
Keep any interest in him a secret.
I AM A TEACHER, AND YOU ARE MY STUDENT.

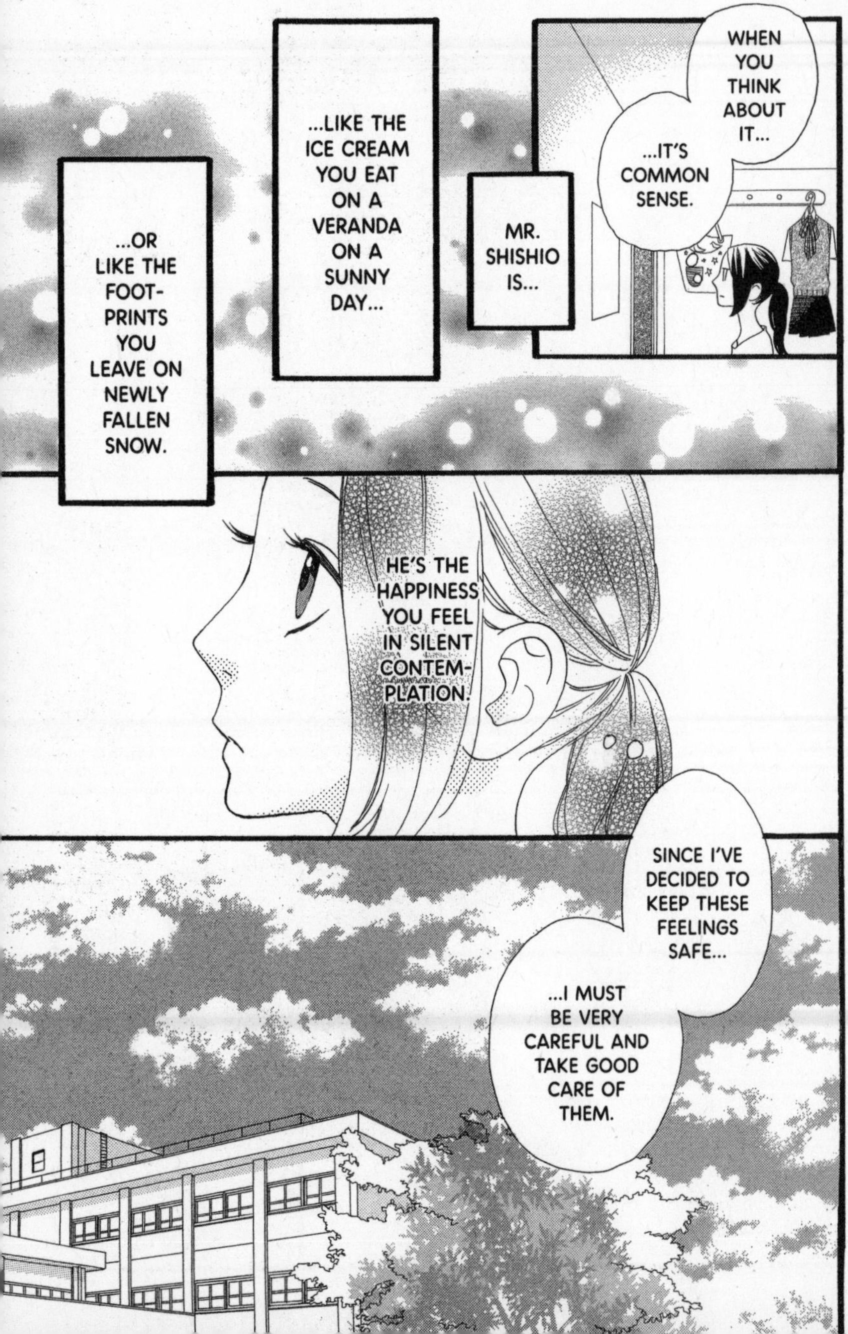
WHEN YOU THINK ABOUT IT...
...IT'S COMMON SENSE.
MR. SHISHIO IS...
...LIKE THE ICE CREAM YOU EAT ON A VERANDA ON A SUNNY DAY...
...OR LIKE THE FOOT-PRINTS YOU LEAVE ON NEWLY FALLEN SNOW.
HE'S THE HAPPINESS YOU FEEL IN SILENT CONTEM-PLATION.
SINCE I'VE DECIDED TO KEEP THESE FEELINGS SAFE...
...I MUST BE VERY CAREFUL AND TAKE GOOD CARE OF THEM.

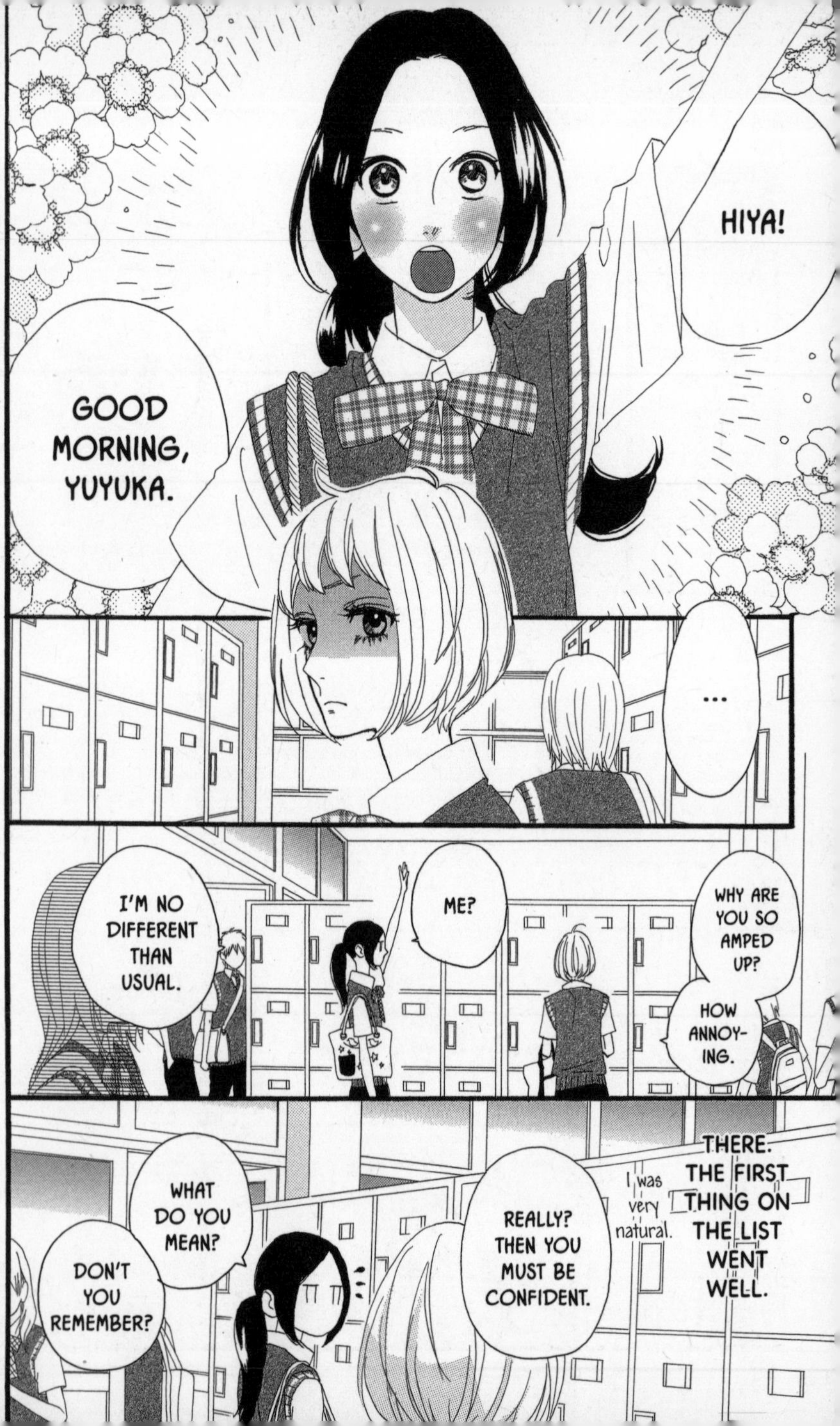
HIYA!
GOOD MORNING, YUYUKA.
...
WHY ARE YOU SO AMPED UP?
HOW ANNOY-ING.
ME?
I'M NO DIFFERENT THAN USUAL.
THERE. THE FIRST THING ON THE LIST WENT WELL.
I was very natural.
REALLY? THEN YOU MUST BE CONFIDENT.
WHAT DO YOU MEAN?
DON'T YOU REMEMBER?

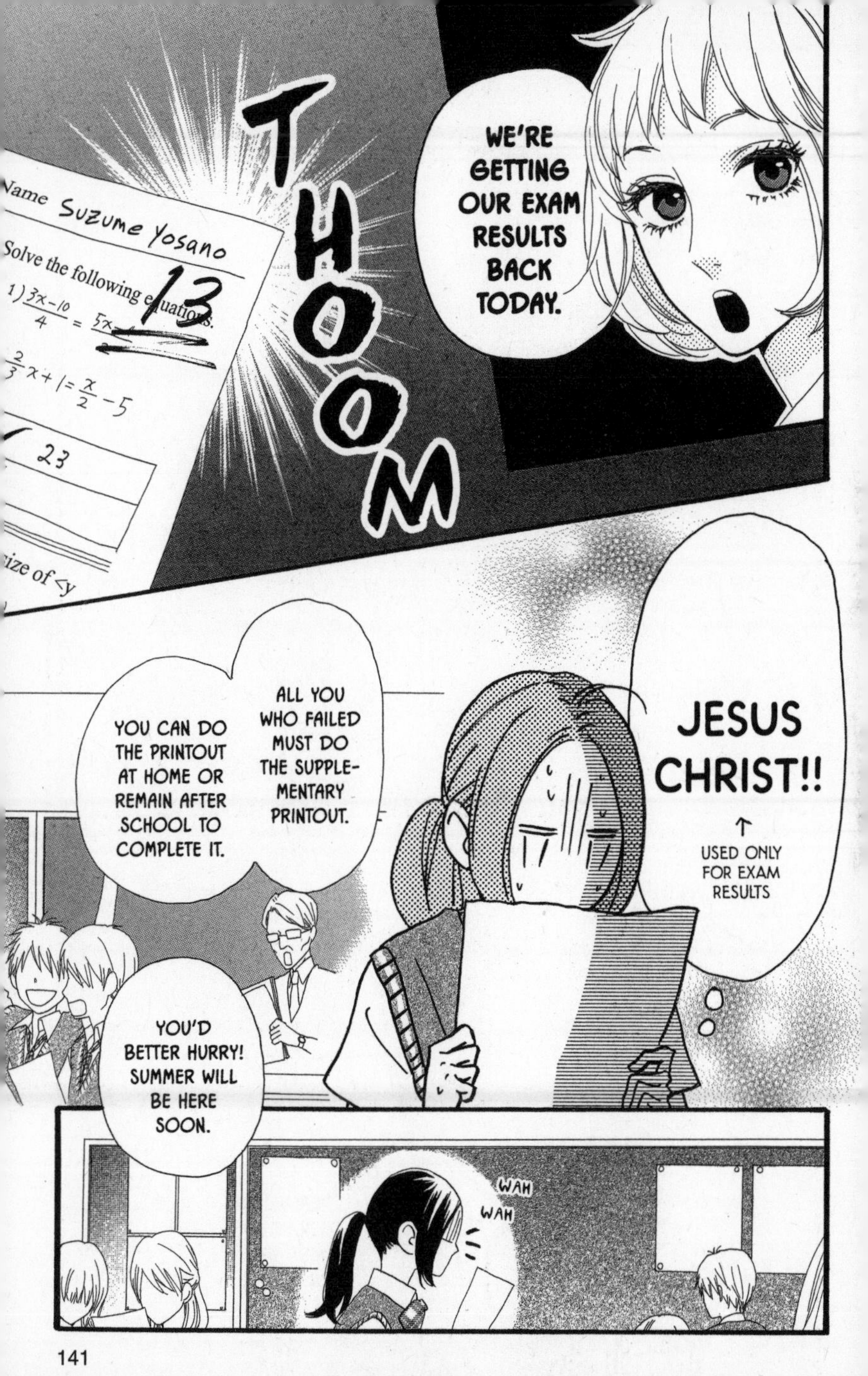
WE'RE GETTING OUR EXAM RESULTS BACK TODAY.
THOOM
Name Suzume Yosano
Solve the following equations.
13
23
JESUS CHRIST!!
↑ USED ONLY FOR EXAM RESULTS
ALL YOU WHO FAILED MUST DO THE SUPPLE-MENTARY PRINTOUT.
YOU CAN DO THE PRINTOUT AT HOME OR REMAIN AFTER SCHOOL TO COMPLETE IT.
YOU'D BETTER HURRY! SUMMER WILL BE HERE SOON.
WAH WAH

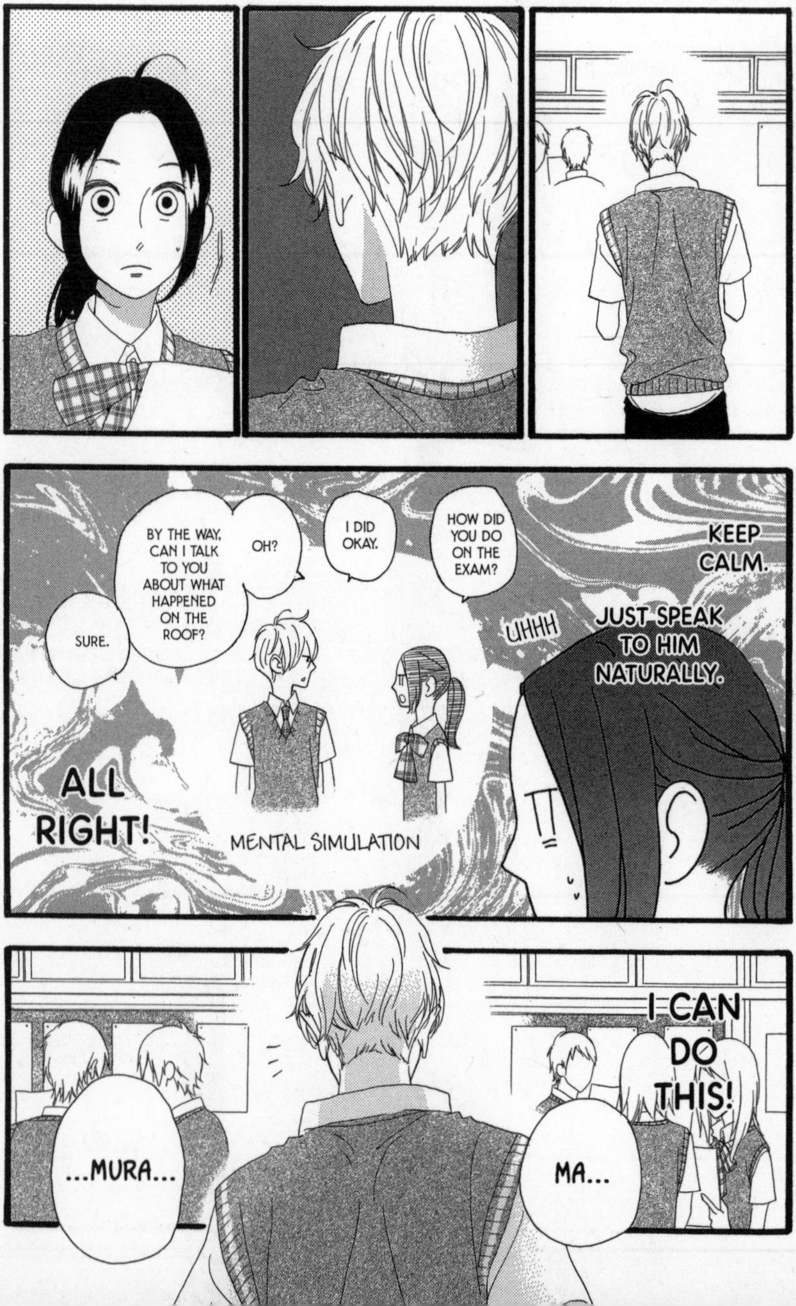
KEEP CALM.
JUST SPEAK TO HIM NATURALLY.
UHHH
HOW DID YOU DO ON THE EXAM?
I DID OKAY.
OH?
BY THE WAY, CAN I TALK TO YOU ABOUT WHAT HAPPENED ON THE ROOF?
SURE.
MENTAL SIMULATION
ALL RIGHT!
I CAN DO THIS!
MA...
...MURA...

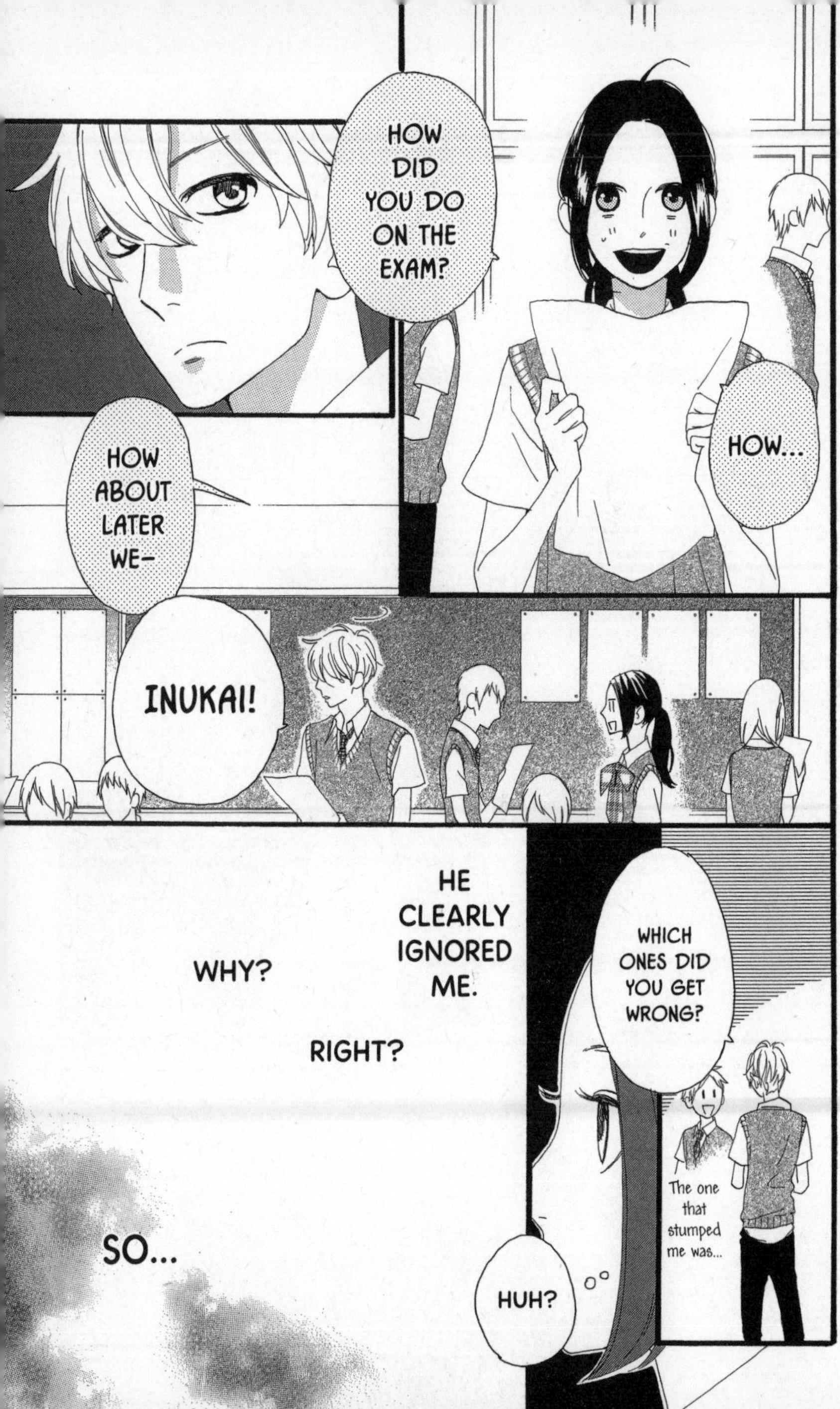
HOW DID YOU DO ON THE EXAM?
HOW...
HOW ABOUT LATER WE-
INUKAI!
WHICH ONES DID YOU GET WRONG?
The one that stumped me was...
HUH?
HE CLEARLY IGNORED ME.
WHY?
RIGHT?
SO...

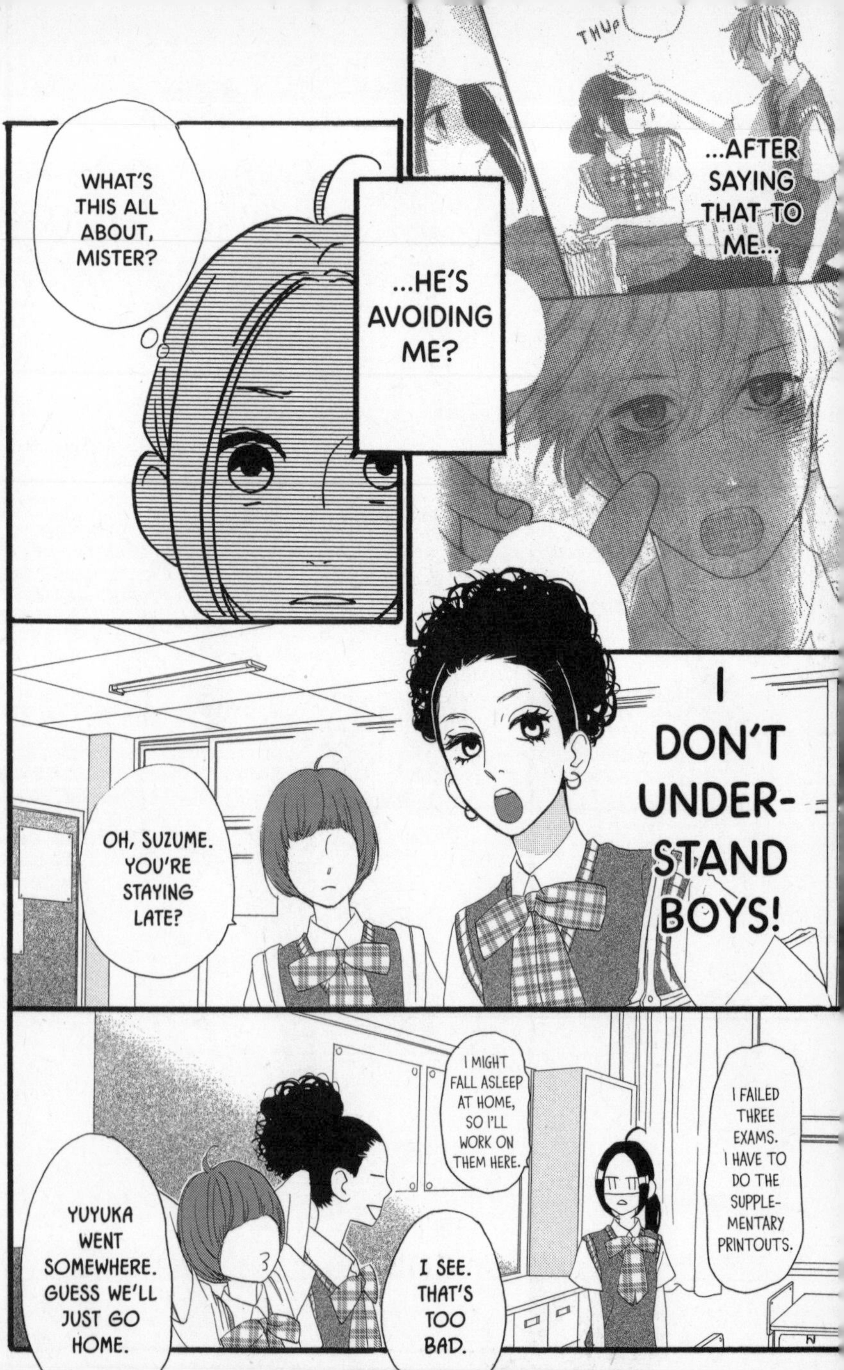
THUP
...AFTER SAYING THAT TO ME...
...HE'S AVOIDING ME?
WHAT'S THIS ALL ABOUT, MISTER?
I DON'T UNDER-STAND BOYS!
OH, SUZUME. YOU'RE STAYING LATE?
I FAILED THREE EXAMS. I HAVE TO DO THE SUPPLE-MENTARY PRINTOUTS.
I MIGHT FALL ASLEEP AT HOME, SO I'LL WORK ON THEM HERE.
I SEE. THAT'S TOO BAD.
YUYUKA WENT SOMEWHERE. GUESS WE'LL JUST GO HOME.

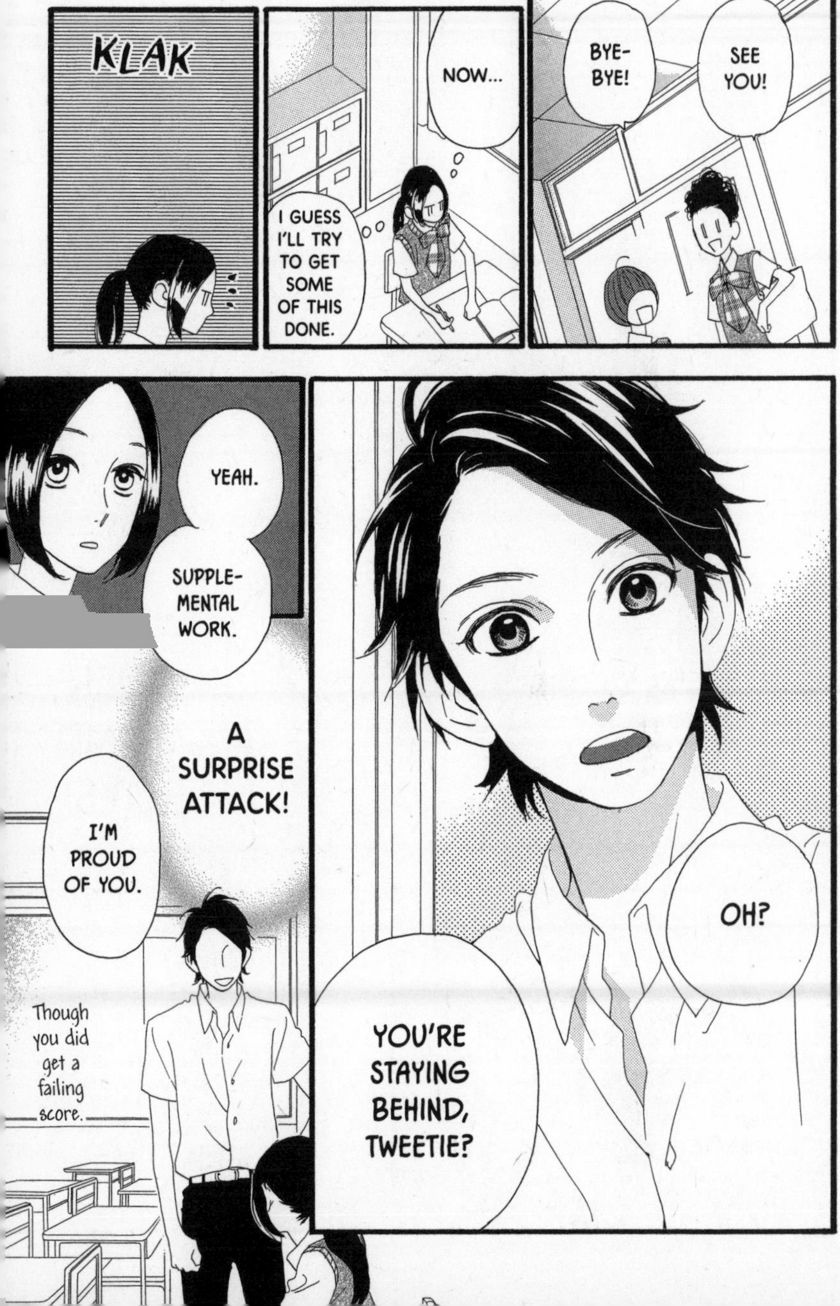
SEE YOU!
BYE-BYE!
NOW...
I GUESS I'LL TRY TO GET SOME OF THIS DONE.
KLAK
OH?
YOU'RE STAYING BEHIND, TWEETIE?
YEAH.
SUPPLE-MENTAL WORK.
A SURPRISE ATTACK!
I'M PROUD OF YOU.
Though you did get a failing score.

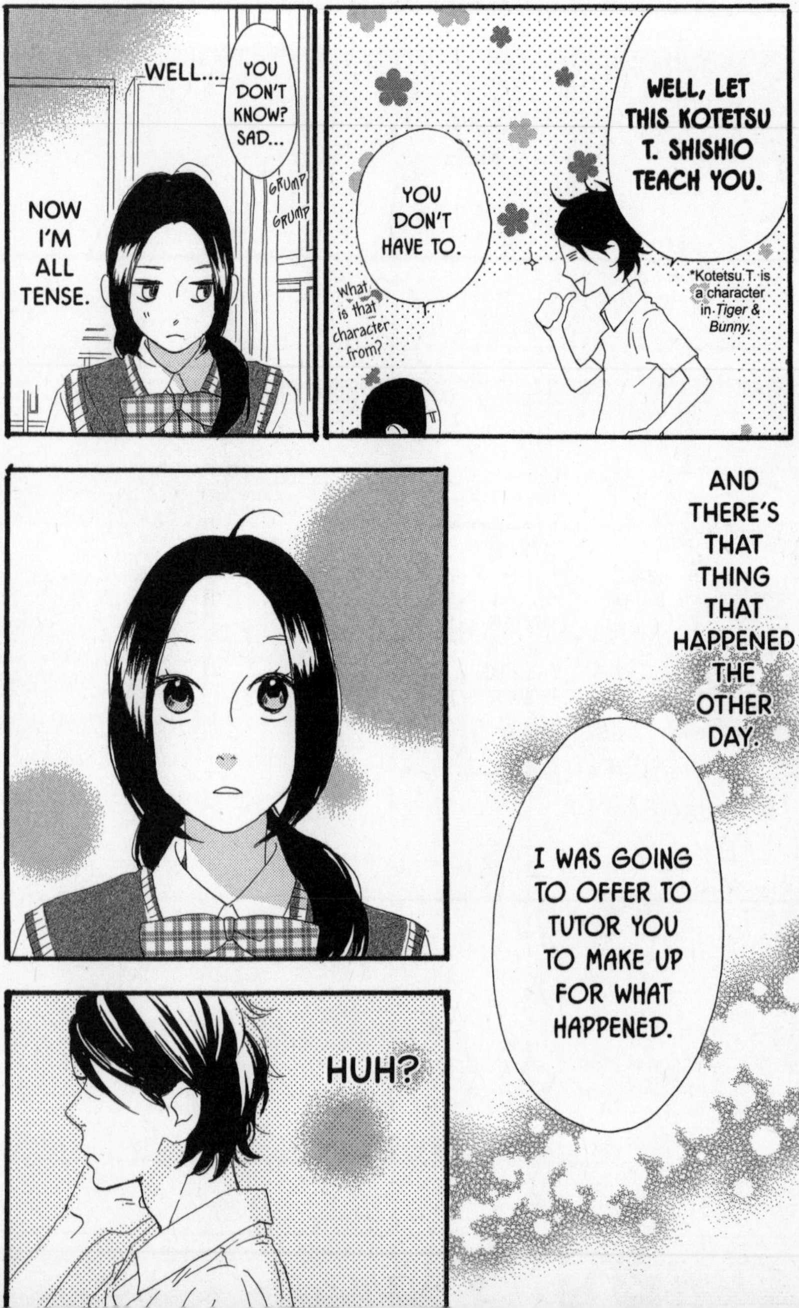
WELL, LET THIS KOTETSU T. SHISHIO TEACH YOU.
*Kotetsu T. is a character in Tiger & Bunny.
YOU DON'T HAVE TO.
What is that character from?
YOU DON'T KNOW? SAD...
GRUMP GRUMP
WELL...
NOW I'M ALL TENSE.
AND THERE'S THAT THING THAT HAPPENED THE OTHER DAY.
I WAS GOING TO OFFER TO TUTOR YOU TO MAKE UP FOR WHAT HAPPENED.
HUH?

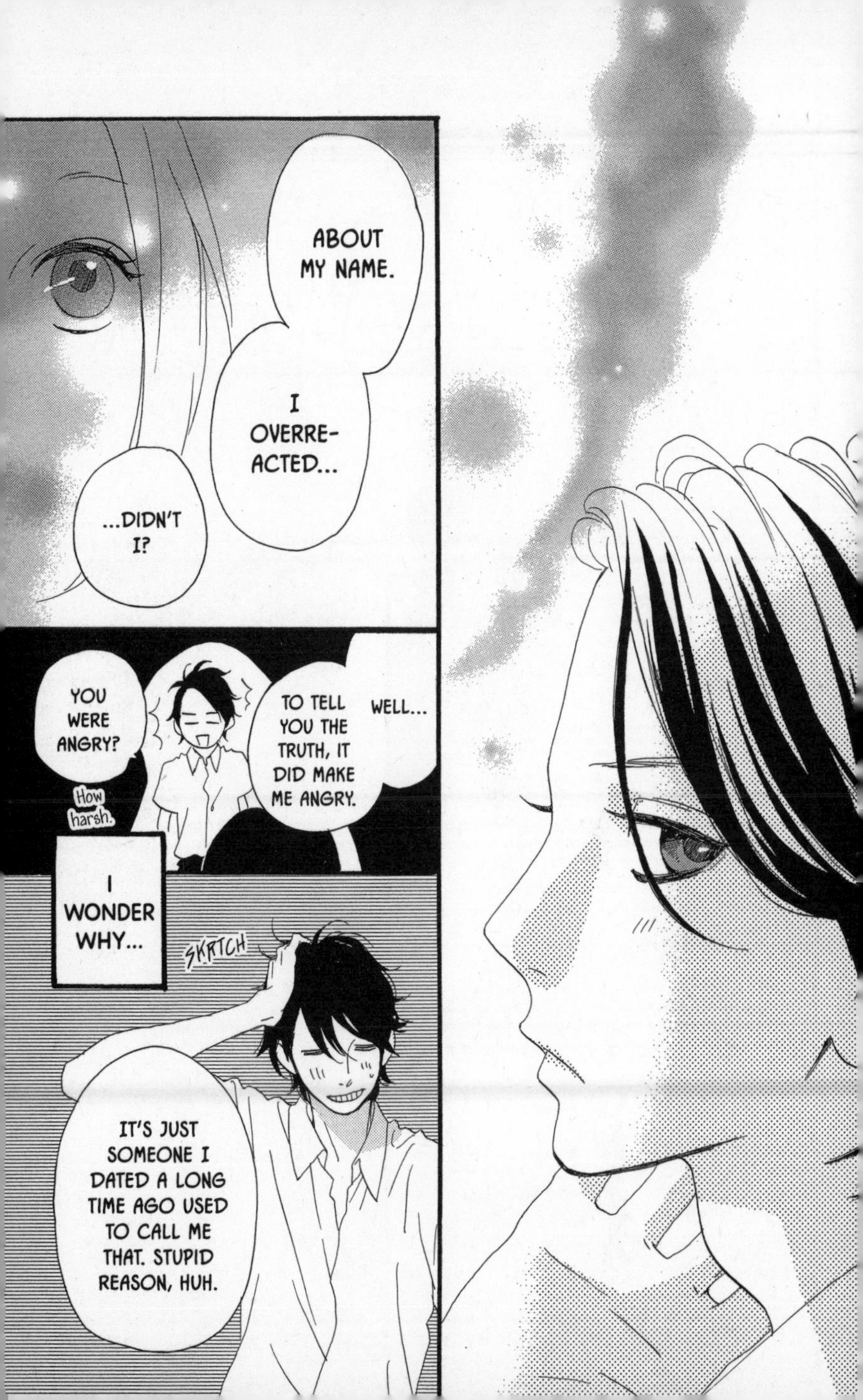
ABOUT MY NAME.
I OVERRE-ACTED...
...DIDN'T I?
WELL...
TO TELL YOU THE TRUTH, IT DID MAKE ME ANGRY.
YOU WERE ANGRY?
How harsh.
I WONDER WHY...
SKRTCH
IT'S JUST SOMEONE I DATED A LONG TIME AGO USED TO CALL ME THAT. STUPID REASON, HUH.

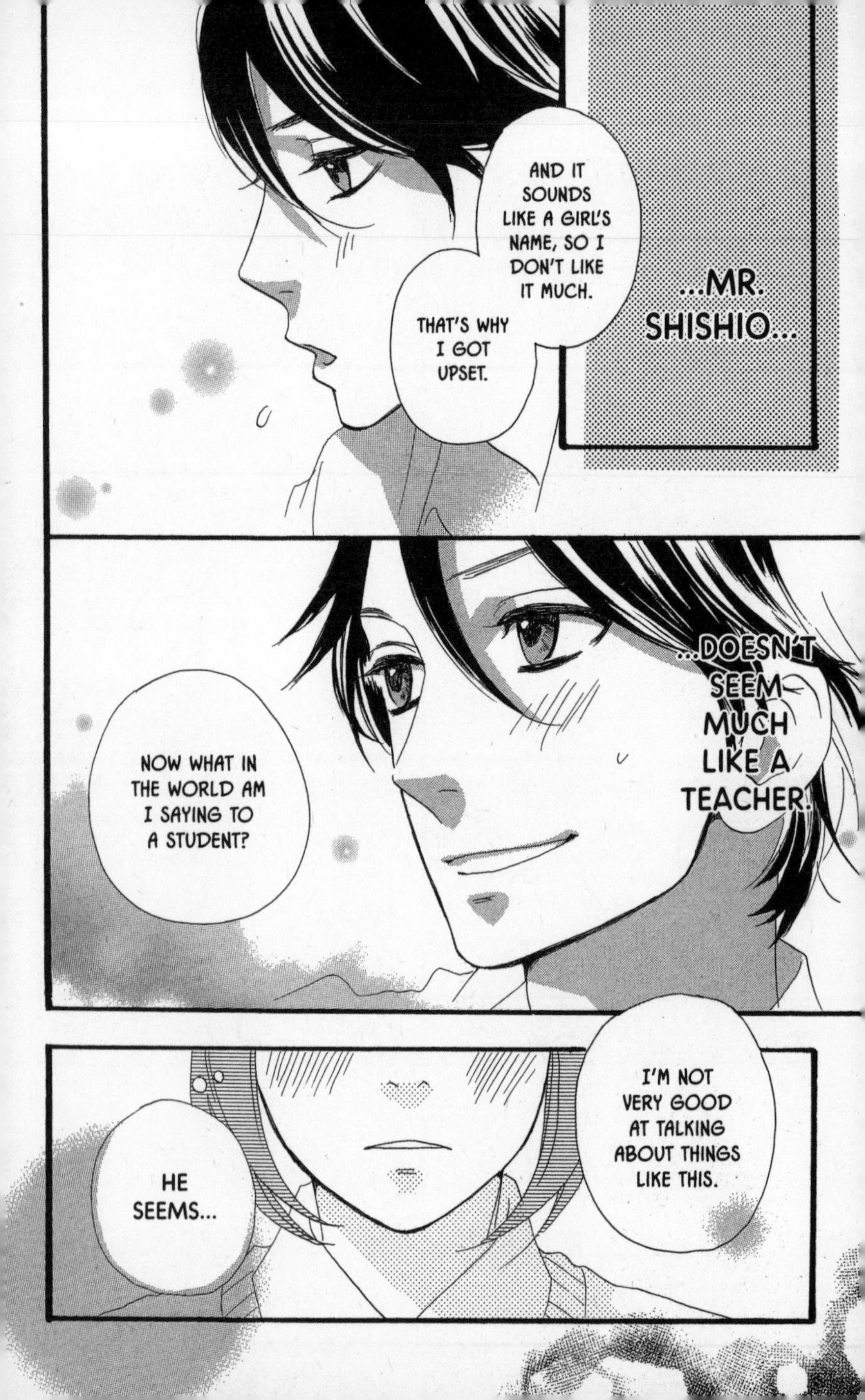
AND IT SOUNDS LIKE A GIRL'S NAME, SO I DON'T LIKE IT MUCH.
THAT'S WHY I GOT UPSET.
...MR. SHISHIO...
...DOESN'T SEEM MUCH LIKE A TEACHER.
NOW WHAT IN THE WORLD AM I SAYING TO A STUDENT?
I'M NOT VERY GOOD AT TALKING ABOUT THINGS LIKE THIS.
HE SEEMS...

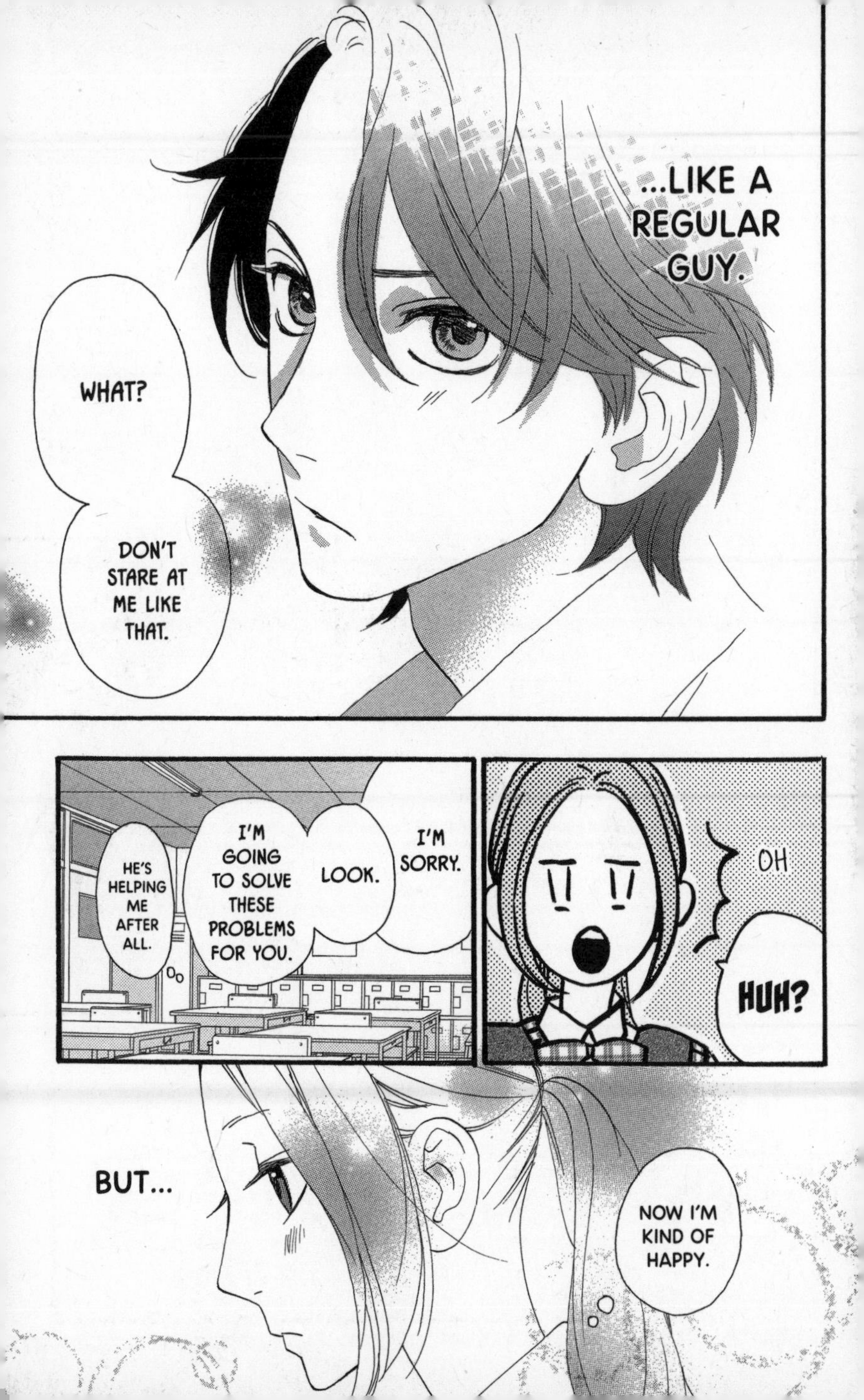
...LIKE A REGULAR GUY.
WHAT?
DON'T STARE AT ME LIKE THAT.
OH
HUH?
I'M SORRY.
LOOK.
I'M GOING TO SOLVE THESE PROBLEMS FOR YOU.
HE'S HELPING ME AFTER ALL.
BUT...
NOW I'M KIND OF HAPPY.

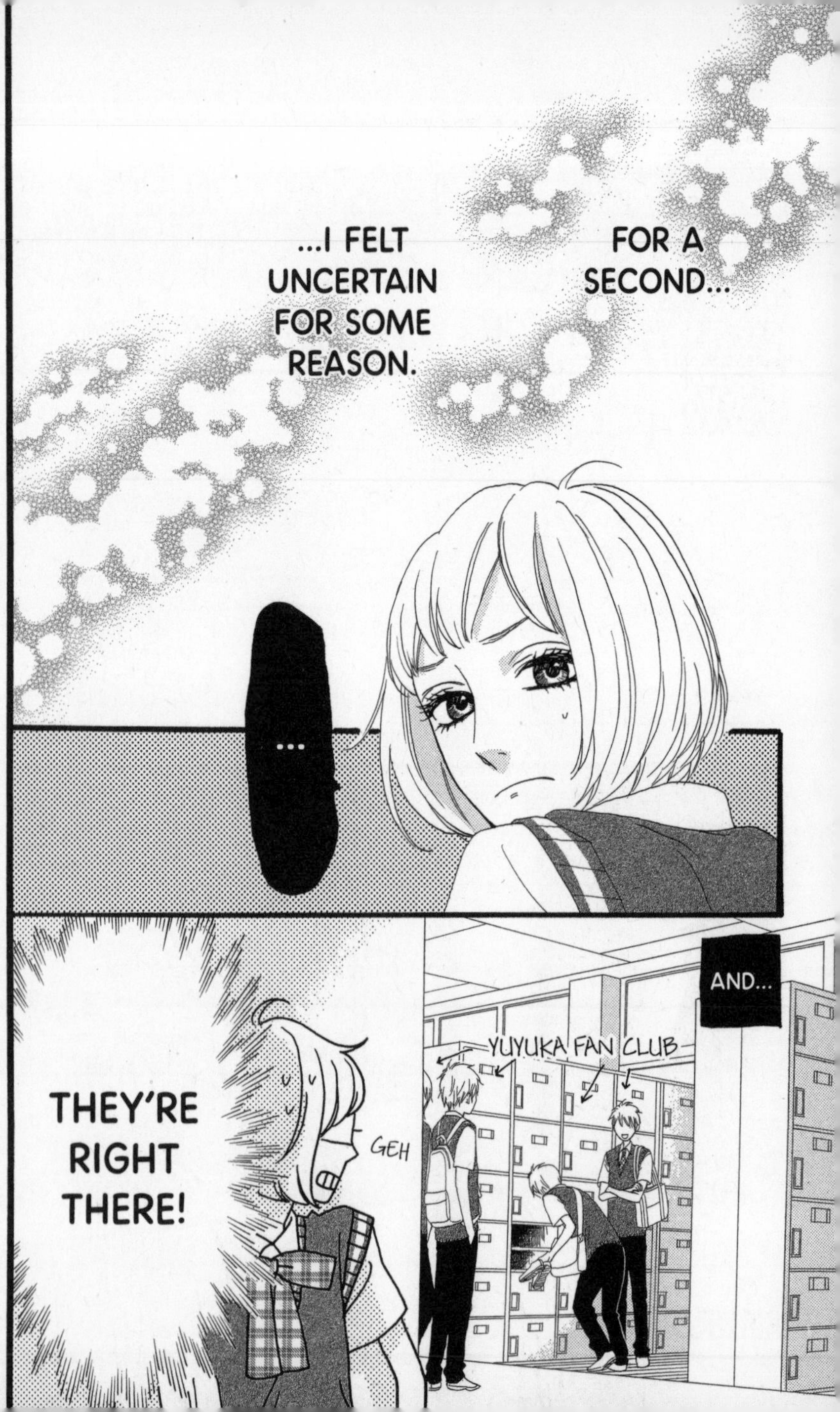
FOR A SECOND...
...I FELT UNCERTAIN FOR SOME REASON.
...
AND...
YUYUKA FAN CLUB
GEH
THEY'RE RIGHT THERE!

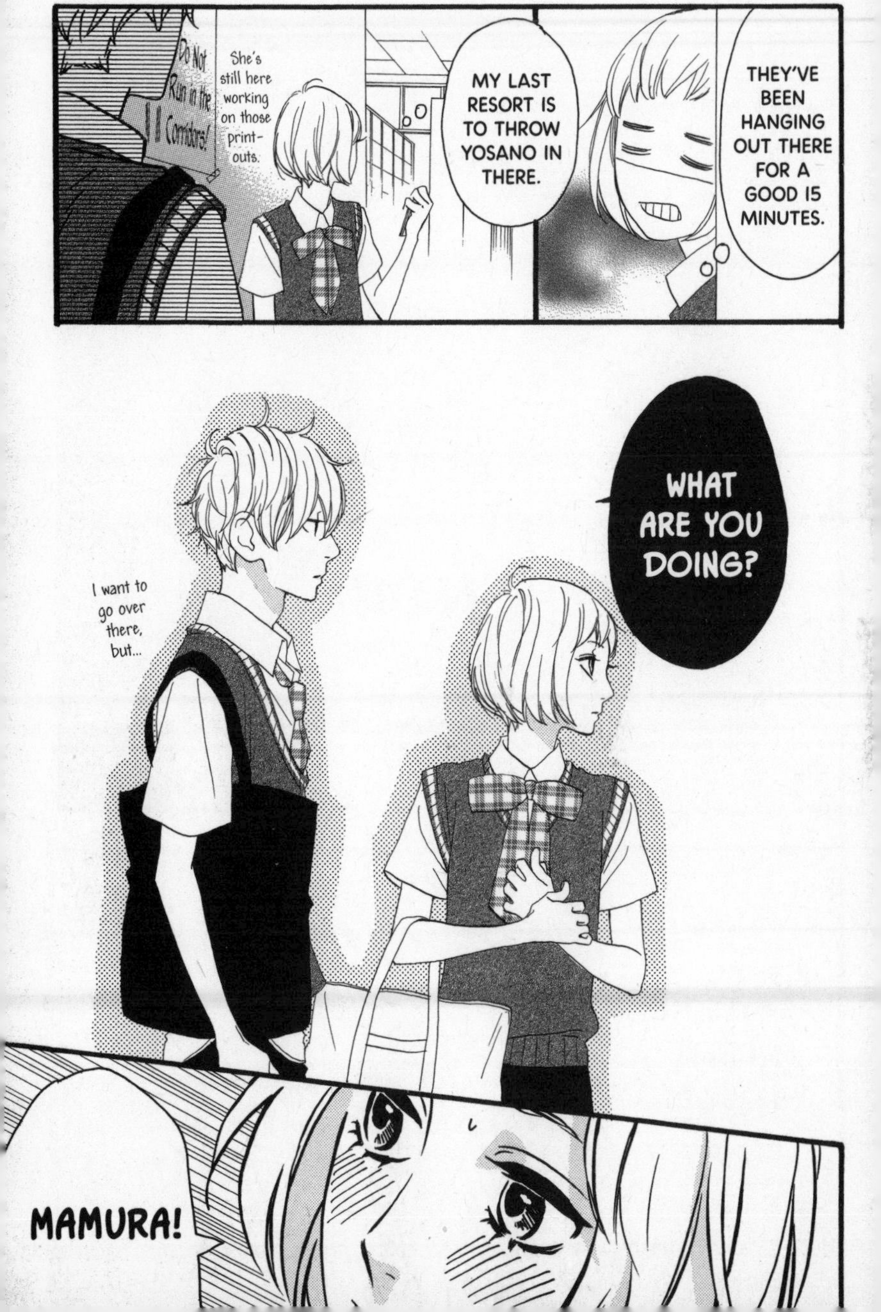
THEY'VE BEEN HANGING OUT THERE FOR A GOOD 15 MINUTES.
MY LAST RESORT IS TO THROW YOSANO IN THERE.
Do Not Run in the Corridors!
She's still here working on those print-outs.
WHAT ARE YOU DOING?
I want to go over there, but...
MAMURA!

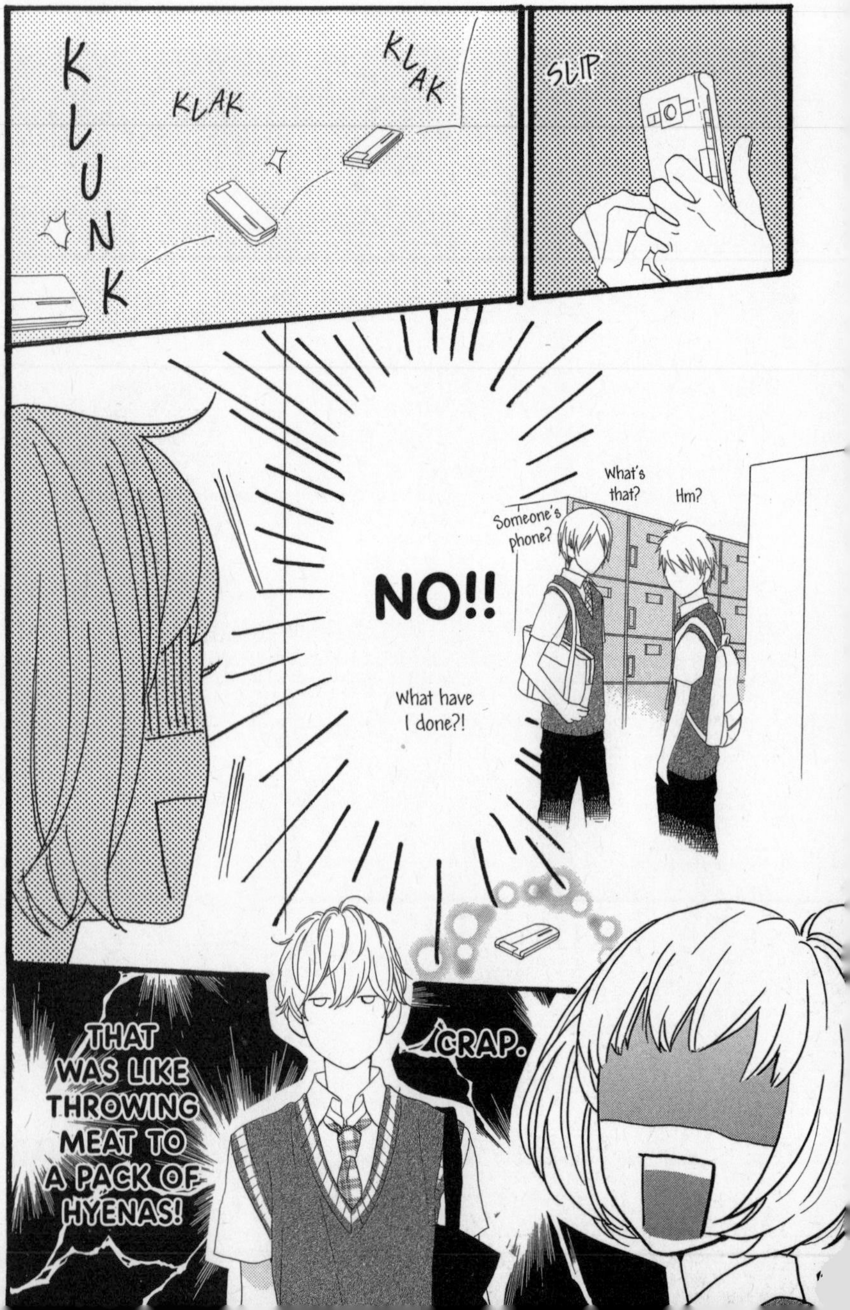
SLIP
KLAK
KLAK
KLUNK
Hm?
What's that?
Someone's phone?
NO!!
What have I done?!
CRAP.
THAT WAS LIKE THROWING MEAT TO A PACK OF HYENAS!

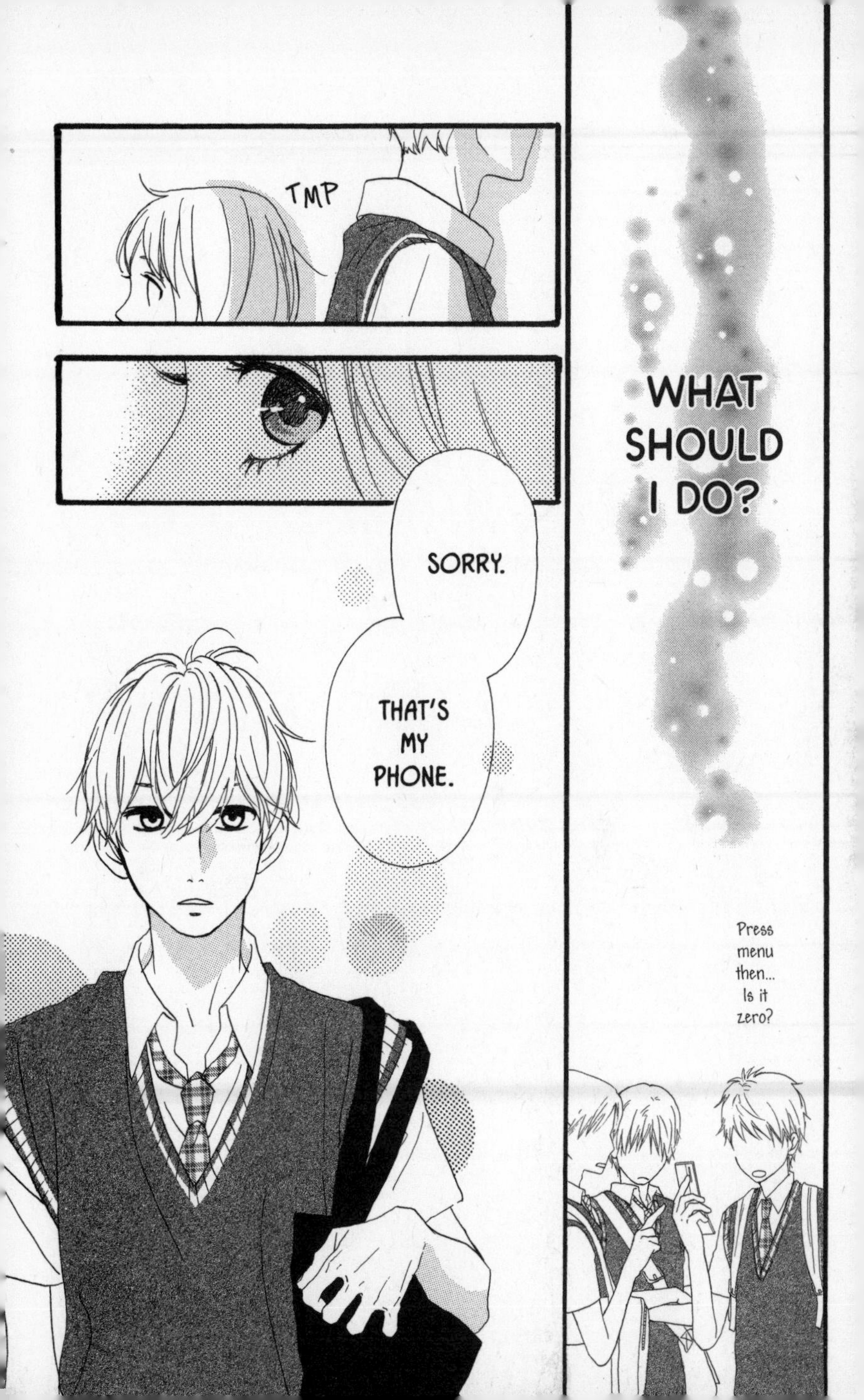
WHAT SHOULD I DO?
Press menu then... Is it zero?
TMP
SORRY.
THAT'S MY PHONE.

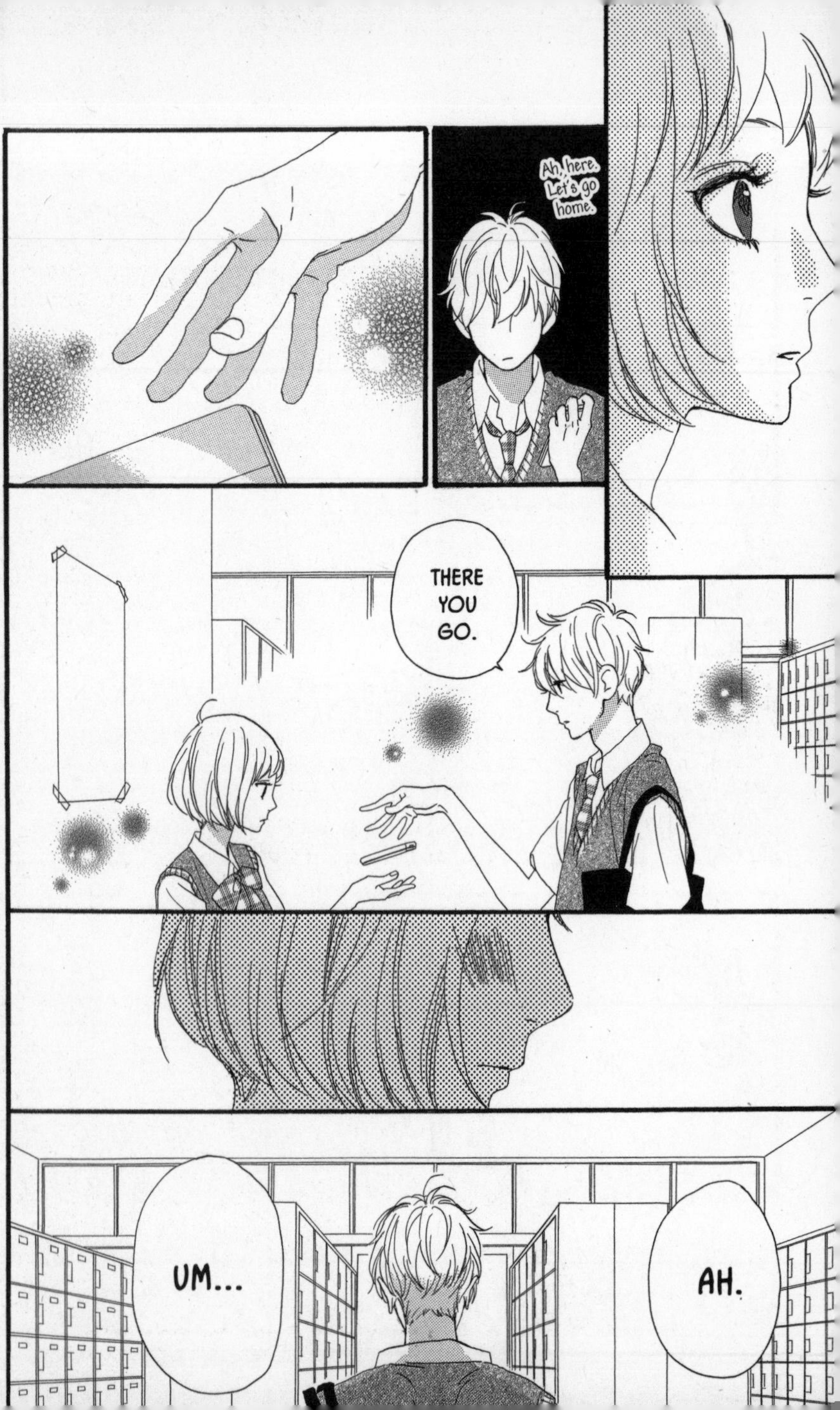
Ah, here. Let's go home.
THERE YOU GO.
AH.
UM...

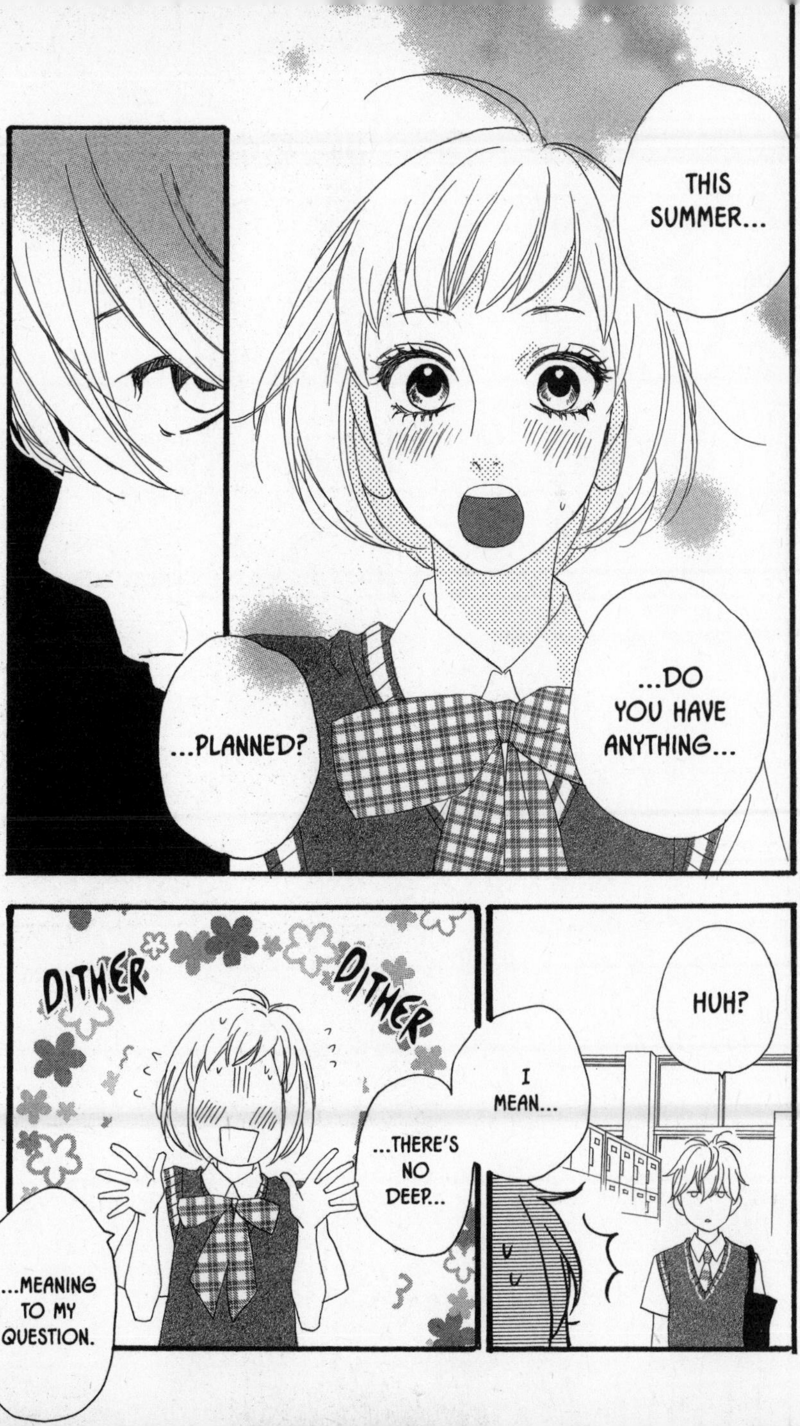
THIS SUMMER...
...DO YOU HAVE ANYTHING...
...PLANNED?
HUH?
DITHER
DITHER
I MEAN...
...THERE'S NO DEEP...
...MEANING TO MY QUESTION.

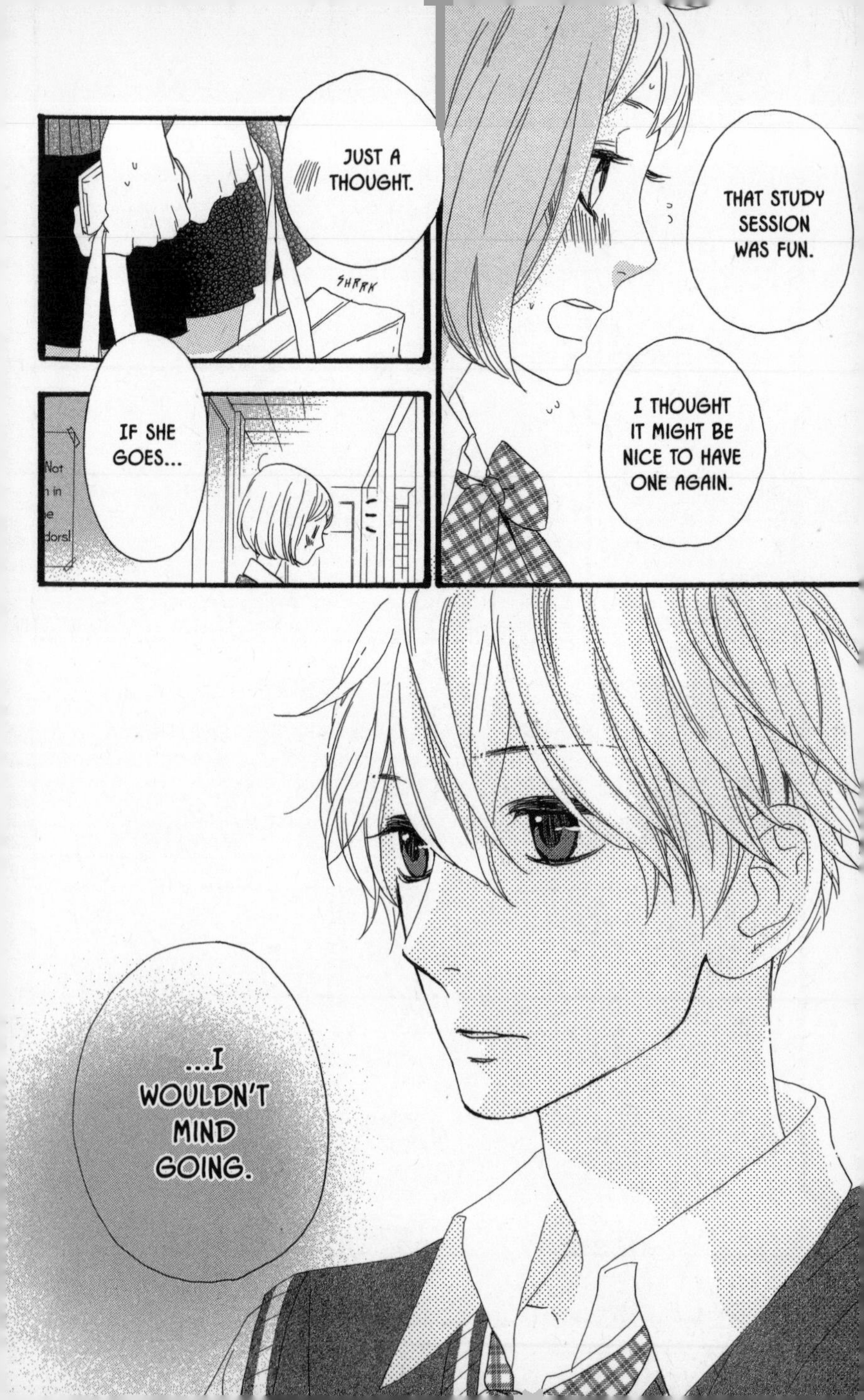
THAT STUDY SESSION WAS FUN.
I THOUGHT IT MIGHT BE NICE TO HAVE ONE AGAIN.
JUST A THOUGHT.
SHRRK
IF SHE GOES...
...I WOULDN'T MIND GOING.

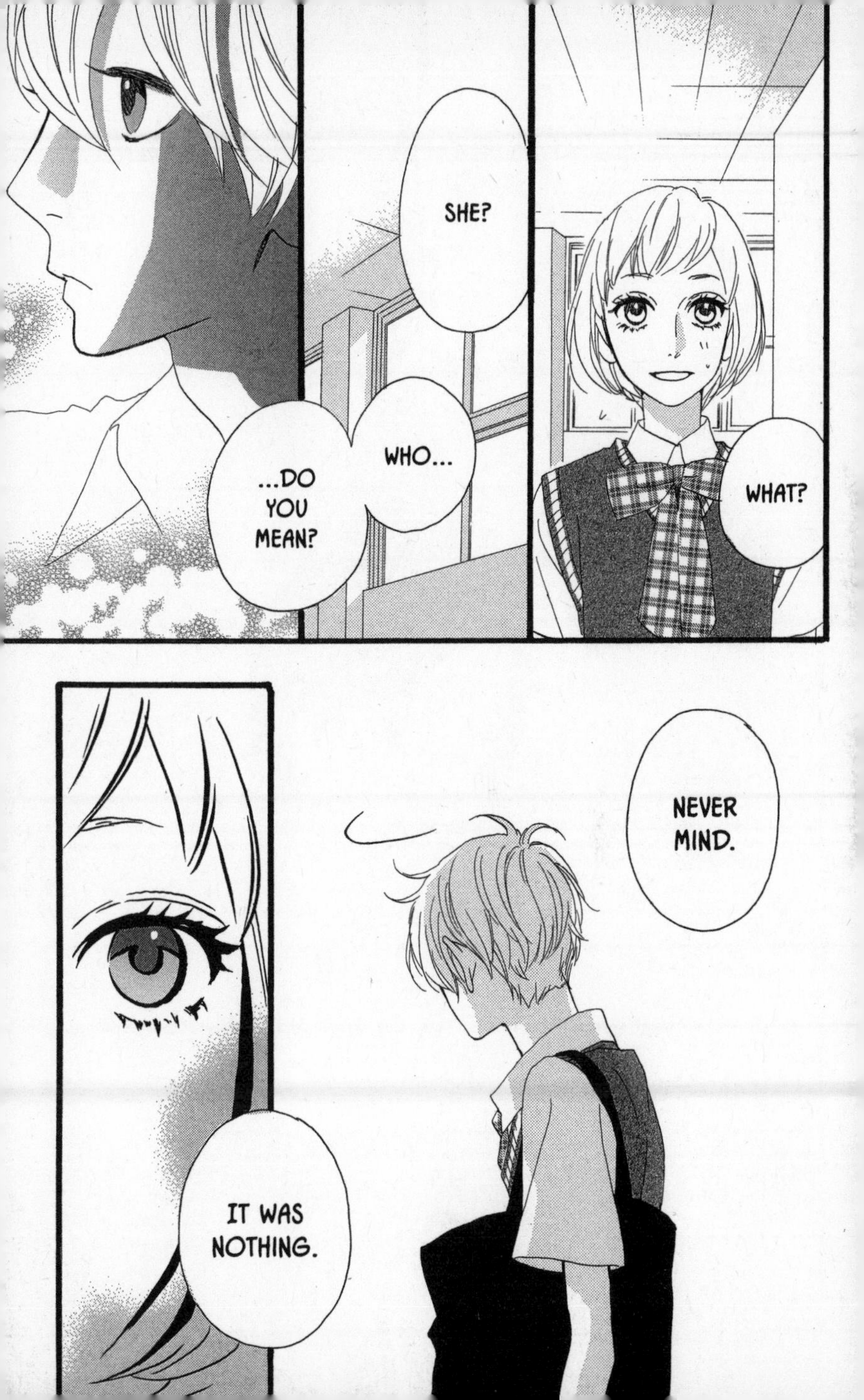
WHAT?
SHE?
WHO...
...DO YOU MEAN?
NEVER MIND.
IT WAS NOTHING.

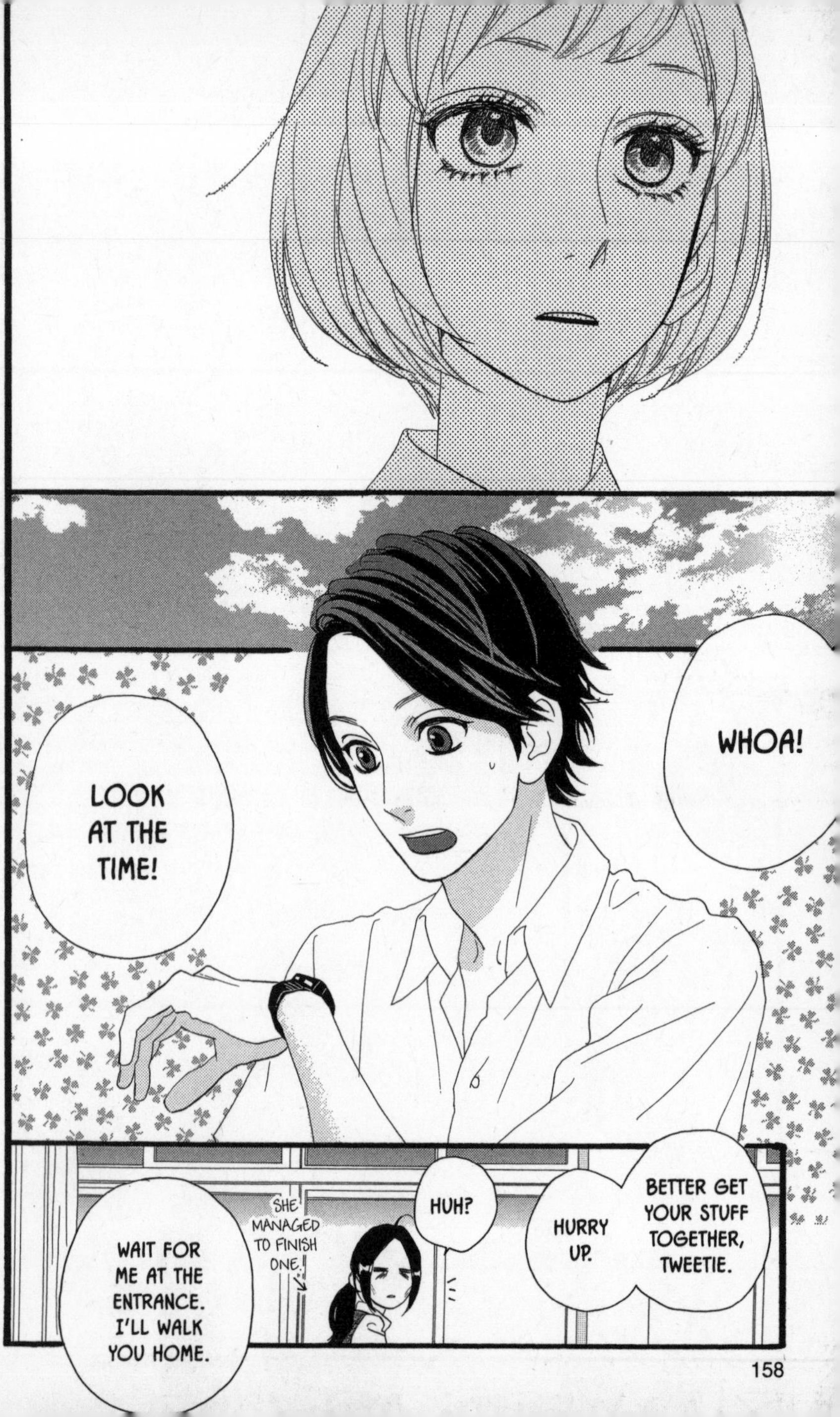
WHOA!
LOOK AT THE TIME!
BETTER GET YOUR STUFF TOGETHER, TWEETIE.
HURRY UP.
HUH?
SHE MANAGED TO FINISH ONE.
WAIT FOR ME AT THE ENTRANCE. I'LL WALK YOU HOME.

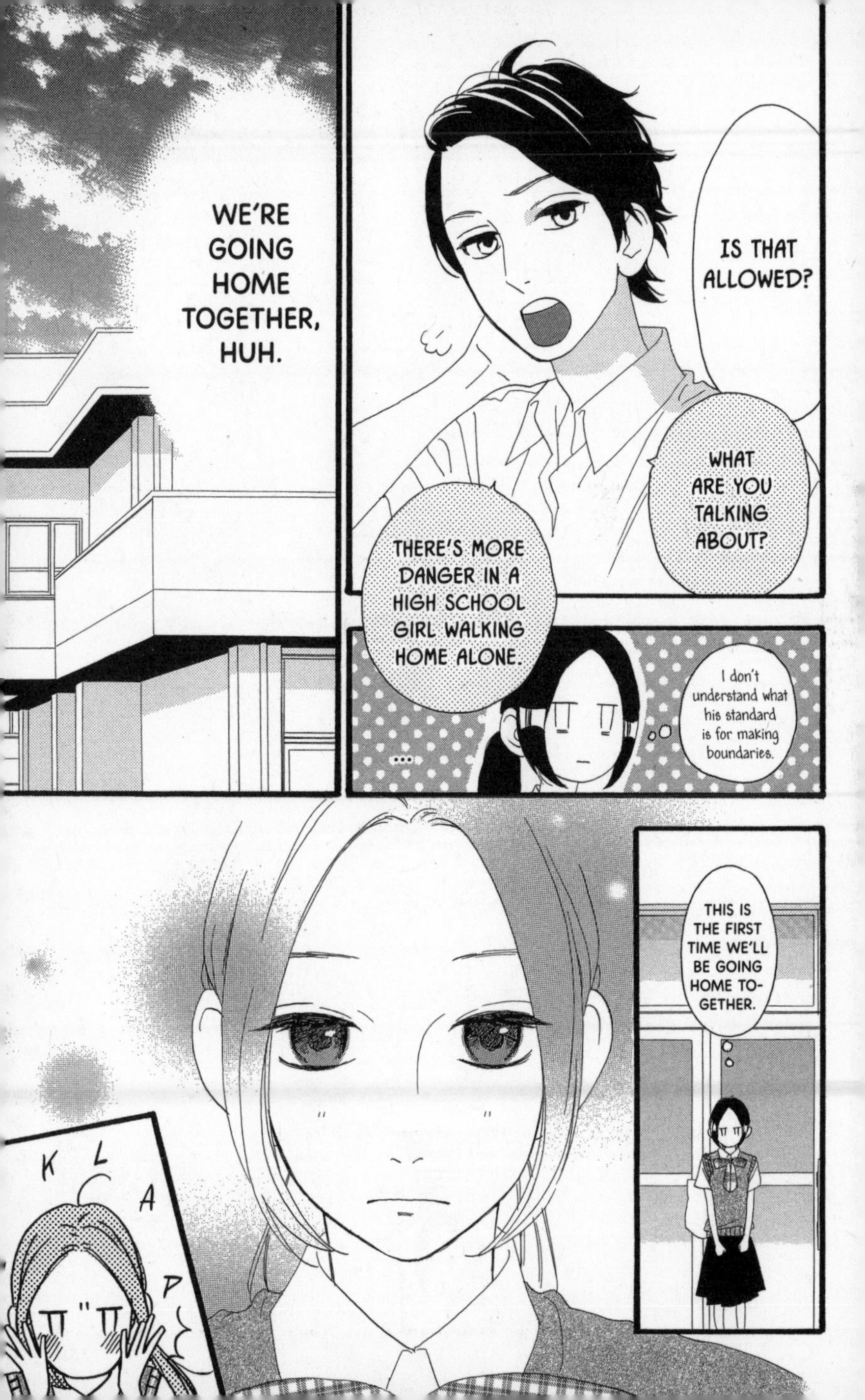

IS THAT ALLOWED?
WHAT ARE YOU TALKING ABOUT?
THERE'S MORE DANGER IN A HIGH SCHOOL GIRL WALKING HOME ALONE.
...
I don't understand what his standard is for making boundaries.
WE'RE GOING HOME TOGETHER, HUH.
THIS IS THE FIRST TIME WE'LL BE GOING HOME TO-GETHER.
KLAP

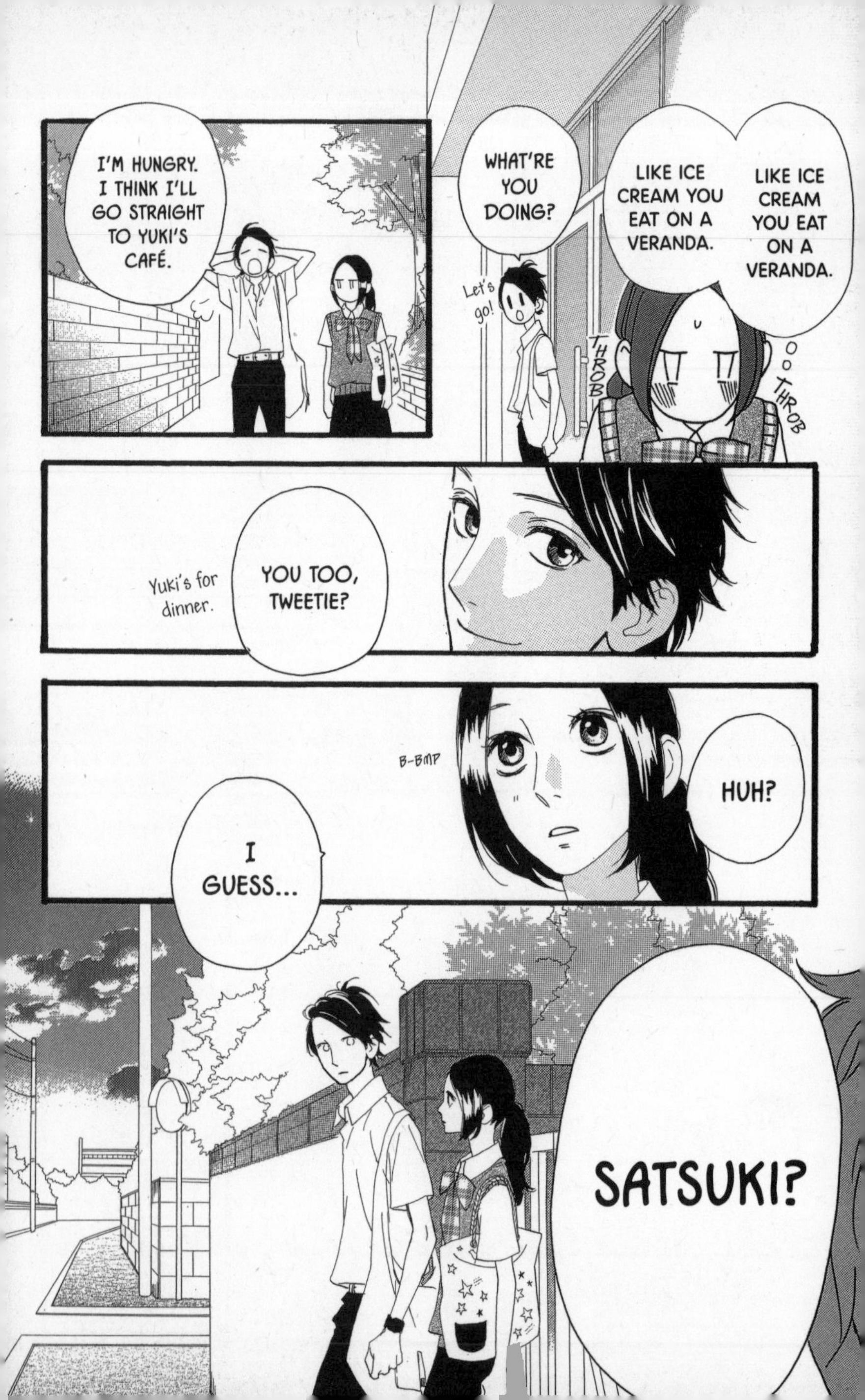
LIKE ICE CREAM YOU EAT ON A VERANDA.
LIKE ICE CREAM YOU EAT ON A VERANDA.
THROB
THROB
WHAT'RE YOU DOING?
Let's go!
I'M HUNGRY. I THINK I'LL GO STRAIGHT TO YUKI'S CAFÉ.
YOU TOO, TWEETIE?
Yuki's for dinner.
HUH?
B-BMP
I GUESS...
SATSUKI?

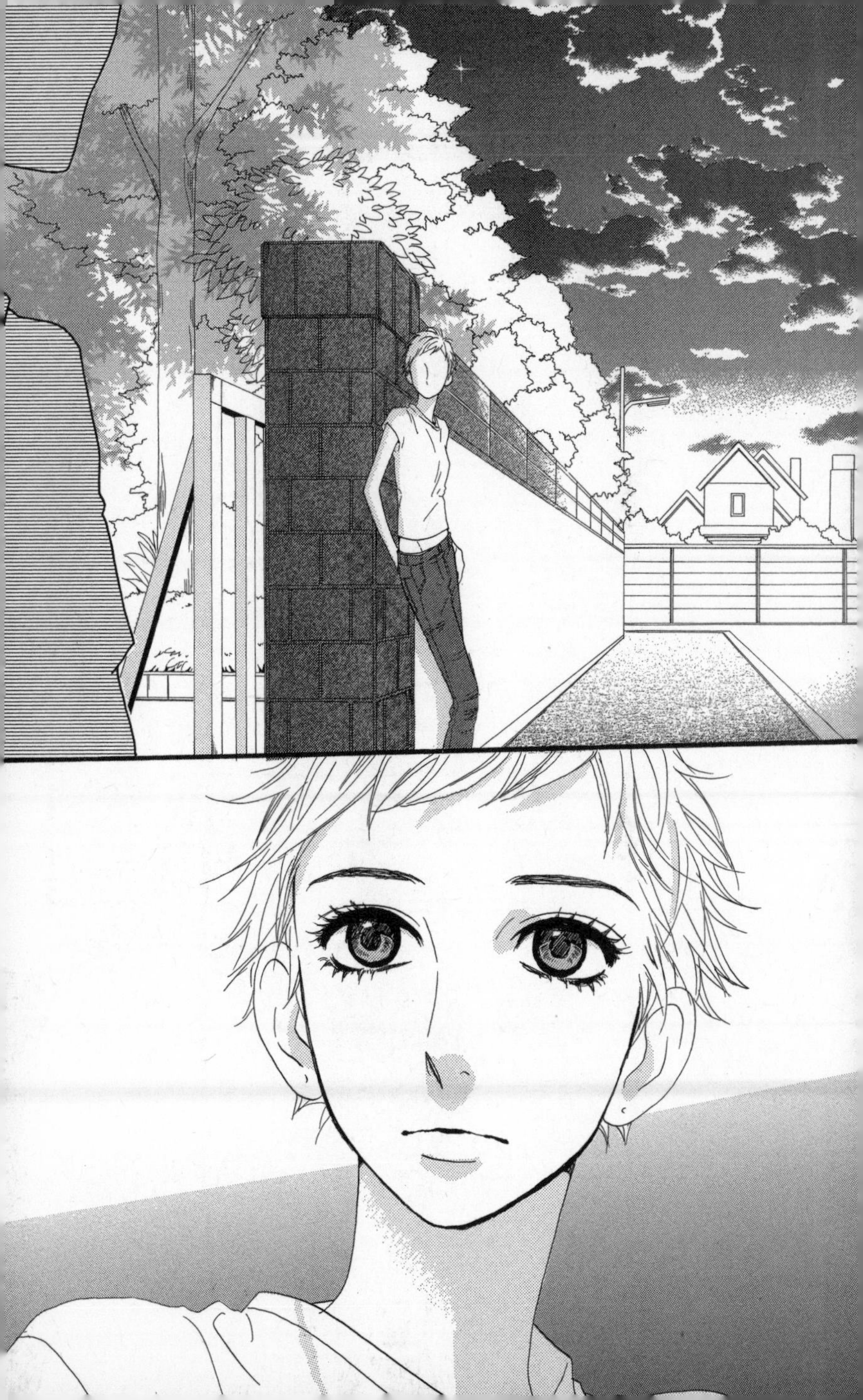

Go! Go! Yukichi!

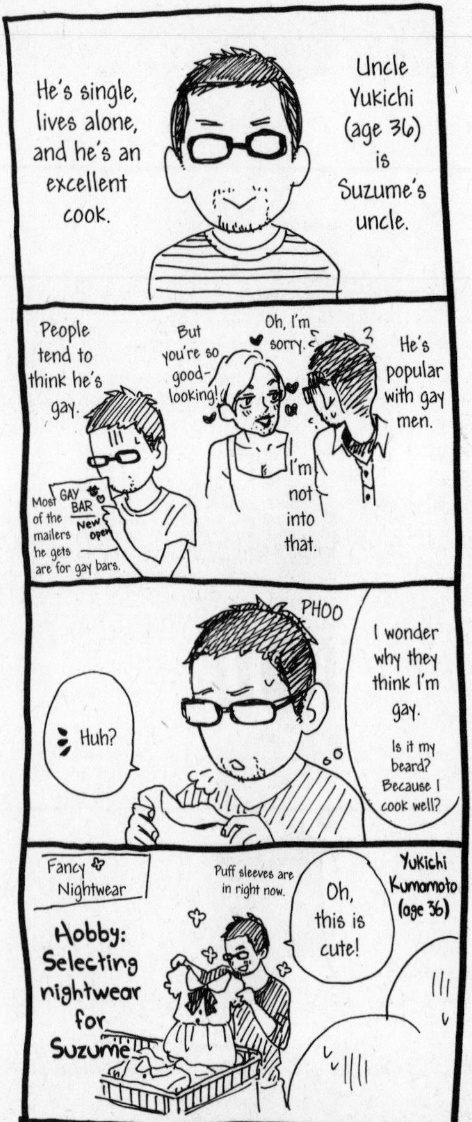
Uncle Yukichi (age 36) is Suzume's uncle.
He's single, lives alone, and he's an excellent cook.
He's popular with gay men.
Oh, I'm sorry.
But you're so good-looking!
I'm not into that.
People tend to think he's gay.
GAY BAR
New
Most of the mailers he gets are for gay bars.
PHOO
I wonder why they think I'm gay.
Is it my beard? Because I cook well?
Huh?
Yukichi Kumamoto (age 36)
Oh, this is cute!
Puff sleeves are in right now.
Fancy Nightwear
Hobby: Selecting nightwear for Suzume

The End

Created by Yukie Noborio
Drawn by Mika Yamamori

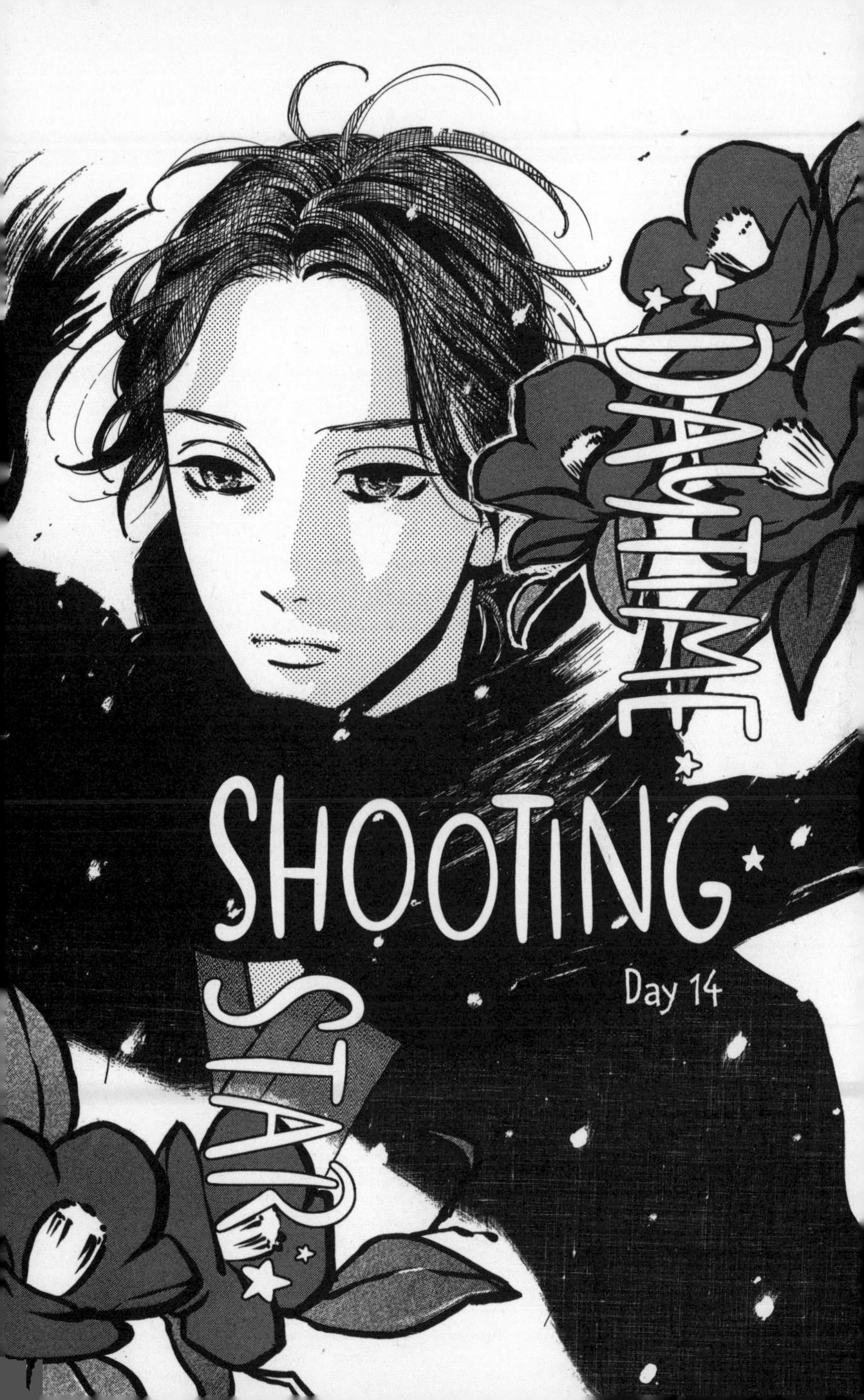
DAYTIME
SHOOTING
STAR
Day 14

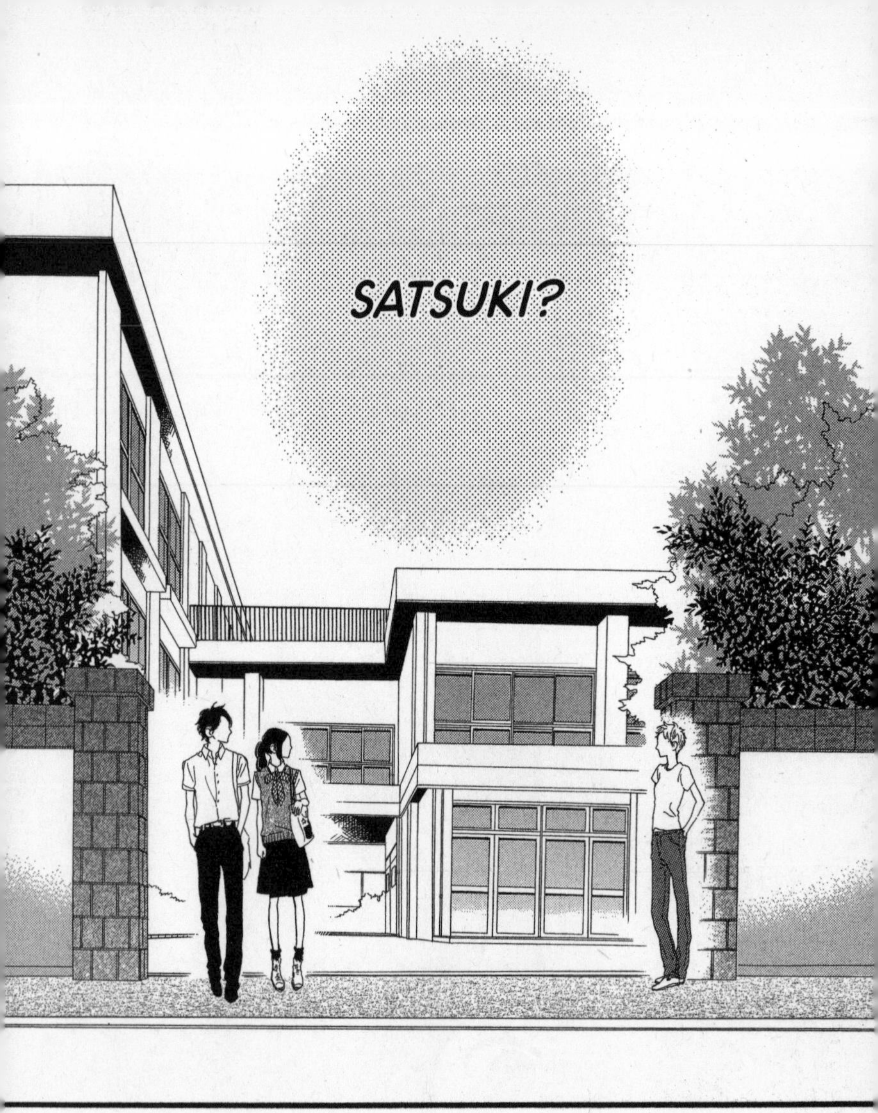
SATSUKI?

And so, did you enjoy this story? It would please me if you enjoyed it even a little.

Until we meet again in volume 3! ♪

Mika

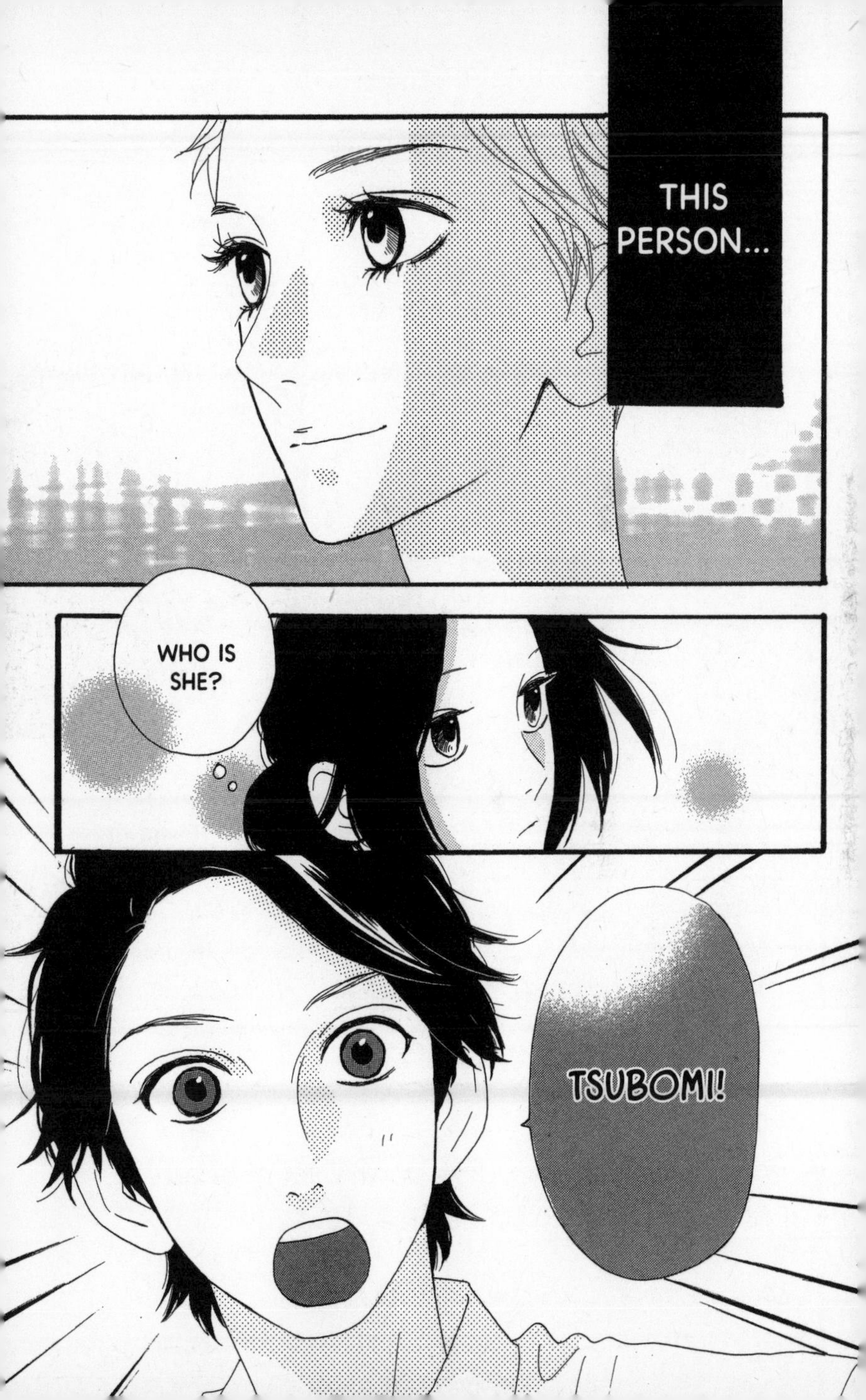
THIS PERSON...
WHO IS SHE?
TSUBOMI!

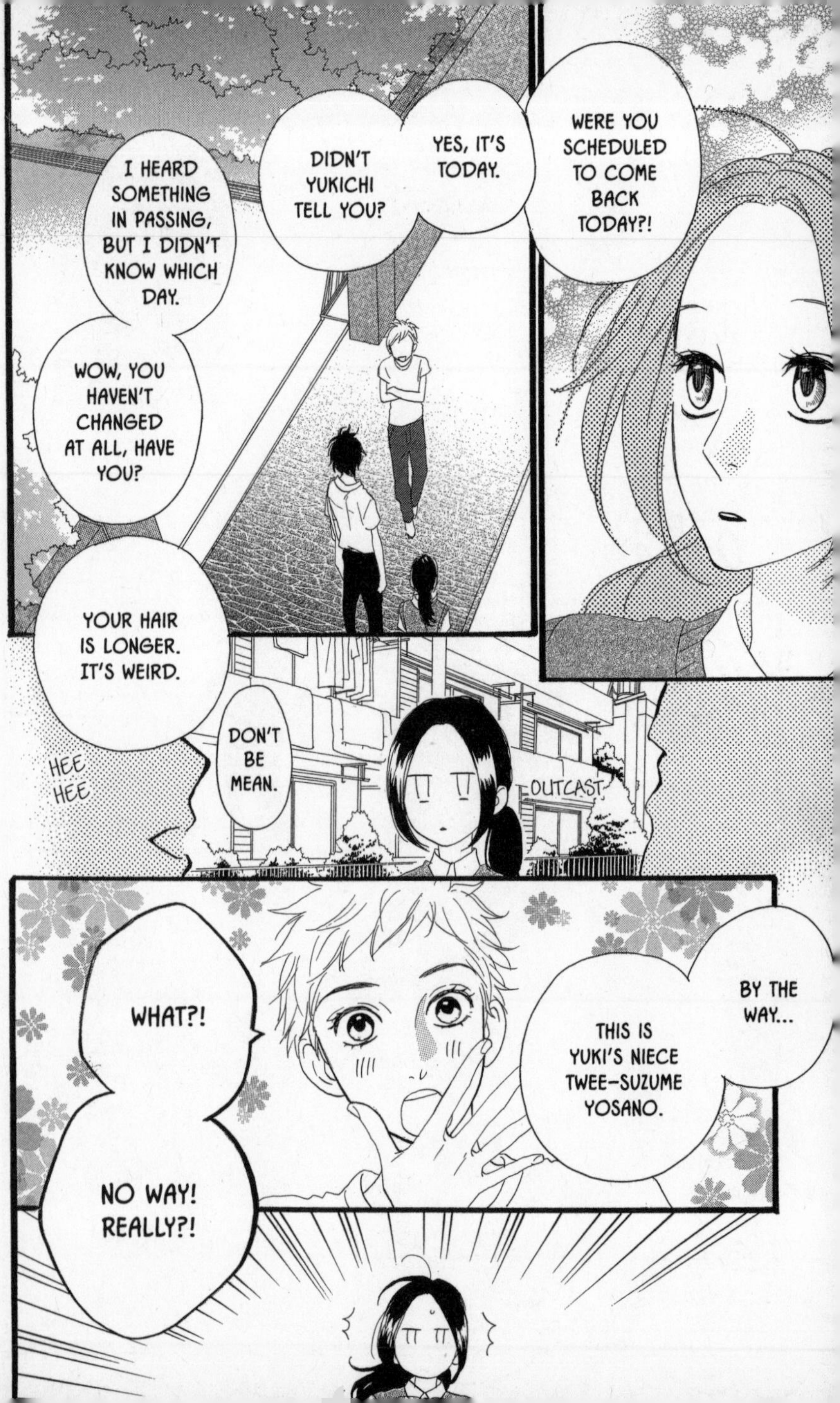
WERE YOU SCHEDULED TO COME BACK TODAY?!
YES, IT'S TODAY.
DIDN'T YUKICHI TELL YOU?
I HEARD SOMETHING IN PASSING, BUT I DIDN'T KNOW WHICH DAY.
WOW, YOU HAVEN'T CHANGED AT ALL, HAVE YOU?
YOUR HAIR IS LONGER. IT'S WEIRD.
OUTCAST
DON'T BE MEAN.
HEE HEE
BY THE WAY...
THIS IS YUKI'S NIECE TWEE-SUZUME YOSANO.
WHAT?!
NO WAY! REALLY?!

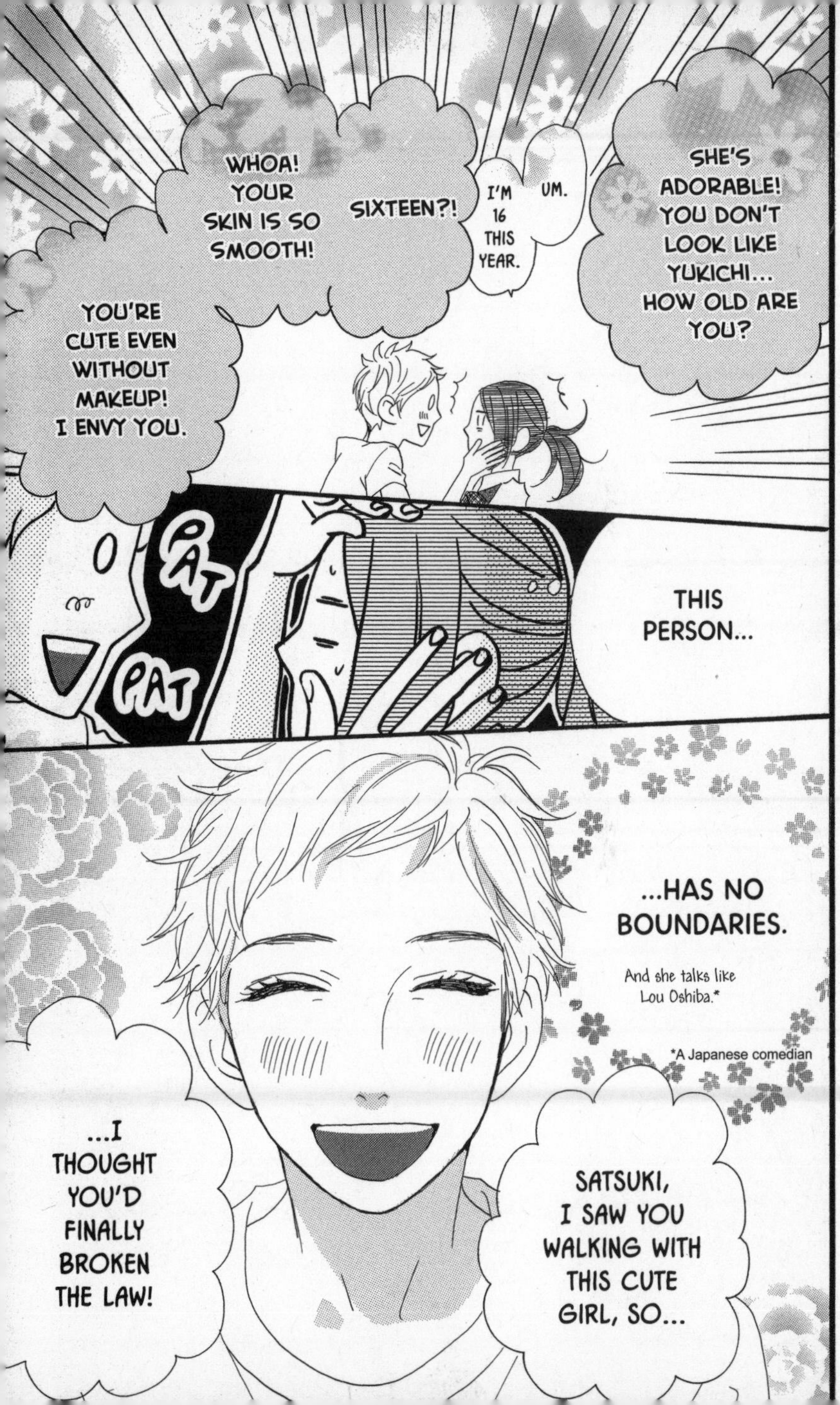
SHE'S ADORABLE! YOU DON'T LOOK LIKE YUKICHI... HOW OLD ARE YOU?
UM.
I'M 16 THIS YEAR.
SIXTEEN?!
WHOA! YOUR SKIN IS SO SMOOTH!
YOU'RE CUTE EVEN WITHOUT MAKEUP! I ENVY YOU.
THIS PERSON...
PAT
PAT
...HAS NO BOUNDARIES.
And she talks like Lou Oshiba.*
SATSUKI, I SAW YOU WALKING WITH THIS CUTE GIRL, SO...
...I THOUGHT YOU'D FINALLY BROKEN THE LAW!
*A Japanese comedian

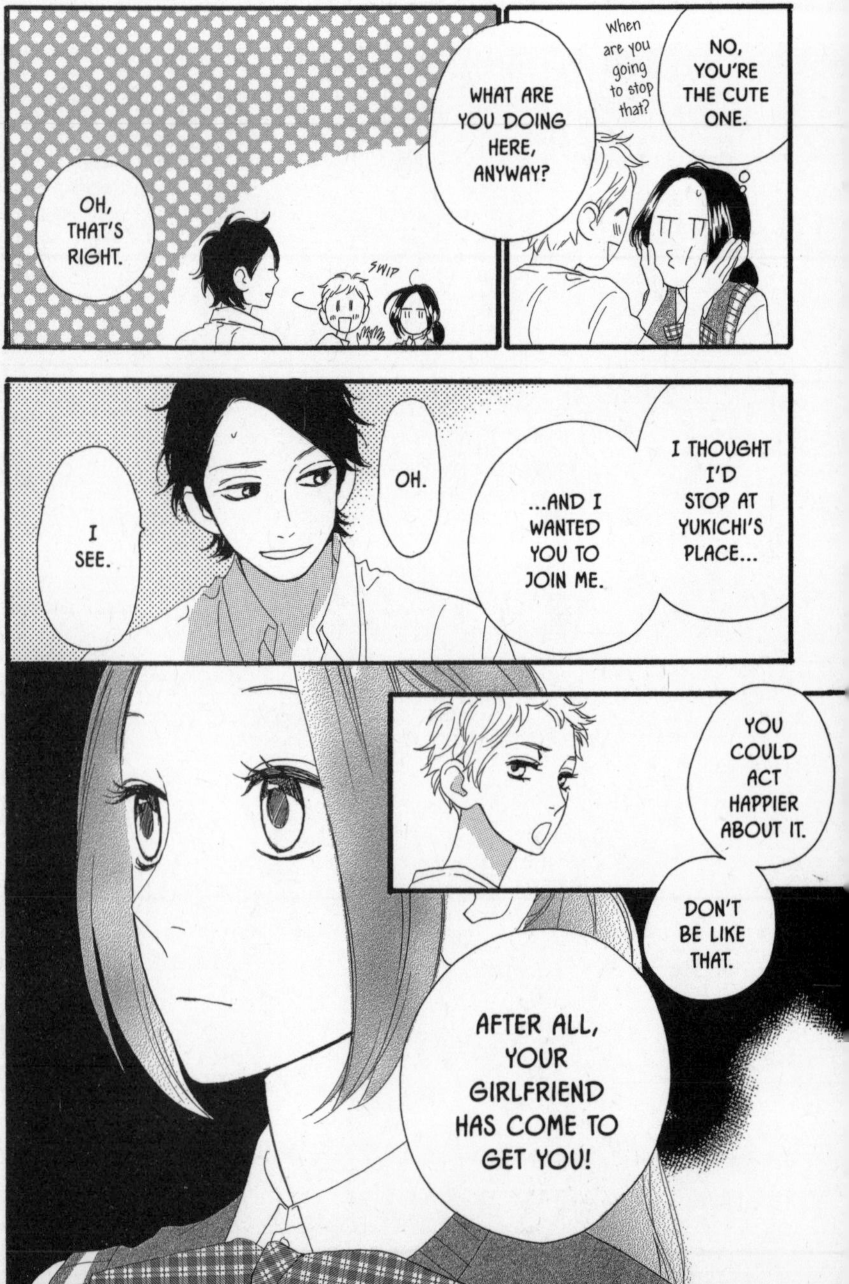
NO, YOU'RE THE CUTE ONE.
When are you going to stop that?
WHAT ARE YOU DOING HERE, ANYWAY?
OH, THAT'S RIGHT.
SWIP
I THOUGHT I'D STOP AT YUKICHI'S PLACE...
...AND I WANTED YOU TO JOIN ME.
OH.
I SEE.
YOU COULD ACT HAPPIER ABOUT IT.
DON'T BE LIKE THAT.
AFTER ALL, YOUR GIRLFRIEND HAS COME TO GET YOU!

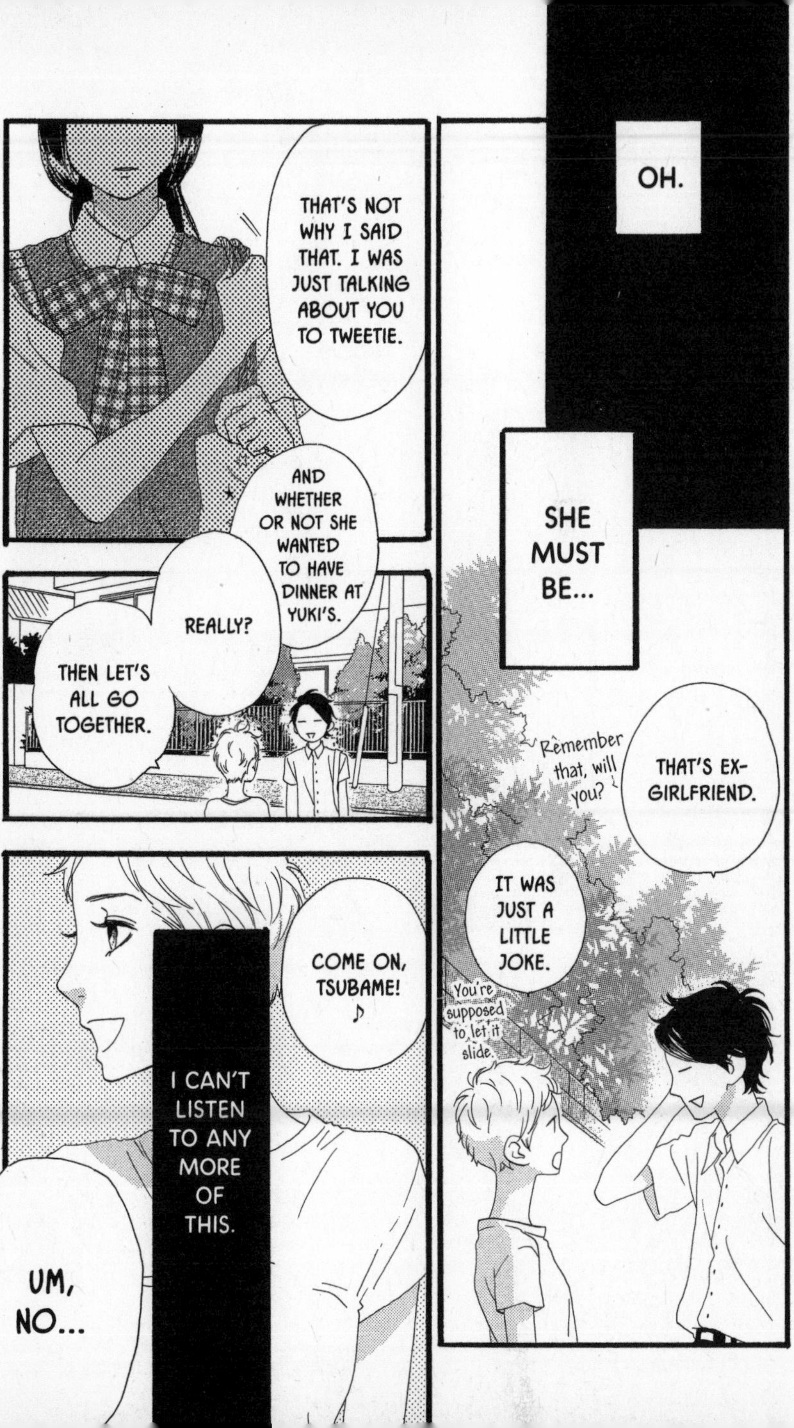
OH.
SHE MUST BE...
THAT'S EX-GIRLFRIEND.
Remember that, will you?
IT WAS JUST A LITTLE JOKE.
You're supposed to let it slide.
THAT'S NOT WHY I SAID THAT. I WAS JUST TALKING ABOUT YOU TO TWEETIE.
AND WHETHER OR NOT SHE WANTED TO HAVE DINNER AT YUKI'S.
REALLY?
THEN LET'S ALL GO TOGETHER.
COME ON, TSUBAME! ♪
I CAN'T LISTEN TO ANY MORE OF THIS.
UM, NO...

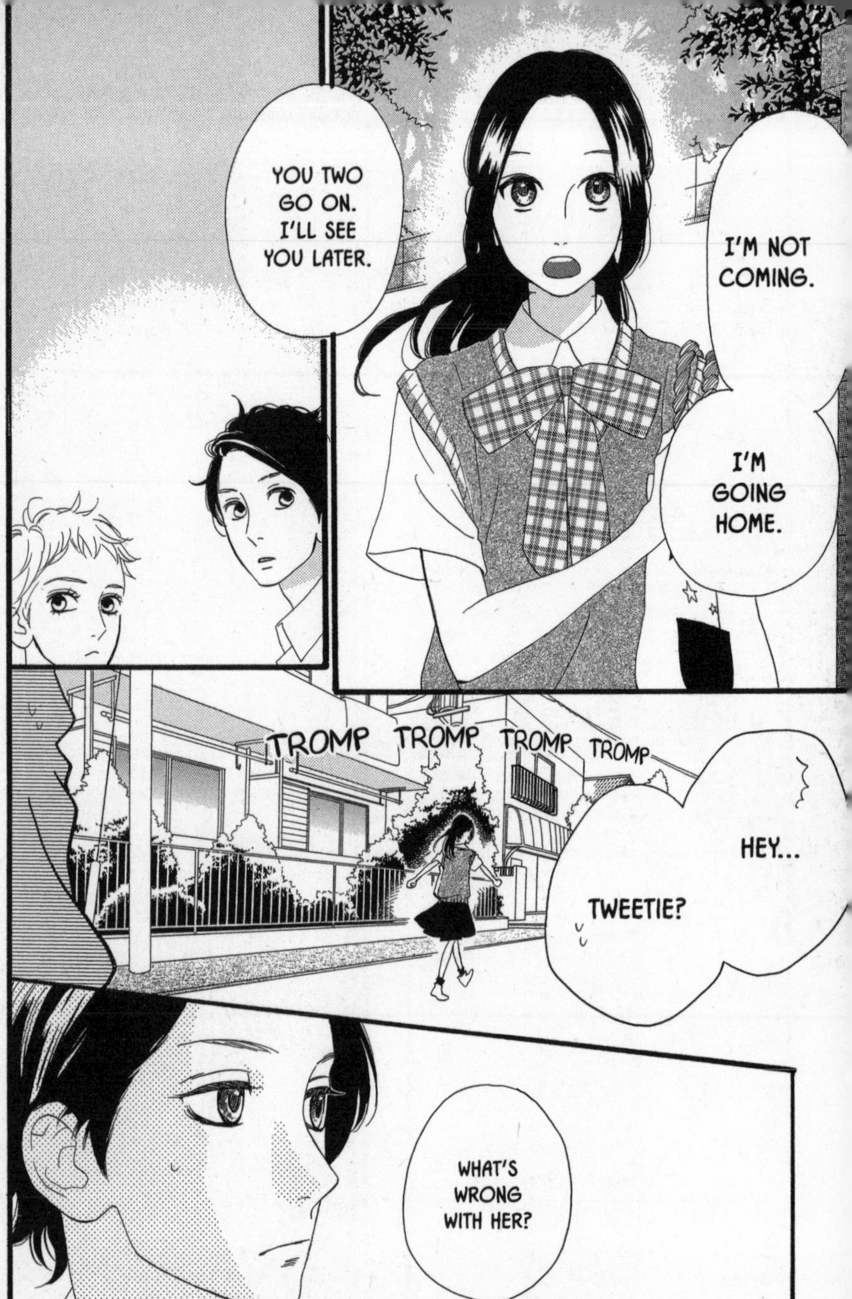
I'M NOT COMING.
YOU TWO GO ON. I'LL SEE YOU LATER.
I'M GOING HOME.
TROMP TROMP TROMP TROMP
HEY... TWEETIE?
WHAT'S WRONG WITH HER?

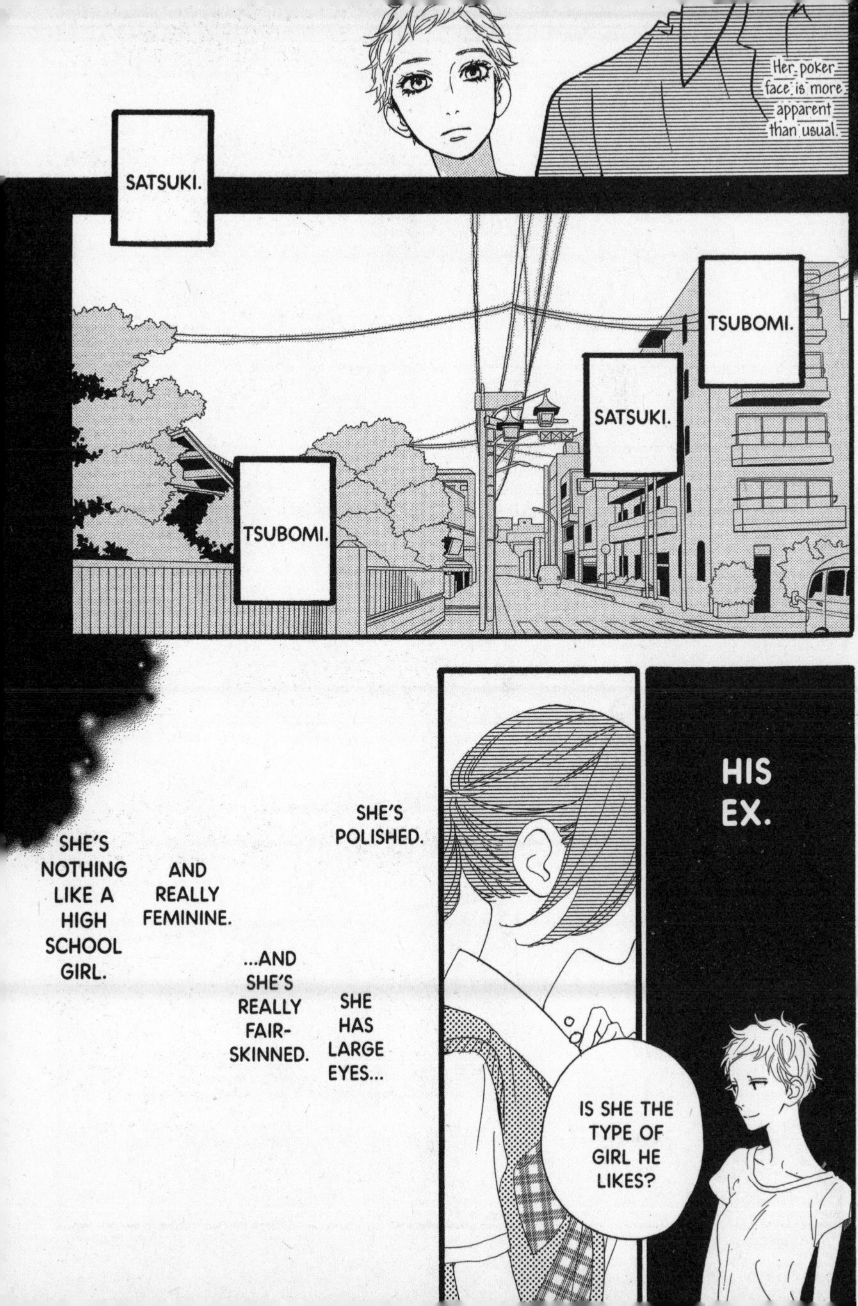
Her poker face is more apparent than usual.
SATSUKI.
TSUBOMI.
SATSUKI.
TSUBOMI.
HIS EX.
IS SHE THE TYPE OF GIRL HE LIKES?
SHE'S POLISHED.
SHE HAS LARGE EYES...
...AND SHE'S REALLY FAIR-SKINNED.
AND REALLY FEMININE.
SHE'S NOTHING LIKE A HIGH SCHOOL GIRL.

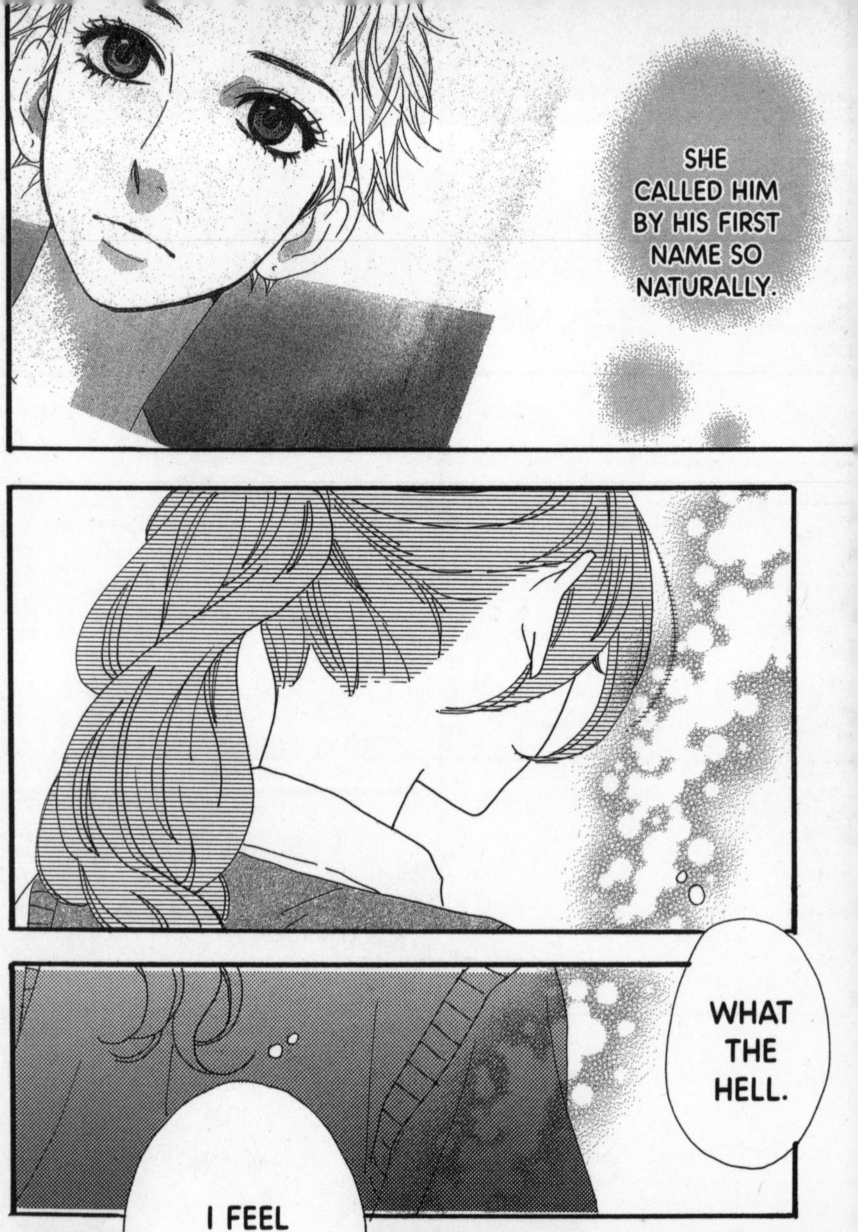
SHE CALLED HIM BY HIS FIRST NAME SO NATURALLY.
WHAT THE HELL.
I FEEL

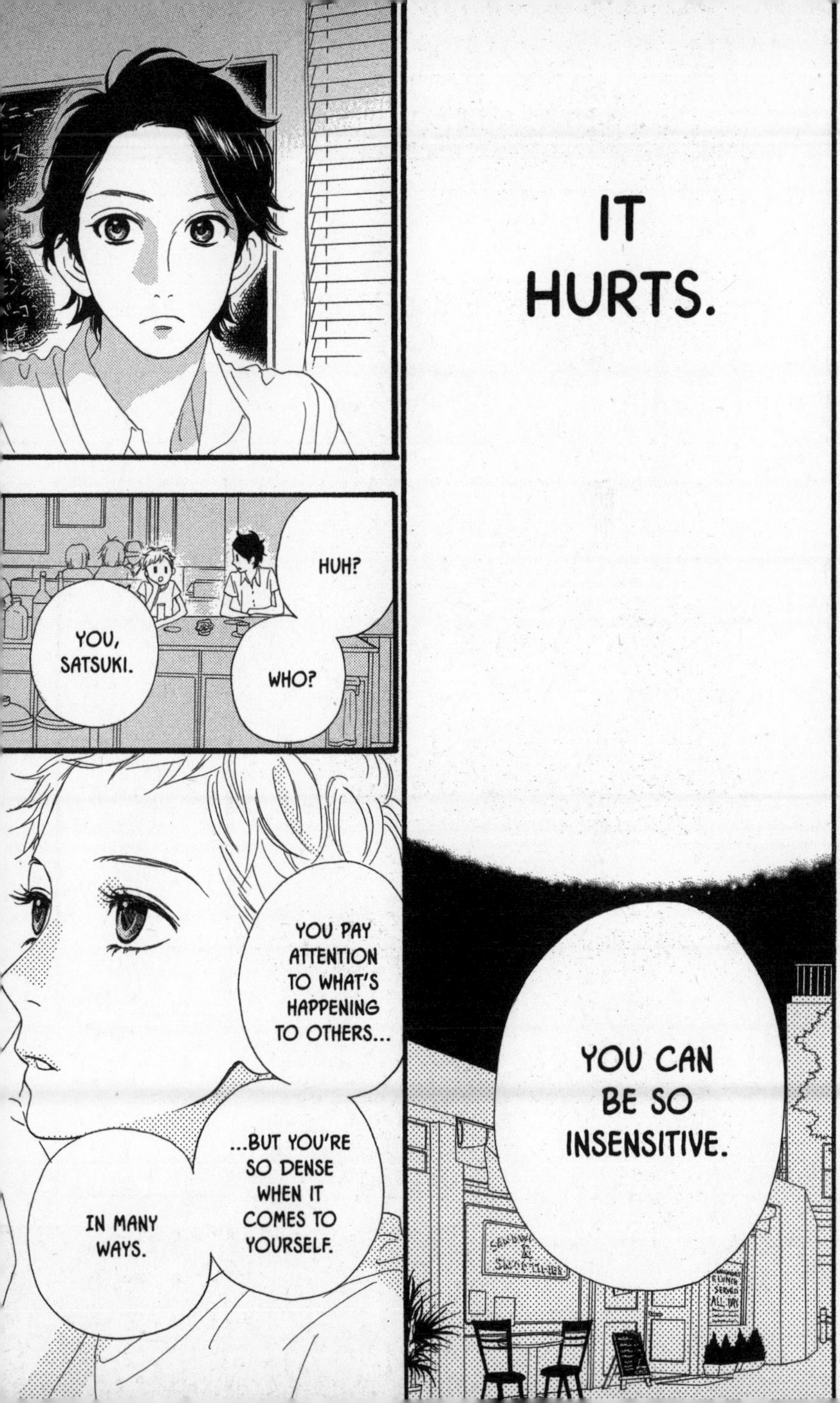
IT HURTS.
YOU CAN BE SO INSENSITIVE.
HUH?
WHO?
YOU, SATSUKI.
YOU PAY ATTENTION TO WHAT'S HAPPENING TO OTHERS...
...BUT YOU'RE SO DENSE WHEN IT COMES TO YOURSELF.
IN MANY WAYS.

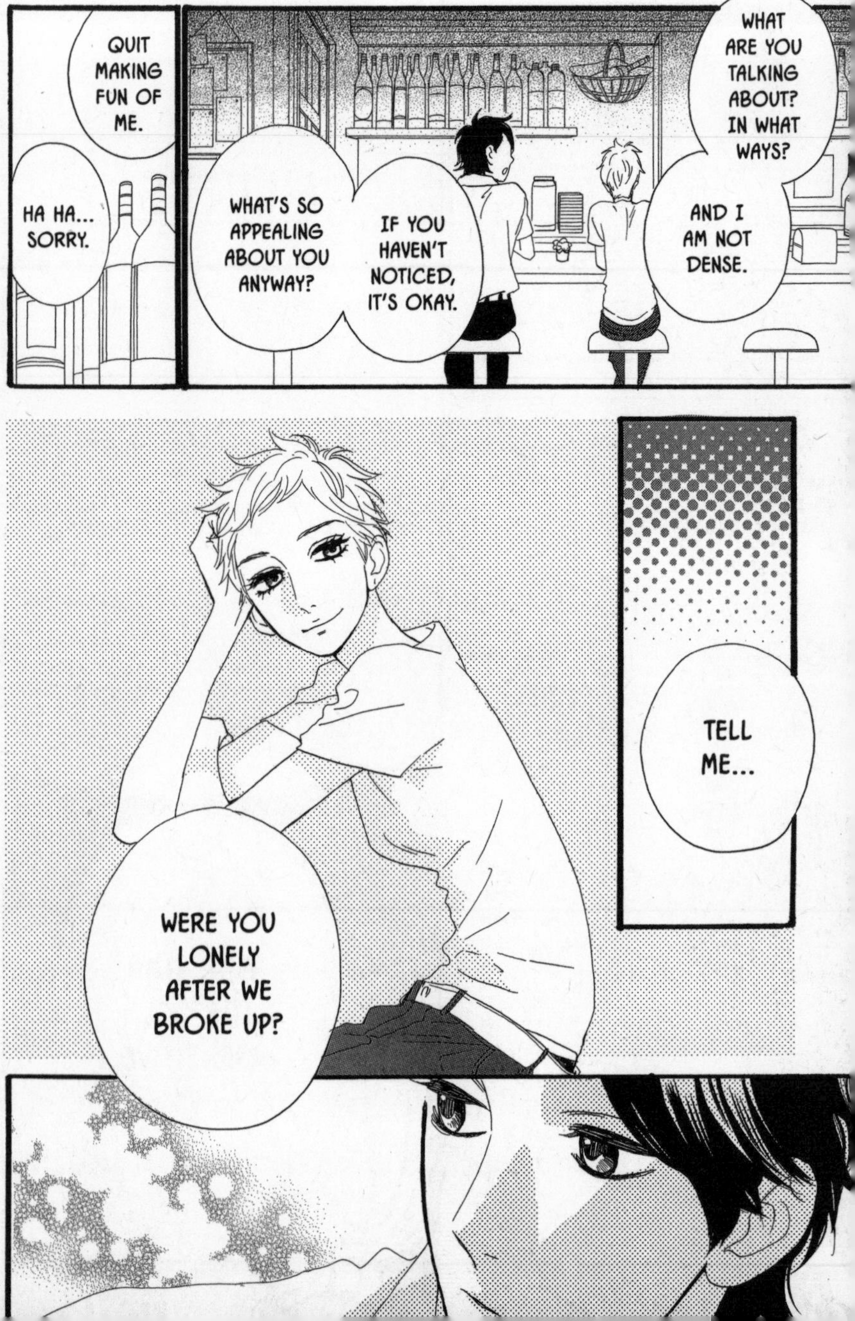
WHAT ARE YOU TALKING ABOUT? IN WHAT WAYS?
AND I AM NOT DENSE.
IF YOU HAVEN'T NOTICED, IT'S OKAY.
WHAT'S SO APPEALING ABOUT YOU ANYWAY?
QUIT MAKING FUN OF ME.
HA HA... SORRY.
TELL ME...
WERE YOU LONELY AFTER WE BROKE UP?

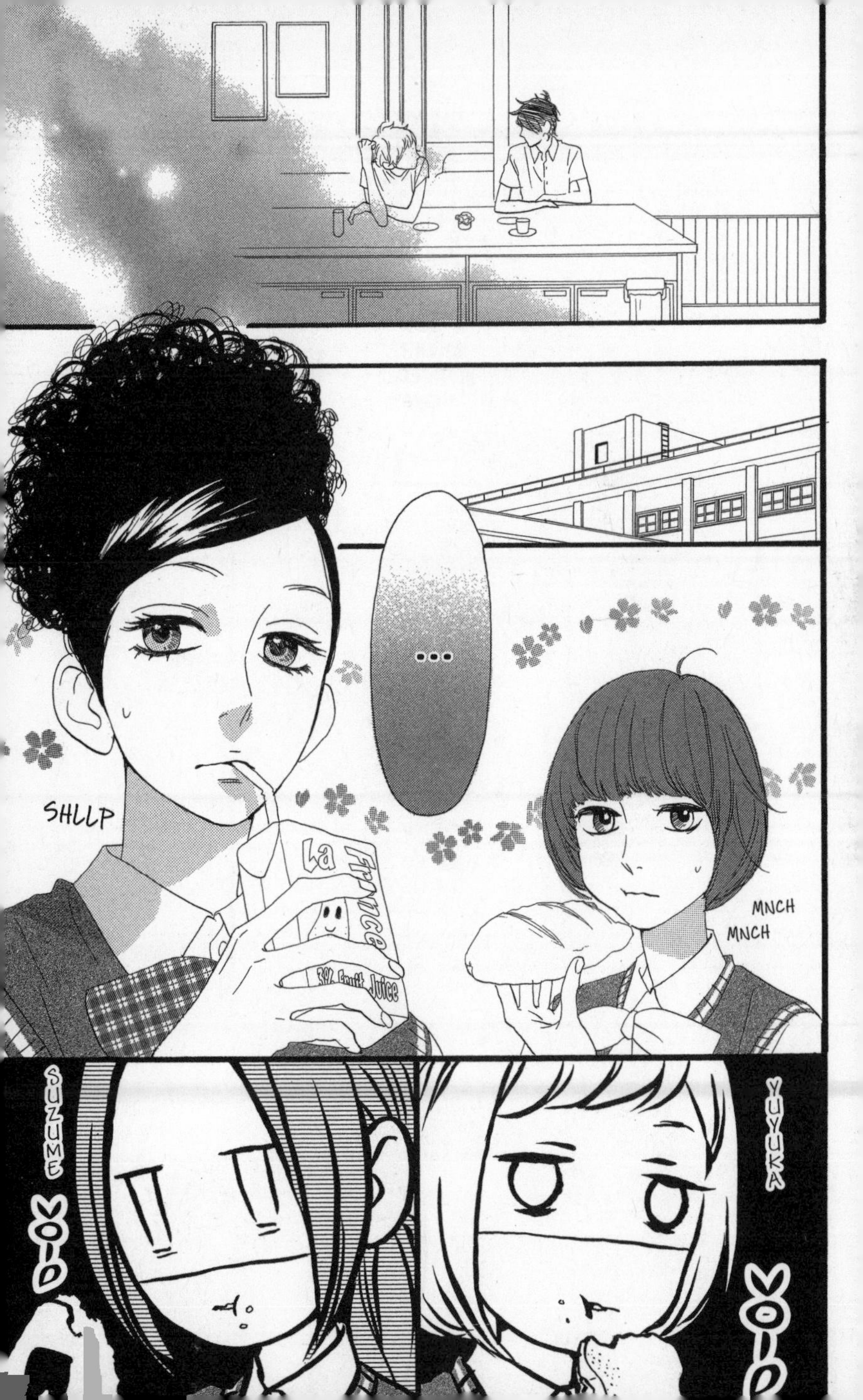
...
MNCH
MNCH
La France
3% Fruit Juice
SHLLP
YUYUKA
VOID
SUZUME
VOID

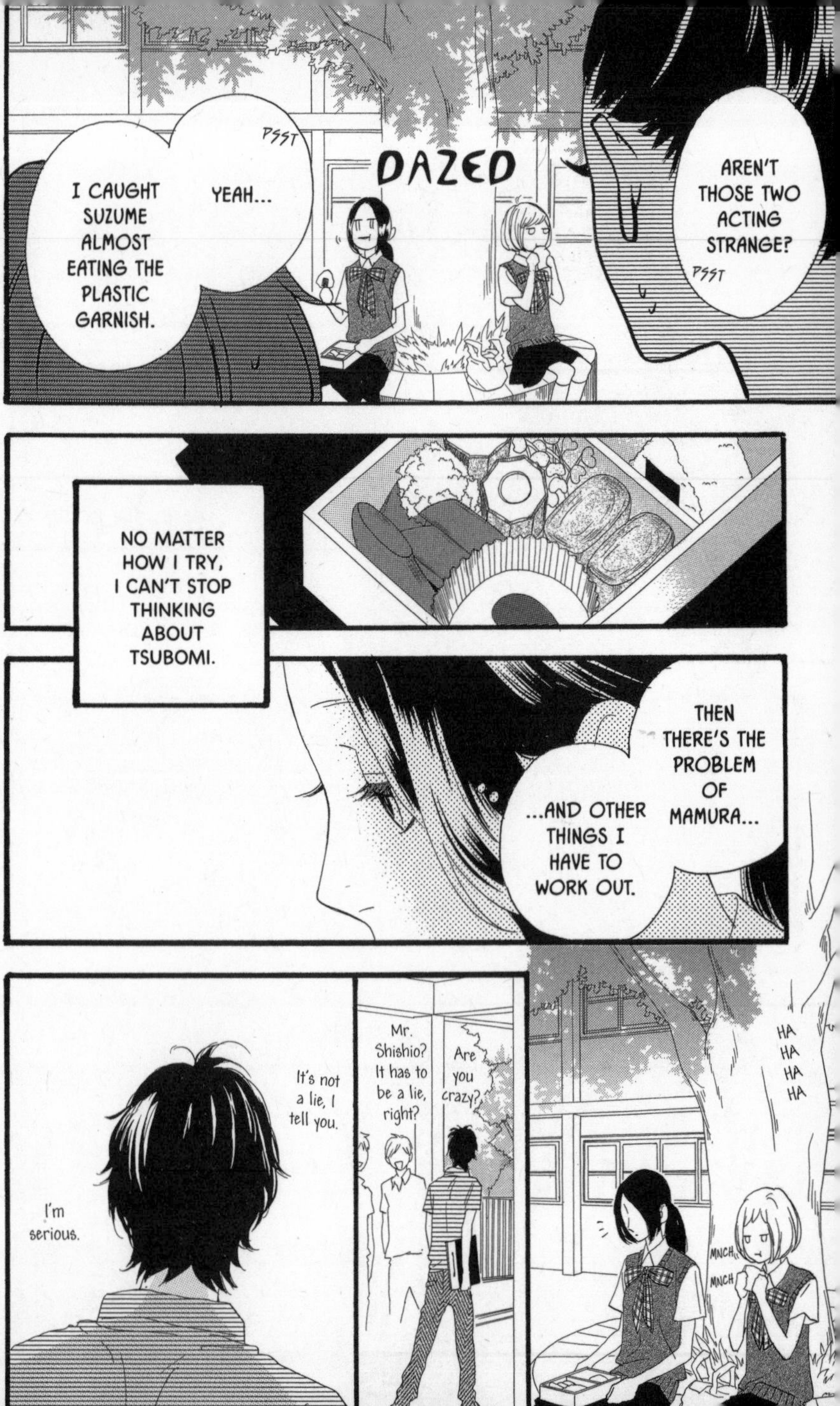
AREN'T THOSE TWO ACTING STRANGE?
PSST
DAZED
YEAH...
PSST
I CAUGHT SUZUME ALMOST EATING THE PLASTIC GARNISH.
NO MATTER HOW I TRY, I CAN'T STOP THINKING ABOUT TSUBOMI.
THEN THERE'S THE PROBLEM OF MAMURA...
...AND OTHER THINGS I HAVE TO WORK OUT.
HA HA HA HA
MNCH
MNCH
Are you crazy?
Mr. Shishio? It has to be a lie, right?
It's not a lie, I tell you.
I'm serious.

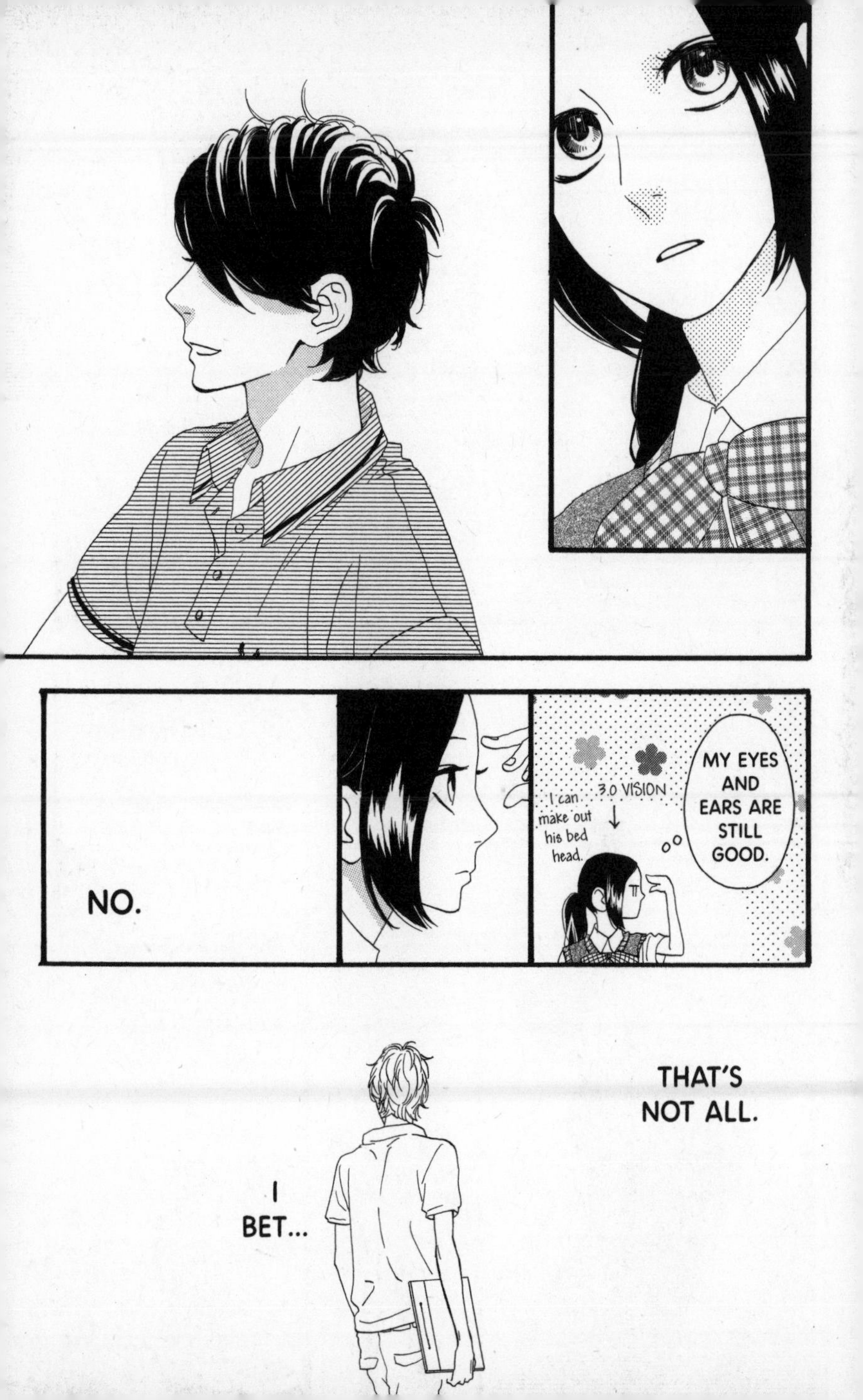
MY EYES AND EARS ARE STILL GOOD.
3.0 VISION
I can make out his bed head.
NO.
THAT'S NOT ALL.
I BET...

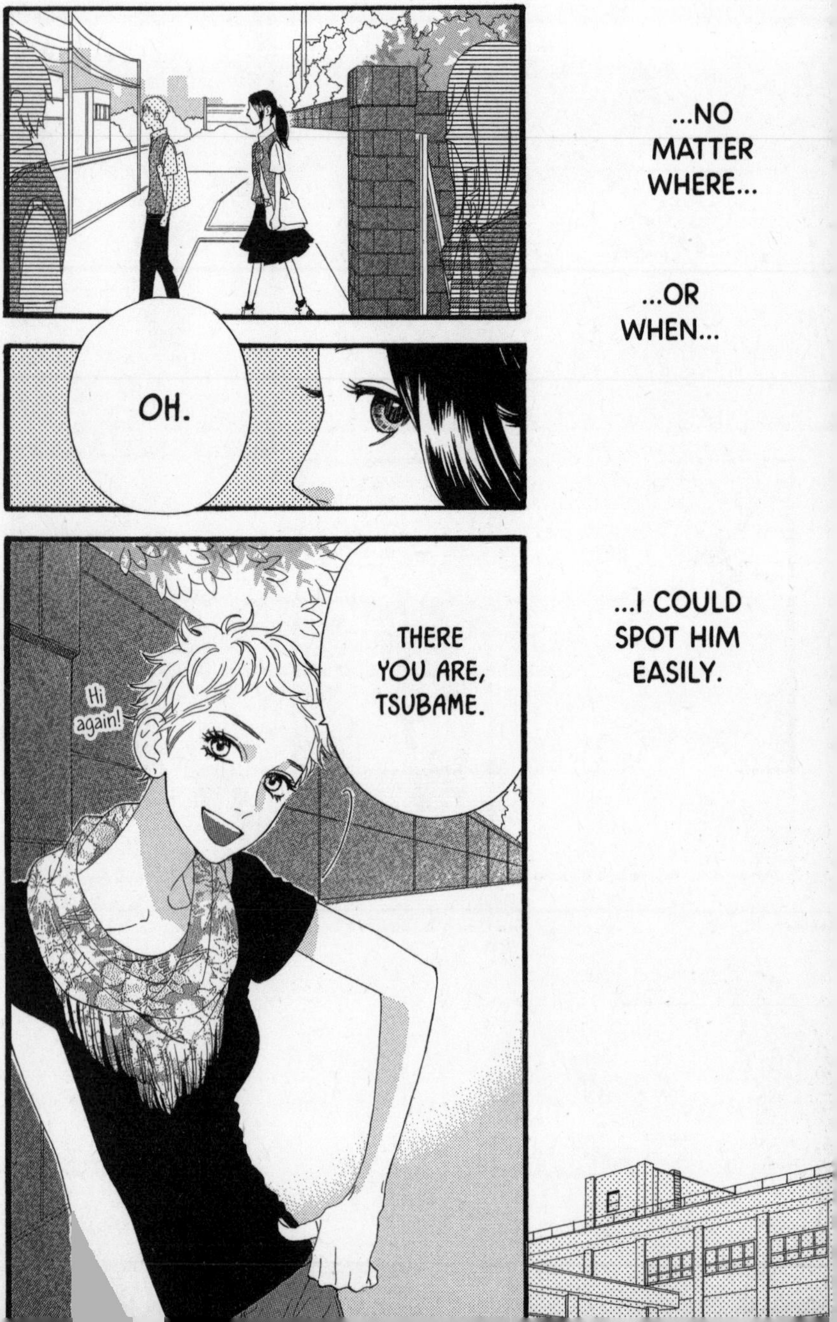
...NO MATTER WHERE...
...OR WHEN...
OH.
...I COULD SPOT HIM EASILY.
THERE YOU ARE, TSUBAME.
Hi again!

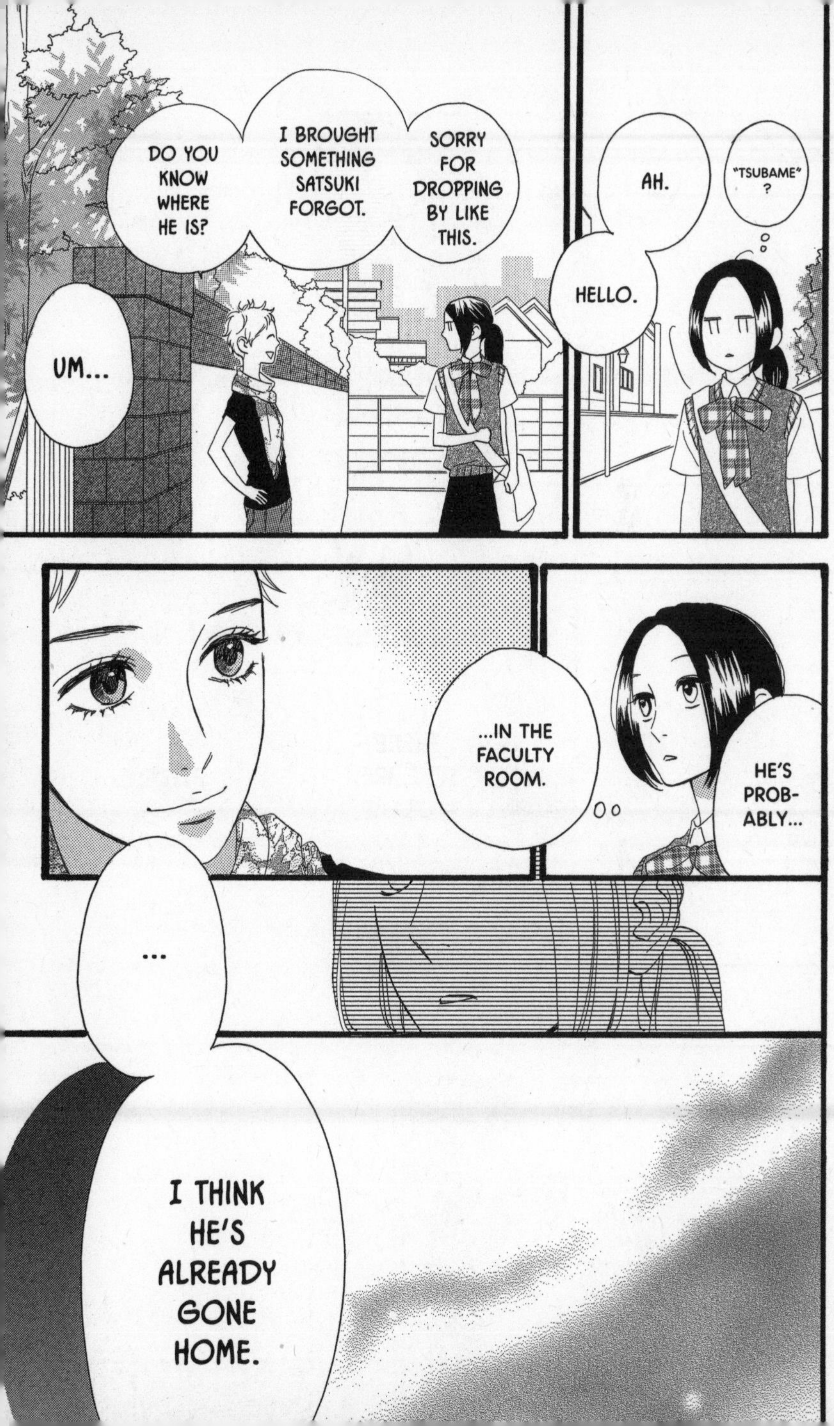
"TSUBAME" ?
AH.
HELLO.
SORRY FOR DROPPING BY LIKE THIS.
I BROUGHT SOMETHING SATSUKI FORGOT.
DO YOU KNOW WHERE HE IS?
UM...
HE'S PROBABLY...
...IN THE FACULTY ROOM.
...
I THINK HE'S ALREADY GONE HOME.

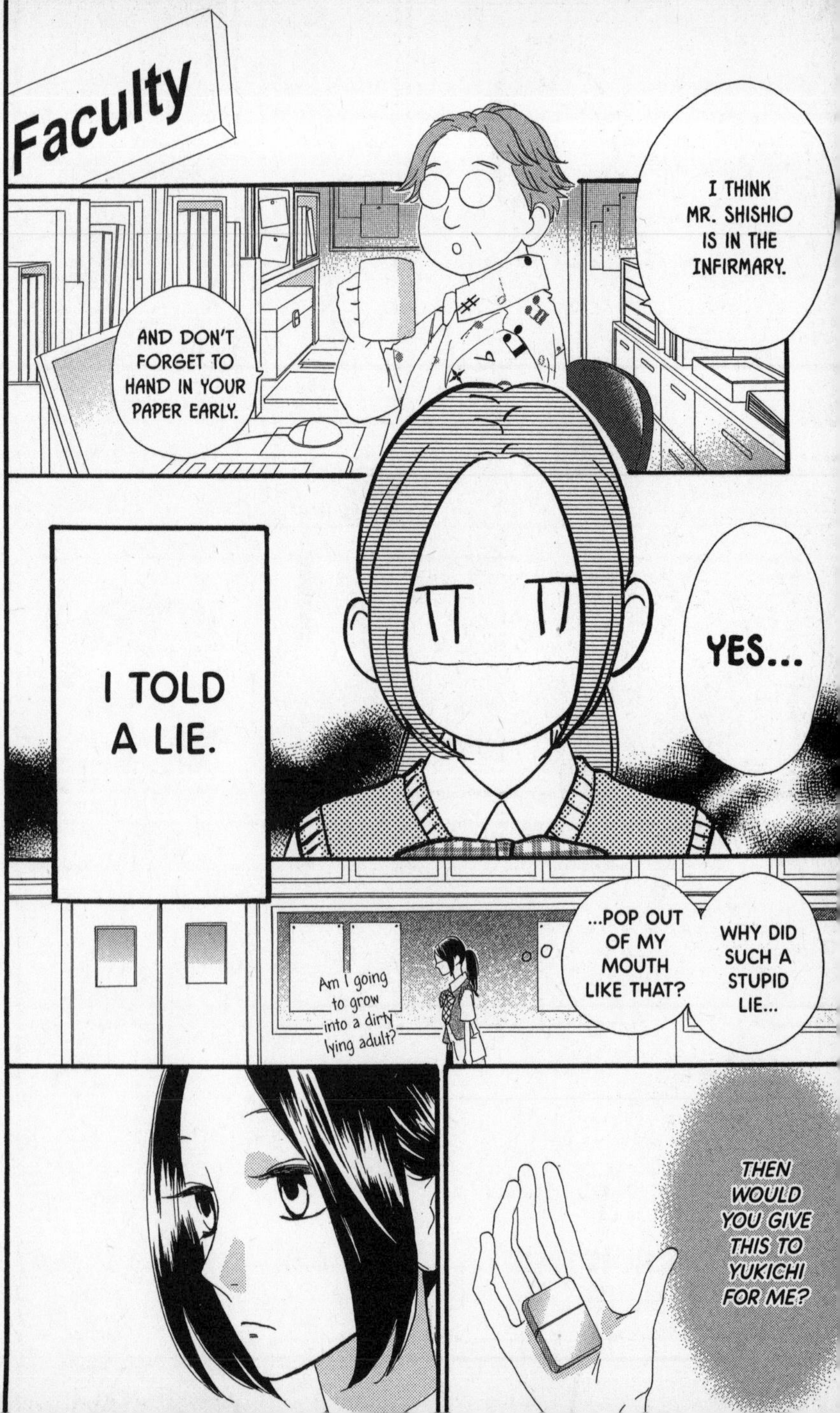

Faculty
I THINK MR. SHISHIO IS IN THE INFIRMARY.
AND DON'T FORGET TO HAND IN YOUR PAPER EARLY.
YES...
I TOLD A LIE.
WHY DID SUCH A STUPID LIE...
...POP OUT OF MY MOUTH LIKE THAT?
Am I going to grow into a dirty lying adult?
THEN WOULD YOU GIVE THIS TO YUKICHI FOR ME?

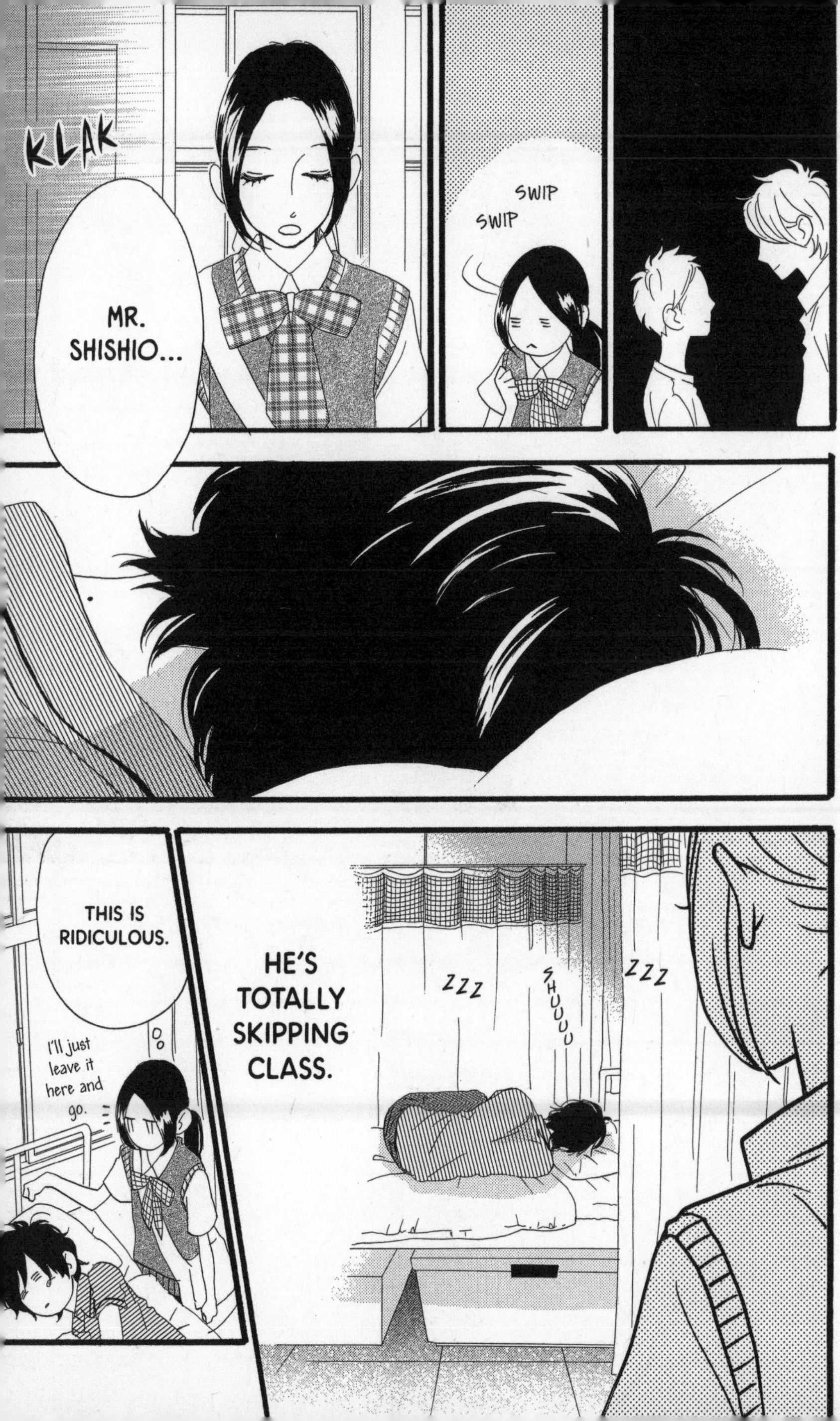
SWIP
SWIP
KLAK
MR. SHISHIO...
ZZZ
SHUUUU
ZZZ
HE'S TOTALLY SKIPPING CLASS.
THIS IS RIDICULOUS.
I'll just leave it here and go.

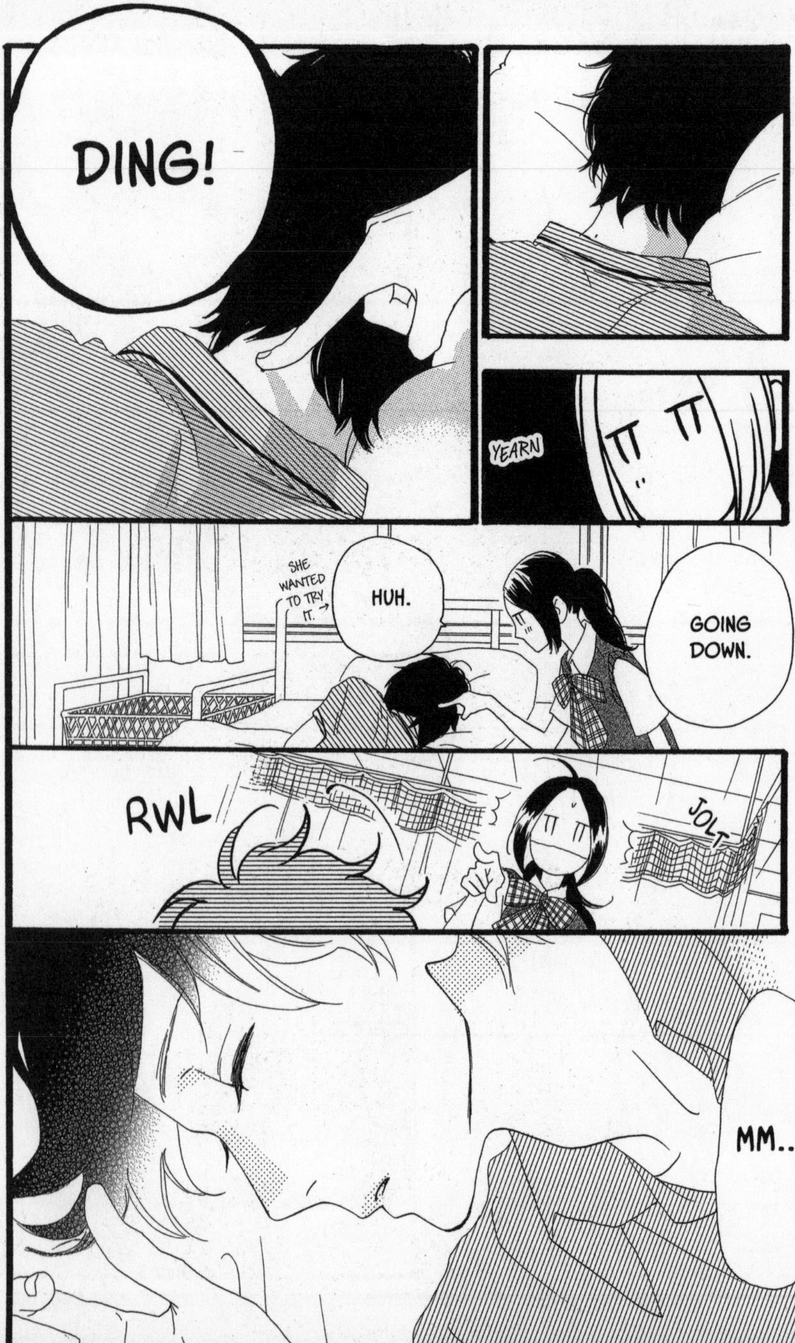
YEARN
DING!
GOING DOWN.
HUH.
SHE WANTED TO TRY IT.
JOLT
RWL
MM...

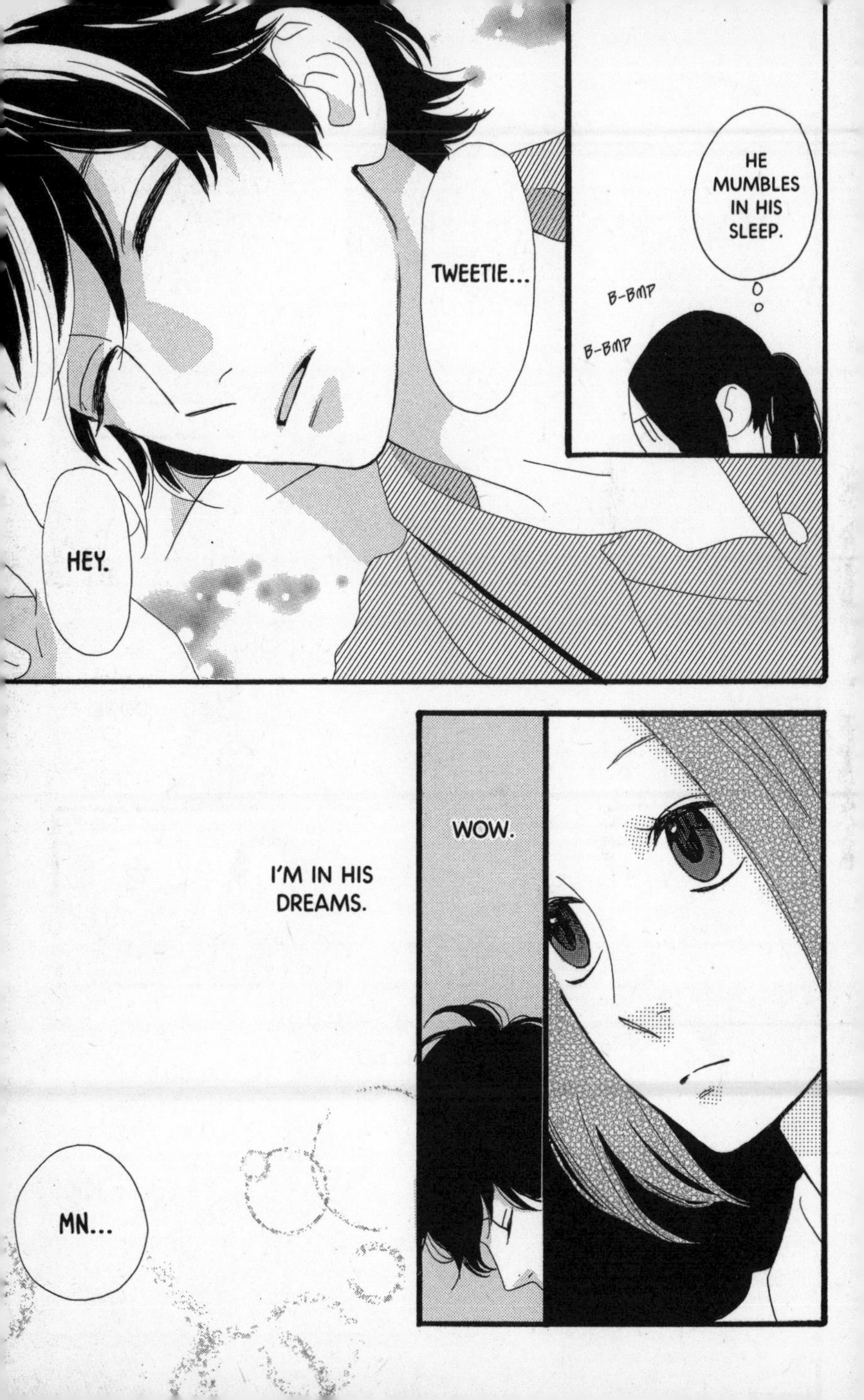
HE MUMBLES IN HIS SLEEP.
B-BMP
B-BMP
TWEETIE...
HEY.
WOW.
I'M IN HIS DREAMS.
MN...

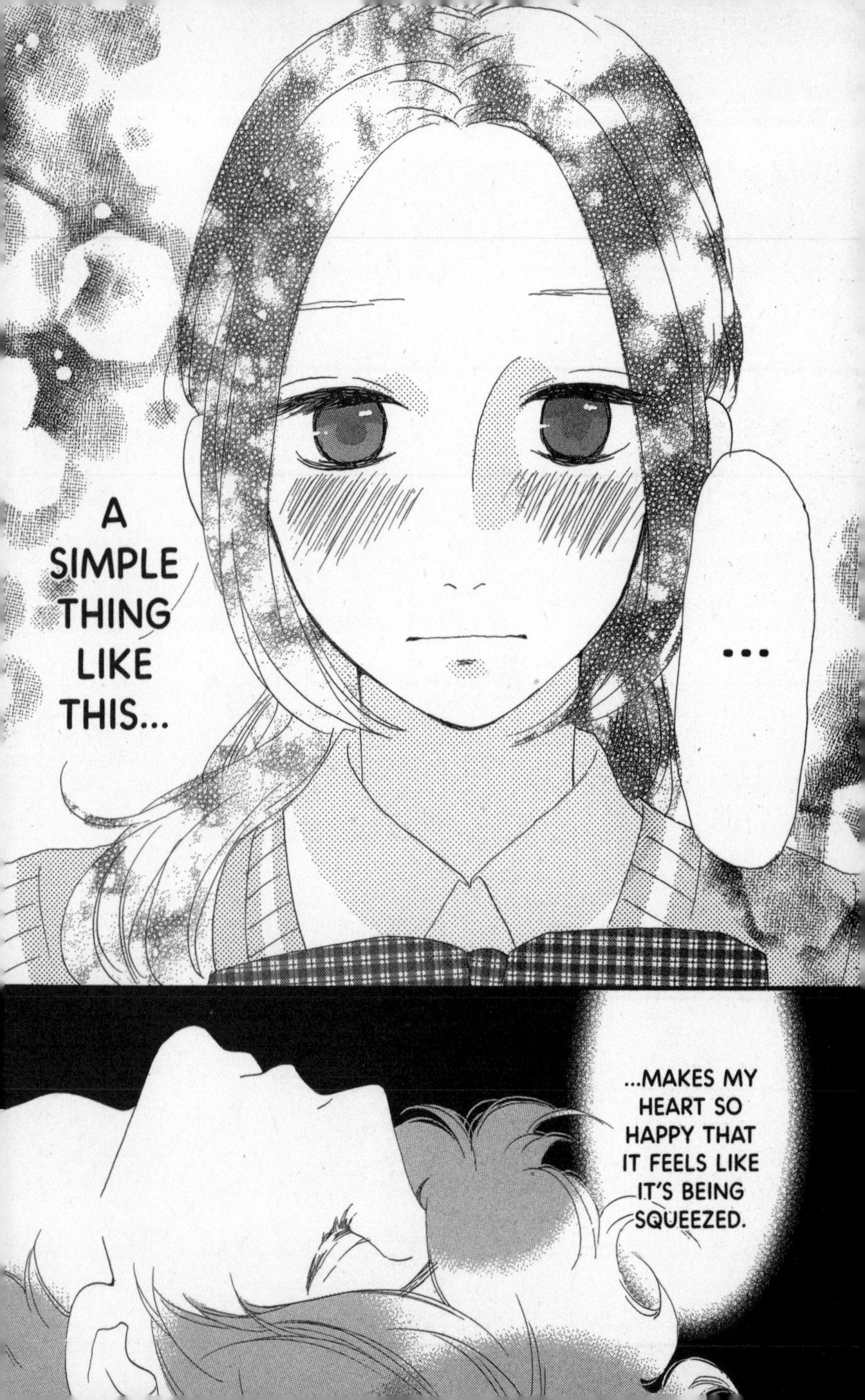
...
A SIMPLE THING LIKE THIS...
...MAKES MY HEART SO HAPPY THAT IT FEELS LIKE IT'S BEING SQUEEZED.

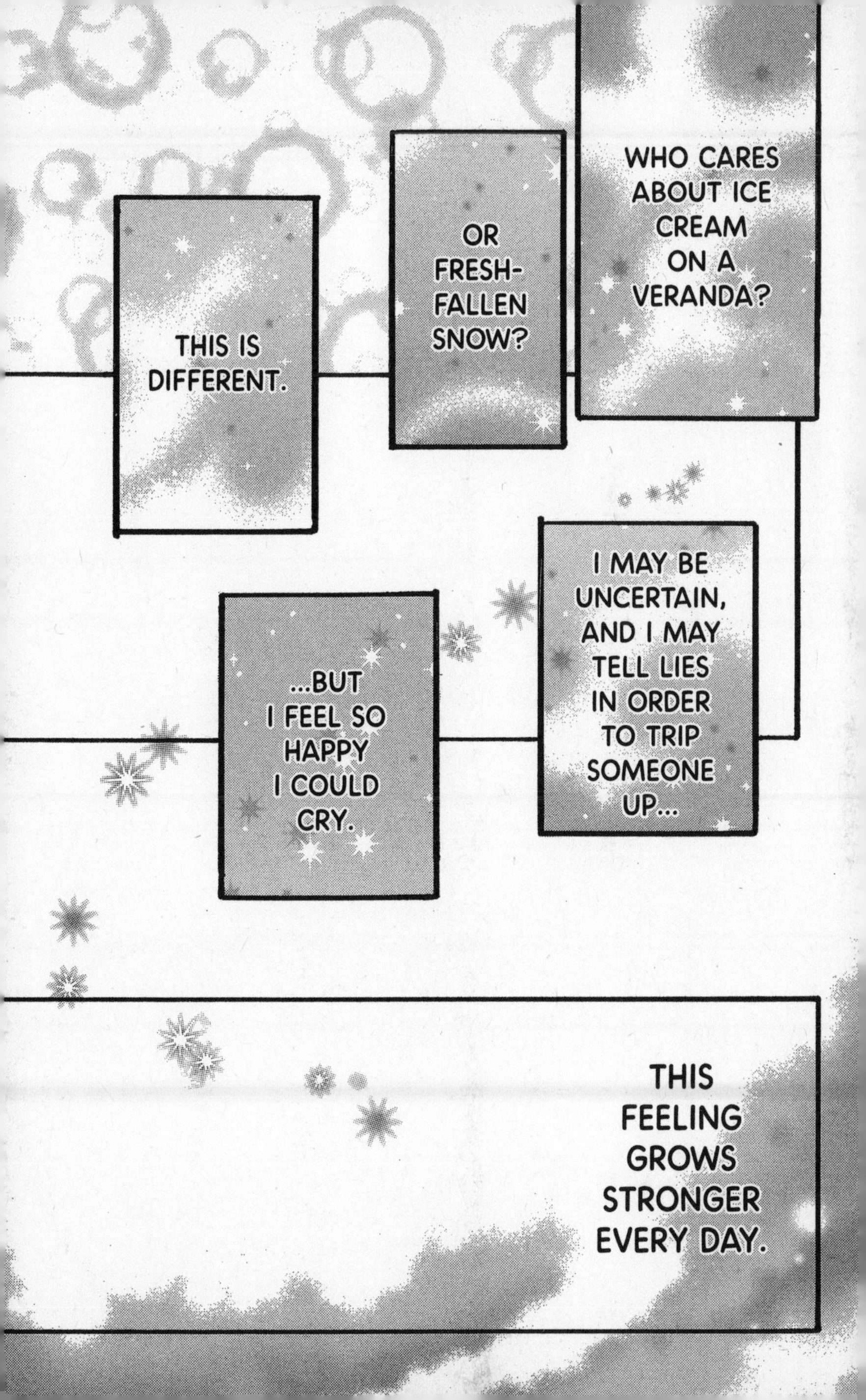
WHO CARES ABOUT ICE CREAM ON A VERANDA?
OR FRESH-FALLEN SNOW?
THIS IS DIFFERENT.
I MAY BE UNCERTAIN, AND I MAY TELL LIES IN ORDER TO TRIP SOMEONE UP...
...BUT I FEEL SO HAPPY I COULD CRY.
THIS FEELING GROWS STRONGER EVERY DAY.

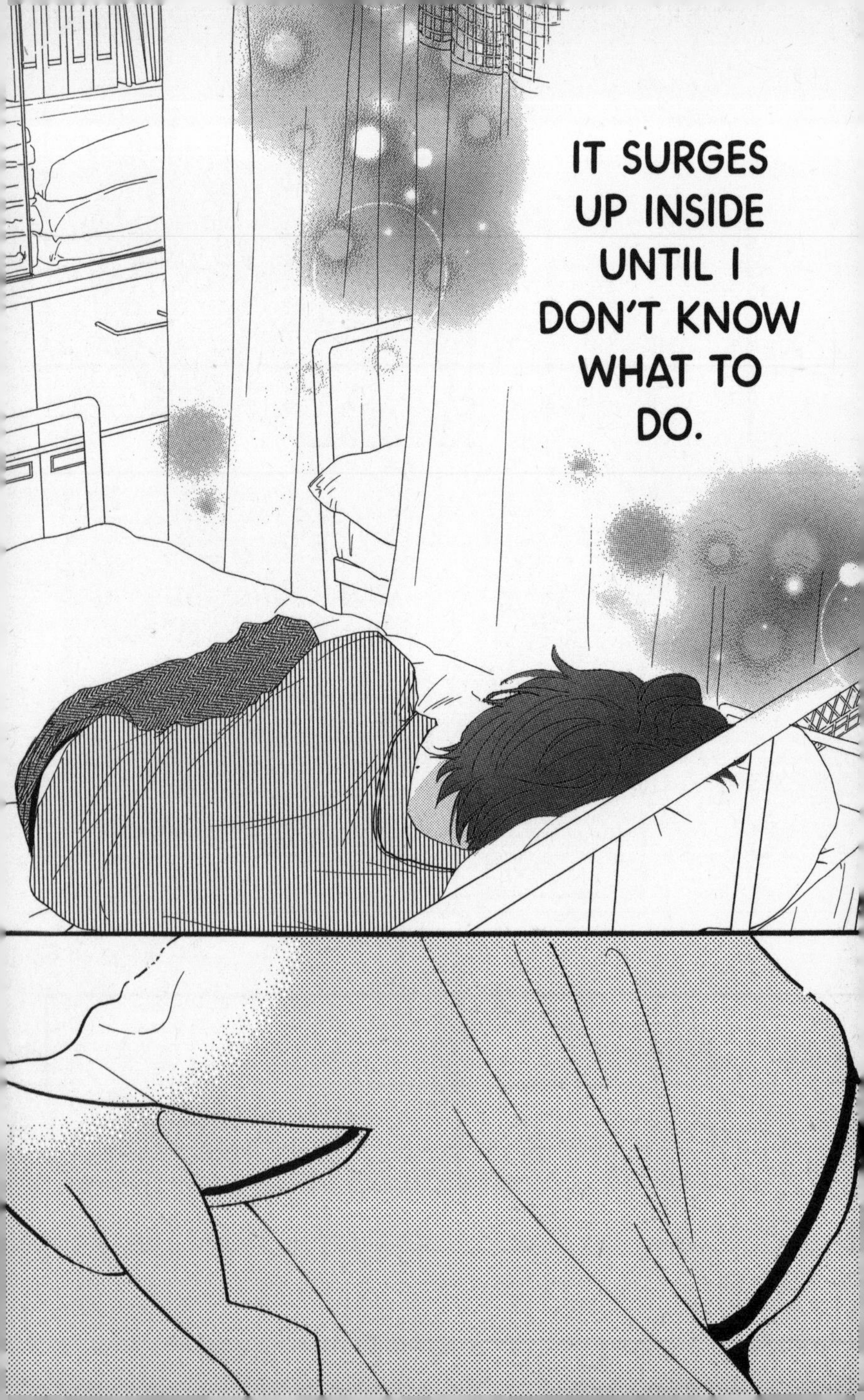
IT SURGES UP INSIDE UNTIL I DON'T KNOW WHAT TO DO.

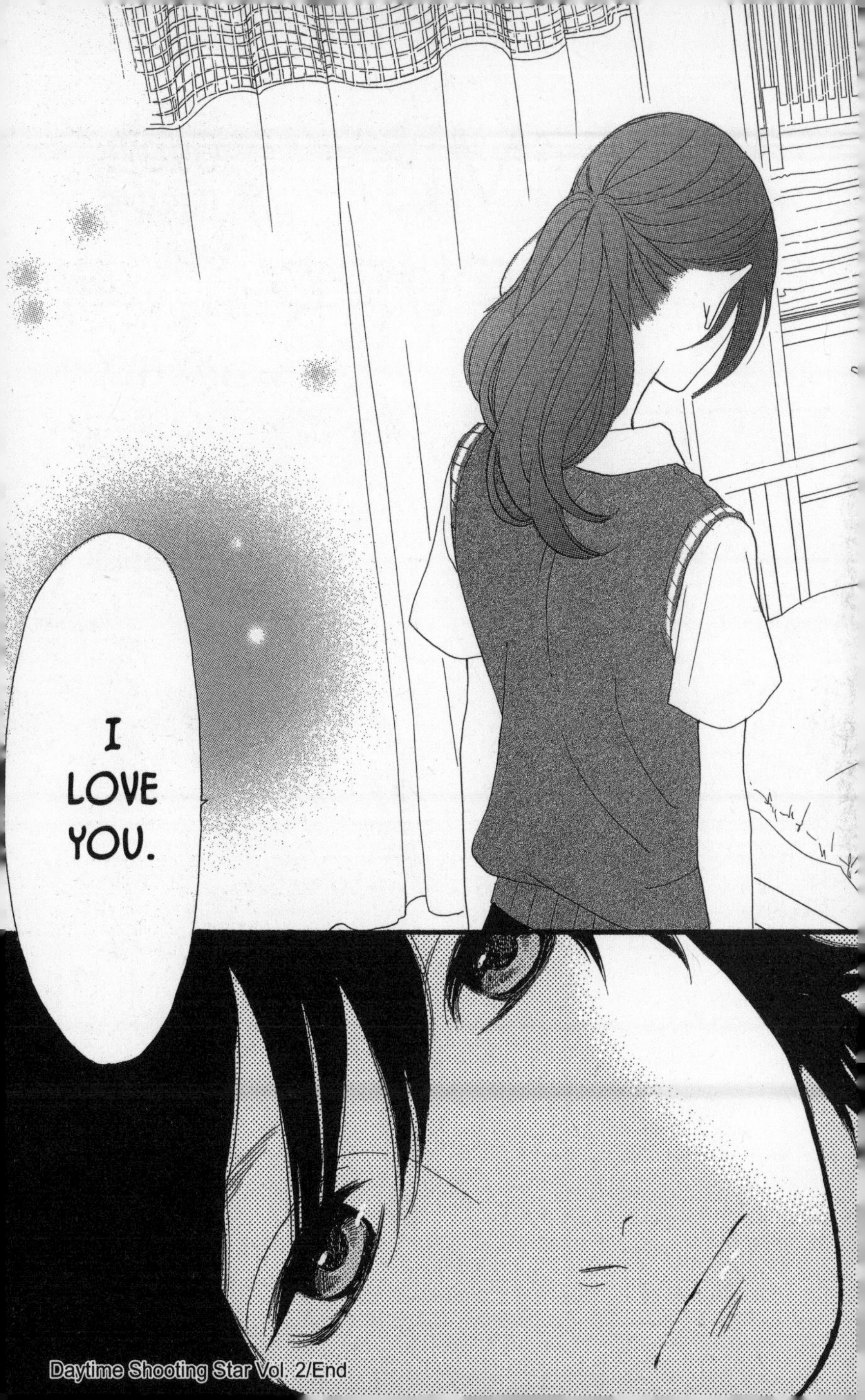
I LOVE YOU.

Daytime Shooting Star Vol. 2/End

DAYTIME WHATEVER

DAYTIME SHOOTING STAR

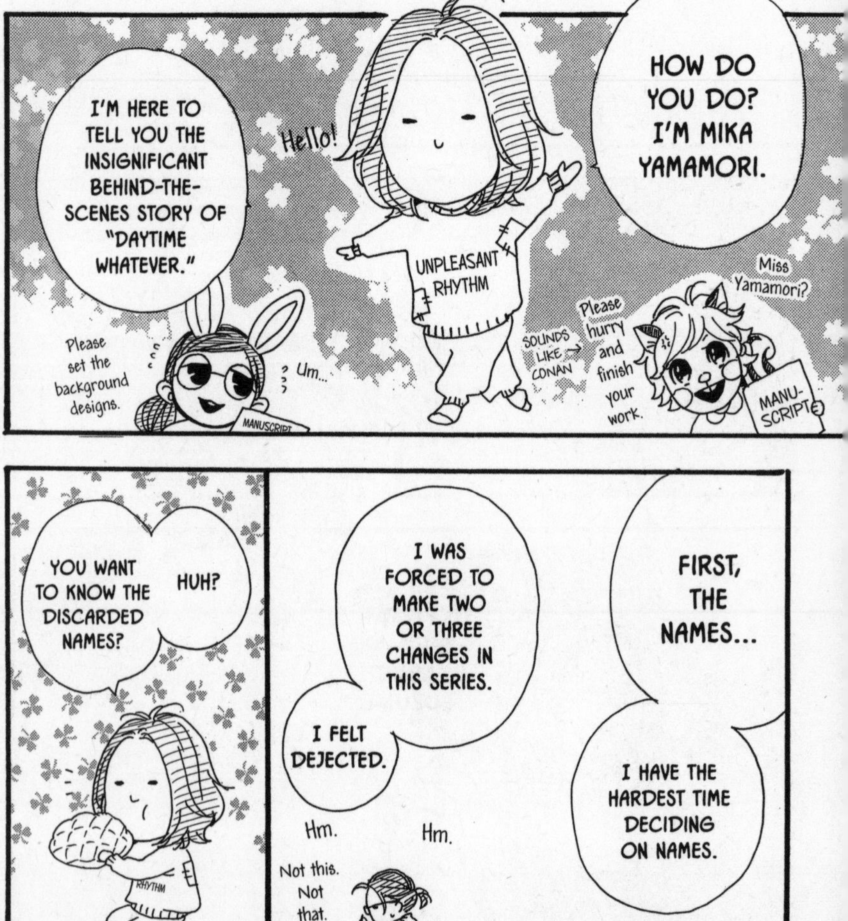
HOW DO YOU DO? I'M MIKA YAMAMORI.
Hello!
I'M HERE TO TELL YOU THE INSIGNIFICANT BEHIND-THE-SCENES STORY OF "DAYTIME WHATEVER."
UNPLEASANT RHYTHM
Miss Yamamori?
Please hurry and finish your work.
SOUNDS LIKE CONAN
MANU-SCRIPT
Um...
Please set the background designs.
MANUSCRIPT
FIRST, THE NAMES...
I HAVE THE HARDEST TIME DECIDING ON NAMES.
I WAS FORCED TO MAKE TWO OR THREE CHANGES IN THIS SERIES.
I FELT DEJECTED.
Hm.
Hm.
Not this. Not that.
HUH?
YOU WANT TO KNOW THE DISCARDED NAMES?
RHYTHM

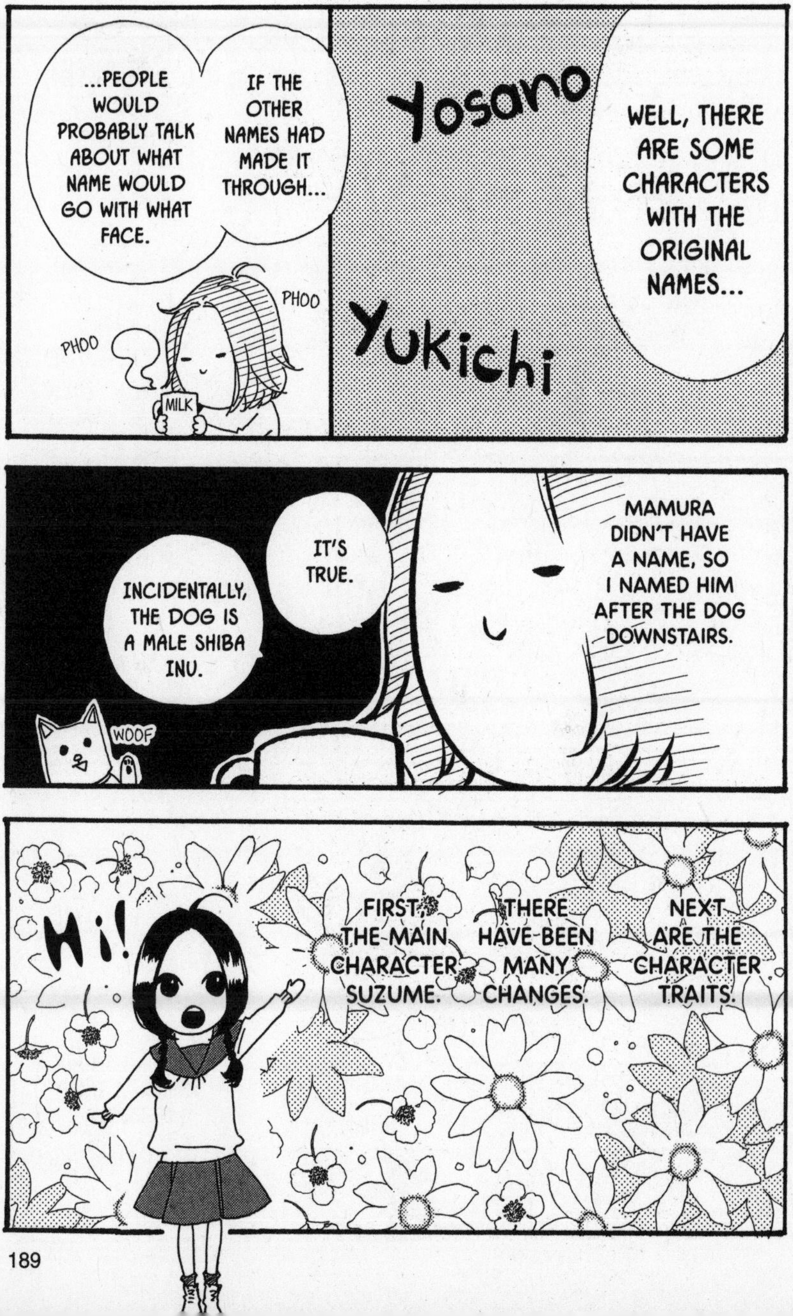
WELL, THERE ARE SOME CHARACTERS WITH THE ORIGINAL NAMES...
Yosano
Yukichi
IF THE OTHER NAMES HAD MADE IT THROUGH...
...PEOPLE WOULD PROBABLY TALK ABOUT WHAT NAME WOULD GO WITH WHAT FACE.
PHOO
PHOO
MILK
MAMURA DIDN'T HAVE A NAME, SO I NAMED HIM AFTER THE DOG DOWNSTAIRS.
IT'S TRUE.
INCIDENTALLY, THE DOG IS A MALE SHIBA INU.
WOOF
NEXT ARE THE CHARACTER TRAITS.
THERE HAVE BEEN MANY CHANGES.
FIRST, THE MAIN CHARACTER SUZUME.
Hi!

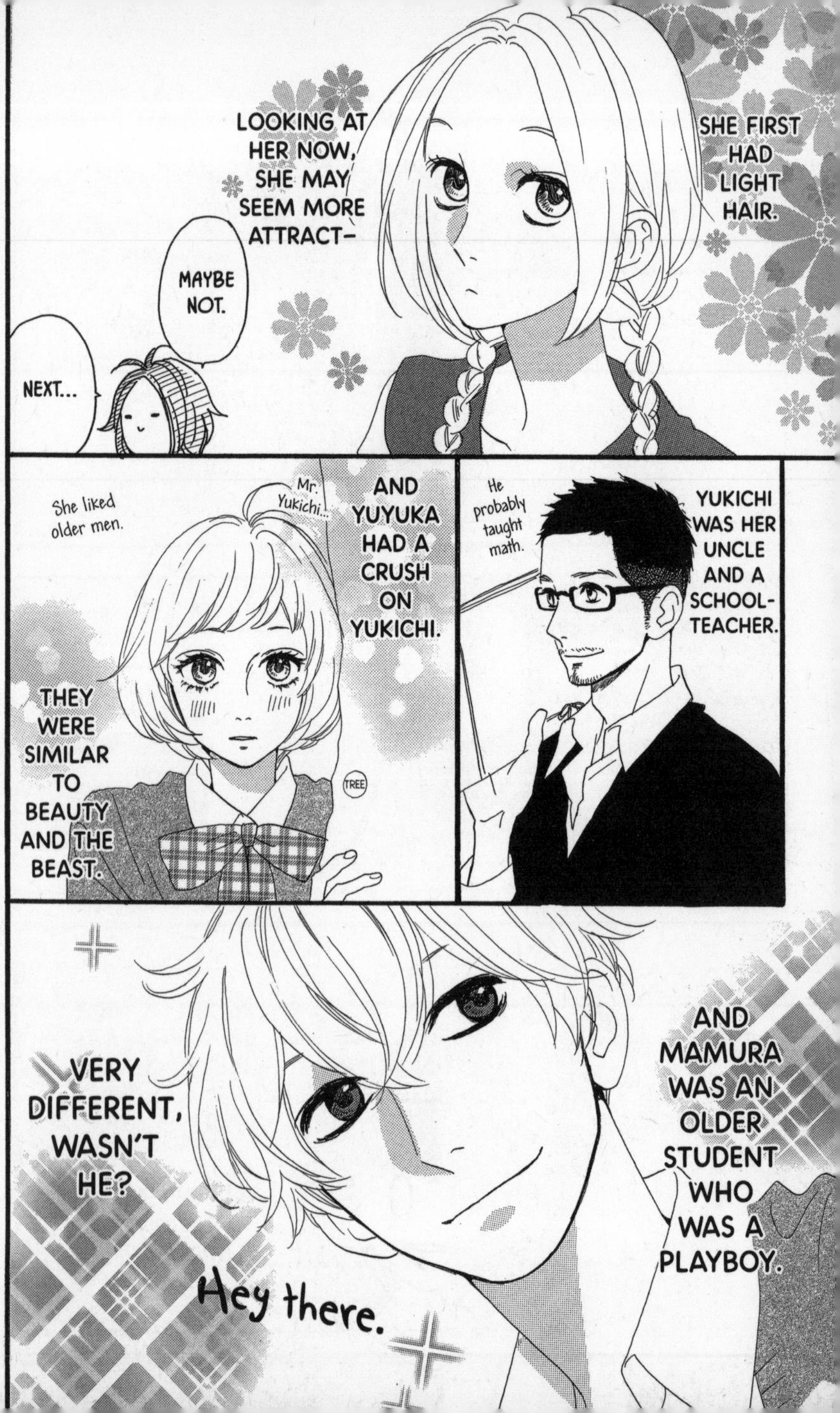
SHE FIRST HAD LIGHT HAIR.
LOOKING AT HER NOW, SHE MAY SEEM MORE ATTRACT-
MAYBE NOT.
NEXT...
YUKICHI WAS HER UNCLE AND A SCHOOLTEACHER.
He probably taught math.
AND YUYUKA HAD A CRUSH ON YUKICHI.
Mr. Yukichi...
She liked older men.
TREE
THEY WERE SIMILAR TO BEAUTY AND THE BEAST.
AND MAMURA WAS AN OLDER STUDENT WHO WAS A PLAYBOY.
VERY DIFFERENT, WASN'T HE?
Hey there.

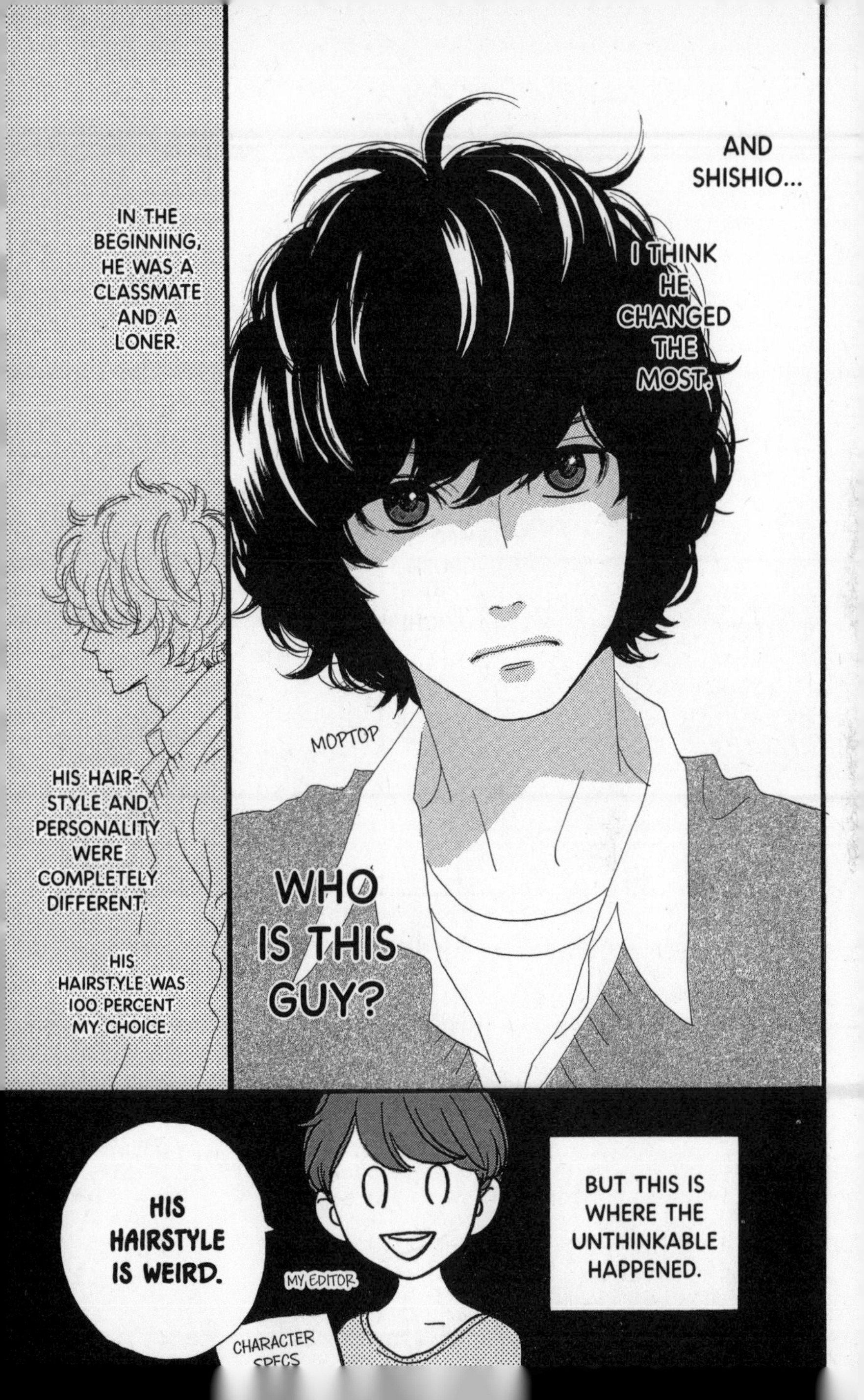
AND SHISHIO...
I THINK HE CHANGED THE MOST.
MOPTOP
WHO IS THIS GUY?
IN THE BEGINNING, HE WAS A CLASSMATE AND A LONER.
HIS HAIR-STYLE AND PERSONALITY WERE COMPLETELY DIFFERENT.
HIS HAIRSTYLE WAS 100 PERCENT MY CHOICE.
BUT THIS IS WHERE THE UNTHINKABLE HAPPENED.
HIS HAIRSTYLE IS WEIRD.
MY EDITOR
CHARACTER

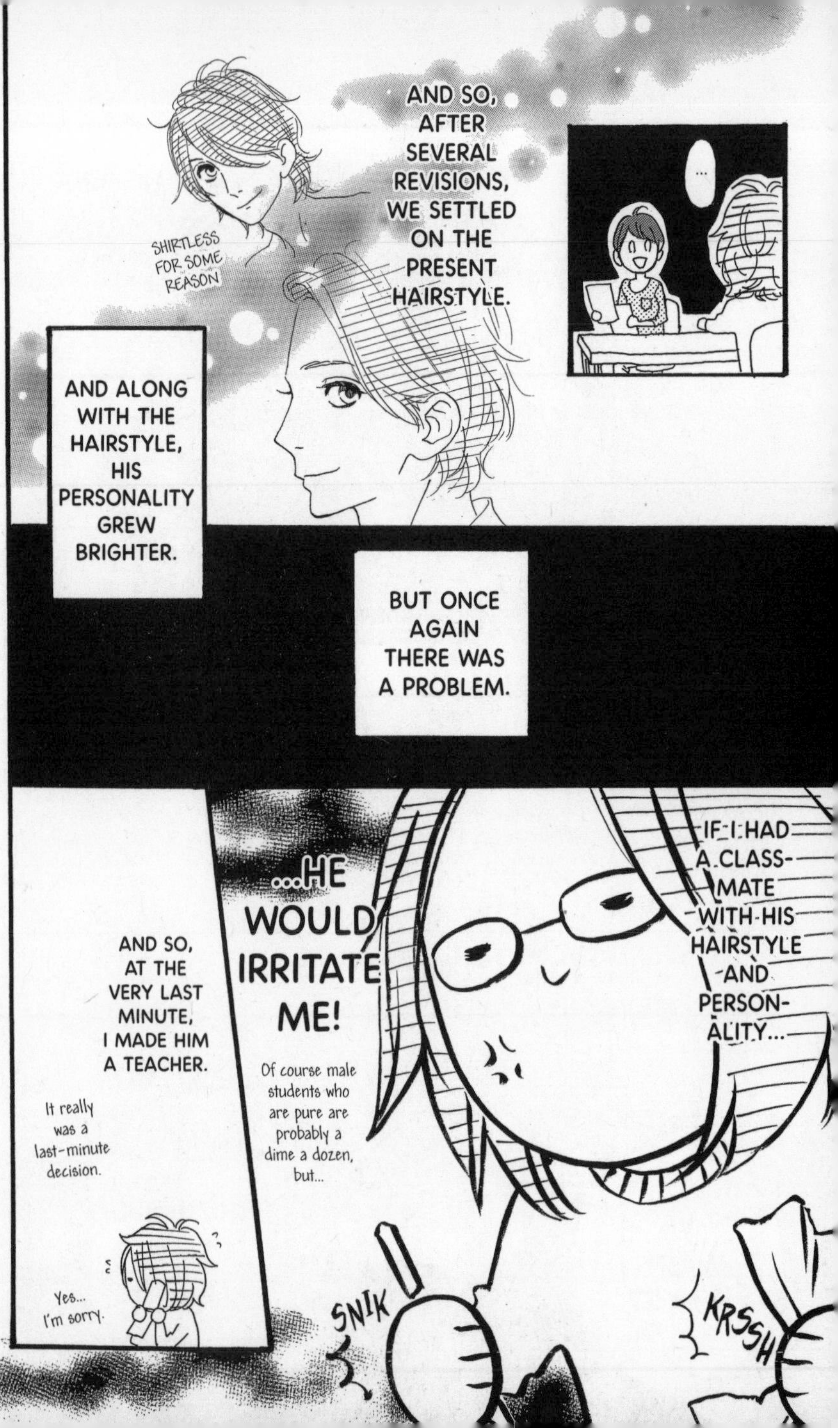
...
AND SO, AFTER SEVERAL REVISIONS, WE SETTLED ON THE PRESENT HAIRSTYLE.
SHIRTLESS FOR SOME REASON
AND ALONG WITH THE HAIRSTYLE, HIS PERSONALITY GREW BRIGHTER.
BUT ONCE AGAIN THERE WAS A PROBLEM.
IF I HAD A CLASSMATE WITH HIS HAIRSTYLE AND PERSONALITY...
...HE WOULD IRRITATE ME!
Of course male students who are pure are probably a dime a dozen, but...
KRSSH
SNIK
AND SO, AT THE VERY LAST MINUTE, I MADE HIM A TEACHER.
It really was a last-minute decision.
Yes... I'm sorry.

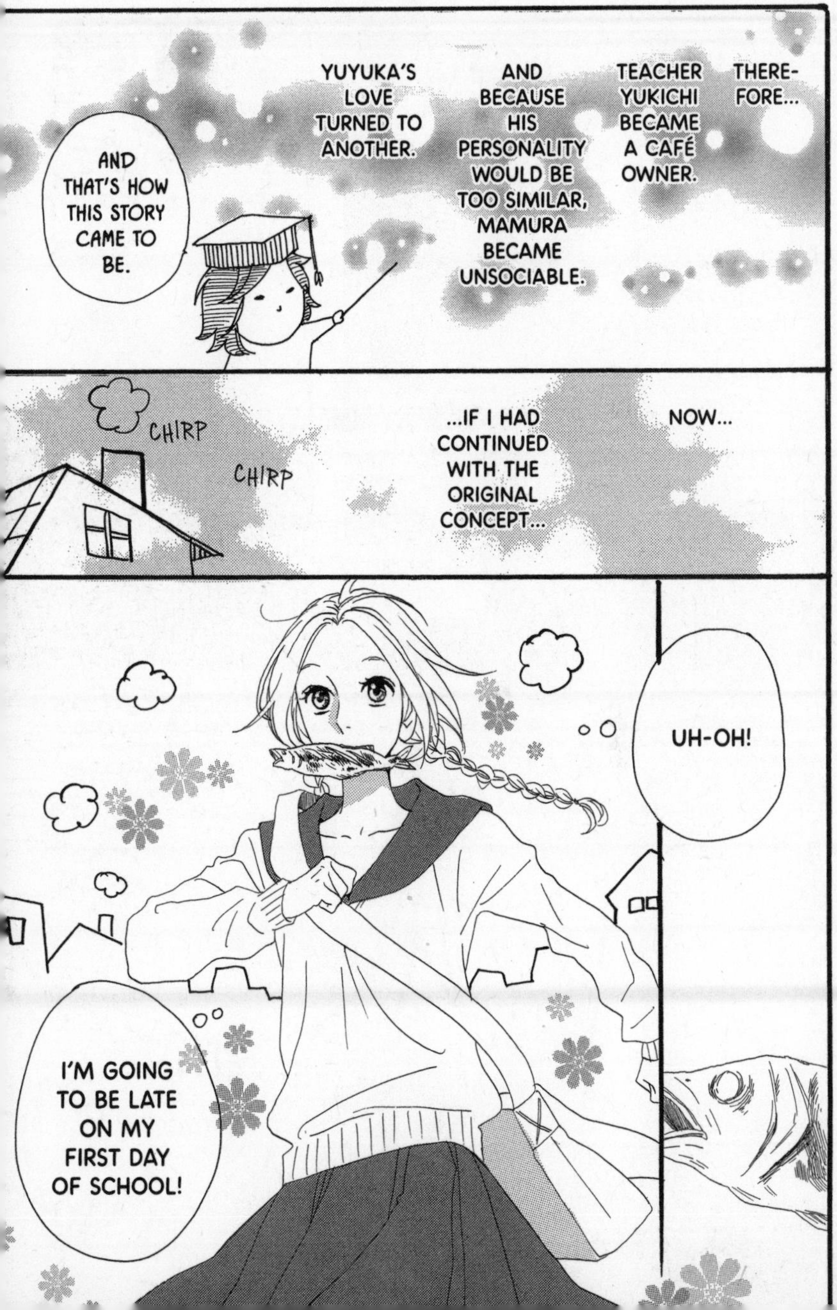
THERE-FORE...
TEACHER YUKICHI BECAME A CAFÉ OWNER.
AND BECAUSE HIS PERSONALITY WOULD BE TOO SIMILAR, MAMURA BECAME UNSOCIABLE.
YUYUKA'S LOVE TURNED TO ANOTHER.
AND THAT'S HOW THIS STORY CAME TO BE.
NOW...
...IF I HAD CONTINUED WITH THE ORIGINAL CONCEPT...
CHIRP
CHIRP
UH-OH!
I'M GOING TO BE LATE ON MY FIRST DAY OF SCHOOL!

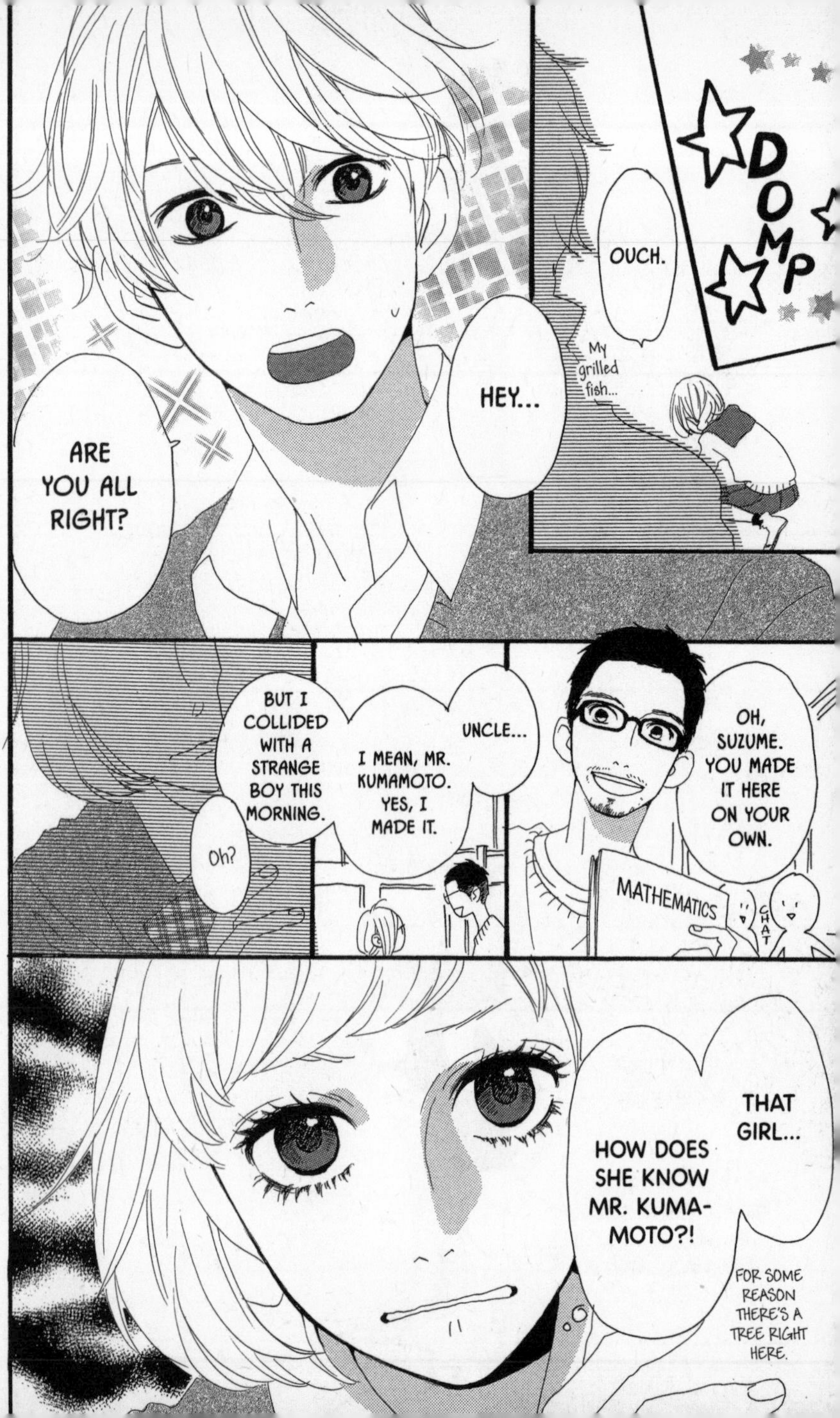
DOMP
OUCH.
My grilled fish...
HEY...
ARE YOU ALL RIGHT?
OH, SUZUME. YOU MADE IT HERE ON YOUR OWN.
MATHEMATICS
CHAT
UNCLE...
I MEAN, MR. KUMAMOTO. YES, I MADE IT.
BUT I COLLIDED WITH A STRANGE BOY THIS MORNING.
Oh?
THAT GIRL...
HOW DOES SHE KNOW MR. KUMAMOTO?!
FOR SOME REASON THERE'S A TREE RIGHT HERE.

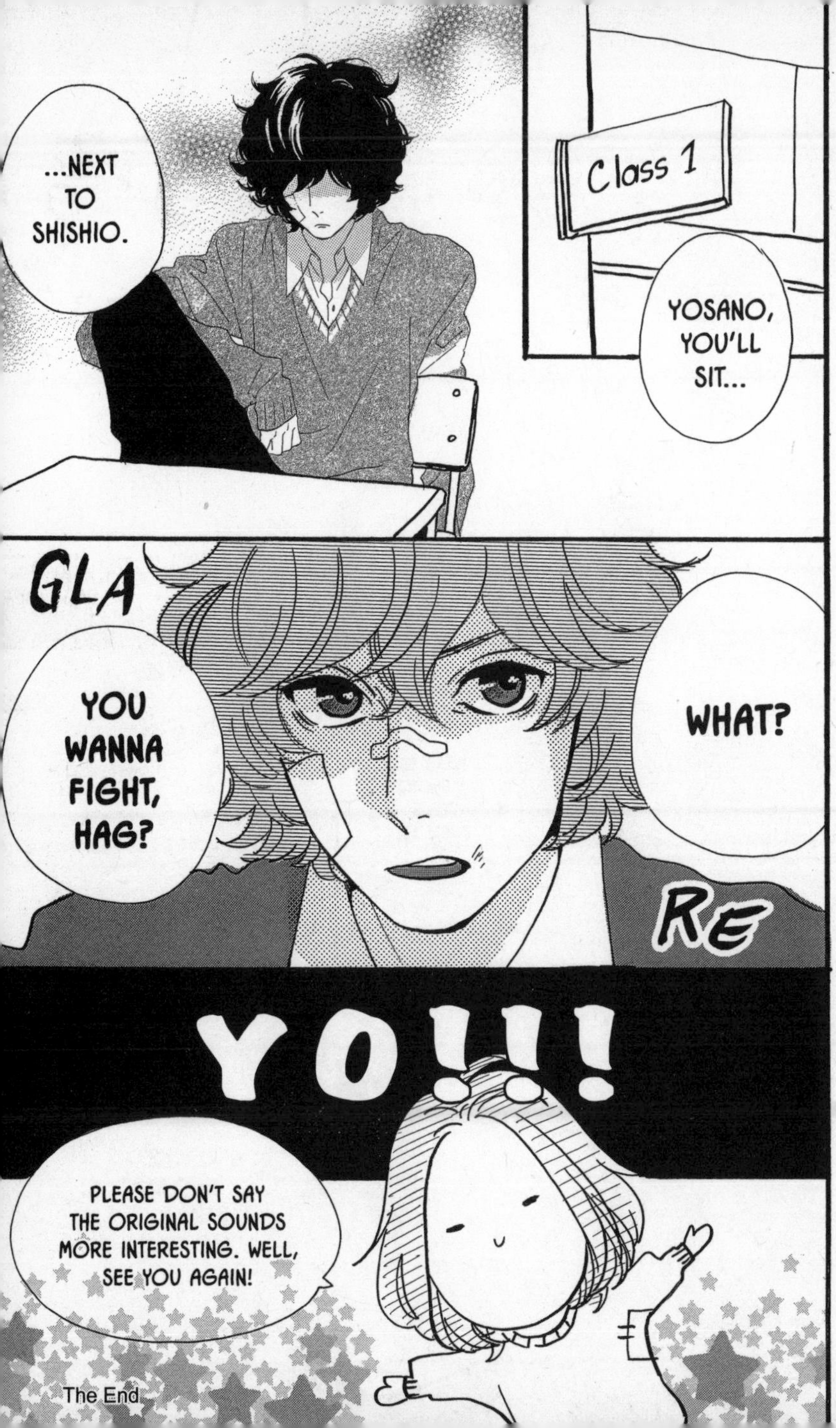
Class 1
YOSANO, YOU'LL SIT...
...NEXT TO SHISHIO.
WHAT?
GLA
YOU WANNA FIGHT, HAG?
RE
YO!!!
PLEASE DON'T SAY THE ORIGINAL SOUNDS MORE INTERESTING. WELL, SEE YOU AGAIN!
The End

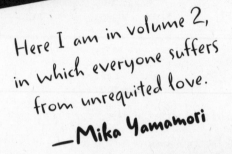

Here I am in volume 2,
in which everyone suffers
from unrequited love.
—Mika Yamamori

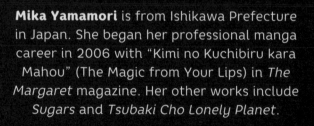

Mika Yamamori is from Ishikawa Prefecture in Japan. She began her professional manga career in 2006 with "Kimi no Kuchibiru kara Mahou" (The Magic from Your Lips) in *The Margaret* magazine. Her other works include *Sugars* and *Tsubaki Cho Lonely Planet*.

⋆DAYTIME⋆SHOOTING⋆STAR⋆ ⋆2

SHOJO BEAT EDITION

Story & Art by
Mika Yamamori

Translation ⋆ **JN Productions**
Touch-up Art & Lettering ⋆ **Inori Fukuda Trant**
Design ⋆ **Alice Lewis**
Editor ⋆ **Nancy Thistlethwaite**

HIRUNAKA NO RYUSEI © 2011 by Mika Yamamori
All rights reserved.
First published in Japan in 2011 by SHUEISHA Inc., Tokyo.
English translation rights arranged by SHUEISHA Inc.

The stories, characters and incidents mentioned in this
publication are entirely fictional.

Printed in the U.S.A.

Published by VIZ Media, LLC
P.O. Box 77010
San Francisco, CA 94107

10 9 8 7 6 5 4 3 2 1
First printing, September 2019

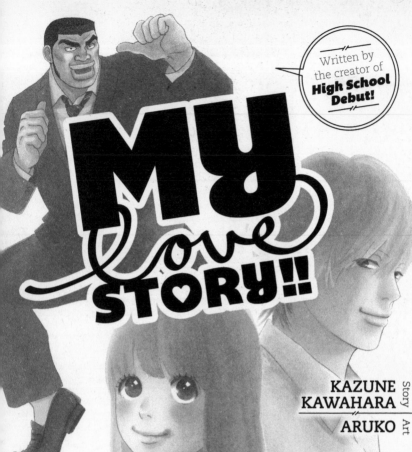

Ao Haru Ride

STOP!

You may be reading the wrong way!

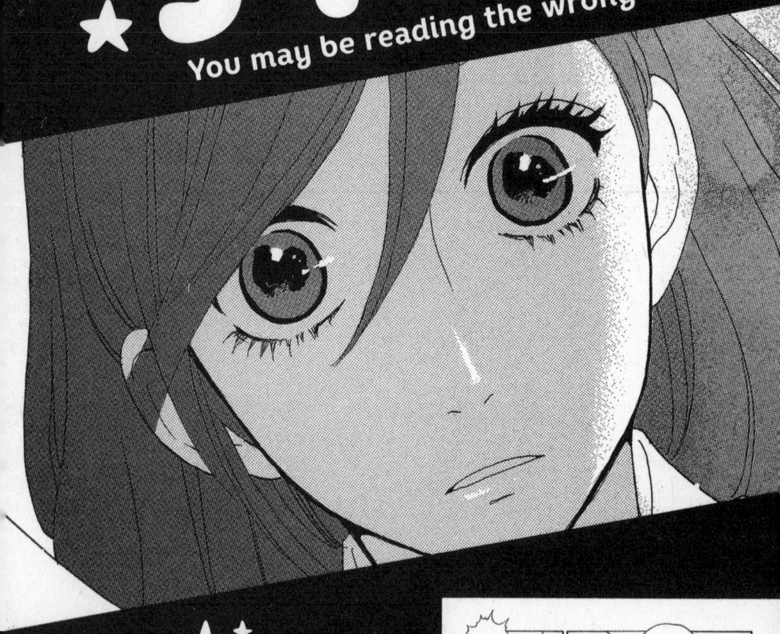

In keeping with the original Japanese comic format, this book reads from right to left—so action, sound effects and word balloons are completely reversed to preserve the orientation of the original artwork.

Check out the diagram shown here to get the hang of things, and then turn to the other side of the book to get started!

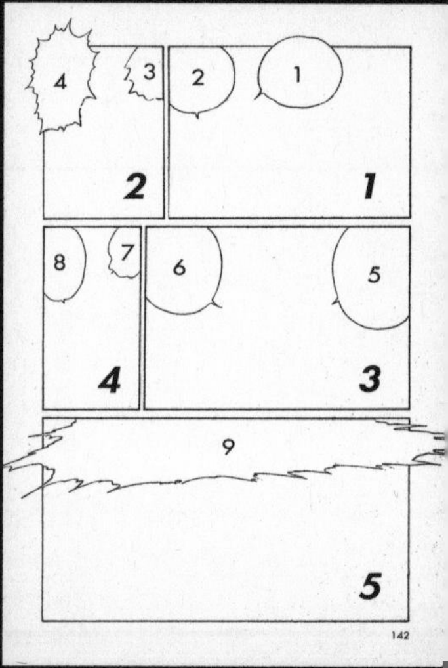
1
2
3
4
1
2
5
6
7
8
3
4
9
5
142